LOCAL UNREST

LOCAL UNREST

THE EXTRAORDINARY TRUE STORY OF THE BIRTH AND RISE OF HAWAIIAN PUNK, INDIE, AND UNDERGROUND ROCK

SHAWN "SPEEDY" LOPES

WORKS OF MERIT

CONTENTS

Preface vii

PREFACE

For those unfamiliar with life in Hawaii, the unvarnished accounts within these pages may shatter long-standing notions of this land as a sort of sunny Shangri-La custom-made for tourism, tanning, and mai tai sipping. For the great majority of the nearly one and a half million inhabitants of these islands, day-to-day reality stands in contrast to the prevailing mythology presented to the outside world. Hawaii is in fact a real place with real issues, a multiplicity of cultures and subcultures, and a complicated history.

This is a story exclusive to its place of origin, with curious social and cultural underpinnings unique to the islands of Hawaii. And yet, anyone who has survived an underground music scene anywhere on Earth will connect with themes of creativity, community, and nonconformity presented here. These filter-free tales speak directly to our need for personal expression, the audacity of youth, and the search for one's tribe along the thorny trail into adulthood.

But why a book on Hawaii's underground music scene, some will ask. Surely the number of indie, punk, or post-punk acts that emerged from a city like Honolulu pales in comparison to the scores of legendary bands from New York, London, Los Angeles, or other renowned settings. The fact is, this was never intended to be a star-studded, big-name record of *who's who* or *who's accomplished what* in the music business. Those well-trodden tales have been chronicled time and again. Rather, the goal here was to track the uncharted history of one of the most colorful, unique, and ruefully overlooked DIY music scenes in America.

As the author of each chapter's introduction and the compiler of the accounts you are about to read, I should probably provide a bit of background to this project. As a preteen in the early 1980s, I first learned of Honolulu's musical underground through AOR station 98 Rock, whose radio ads for local nightclub Wave Waikiki heralded the presence of homegrown bands like The Squids, Deviant Sheep, and Obscene Routine. Although the station never bothered to play any of their music, those inventive, whimsical names certainly piqued my curiosity and stuck with me through the years. It wouldn't be long before indie publications like *Novus* and *Brouhaha* tipped me off to active punk, reggae, and new wave acts gigging around Oahu as well as major headliners blowing through town.

Of equal significance was a fateful discovery that in a certain corner of my room, in a certain corner of my bed, my Walkman could pick up the signal of a then-little-known station broadcasting from the University of Hawaii at Manoa's campus called KTUH, which played damn near anything you could think of, including some of the most obscure yet forward-thinking bands in and around Honolulu. I soon developed a lifelong obsession with this secret society of musicians and decided only several years ago that I would commit to paper the shadowy origins of my local underground.

It was an easy choice to go with an oral history format as seen in such popular works as *Grunge Is Dead* (Seattle), *Complicated Fun* (Minneapolis), *A Curious Mix of People* (Austin), *Gimme Something Better* (Bay Area) and the granddaddy of them all, *Please Kill Me*, the hugely influential story of the birth and rise of punk rock in New York City. Since *Please Kill Me* appeared on bookshelves in 1996, the oral history has shown to be an effective and popular approach to storytelling, particularly with books centered on regional music scenes. By harvesting anecdotes from interviews with key figures of a particular community, a truer understanding—or at least a sense of "how it must have been" and "how it happened"—surfaces. That's precisely what I hoped to convey here.

For more than five years, I endeavored to document the story of Hawaii's music underground as told by the people who lived it: the musicians, DJs, promoters, nightclub owners, and others who left their mark through the decades. As someone who has consumed numerous books on renegade music scenes from around the world, I firmly believe that in terms of entertainment and enlightenment, *Local Unrest* compares quite favorably with similar published works. Believe me, I would not have invested such time, pursued my subjects so diligently, nor put my name on this project otherwise. I do hope you will enjoy these engaging, true-to-life tales as much as I relished collecting them.

Aloha.

1

ROOTS

There are those with roots that date back a thousand years to the earliest Polynesian settlers of this remote archipelago. Others can trace their lineage to the first Protestant missionaries in the Islands, or sailors and whalers who jumped ship here. Many are descended from plantation laborers brought in from China, the Philippines, Puerto Rico, Japan, Korea, the Atlantic islands of Portugal, and other far-off lands. A great number in Hawaii lay claim to some exotic combination thereof.

In more recent times, visitors, itinerants, and wanderers have settled here, drawn by the island chain's natural charm, while countless students, immigrants, and members of the U.S. armed forces came and never left. Some chose this land to build a new life, and an exceptional few have left behind significant legacies.

In the realm of popular music, none have had quite the impact of the late Tom Moffatt, the legendary concert promoter and radio man whose influence in these islands spanned six decades. Moffatt, who arrived in Honolulu from the American Midwest in 1950, was an early rock convert and is credited with playing the first rock-and-roll song on Hawaiian airwaves: Bill Haley & the Comets' "Rock Around the Clock" in 1955. In time, he would entice many heavyweights of pop and rock to come through: Elvis Presley, The Kinks, The Animals, Jimi Hendrix, Led Zeppelin, Elton John, Stevie Wonder, the Rolling Stones, and Michael Jackson, to name but a handful.

After early stints at KGU, KIKI, and KHVH, Moffatt migrated to K-POI (hyphenated in those days), the fabled Honolulu station where rock and roll was broadcast 24/7 and disc jockeys readily engaged in preposterous promotional stunts. There was the Donkey Derby, featuring K-POI DJs riding donkeys in a race that stretched from Pearl City to Kahala, and a

"Wake-a-thon" in which News Director Tom Rounds fought sleep for a then-world record of 203 hours, 44 minutes and 40 seconds. One imprudent caper required Moffatt be suspended in a car by a crane for an entire week, though perhaps by good fortune, a state safety inspector who had tuned in that day duly shut down the operation an hour into the stunt.

Hawaii became a U.S. state in 1959, and by the mid-1960s, its population was on the rise, but even at 700,000 or so residents, it was still half what it is today, and the 8,500-seat Honolulu International Center was by far its largest indoor concert venue. The first concert at the HIC (now Blaisdell Arena) was K-POI's Million-Dollar Party, a star-studded musical showcase featuring Jan & Dean, Teddy Randazzo, Bobby Rydell, Paul Revere & the Raiders, and The Dovells, among other name acts.

A flourishing local rock scene, centered around high school surf and garage bands, was all the rage then, with several outdoor Battle of the Bands-type events at the Waikiki Shell. The first, in 1963, drew a record-setting 9,200 screaming fans and another estimated 1,500 latecomers milling about outside. Teen clubs catering to the new generation sprouted up around Oahu with names like The Wherehouse, The Happening, The Quonset, The Hoot, and Peppermint Mist. In the summer of 1965, Moffatt and Rounds opened their own teen nightclub, Fat City, just across Kalakaua Avenue from the Moana Surfrider, the majestic oceanfront hotel which still stands on Waikiki Beach. Another fondly remembered hotspot, the Funny Farm, reportedly drew 1,000 attendees regularly to the site of the former Chinese American Club on Kapiolani Blvd., where the Marco Polo Condominiums now sit.

Old-timers will also recall Forbidden City, the popular cabaret and strip club near the corner of Kalakaua and Kapiolani owned by nightlife impresario Jack Cione. A bold and visionary promoter, Cione often made headlines in the '60s and '70s by featuring nude help such as topless shoeshine girls and naked waiters at the Dunes, the most infamous of his many nightspots. He also hired famous acts like Della Reese, Pearl Bailey, and Redd Foxx to perform at his venues. Outrageous rhythm-and-blues wild man and shock rock forefather Screamin' Jay Hawkins, who lived in Honolulu from 1962 to 1971, played at Cione's clubs and recorded the rare and long out-of-print album *A Nite at Forbidden City* on Sounds of Hawaii Records in 1963.

While Hawkins enjoyed his residence in the Islands, it wasn't always a picture-perfect existence. A professed womanizer, Hawkins's romantic life was knotted and convoluted. One fateful night in Waikiki, after disclosing his recent marriage to Virginia Sabellona, a waitress at one of Cione's clubs, he was stabbed by co-performer and fiancée Shoutin' Pat Newborn. A Sunday edition of the *Honolulu Advertiser* noted that Hawkins had been attacked with a kitchen knife and was subsequently found lying nude at the front door of

Newborn's Kalakaua Avenue apartment. The twenty-year-old Newborn (real name Patricia E. Williams) was charged with battery with a weapon and given the option of exiting the Islands or serving time in Hawaii State Prison. She chose to leave.

According to legend, it was during his stay at Queen's Hospital that a recovering Hawkins wrote the comical cult hit "Constipation Blues," in which he depicts the cursed bowel condition through assorted grunts and impassioned howls.

Through Sabellona, Hawkins had married into the family of Dennis Apeles, a local drummer. Apeles, still in high school at the time, was recruited, along with his guitar-playing cousin Larry Gealon, to form a trio with Hawkins. Hawkins held court behind his Hammond B3 organ on which he played bass lines with his feet. "It was a trip," recalls Apeles. "I liked rhythm and blues, but he was off the wall. He would be there with his crazy hairdo, bone in his nose, and what he would call his 'juju stick.' Good fun."

Shock rock pioneer Screamin' Jay Hawkins lived and performed in Honolulu from 1962 to 1971. *Pictorial Press/Alamy*

In time, the nutty, unpredictable antics employed by Hawkins would be matched, and possibly even outdone, by some of the more radical elements of Honolulu's rock community. A great number of unshackled personal accounts, which until now have been largely undocumented or consigned to the recesses of social media, comprise this captivating and sometimes shocking story of Hawaii's underground music scene.

Michael Corcoran (writer for *Rolling Stone, Creem, Spin, Sunbums*, etc.): We came from Idaho, where we had lived for six years. The first year in Hawaii, 1971, we had to live in Halawa Valley. You had to wait about a year to get base housing, so I went to Aiea High School for my sophomore and junior years and then we moved to Hickam Air Force Base my senior year, and I went to Radford High.

It was a terrifying experience to be a *haole*. I would say 90 percent of the white people in Hawaii are just terrified all the time, at least back then. You'd see some fights where you could not believe the person did not die, they were beat up so bad. It's like, God, if that was ever me, man, I'd be *dead*. So you just avoided all that shit. It's like if you get the first pet in on a dog, you know, then he's your friend forever. But if you hesitate or are a little worried, the dog's gonna bite you. It was kind of like that with some of the locals, the hardcore Hawaiian guys. What I did was I went right up to them and shook their hand right away, and they would look at me like I was maybe a little retarded, but at least they weren't gonna fuck with me. You had to figure out a way to survive it. It was a violent place.

My junior year, on Kill Haole Day, my parents insisted I go to school. They made me get on the bus—they *watched* me get on the bus. I did not want to go to school on Kill Haole Day and get beat up, so when I got off the bus at school, I went right to Mabel's Crack Seed in Aiea Shopping Center. I spent all day at Mabel's reading the magazines, and it was the first time ever I'd seen *Creem* magazine, *Rolling Stone,* and *National Lampoon,* and I read 'em all, cover to cover. Those were the three main magazines in my life, really, and I ended up writing for all three of 'em, and it was all because of Kill Haole Day.

But Kill Haole Day is a total myth; it's like a scarecrow. It's fun to scare the white people.

David Sumida a.k.a. Beano Shots (guitarist: The Squids, Oriental Love Ring, Beano's Black Sheep, etc.): I was born and raised in Aiea and lived on the family farm. My grandparents started Sumida Farm back in 1928. We're a landmark; a watercress farm surrounded by four shopping malls. It used to be sugarcane all around us, and now it's all developed, but we're still here thanks to my parents' efforts to keep the lease. The developer of Pearlridge Center believed he had the power to take away our lease, but my dad fought the developer in court and won and so we got to stay.

When I was old enough to go to high school, I went to Mid-Pac, or Mid-Pacific Institute, and I started learning the guitar and got into a surf band. Surf music was really big when I was a freshman. By the time I was a sophomore, the British Invasion hit, and I was totally into British bands. I think the Yardbirds and the Stones were my favorites, and I totally got into that LA band Love, and the Left Banke.

But as far as playing music, I was just fooling around 'cause I really wanted to have an art career. I went to University of Denver to study art, and later on I transferred to University of Hawaii and fell in love with the sculpture department. I didn't start getting serious about music at all until I saw the band Television.

Dave Rorick a.k.a. Dave Roe (bassist: Al Poe & the Fleas, Whitey & the Gooks; bassist, session player: Johnny Cash, The Pretenders, Dwight Yoakam, etc.): I grew up in Makakilo, and I went to Campbell High School in Ewa Beach. I was born in the early '50s, and my father was in the service. I got here when I was eleven. When the Beatles hit, that's what started it for me. My stepfather hated it. He thought they were a bunch of fags with long hair, but my mom totally got it because she was totally into country music and rockabilly—of course, they didn't even call it rockabilly back then—but I remember they played three weeks in a row on the *Ed Sullivan Show,* and the second week she looked at me and said, "It's the Everly Brothers—that's all they're doing!" Intuitively, she got it.

The local influence on me was all the cats I was playing with, all the young guys. It was the era of the Mopp Tops, you know, guys like that; Leeward Oahu guys in rock bands who were out there doing soul music and the Young Rascals. I was still banging around in garage bands, but I was very affected by the surf music scene as well. I used to watch all the other haole kids get their ass beat, and I was the hippie kid with an acoustic guitar running around singing Beatles songs on campus, so they left me alone.

Gary Chun (writer for *Honolulu Star-Bulletin*, editor for *Novus, Brou-haha*; co-host of KTUH's *Rough Take*): I was born in 1955, the year rock and roll was born, and grew up basically in the Kaimuki area of Honolulu. Music was always something I could get lost in because I was kind of a loner kid and it was the thing that sort of helped bring me into social circles.

When I got to UH, I worked at *Ka Leo*, the student newspaper, and started a record review column. I made a concerted effort to get material for my column and feed my music addiction habit, so I'd go to the Yellow Pages and look up music distributors, and I'd drive to various distributors around town and pick up records. Sometimes it would be Hawaiian music mixed in with obscure, independent stuff. I built up a record collection of up to 3,000 albums.

Dennis Apeles (drummer: Screamin' Jay Hawkins, Bobby and the Rebels): I was playing with my cousin, and we had a band called Bobby and the Rebels. We were playing the military circuit when we were young teenagers, still in high school, seven days a week.

When I was fourteen, I played at Hoffman Cafe, which was next to Club Hubba Hubba and the Swing Club on Hotel Street. It was a dive. They used to put chicken wire around the band because of the fights and the flying beer bottles.

I used to have a fake ID 'cause I was underage. All the guys I played for were older than me, and they would tell my mom, "Oh, we're gonna take Dennis to play drums for us at a party." My mom would say, "Okay, take care of him—make sure he eats!"

I quit playing when I got married. I was twenty-two. That was 1969.

Jack Law (owner of Wave Waikiki, Hula's Bar & Lei Stand, Malia's Cantina): When I graduated from high school, I got a job in downtown Detroit. I was working at a wholesale record distributor called Music Merchants. It was right when Motown was breaking wide open. I was relatively young—eighteen, seventeen years old, something like that—and the only white kid working at this warehouse in the middle of the best years of Detroit.

The automotive industry was happening—it was still cool—and Berry Gordy had Hitsville, USA, which was just a few blocks from where I worked. I just wanted to be in the music business somehow; I wanted to be in show business.

I was going to a community college, and I met a couple of guys. One of them had the bright idea of attending the University of Hawaii. Tuition was real cheap, so the three of us ended up going to Hawaii for school, which was a real big thing back then. It was 1966, and to go to that exotic place in the middle of the Pacific was quite an adventure. It was pretty neat, it really was. There were hardly any high-rises in Waikiki, and the Royal Hawaiian Shopping Center wasn't built yet, so it was all low-rise businesses along Kalakaua Avenue. The center of Waikiki around the International Market Place was where everything happened, and there was a lot of live music—Hawaiian music, dance music, Don Ho was performing at Duke Kahanamoku's—and you couldn't swing a cat without finding a bar with live music. There were a lot of gay bars too.

This was before the jets would go across the Pacific without stopping in Hawaii for refueling, so there were a lot of different people here from the mainland U.S., people from Australia, people from Asia, on their way to somewhere else. Fort DeRussy was a major rest and recreation spot for the military, and there was a big anti-war movement on the University of Hawaii campus. For a kid from the suburbs of Detroit, it was really quite exciting.

Within six months of living in Hawaii, I met Bob Magoon. He was the first person of Hawaiian ancestry to have a Broadway show. He was always working on music. Bob had a house on the beach at Diamond

Head, and I went there one afternoon with a mutual friend. Bob and I ended up putting together this band called the Potted Palm, and we put out a couple of records. That's how I got started in the music business.

Kit Ebersbach (keyboardist/pianist/composer: The Squids, The Tourists, Pacific Ethno Techno, Don Tiki, etc.): I went to Yale. I was a Yalie and I graduated DA there. I wasn't much of a scholar, so they sent me where they thought I would fit in the best. I came to the University of Hawaii to go to graduate school for linguistics in 1967. It was completely alien to me, everything about it, even the way people talked. I'd only lived in New Jersey and New England my whole life. It was just an acculturation thing. But once you've lived in Hawaii, it's hard to live anywhere else.

When I was younger, it was the era of Chubby Checker and these kinds of silly songs that were popular, and they didn't appeal to me at all. I came up more like a jazz guy, and my first love was Bill Evans, being a piano player. I liked jazz and it took me a bit to get out of a strictly jazz mode. Like a lot of people, it was *Sgt. Pepper* that really made me see the art in rock and roll and what it could do, and after that I was all for it. I decided I didn't really want to be a linguist; I really wanted to play music.

Gerry Ebersbach a.k.a. Rubella Shotz (bassist: The Squids, Fun and Profit, Pacific Ethno Techno): I hate pop music. It's so simple. It's just really boring. And I don't know if you listen to any early rock or punk, but they were out of tune, and it just drove me crazy. Guitars are not in tune with themselves and not in tune with other instruments; they're not necessarily playing on the beat, and the singers were flat or sharp or whatever. It was like, "This is just awful!"

Well, my mother was really determined that everything be perfect. When I was five, every day after school, I came home and she chose a poem for me to memorize, and I had three chances to say it to her; otherwise, she'd be furious. So I learned to memorize really fast and be really accurate. That was her criteria. I remember crying when I couldn't remember something and she'd be furious and wouldn't talk to me. And I was five. So I was set up, by her training, to want things to be precise.

I learned much later that she really loved classical music. I had no idea because she never listened to it, and I wasn't allowed to buy music, and I wasn't allowed to listen to anything in particular. So all I had was the piano.

Kit and I met at a party, and he asked for piano lessons. I said, "Well, I have to audition you." So I did. He was really awful. *Really* awful. The worst thing I'd ever heard. I couldn't believe it. He was very florid and had no technique. It was really bad. But, you know, he was an adult, and I thought, *Well, I can't insult him,* so I said, "Let's go for a walk." And that's what we did. We got married after three months, something like that.

He took me in and took care of me, and he was kind and smart. And then he had an interesting kitchen with all kinds of spices, and he had interesting books and interesting things to say. He listened to Bill Evans. I'd never listened to jazz before, didn't like jazz, but Bill Evans was a real big entry into jazz. Just beautiful and thoughtful and introspective.

Jeff Dahl (vocalist/multi-instrumentalist: Angry Samoans, Vox Pop, Jeff Dahl Band, etc.): I was a typical army brat, born in Germany. We moved around quite a bit until I was about four years old. Then my parents split up, and my mom, myself, and my brother moved to Hawaii. That would be 1959. This is right after statehood.

The mystique of Hawaii was not lost on a four-year-old. We were at the beach five days a week. That was Waikiki before it was built up and crowded. It was a different place. Eventually, we bought a house in Kailua, and that's where I grew up. Kailua Elementary, Kailua Intermediate, and then Kailua High School, class of '73.

In Hawaii, I'd been listening to bands that you would call the roots of punk: The MC5, The Stooges. And you know how I found those records? They would have a cut-out bin at Longs Drugs in Kailua of records that nobody would buy. You'd get ten records for a dollar, and so you'd buy whatever had a cool cover. The first MC5 record, *Kick Out the Jams.* Wow, cool cover. The Stooges' first record. These guys look nasty. Cool cover. This was stuff that they released that nobody bought, so they didn't want 'em in regular stores taking up space; they would just put them in these junk bins in your neighborhood drugstore at some outrageously low price. They were a dime each, so it wasn't any real investment.

I can understand why a record like *Kick Out the Jams* was in the bargain bin, because even for some of the people who liked hard rock, it was beyond their taste. If a record starts off with some guy screaming *"Kick out the jams, motherfuckers!"* I mean, that was something you had never heard before. I had a girlfriend at the time, and I played her the first Stooges record. "I Wanna Be Your Dog" came on and I'm just freaking out, like, "Man, this is the best song I've ever heard in my whole life!" and she's like, "Really?" and she broke up with me right then and there.

Chris Planas (guitarist/vocalist: Pagan Babies, Cool Runnings, Nuclear Tan, etc.): I was born in Chicago, actually. My dad is Filipino/Japanese from Hawaii. He was in the 442nd. And my mom was Mexican American. She was from San Antonio. She was a farm laborer from when she was a kid. They met in Chicago, got married. I was born, my brother was born, and when I was five, my dad wanted us to move to Hawaii. We lived off Lusitana Street, right at the foot of Punchbowl.

Because my mom was Mexican American, when she moved to Hawaii, there was nobody around to share her culture with, so one thing that she would do is play her records, either Mexican or Tex-Mex music. When I was eight, I remember it was a Sunday night, the Beatles played on television, and within a few days, she had brought home the first Beatles album, *Meet the Beatles.* She was young enough to like them, and we liked them too, me and my brother. Probably me more than my brother.

For most of high school, I was playing guitar, but not in public. I started to take my cues from *Rolling Stone* and other magazines that were starting to write about rock music as a serious form of expression.

I was at UH for a couple of years, then transferred to UC Berkeley in 1975. When I was at Berkeley, there was a shift from people who wore corduroy and plaid shirts to skinny ties and leather. The thing is, I'd come back to Hawaii for summer, and I didn't see that in Hawaii. When I moved back in 1980, I wanted to put together a rock-and-roll band similar to Rockpile and Elvis Costello, but I didn't realize how hard that was going to be.

George Kail (owner of 3-D Ballroom, Pink Cadillac, Blue Zebra, etc.):
I was an award-winning hairdresser from Pittsburgh. I used to teach in front of like, a thousand people when I was around eighteen years old, so my background is hairdressing and fashion. I kind of got bored in Pittsburgh. I mean, I was a workhorse, doing thirty people a day, cutting and blow-drying. When I left Pittsburgh, I left as one of the top hairdressers there and moved to Los Angeles. I always had that adventure in me to want to do something more exciting.

In Los Angeles, I continued to do hair, and I used to do a lot of celebrities: Diana Ross, Cher, Marsha Mason. I did Linda Ronstadt's hair. I used to be roommates with a guy named Greg Ladanyi, who was a Grammy-winning producer for Jackson Browne and Toto, so I was always around entertainment. A lot of it was a blur. It all happened so fast, and I wish to this day I kept a diary because so much of it I forgot. I was very much caught up in that whole LA scene, and I was also in a lot of bad things there, the LA drug scene and so on.

I became very good friends with Paul Mitchell. Paul Mitchell's pretty well-known in the salon business. He migrated to Honolulu and I always kept in touch with him, and one day I said to myself, "I want to be where that man is because he's a genius."

Gary Owens (DJ at 3-D Ballroom): I moved to Hawaii when I was six years old. My dad was in the military, stationed at Schofield Barracks. It was 1966, before there were any freeways. My dad was off at war and did a couple tours of duty. So my brothers and I were bored hanging out at home, and one day my dad brought home surfboards from a guy in Wahiawa who used to take old longboards and repurpose them. The boards were funky. They didn't look anything like what people are riding today.

My parents bought me a skateboard too. That was it. I'd go skateboarding with all my friends on the mainland every summer. They had better stuff to skate, and all we had was A'ala Park and whatever pool I could find. They'd start cutting their hair and listening to Devo and Blondie and The Cars. From there it went to Sex Pistols and then Dead Kennedys and all the American hardcore bands. That's when all the hair came off and the fuckin' topsiders and Jordache jeans were left behind, burning in a big pile.

Sonya Mendez (vocalist/multi-instrumentalist: Sonya & Revoluçion): I was born on Oahu, and in the early years of my life, I was raised on a dairy farm in Red Hill. There used to be three dairy farms on Red Hill, in the back of Foster Village. We lived in a Quonset hut, and the nearest neighbor was probably a half a mile away. It was a fun farm life. We had chickens, we had pigs, we had ducks. We'd go down and watch all of the cows, and every Sunday when we had nothing else to do, we'd tease the bull and run through the pen with a red T-shirt just to see if he would chase us.

My father, when he first came from the Philippines and settled here, used to sing live on the radio with the local Filipino radio station way back in the 1950s. So I got my musical talent, I guess, from my father, who was a singer, in addition to being a taxi driver, a landscaper, a milk pasteurizer, and a carpenter. As an immigrant from the Philippines, you do whatever jobs you can, right? But performing, I think, is just in our DNA as Filipinos. We can all sing, we can all dance. It's just in our blood.

Frank Orrall (Drummer/vocalist/multi-instrumentalist: Poi Dog Pondering, Hat Makes the Man, The Squids, Mumbo Jumbo, etc.): I was born in New Mexico, in a small town of maybe 200 people. It was all astronomers and their families. My father was an astronomer, and that's how we got out to Hawaii, because there's good observing on top of the volcanos out there.

My mom kind of taught us about music. She would play guitar around the house, and my sister and my brother and I all picked it up. My first exposure to punk was the Ramones' *Rocket to Russia*. I remember hearing that album in the mid- to late '70s and just having my mind blown. Then the Sex Pistols. I started playing in high school party bands. I was in a band called Urban Project that was all Hawaii Kai guys, and we did Tom Petty, the Stones, and a smattering of the kind of stuff that was approaching punk and new wave.

There was this feeling then that you're in the middle of the ocean and you're separated from everything. I used to go to the University of Hawaii bookstore and read *NME* and *Melody Maker,* and my imagination would just blow up reading about these scenes that were happening around the world, and I feel like the gift that we got was we got to imagine it with the whole of our imaginations. It was like we couldn't be in New York or London or wherever and see it, but being in the middle of the Pacific just made us dream harder.

2

EVERYTHING CHANGED

When Richard Upper caught the Steve Miller Band in concert at the University of Hawaii's Andrews Amphitheater in February of 1970, rock photography was an emerging discipline with few professional practitioners. Camera-toting concertgoers were a rarity then, usually ignored by security and given free run of the place. As Upper remembers, it was while pacing the length of the stage, camera in hand, that he was approached by a band official requesting several of his choicest shots. "I sent them pictures," Upper recalls. "And they said, 'This is great—can we use one for our album cover?' and they sent me a hundred bucks."

Upper's photo of Steve Miller, caught mid-song, strumming a twelve-string guitar, graced the cover of the Steve Miller Band's album *Rock Love* the following year, placing the Roosevelt High School freshman in rare company as a paid rock-and-roll photographer. Over the next decade, Upper would become known for his iconic photos of the Rolling Stones, Van Halen, Carlos Santana, Rory Gallagher, and Rod Stewart.

At the time, Upper saw school as a hindrance to his aspirations and a bit of a drag. He stopped attending classes the following year and negotiated a deal with the school's principal to complete his studies at home in a bid to pursue photography full time. Initially, his parents weren't thrilled with the idea, but recognizing a uniquely auspicious future for their talented, headstrong son, they capitulated. Upper even built a darkroom upstairs at his home in Makiki. "I had a bed in there, a refrigerator, and my stereo, printing and processing and making montages," he says. "I wouldn't come out for days."

To his credit, Upper graduated high school a year ahead of schedule, which allowed him to plunge headlong into photography and attend a non-stop string of concerts with an older, freewheeling crowd. Among his colleagues was Robert Knight, a working lensman who had first introduced Upper to the idea of shooting concerts with photos he had taken in San Francisco of Jimi Hendrix and Jeff Beck. Like Upper, Knight was already on track to becoming a distinguished rock photographer, and the pair formed a partnership they branded Black Sun, doing work for Milici Advertising Agency out of a Fort Street darkroom in the early 1970s. They often photographed visiting rockers in their spare time. "Richard had a very good eye," recalls Knight of his young cohort.

A working relationship with Tom Moffatt secured Knight and Upper's entry to many concerts on the island, including several legendary shows at Diamond Head, the 500,000-year-old volcanic crater overlooking Waikiki Beach and the most famous of Oahu's natural landmarks. These music festivals, known by several names and run by various promoters, occurred annually around the New Year holiday, with another separate gala, most years, in summer or fall. The first drew 12,000 attendees on New Year's Day 1969, more than seven months before Woodstock, and starred local rock, folk, and slack key musicians. The laid-back inaugural affair commenced at the break of dawn with sitar music, a meditation session, and skydivers, who, after delighting the early risers in attendance, quietly returned back to Earth, where they were greeted with a lit joint.

In 1971, Yvonne Elliman, two years removed from her time at Roosevelt High, returned home from a starring role in the smash rock opera *Jesus Christ Superstar* to perform at the Sunshine Music Festival inside Diamond Head. This just days after an opening slot with Lee Michaels at the Honolulu Civic Auditorium. By the mid-'70s, Elliman would tour and record with a resurgent Eric Clapton before transitioning into a soul and disco sensation with a string of hits to her credit, including the number one smash, "If I Can't Have You," from the multi-platinum soundtrack to *Saturday Night Fever*.

Throughout the 1970s, crater-goers enjoyed performances by such luminaries as Santana, Big Brother and the Holding Company, Boz Scaggs, Richie Havens, Graham Central Station, BTO, Seals & Crofts, Cheech & Chong, Styx, Journey, Little River Band, and War, among others.

Most years saw few problems at the crater as the masses were often respectful and well-behaved and policed themselves quite nicely. When a fire broke out on the festival grounds in 1973, for example, there was no panic. Attendees calmly put out the blaze by beating it with palm fronds, while a few helpful souls chipped in by urinating on it, reported the *Honolulu Star-Bulletin*. Mellow vibes all around.

With tens of thousands in fellowship basking in the balmy rays of the Hawaiian sun, the crater fests were a wondrous experience for Upper, who saw in them the coming of a new age of free and uninhibited expression. "I'd walk through the crowd and there'd be people doing their trippy dancing and girls with their tops off, and I thought this must be happening all over the world," Upper recalls. "Hippies are taking over."

Jeff Dahl: The first FM station that I took note of was at the University of Hawaii. They had this great station, and they would have a show of big band music and then a show of Hawaiian music and then an FM underground stoner show where they'd play deep cuts of, like, Steppenwolf and The Animals. Psychedelic stuff. The best shows were the midnight overnight ones.

We had the old radios back then, the tube ones from the '50s and early '60s, and they were much more powerful. We would rig up these antennas that would go up the wall of my bedroom and circle the whole ceiling to get good reception in Kailua. Me and my buddies were little mad scientists. We figured this out and we all did this.

With the advent of FM radio, you started seeing local rock bands come out that were actually playing original music. It was the biggest thing you could possibly do if you were a band in Hawaii, like, "Yeah, we play original music; we write our own songs." That was *huge*. I mean, you couldn't even believe someone could actually do that. "You're not The Beatles, you're not the Stones—how can you write your own songs?" And they would write great songs too.

Richard Upper (rock photographer): I applied to *Rolling Stone*. Ben Fong-Torres, their senior editor, even came over to my house in Makiki. I'm not sure why he came to Honolulu, but this was maybe '69 or '70. I sent them pictures of what I had shot. At that time it might have been Blind Faith, Joni Mitchell, Steve Miller, probably. But when he came over, I had all my pictures spread out on the floor in the living room. We sat down and he said, "Well, these are really good." He looked at my stuff some more and looked at me and said, "You know, you're a little too young for this job." So he gave it to Annie Leibovitz.

Dave Roe: Al Poe and the Fleas were a power trio. We were pretty big in 1970. We played the HIC, opening up for Grand Funk Railroad and a lot of big bands. It was just basically three-chord rock and roll.

The guy that ran the band was named Vic Burke, and he eventually became the head of the Sociology Department at Ohio State. He was really the first punk rock guy, I gotta tell you, that I ever met. He said, "Man, everybody's growing their hair long." He goes, "Fuck that, let's shave our heads!" So we shaved our heads in the middle of all the hippie shit. He used to stand there and preach to me and the drummer about where all of this was probably gonna end up. I didn't realize how forward-thinking he was until about ten years later. If we had come out in '78, we would have been considered super punk rock.

Jack Law: I was into whatever music was happening at the time, but slowly, because of my association with Bob Magoon, I also got into enjoying Hawaiian music. Peter Moon asked me if I would consider managing the Sunday Manoa Trio. They were playing at the Outrigger Canoe Club, and I was asked to come and listen to them one afternoon. I had hair that came down to my collar, but by today's standard it wouldn't have been considered long. Somebody came up to me, tapped me on the shoulder, and said, "I'm the manager of the Outrigger Canoe Club, and I've got to ask you to leave. Your hair's too long, and we have a rule against long hair."

The Vietnam war was still going on and the country, including Hawaii, was divided between the hawks and the doves. The people who belonged to the Outrigger Canoe Club were a bunch of conservative haoles who drew a mark in the sand by passing a rule: no long hair and no medallions.

Looking back on it, it was just so silly. Bob Magoon's father helped start the Outrigger Canoe Club, and Bob was going to join the club, sponsored by his parents. This was a Yale graduate, an ace in law school, a *kama'aina* with royal Hawaiian roots, and they turned him down because he was gay. I still can't go to the Outrigger Canoe Club and feel completely comfortable. It sort of sticks with me. I've been asked to join a couple times and I won't join.

Michael Corcoran: There was a guy, a surfer named Paul Maddox. He and his wife started *Sunbums* in the late '60s. It was more of a surf newspaper, surf culture, you know? They had music reviews in there too. So I went to a show and wrote a review just for myself and sent it to *Sunbums* thinking they might want to print it, but they had already assigned it. The editor, who was Kathy Hellenbrand, liked what I wrote, and so she invited me to come in and talk to her about doing more writing and I did. In January of 1975, I met with her and from that time on, I was kind of her right-hand person.

They had an art director named Blue Johnson. He was a Black guy from LA who looked like Jimi Hendrix. Bass player. He was real cool. And they had PF Bentley as photographer, who's a big deal now. They had guys who had shows at KTUH, a guy had a surf column, someone had a food column. It was basically an alternative biweekly. It was kind of before its time. There were a lot of papers that started on the mainland, too, in the '70s, but *Sunbums* was really early.

By that time, John Leonard—JFL—was the owner. He'd put on concerts and we'd have to work the concerts. We would do odd jobs. My job was usually to go to the airport, pick up the luggage of the band that was playing, and take it to the Kahala Hilton. I did that for The Faces, Loggins and Messina, Leo Kottke, Dan Fogelberg, Deep Purple, too.

Deep Purple's flight was delayed, and their planes didn't come in 'til three in the morning, and I had to go pick up their luggage. They were supposed to have all these limos, and it was just a real nightmare. They were all screaming at me, but what the fuck am I gonna do, you know? That was Tommy Bolin's very first gig playing with Deep Purple, at the HIC.

It was real exciting to me too, though, because you never really saw anyone real famous in Hawaii. Talking to Rod Stewart while he's waiting for his luggage? I mean, Jesus Christ, I couldn't believe it. Paul McCartney came backstage once with Linda. The show was Loggins and Messina with Leo Kottke opening. They were smoking a joint, and Paul handed it to me right before they went on stage. I should've kept it but I smoked it.

Gary Chun: *Sunbums* was a great local documenter of the scene and a good reflection of that time. Also, the first big venue before the HIC was the Honolulu Civic Auditorium on Beretania Street. They had boxing, roller derby, and then later on you had these rock shows, like the Grateful Dead did a show there, then Led Zeppelin. The Civic Auditorium and the old Honolulu Stadium were two of the biggest venues in town.

Richard Upper: *Sunbums* was the rag, for sure. I don't want to necessarily commit to the comparison, but it was like the *Rolling Stone* of Honolulu. They covered all the shows and what was happening in town with concert reviews and stuff like that. Let's face it, everybody wanted to play Hawaii. There were ads in there from what we would call "hippie stores," where you could get bell bottoms and imported stuff and all the latest fashions from San Francisco.

Jack Law: I got my real estate license, and I was doing business with Bob Magoon, whose family had land in Waikiki. One of the pieces of land was across from the Kuhio movie theater and he wanted to open up a bar there. I said, "Bob, we don't know anything about the bar business," and he says, "How hard could it be?" That's how Hula's got started in 1974.

It wasn't an overnight success, but when it took off, it became a centerpiece of Waikiki. Before, Halloween was just something for kids, but we went all out and our customers went all out and it became an adult holiday. It was everything.

When Studio 54 was happening, I'd go to New York maybe two times a year just to check out what was going on and try to bring some of it back to Hawaii. We were the first video bar in the state. It was before MTV and we had to make our own music videos. I had to hire somebody who worked at a bar on the mainland who would take all this stuff off the airwaves or wherever he could find it and then cut it all to the beat of the music on an analog editing console.

Michael Corcoran: Aerosmith was bigger in Hawaii than anywhere else except Boston and that's because there was a radio station called KIKI in Kaka'ako. I think it was 83 AM. The DJs could play whatever they wanted to. There was no playlist, so it was a really progressive radio station.

When the first Patti Smith record, *Horses*, came out, I used to write for *Sunbums*, which was also in Kaka'ako. I got that record and I played that first song, "Gloria," and I took it right over to KIKI. The DJ, Steven B. Williams, played it on the air that day. Things could happen like that back then.

Steven B. Williams was the biggest DJ in town, really. He had a great voice, was really funny, and he kind of discovered Aerosmith. He was going through the alphabetized albums and saw the second Aerosmith album, *Get Your Wings,* and he played a song from it, and another song, and before you knew it, Aerosmith was huge in Hawaii. The first time they came to Hawaii was in December 1974, and they opened for Guess Who at the HIC. It sold out and there were maybe 300 people left when Guess Who finished their set. Everybody left after Aerosmith.

Probably the main record store in Hawaii back then was DJ's Sound City in the Ala Moana shopping center, and when Aerosmith did an in-store appearance, probably 5,000 people showed up. It was really crazy. Steven Tyler—I interviewed him during that thing—was just blown away. He couldn't believe what was going on. It wasn't long—maybe six months later—that "Dream On" from the first album was re-released and became a hit nationwide.

So yeah, when Patti Smith's *Horses* came out, I played it and it was like, "Oh my God." It was poetry and beatnik rock and she had that song "Land" and—my God, the guy getting basically raped and stabbed in the locker room, and he sees horses while it's all happening—it was this whole different world where music was about more than I thought it was. It really opened up the idea that you can have music be about really horrible things, to not be about love or heartbreak. It can be about sexual assault and racism and all this other stuff. Everything changed in the '70s.

Richard Upper: By today's standards, Hawaii could have been the most racist place on the planet. I'd get called "haole crap" all day long. People would say about a Chinese guy, "That *pake* over there is a jerk." Everybody was calling everybody by color.

Michael Corcoran: A lot of haoles hated Hawaii. I know I did. To me, it was the worst place in the world because only about once every three months there'd be a national band that would play HIC: The Faces, Lynyrd Skynyrd, ELO, Savoy Brown. You went to every show that came through because it'd be, like, three months before another one would come through.

In the '70s, I thought there was nothing less cool than Hawaiian music, but when you look back, that was really the coolest shit that was going on. You know, like Gabby Pahinui. That's like living in Jamaica and not liking reggae. I mean, Sonny Chillingworth, all those guys, they were around. You could see them at Alakea Grill over there down by Chinatown.

Cecilio & Kapono would sell out the Waikiki Shell two nights in a row. There was Country Comfort and Kalapana. Olomana was big too. When C&K got signed to Columbia, that was unheard of that a Hawaiian group would get signed to a major label, and in Hawaii, you'd think they were the biggest thing in the world.

Jeff Dahl: There were the crater festivals, of course. It was like our Woodstock, done in Diamond Head crater. Man, it was like you never knew so many kids had long hair or that there were that many hippies on Oahu. It was amazing.

All these great bands would play, local bands and bands from the mainland. Santana and Buddy Miles made a record there, Blue Cheer played once, Styx played, Frank Zappa. It was a cultural thing, you know? Just a coming together of all of these freaks. I went to every single one while I was in high school.

Richard Upper: Those shows were fun, but I didn't hang out in the front. I spent most of my time backstage because I wanted to shoot the musicians. I wasn't there to party with friends.

I did have friends—girls I knew who were actually groupies. Back then you could just go over to the Otani House. It was owned by a businessman who was friends with Tom Moffatt, and it was a beautiful house, right at the foot of Diamond Head. That's where they put the stars who came into town, and if you knew that, you could just sort of

A festival crowd takes in Japanese rock band Gedo at Diamond Head Crater. *Courtesy of Richard Upper*

drive up, park in the driveway, and knock on the door and just talk to 'em. I mean, they didn't have security guards or anything. But in those days, people weren't like they are now, where you have to be careful. People were very polite. There was a cultural standard that people had back then. Sure, you screamed when you were at the concert and stuff, and maybe followed them around if you saw them, but you didn't stalk 'em. You could approach them.

Robert M. Knight (rock photographer): A lot of major rock bands like Jimi Hendrix and Led Zeppelin stayed there. I remember driving down and hanging with the Hendrix band, spending time talking with the guys. I was given a heads-up not to eat any of the food and drinks because they were spiked with LSD.

I took photos of Led Zeppelin around the pool and beach area of the house. One time, John Paul Jones was sound asleep, and they put a garden hose in the window and flooded his room with water so when he woke up, he probably thought he was sinking on the *Titanic*. It was a fantastic place, but years later it was abandoned and bought by David Geffen and torn down.

Richard Upper: You could walk around the house and go to the beach. They had a very narrow strip of land before you get into the water, and Steve Miller was sitting on a wall there one day. Me and Robert started talking to him, and I took a few pictures and got this really great picture of him. When I showed it to him, he goes, "Oh, that's great! Can I get one of those? I'd like to use this." I said, "Okay, I'll trade you for two plane tickets and two tickets to the Rolling Stones." So me and Robert flew to LA. Robert was old enough to rent a car, and we went to the LA Forum to see the Rolling Stones. We got a lot of pictures.

Michael Corcoran: The thing about Hawaii in those days was that if you were a club and you wanted to stay open until 4 a.m., you had to have live music past midnight. All the gay bars had rock bands because they wanted to stay open until 4 a.m., so they'd have a rock band that played until 12:02. Two minutes after midnight, boom, they would shut down the music and play disco and that was it. So a lot of the rock bands played the gay bars: the Gay Ninetys, the Stuffed Tomato, the Dragon Lady. There was a live music scene based on the gay bars because the bands were sort of glam rock bands.

I knew this band called Widow, who was very influenced by Aerosmith. They had the scarves on the mic stands, and they played at the Gay Ninetys. Some of their original material was more Alice Cooper than punk rock, but some of the glam rock bands were starting to happen.

Ronnie Ravelo (bassist/guitarist: Widow, Collision, Mumbo Jumbo, etc.): In the mid-'70s I was in a band called Widow. We would get dressed up. I had bell bottoms and my sister made me this kick-ass shiny silk shirt. Every band was under an agency back then. They would book the bands, and they took 10 to 15 percent. Our agent hated us because we never played the Top 40 stuff.

There was one time I went with our drummer to pick up a check at the agent's office, and when we get there, the guy's just standing there with his hands on his hips, yelling at us, commanding us, "SIT DOWN!"

Just like that. "Sit down!" Like, whoa, what the fuck, you know? And he goes, "I got fifty-four bands under my belt. Fifty-four! Fifty-three of them are working constantly...one isn't!"

He says, "These are the songs you gotta play..." and names a bunch of songs. Our drummer goes, "We got it. That's what we'll be playing at our next gig." The guy would shout out other songs—*boom, boom, boom.* "Yeah, yeah, we're learning those. I got it."

We leave and I tell the drummer, "Okay, we have to home in on these songs. I guess I'll go buy the records," and he's like, "Nah, fuck it, man. We'll just play what we want to play." We did Alice Cooper, David Bowie, and of course, the Stones. We played whatever we liked.

Jeff Dahl: The best place to see real rock and roll in the clubs were the gay bars. So we'd be sixteen years old going to a place called the Gay Ninetys, which as you might imagine, was a very gay club and they had a band there called Saloon Pilot that would be playing Jeff Beck Group, Led Zeppelin, Stones, you know, just great stuff from that era. They were really, really good. Across the parking lot they opened up another gay bar called the Stuffed Tomato. They had a band called the No Name Band, and they were playing the same stuff, so you'd just go back and forth.

We were sixteen years old and going to these clubs and they let us in. They weren't bothering us. No one was trying stuff like, "Hey, little boy, let me buy you a beer" or anything like that. We were dancing and having fun, and it was a great time. We would go every single weekend once we discovered this. It was safe. We'd go there with our girlfriends and jump around, and the people who were there just laughed at us and danced also. They were nice people.

Ronnie Ravelo: Widow got picked up by a promotion and management company called Papa Productions. They were doing a show in Hawaii, and I guess they liked what they saw because they put us on the Deep Purple concert at HIC. I remember standing behind the curtains and watching the arena fill up. I'm going, "Wow, I've never seen anything like this," you know? And this guy's standing next to me. I'm looking at him, and I go, "Hey, you're Tommy Bolin! You're playing with Deep Purple?"

He goes, "Yeah, Ritchie Blackmore quit and I'm filling in."

I said, "My goodness, it's such a pleasure to meet you. You must be used to this, huh?"

He goes, "Oh, fuck no!" He pushes me aside and stares out the curtains, going, "Wow, that's a good crowd!"

We got to talking and he says, "Hey, would you like to meet the band?" So he took me backstage, and I met a couple of the guys and then the security guard just grabbed me and threw me out. He looked at Tommy and said, "Don't ever do that again."

But that show led to us doing another show with the same promoter for Steppenwolf in Albuquerque, New Mexico. It was a sellout crowd. I remember I was going like, "For Steppenwolf? In the '70s? Wow, this is kinda cool!" We had a half-hour set, played our hearts out, and went backstage. I chug two beers and somebody slams the door open to our room and says, "What the hell do you guys think you're doing? Get the fuck back on stage! They want more!"

Then everything just kind of turned sour. There were too many off-the-wall incidents. The police were called on our drummer for making too much of a commotion one night at our hotel, and our singer injured the guitar player, and the promoter's driver told the promoter we weren't practicing very much. The promoter wanted my singer to come out on stage dragging a shotgun, shoot it in the air, and all this confetti would come flying out, and I thought that sounded pretty cool, but he said, "No, no, no, I don't do guns. Here's what we want..." We were supposed to play with Ritchie Blackmore's Rainbow and Argent and all that, but I guess the promoter canceled those plans. He hated us already.

Richard Upper: I met an A&R guy who was at Warner Brothers through some friends. I think they knew somebody he knew. We all hung out, maybe it was at the beach at Makaha. We got to talking and he saw some of my photos and a book I had printed up with Rolling Stones photos I had taken of their shows in Hawaii and he said, "I want to take your Rolling Stones photo book and show it to somebody." Turns out it was the manager of The Faces, who said, "Can you do one for us? We've got some tour dates coming up." So I did ten or twelve shows with them, something like that. We even came to Hawaii.

So then I got to show off. I came into town with The Faces, they played the HIC, and all my friends got to see me on stage with Rod Stewart. I'm standing on stage behind one of the big monitors, and he says, "You got your Polaroid SX-70?" and I reach in my camera bag and give it to him, and he takes pictures of people in the audience and throws 'em out. They used one of my photos for the inside of Rod Stewart's solo album, *Atlantic Crossing*.

Sonya Mendez: When I was a senior at Aiea High School and tired of making $1.25 an hour as a hula model at the airport, I saw an ad in the paper that said *WANTED: singer and dancer for show in Waikiki,* and I thought, *Hey, I can do that!* So I called up and this woman answers and she goes, "Oh, it's for my daughter's show—it's for Carole Kai."

Back then, all the top entertainers had their own showroom in Waikiki and at least a six-piece band and a few singers-dancers. They were real Vegas-style presentations, fully choreographed with costume changes. The Society of Seven was at the Outrigger, Dick Jensen was at the Oceania, and Carole Kai was doing two shows a night, six nights a week at the Garden Bar in the Hilton Hawaiian Village Hotel.

So Carole called me back and asked me to audition at her house, after which she hired me to be a backup singer for her show. During my senior year in high school, *BOOM*, I was in show biz. I was making $185 a week, which in 1972 was like, "Wow, this is big money!"

I was with her for a few years, and that's when she said, "Okay, it's time for you to go on your own as a solo performer." She was my manager for a little while.

Dave Roe: I was playing in a seven-piece funk band in Waikiki. We sort of bridged the gap between '75 or '76 and '77, when it all went from funk to disco, which are two different things. The club had a four o'clock license, which meant they had to have a live band, and it was completely controlled by the Japanese mafia. I mean, it was Yakuza to the max.

In the early '70s, a teenaged Sonya Mendez, bottom left, was in a showroom act headed by Carole Kai, bottom center. *Courtesy of Carole Kai*

The guy who ran the club, he had a meeting with me 'cause I was the band leader and he said, "Hey, Dave, you know, this disco thing… It's really popular right now."

I said, "It is."

So he said, "Here's the deal, brah. Your band is too big. I have to stay open 'til four. I want you to put a smaller band together, so you'll play from 10:00 to 10:30. You won't talk, you'll mix in and out from the DJ, and that's the only set you're going to do, then you're outta here. You can make the same money, I don't care, but it's all about the DJs now."

All the guys were happy, like, "Brah, we only play for half an hour! That's fucking great!" and I'm going, "Yeah, but this sucks. This is awful shit, it's commercialized crap. Look what they're doing to us!"

At that point, nobody gave a shit about the bands anymore. There was an abrupt change. It was all about the disco dancers. That's the thing that propelled me to play rock and roll again. I started writing songs. It wasn't about being a cover band.

Michael Corcoran: Seconal was really big then. They called them reds. A lot of locals would take a red and drink a couple beers, and they would be fucking *out*. They'd be blackout drunk. There was every kind of downer you could think of: Seconal, Quaaludes, a lot of pills. The locals were into a lot of pills, which usually came from China or the Philippines. It wasn't rare to go to a club and see someone totally out on drugs.

Drugs were very prevalent in Hawaii in the '70s. People smoked weed out in the open. In Waipahu, there's a really big Filipino community, and the Filipinos who lived in apartments had no place to garden. A lot of them love to garden, and so they would just take over a median strip and have these intricate gardens where they would harvest vegetables or whatever, and a lot of times they'd have pot plants growing in there. It was wide open.

Jeff Dahl: Your parents back then would just go to the doctor and say, "I can't sleep," "I want to lose weight," or "I feel nervous," and with absolute impunity, doctors would prescribe pills for them. People would sneak into their parents' medicine cabinets and take a few of these and a few of those and see what they did.

Michael Corcoran: For some reason, the City and County of Honolulu thought it was a good idea to have the buses go right down Hotel Street to transfer at Fort Street Mall. They could've gone to King Street, one block over. Instead, you're a fifteen-year-old kid on a bus and you're looking out the window, and there's all this porno stuff, prostitutes, and transvestites and the "Boys Will Be Girls" revue. You're going right down the middle of the sex capital of Hawaii, and I think that really warped me, you know? There was nothing like that in Idaho. It was a culture shock like you wouldn't believe.

That's when we started hearing about *mahus* too. They could fight. A lot of them were big local guys with wigs, and people didn't want to fuck with them because, man, a mahu could insult you in such a way that made you look like the biggest fucking fool if you fucked with them. They didn't give a shit. Mahus were really tough. They had to be. Kill Haole Day and mahus were the two things you found out about right away.

Jeff Dahl: The best music store in Hawaii was on Hotel Street. That was where you would go to buy, like, a Les Paul or a serious guitar or a serious amp. That's what we went to Hotel Street for. I don't know about everybody else.

Richard Upper: I'd want to go see new ghost movies or a samurai flick, and my mom used to say, "Now, it's okay if you want to go see that movie downtown, but just stay away from Hotel Street."

Michael Corcoran: My editor Kathy Hellenbrand moved to LA to learn tattooing from Ed Hardy. She worked at Ed Hardy's shop called Tattooland in East LA. So I was in Hawaii and she said, "You're not going to believe what's going on with this music scene in Hollywood!"

I knew about the records and stuff, but in Hawaii, you learned it through the magazines, like *Creem* and *Rock Scene*, so you'd read about this music, but you'd never see it.

I remember the first punk rock record I ever got was the Ramones' *Leave Home*, the second Ramones record, not even the first one. So I was a little bit late to the game, but the same day I bought it, I also bought *Marquee Moon* by Television and *Powerage* by AC/DC, and to me, AC/DC was so much better than punk rock. If you listen to AC/DC's *Powerage* and then you listen to the Ramones, the Ramones sound like crap. I was still really into hard rock, but I loved the concept of punk rock; the whole idea that you could just start a band even if you didn't know how to play.

So anyway, Kate says, "This punk rock shit is crazy here in LA. You need to get your ass over here." She sent me a 45 of Devo doing "Satisfaction," and I thought, *Oh, this is great. I need to go to LA.* I bought a one-way ticket for, like, 150 bucks. It was in November, I think, '78, and I stayed there several months. Once or twice a week, I'd take the bus and see punk bands and go to the record stores and get fanzines and buttons. I was really into the whole punk rock thing.

The fanzines really turned me around because they weren't well made like magazines; they were xeroxed and stapled, and any idiot could do this. I got back to Hawaii in February or March of '79 and decided I had to do a fanzine.

There was a guy named Jim Wood from the Honolulu Doggs. The Honolulu Doggs were a great blues band. They were into listening to punk music, but the music they played was blues music. Jim Wood had this idea, same time as I did, about doing a fanzine. He wanted to call it the *Oahu Lie,* and he wrote this really scathing article about a guy who owned three or four rock-and-roll nightclubs in Hawaii and was a total scumbag, ripped off all the bands. He was a complete asshole, and Jim Wood just outed him about what a scumbag he was. I thought, *Shit, I didn't know you could do that in a public publication,* you know? So I did the "Ten Biggest Dildos on Oahu" article about people like that who were fuckin' worthless.

Jim Wood left for the mainland, so I changed the title to *Honolulu Babylon* and put out the first issue, maybe 20 percent written by him and 80 percent written by me. It looked like shit. It was basically hand-written and xeroxed.

I knew Michael Malone through Kathy Hellenbrand. They were a couple for about seven or eight years and lived together. So even though I was best friends with Kathy, he and I weren't very friendly because he always thought I was trying to screw his woman or something. He had Sailor Jerry's tattoo shop at 1033 Smith Street, bought it when Sailor Jerry died in '73, and he called it China Sea Tattoo.

I slid the issue of *Honolulu Babylon* under the door at China Sea. I ran into him about a week later and he says, "Hey, man, that paper you put under my door, it was great! Let me do the art. You need someone to do art for you. I like the attitude, but it doesn't look very good."

He kind of took over from that point and started doing all the covers and made it look really good. He made it into something special. I was basically the writer, and he was the designer. I went by Yikes! Crawford, and he was Rollo Banks.

3

RAW ENERGY

In the Honolulu of the late 1970s, the Internet would have been difficult to imagine by the average citizen. Music streaming, YouTube, and social media were much closer to science fiction than real-world living. Cues on pop culture, however, could be gleaned from magazines, movies, or TV, and news traveled quickly enough that stories sent by wire would appear in the papers the following day, photographs included. Record reviews, produced by *Rolling Stone*, were sent to newspapers across America, and quick-read essays on ingenious new platters by Patti Smith, Elvis Costello, The Cramps, Garland Jeffreys, Iggy Pop, and Blondie were occasionally found in the entertainment sections of Honolulu's two dailies, the *Honolulu Star-Bulletin* and *Honolulu Advertiser*, usually abutting ads for Japanese and Filipino action films and X-rated movie houses in Chinatown.

No punk act gained more notoriety in this time than the Sex Pistols, whose deliberate antagonism of reporters and concertgoers, general boorishness and misbehavior, as well as unfounded yet widespread rumors of sex and vomiting on stage gained media attention the world over. Though it consistently garnered headlines, punk rock was largely dismissed by the general populace as vile and vulgar theater.

In 1978, when the Sex Pistols ventured across the Atlantic for their first and only U.S. tour, wire services detailed the event, starting with their first gig at an Atlanta shopping mall, where they played to an audience of mostly long-haired youngsters keen to see what this punk rock fuss was about. For all the hoopla, the band dissolved nine days later without much fanfare. The arrest of Sid Vicious later that year for the alleged murder of girlfriend Nancy Spungen and his subsequent death of a heroin overdose certainly did punk no favors.

Back in the Islands, a number of young upstarts, inspired by the exciting and rapidly evolving developments in rock, began experimenting with the sounds of punk and new wave. Unbeknownst to this audacious, fragmented assemblage of artists, a new era in underground music in Hawaii was already underway.

Byron Lai (guitarist: Hat Makes the Man, Diamond Hedz/New Dreamers, Whitey & the Gooks, etc.): Toward the end of 1977, I went to stay with my sister in San Francisco, and that's when I got exposed to a lot of punk and new wave music. In fact, that's when I first heard the Sex Pistols. It was on the radio in San Francisco, probably on KSAN. I thought, *Oh, so that's the Sex Pistols. Wow, that's pretty awesome.* Another band I heard on the radio there that I liked was Eddie & the Hot Rods. I also saw them in concert there.

I did get to see the Sex Pistols for their last concert before they broke up, at Winterland. I remember the crowd throwing stuff on stage, like, non-stop. It was sort of like a sign of tribute. It wasn't like they were insulting the band; it was just the thing to do. The band was really good, especially Paul Cook and Steve Jones, except Sid Vicious wasn't much of a bass player.

I thought about moving there, but I ended up coming back home, and when I came back, I wanted to start a band because I felt with the punk and new wave movement there was room for people like me. Actually, I wanted to start some kind of power pop band.

Beano Shots: I graduated from UH in 1975 with a BFA degree and was working as a carpenter. I went to visit a friend in 1978 in New York City. Up until then, I was a struggling artist, and when I saw Television at the Bottom Line, it just blew me away. Everything started making sense to me, seeing Television and how proletariat they were.

The last concert I saw before I left Hawaii was Rod Stewart and The Faces, with Ronnie Wood—you know, that caliber—and when I saw Television, I was like, "Oh, I can do that!" It was accessible. I mean, prior to that, I was a struggling artist spending, like, two months on each piece and having to sell it for a lot of money, prices most people couldn't afford. When I saw Television, I was thinking, *Wow, this is a great art form because this is totally accessible. All you need is to pay a small cover charge, and you get to hear an original band play their own music.*

There was all this punk fashion, punk record stores. New York was just so alive. That whole scene, the street people, everybody. It was something new to me and I totally embraced it. I thought about it all that night, and by the time I came back to Hawaii, it was like, "Okay, fuck being an artist; I'm gonna be a musician and I'm gonna play punk rock."

Dave Roe: When the Sex Pistols came out, everybody hated them. It was a unified front of hate, you know? Hawaiian music's so melodic, and the local guys sing so great, and so with the punk stuff, it was like, "Why's he singing li' dat? Sounds like shit, man!" But that rhythm section in The Attractions, that spoke to me, and I've become friends with those guys throughout the years. That was the most powerful rhythm section in rock and roll the whole time, I thought.

I put together a punk band called Whitey and the Gooks. Byron Lai was in that band. We were the first band I knew that cut tape of all originals. I still have tapes of all that stuff. I was most deeply influenced by the Ramones at that point and Elvis Costello.

Kit Ebersbach: I was always trying to write songs, and I wasn't very happy with the songs that I wrote. It was right after disco kind of took over that I would read about these new bands in *Rolling Stone* and the whole reaction to disco. I wasn't interested in Johnny Rotten or any of those guys, but I was intrigued by Talking Heads and Elvis Costello, and when I bought *My Aim Is True* and listened to it, it was hard to take because it was so different from disco or Michael McDonald or any of that kind of stuff. But some of the lyrics caught me, and I realized they were singing songs not necessarily based on love or anything like that, but more like their own life experiences. That gave me encouragement. That kind of sealed the deal for me with Talking Heads and the stuff David Byrne did and how he was so geeky. It was so anti-rock and roll.

Ronnie Ravelo: Widow moved on to LA and tried to do things there. We got a few gigs just doing Top 40 music. Nobody wanted originals.

After a while, the drummer, guitar player, and I wanted to leave. We'd had enough already, you know? But I wound up staying out there from about '75 to '79.

There was a lot going on in LA, but I didn't realize the amount of people who were digging punk until I saw my first punk show and I kind of started changing my attitude. Punk put a different light on music, and I liked it because it was rebellious. It was something I was looking for because I was just playing regular rock and some fusion stuff like Yes, and I was getting really bored, so all this new stuff was really intriguing.

There was this one time, my car broke down and I was at a bus stop and a car pulled up. The guy got out and he was dressed in a multicolored outfit; half of his hair was red and blue, and the other half was shaved off. I was in my brown leather jacket and jeans. He was pumping gas and we were looking at each other. He was staring at me and I was just staring at him. I don't know what he was thinking, but all I could think was, *I'm the past and that's the future.*

Jeff Dahl: I was in the army, stationed in the Washington, D.C. area at the Pentagon Heliport, and there were some great record stores there. Oh man, they were fantastic. I would go to these record stores two or three times a week. They would have these big import sections with records that weren't released in the U.S.

In *Creem* magazine, which was the Bible to me growing up, I'd heard about The Dictators and the New York Dolls and these bands at the end of the glam scene that were really the bridge to punk rock. I saw this single that one of these stores had just gotten by this English band called The Damned, and that was the first English punk rock single. I bought that and took it home straight away like it was a little jewel or something, like, "Wow, my prize!" I put it on for the first time and just went "Holy shit! This is the music!"

I actually started out as a drummer, but I decided to start playing punk music when I bought that Damned single. I bought a guitar and a little tiny amp and taught myself a couple of barre chords. To me, the magic thing was writing your own song. So actually singing it and learning guitar for two months to be able to play it and write the chords, that was just a means to an end. But the whole goal was to write this song and record it. That just seemed like the coolest thing in the world. I couldn't think of anything cooler than that.

Two months after I bought my first guitar, I recorded "Rock and Roll Critic," my first single, at a four-track recording studio at three dollars an hour. This was, like, in '76. I had to play everything myself because although there were different outlets for finding musicians, there was no mention of punk then. I finished my time in the service and had gone back to Hawaii to go to UH, and somebody in D.C. heard it and said, "Hey, man, let me release this."

Byron Lai: The first serious band I was in was with Rudy Trubitt and Dave Sumida and Dave Lassiter, and we were called the Diamond Hedz, which became New Dreamers. I was more into pub rock and power pop: Dave Edmunds, Nick Lowe, and Rockpile, that kind of music. A lot of it reminded me of the '60s, the early British Invasion, or even '60s garage rock. I'd gotten really sick of the typical '70s arena rock-type bands like Styx and Journey and Kansas, so when punk and new wave came out, I was totally on board with that.

David "Rudy" Trubitt (guitarist/vocalist: Diamond Hedz/New Dreamers, The Squids, Fun and Profit; solo artist): Beano and Byron are kind of contemporaries, age-wise, and Dave Lassiter and I are about the same age. So the New Dreamers had a couple of twenty-year-olds and a couple of thirty-year-olds. At one point, I thought that we should have called the New Dreamers "The Decades," and both Byron and Beano thought that was a really bad idea. That got shot down right away.

Beano Shots: I had friends who were about ten years younger than me. They were already listening to punk rock and turning me on to punk rock. My girlfriend at the time, her friend's son and I became friends, and I met all his friends. We were jamming, practicing. They were all basically from Manoa. Peter Bond was one of those kids.

Peter Bond (guitarist/vocalist: Hat Makes the Man, Oriental Love Ring, Spiny Norman, etc.): You could get beat up for wearing a Devo shirt. I mean, it was just nuts how hostile everybody was to punk and new wave music when it came out. It was crazy. The first Elvis Costello album, people frickin' hated it. They just couldn't stand him. So that made it more fun to be a part of it. You wanted to be in this group that everybody hated.

The Sex Pistols were the moment that I saw it all change. The English thing just exploded. I'd heard a little bit of propaganda about the Sex Pistols, just tiny little snippets here and there, and I remember when a promo of it came in when I worked at House of Music, one of the guys who was into jazz started to try and break the record, and I was like, "Don't! Give it to me!"

David "Rudy" Trubitt: What was kind of the awakening to this whole style of music was being friends with Peter Bond, who worked at House of Music at the time. They were getting all of these promotional albums that would come into the store that they would never play. Peter would bring home these records, and he was very generous and started sharing them with our group of friends. That was my introduction to The Stranglers, The B-52s, and just a ton of obscure bands that never really stuck around like The Shirts and Radio Birdman. The day he gave me that first album, I remember we went surfing; he gave me this record, Skylab fell to Earth, and I listened to The B-52s for the first time.

Peter Bond: The first new wave song that I remember getting played in Hawaii was on this one station, and they were really nervous about playing it. They were, like, "We're gonna play this song...We know a lot of our listeners don't really like this kind of music..." Almost two days of leading up to, "Okay, hang on to your hats...Don't freak out..." It was The Knack's "My Sharona." That just sounds so crazy now.

Jeff Dahl: I was hoping there was something I could put together in Hawaii, musically speaking, and it was absolutely not possible. There were no clubs or venues that would allow you to play the stuff I wanted to play, so it was either New York or LA, and I fucking hate New York, so I went to LA. I went to Hollywood, man, and it was all right there. This was the promised land. Here were the people I was searching for.

I got off the plane, went to a show, and it was X, Flesh Eaters, The Screamers, and the Alley Cats. It was, like, two dollars to go see that. All the legendary bands from that era, you'd see 'em all, and it was never more than a few bucks.

The scene then was smaller, and it was really incestuous: Everybody knew everyone, everybody had sex with everyone else, everybody had been in a band with somebody else. There was not a lot of posing. It was really down to earth. I had run into Don Bolles from The Germs, and we had started jamming a couple times a week. Out of that came Vox Pop. We would get as stoned and drunk as humanly possible and just play and see what would happen. So we would start playing these shows, and we were really, really loud and really obnoxious and people loved it. Right from the get-go, our shows were pretty well attended.

From Vox Pop came 45 Grave. Three of the guys had started 45 Grave as kind of a fun offshoot, and then I started singing with the Angry Samoans, and Mikey, our keyboard player, was playing in Nervous Gender. Like I said, it was really incestuous how everybody played with everyone.

Frank Orrall: There was a band from Chicago called Piranha Brothers. They came out to Hawaii, and they would do a residency at Lucky Pierre's in Puck's Alley. This was big for me. I used to go see them on the weekend and drink seven and sevens or vodka and whatever. You had to buy two drinks, and you could watch the band. But these guys were fucking showmen, man. They used to do, like, David Bowie stuff, they did some Ramones stuff, they did Bruce Springsteen, and everything kind of worked together in some way that was part of this wave. You definitely had the feeling that something new was happening, you know? It felt like there was this raw energy that was coming. What I liked about it was they put on a show. They were total showmen. They took that little stage and they rocked it.

Michael Corcoran: One of the first punk rock shows ever, from a touring band, in Hawaii, was Talking Heads at Little Orphan Annie's. I think the cover was $2.50. Little Orphan Annie's mainly catered to military guys since it was really close to Pearl Harbor.

Talking Heads played Japan, and on the way back to the mainland, they wanted to stay in Hawaii for a week, do a couple gigs, make enough money to pay for the hotels, and that's what they did. They were really cool, too. They sat at a table at the club, and anybody could walk up to them and talk to them. They were very nice. I asked David Byrne, "I'm going to be a music critic. Who should I read?" And he said "Well, you should read Glenn O'Brien from *Interview* magazine. He's my favorite music critic." You could get *Interview* in Hawaii. It was really weird; every magazine you could think of you could get in Hawaii, for some reason, but nothing else. Very few live concerts.

Gerry Ebersbach: We went to see Talking Heads. Kit really loved listening to David Byrne, and I said, "Do you need to talk to him?" and he said, "No, no, no..." and I said, "No, you have to!" So I went over to the people who were taking care of David Byrne and I said, "Kit Ebersbach, he's a member of the top punk band here in Hawaii. He really loves David Byrne, and he needs to talk to him." So they let him in and they ushered him over to see David Byrne, and Kit said he couldn't talk. He was tongue-tied. I said, "Why did I go to all that trouble if you couldn't even talk to him? What's the matter with you?"

Frank Orrall: The B-52s were fucking great. I remember the feeling at the show was fun. They played "Rock Lobster," and you'd get on the ground, and half the people didn't know what to do. They're like, "What the fuck is going on here?" They had all these interesting instruments and quite a few toy instruments like kids' walkie-talkies and little toy pianos to make little interesting sounds. It was very close to the record. They were very well rehearsed.

A big new wave moment for me was listening to the B-52s album on my first Walkman and hearing that stereo fidelity right in your ear. That was pivotal for me. And Talking Heads' *More Songs About Buildings and Food* and *Fear of Music* were huge records for me. There was that post-*Rocky Horror Picture Show* vibe with that whole era.

Gary Chun: When The B-52s and Talking Heads were just starting to break out and they both did their gigs at Little Orphan Annie's, those

The B-52s performed at Little Orphan Annie's in December 1979, just
a few months after a Talking Heads show at the same venue.
dpa Picture-Alliance/Alamy

were memorable shows because the local attendance was so small, but the
young people like myself just loved this music to the bemusement of the
military folk there. The B-52s more than the Talking Heads because when
Talking Heads came out, "Take Me to the River" was a big hit, so I think
that they had a more appreciative audience, but The B-52s, I mean, the
military guys just did not get this music. Years later, when I interviewed
David Byrne for the *Star-Bulletin*, he said he remembered seeing military
guys at the club going into the restroom and dropping acid.

Gerry Ebersbach: We were backstage at the Police show, and Andy
Summers kept looking at me and coming toward me, and I kept trying
to get away, thinking, *Well, that's really weird because here I am, standing with Kit's arms around me and our two kids, and he's trying to hit
on me. This is just too bizarre.* I'm pretty anti-social.

Gary Owens: I saw Talking Heads at Little Orphan Annie's. I saw The
B-52s there too. We used to go there, and they had a thing called "The

Three Dollar High" and it was three dollars for all the alcohol you could drink from seven to nine. We'd go in there and just get shitfaced. Three bucks, you could afford that in high school. I graduated a year late, so I was eighteen and could go to bars, so I was the man, kinda. All the girls wanted to hang out with me and go to bars. I had a car, my mom's Ford Granada. I borrowed it every evening.

Then I saw Devo at Campus Center Ballroom, which was pretty cool. They were all in their yellow suits, before they got radio-friendly. I also saw The Police there when they had their first album out. The Police were kinda punk rock in the beginning.

As far as a scene, though, I just knew my friends. We'd go to shows and see some of the same people, but it wasn't until 3-D came along that we all started hanging out and got to know each other.

Devo first played the Aloha State in
1979 at the University of Hawaii.

4

1980

Just past the Ala Wai Promenade and over the Kalakaua Avenue Bridge, revelers rolling into Waikiki would have come upon Lava Lava Disco Cabaret. It was, according to local gossip and entertainment columns, Honolulu's trendy new gay nightspot. With the opening of his club in the summer of 1979, Lukas Martin, who also headed a local carpet company, was said to have been living the high life, cavorting with various creatures of the night and inviting select guests up to his Chateau Waikiki penthouse.

One evening, several months into this new venture, Martin failed to appear at his nightclub. When he was a no-show for a second straight night, his hires began to worry. Just the previous week Martin had recounted to police an assault by two men he brought back to his condo who pummeled him and ran off with his keys.

Concerned by Martin's absence, an employee went up to Martin's apartment overlooking the club and knocked on the front door. Hearing a radio and Martin's dog inside but no reply, the employee grew uneasy and called the authorities. Once inside, police discovered Martin lying on the living room floor, naked, his limbs entangled in a bedsheet, and his apartment ransacked. He had been beaten and strangled to death.

In terms of murder, 1980 was Oahu's deadliest year ever. A homicide detail of six detectives oversaw 595 fatalities that year—slayings, suicides, and accidental and unattended deaths included. "That is a lot of work," Maj. Lester Akeo, top man at HPD's Criminal Investigation Division, told the *Honolulu Star-Bulletin*.

Other unsolved homicides that year included the executions of a pair of underworld gambling figures: one hammered by three .38 slugs while sitting in his Cadillac in Chinatown, the other mowed down on a barstool by automatic rifle in a Kapiolani Boulevard lounge. Most disturbing of all was the case of the eight-year-old Halawa Heights girl who was snatched on her short walk to school, confoundingly, without a single witness. Not long after the girl's lunch bell rang at Webling Elementary, a terrified tourist out on the North Shore happened upon her delicate, inanimate form dumped before a concrete culvert at Leftovers Surf Break with a mortal incision stretched across her throat.

The writers for the original *Hawaii Five-O* would have been hard-pressed to dream up episodes this brutal, though in 1980 they wouldn't have to: TV executives drew the curtains on the venerable cop series, ending a storied twelve-year run in the Islands.

Certainly, 1980 was a tumultuous year for Hawaii. In many respects, it was also an unfolding of sorts; an uncommon year of upheaval and change, when perennial figures of the old eon fell away to make room for the new.

The dawn of the '80s saw the hunky, Ferrari-driving *Magnum P.I.* quickly supplant the suit-and-tie gumshoes from *Hawaii Five-O* to become an early icon of the new decade and Hawaii's favorite celebrity sighting. Disco, once all the rage, was suddenly on the wane, and local youth started to take to exciting new sound forms like rap, punk, new wave, and heavy metal.

In and around town, a motley band of upstarts and artists had already begun to fraternize and collaborate with one another in novel modes of expression. Before year's end, new gathering places would make Waikiki ground zero for this postmodern convergence of music, style, and subculture; 1980, it could be said, was the year the freaks, misfits, and rebels forever changed the Honolulu nightlife.

3-D BALLROOM

George Kail: I came over here to Hawaii after probably ten years in LA. You could get caught up in the LA scene in a good way and a bad way. You know, there were a lot of drugs, a lot of nightlife, a lot of good and bad.

So, it was another adventure to come to Honolulu. And the reason I came here was my best friend, who I worked with in Pittsburgh, a guy named Maurice Damien. Maurice was already established here in the hairdressing field. He owned salons and did the Governor's wife's hair and so on and so on. I came here and worked with him for a short time and then I ended up opening my own salon in Waikiki, which was kind

3-D Ballroom occupied the top floor of 2260 Kuhio Avenue in Waikiki.
Courtesy of Wade Allen

of like a combination hair salon and clothing boutique that sold designer clothing and antique clothing. It was called La Bamba. La Bamba was right above Hamburger Mary's, which was next to the gay club Hula's.

I met this guy who used to come to my boutique at that time. His name was Kim Bloss. He was a crazy guy who'd always come in with a top hat and a cane. He was a very, very interesting, eccentric person, like something out of a comic book. Very creative. He was like me in a way, where he had all these abstract ideas, and his musical taste was Iggy Pop and all this underground music. He loved my store because I carried all kinds of crazy shit, and he said, "Hey, my dad has a place on Kuhio Avenue, and we could rent it really cheap." I said, "Sounds good. Let's open a club!" That's what started the 3-D Ballroom, my first nightclub.

Peter Bond: 3-D was such an epic, epic place. It couldn't have existed at any other time.

George Kail: It was an abandoned residence. There were apartments up there, and me and Kim gutted everything and actually had a dumpster on Kuhio Avenue and were throwing shit over the side, off the third floor. I don't know how we got away with it, but we did. We did it on a shoestring. I didn't even have any money in those days. I think we built that damn place for, like, $15,000 or something like that.

Frank Orrall: I actually lived there before they opened. The word was on the street that Kail and Kim were opening this club, and I knew them from around the scene. I didn't have a place to live, and they let me sleep at 3-D. They were doing construction there during the day and then I'd sleep there at night. Downstairs was an arcade, and I just remember hearing Galaxian, you know—*BLEEP-BLEEEEEEP BLEEP-BLEEEEEEP* and then Pac-Man—*WAKWAKWAK*—shit like that while I'm sleeping. I remember also going into the girls' bathroom and writing "I want to fuck the drummer" before they even opened.

Matthew Miller (bassist: Hat Makes the Man, Poi Dog Pondering): The whole electrical setup in the place was crazy. I remember one of the first times I played there, I touched my lips on the microphone, and all the lights in the place flickered, and I thought I was gonna fuckin' die. I got an electric shock through my lips. It was a slapped-together place for sure.

George Kail: 3-D was not a real big club. It was about 2,000 square feet, which is pretty small for a nightclub. It had a small stage where we did all our bands. The dance floor itself was sort of in the middle. Records—45s and 33s that I'd pick up from the Salvation Army or whatever—were laminated onto the floor.

It was a pretty innovative club because it was the first club in Honolulu that went with another format other than regular disco stuff. We had a new wave/punk rock mishmash, and we would play music from the Sex Pistols to the Cocteau Twins, whatever the cool music was at the time, but absolutely no disco music. More Depeche Mode, Bauhaus, Joy Division. It was the only club that, at times, had slam dancing on the dance floor.

The DJ who kicked off the club was a very, very innovative DJ named Crazy George. Well, Crazy George was really pretty crazy. The guy was the most unsanitary person, but he would bring his records, and he knew his music. People had a lot of respect for him because he would save every goddamn dime he ever owned to go out and buy the latest underground music. Gary Owens was also one of my DJs.

Gary Owens: Crazy George was kind of a nerd. He was a nerd who liked to take a lot of acid. When I first met him, he had a girlfriend and then I guess she just didn't like him anymore because instead of taking her out to eat, he'd buy more and more records. He was a vinyl addict, and his whole apartment started filling up with records. I think she just went, "Well, I gotta get out of here." From there on out, George would just hang out at 3-D.

Peter Bond: Crazy George, he was like the beloved DJ, the main guy for a long time, the most cutting-edge guy out there, and he was just out of his mind smoking weed in the DJ booth. We'd go in there and smoke with him all the time. Kim, the blackout drunk owner at 3-D, would just abuse the living shit out of Crazy George, who was so fucking stoned out, it was just hilarious and sad at the same time. He'd yell and call him all kinds of names: "Fuck you, George! You fucking suck, you fucking piece of shit! Why the fuck do I let you into my fucking club?" That kind of shit. It was amazing.

George Kail: Kim was an abusive alcoholic, and he would be like a Jekyll and Hyde character. During the day, he was calm, he was creative, he was normal. He would never drink during the day. But at night he would put away at least fifteen or sixteen Heinekens, and once he'd start drinking, he couldn't stop. It got to a point where I said, "Look, if you're gonna do all that drinking, you better keep track of it!" He would go to the bartender and down one after another after another, and the bartender would say, "Kail...he's up to eighteen!" *Eighteen Heinekens*—can you imagine that? That's a case of Heinekens. After a while, he would get to a point where he didn't even know where he was or who he was, and he would piss off a lot of people. He was very playful in a bad way. He would go up to girls and just hoist up their dresses and act like a little kid. He was nuts.

Peter Bond: He was an insane madman. I remember him one time throwing a mannequin on the dance floor and humping it. Everybody's there watching this guy too. He was just slurringly fucked-up drunk.

Matthew Grim (promoter/owner/DJ: The Faktory, Zone 24, Sanctuary, Sub Club, etc.): He would come out in a trash bag, just ridiculously wrecked, with his dick hanging out, and none of the security would touch him, and everybody would just get away from him because he was seriously a fucking drunken, horrible piece of shit person that everybody hated. He'd be, like, "What are you fuckin' fuckers doing in here?" 'cause he knew we were underage, and we'd always have to hide from him 'cause he was just an alcoholic, shitty, drunk fuckin' dick.

Gary Owens: He'd get so psycho too, man, you didn't know if he was your friend or your enemy. He'd be yelling at you: *"YAAAAAAAARGHH!"* and ten minutes later he'd be like, "Hey, man, how's it going?"

One night, we all got arrested out front, me and a couple of the Hawaii Kai punk rock kids. We were just being belligerent idiots. We were wasted too, and we all got taken down to jail, and who comes walking up with bail money and gets us all out? Kim. I was kinda trippin' on that. Fuckin' A. I had a little newfound respect for him after that.

John Dahlin (vocalist: The Accüsed, ADMS Family, Crib Death, etc.): Kim was from Detroit. He grew up on the Stooges, like, seeing Iggy Pop back in the '60s and '70s, and he was walking a fine line as far as sanity, I think. The mountains of cocaine he was doing probably didn't help. I can remember him closing the club; we'd be standing across the street, and he would be just *screaming* at the top of his lungs at nobody, out the window into Waikiki. At nothing. Not angrily, just like a howling at the moon or something.

George Kail: We built the place with love, very little money, and a lot of crazy, cool ideas. I remember we used to have mannequin hands holding roses and champagne glasses, coming out of the walls. We had a lot of three-dimensional ideas. We had a mannequin on a surfboard out in front of the place, and that was our sign on Kuhio Avenue.

The bar had razor blades and coke spoons laminated into it, and for a nightclub in Honolulu to do that was sacrilegious; it was a no-no. It made it look like we were doing lines of coke—which we did at times—but it wasn't a drug house or anything like that; it was just a crazy, creative club. In those days we got away with things because people more or less thought I was out of my mind. I had pink hair and cockroach-killer boots, you know, with the points, and I was a wild, crazy guy, and Kim was the same way—a little bit too wild and crazy—and I had to eventually get away from him.

Peter Bond: They couldn't get a liquor license at first, from what I recall, so to go there you had to be invited, but to get an invitation, you paid ten bucks and you could bring your own. Guys were bringing in these cases of beer. There were all these runaways in there and these way-underage kids—fifteen-, sixteen-, seventeen-year-old kids in there. Everyone was drinking, everyone was partying.

We were all slightly different, you know; some people might like Siouxsie and some people might like the Sex Pistols, but at the same time, everyone was cool with what everyone else liked. We hadn't started separating into the punks and the mods or any of that stuff. Everybody got along.

John Dahlin: The Boys Club, they were all these Navy guys, and they lived in Waikiki. They were, like, really into ska, and a bunch of them were in a scooter club. They were hell-raising Navy guys who'd always have your back if somebody was harassing ya, great dancers and all-around good guys to have as big brothers. They were stalwarts of the scene.

I remember I was a block up from 3-D with my friends Tom and Liz, and this local kid walks by, "Eh, you like score bud?" and we said no, and Tom said something smartass to him, and he says, "Fuck you, brah! I coming back wit' my friends!" and he did. He came back with, like, six guys. The next thing you know, I'm against the wall, and one guy's threatening to rape Liz, and Tom's mouthing off, just pissing them off more 'cause he's good at that. Right then, I see a fist coming out of the corner of my eye. Some guy got me in the jaw, cracked my jaw, and Tom said, "Go get help!"

So I ran down the street to 3-D. I got upstairs and sat down. A couple of guys from the Boys Club were there, like, "Johnny, Johnny, what's going on? What happened?"

"I don't remember!"

I had amnesia. Meanwhile, there's six guys beating up on Tom a block away and finally I remember: "Oh shit! There's a bunch of *mokes* beating up on Tom! Go down there!"

Five guys from 3-D go tearing down the stairs, and there was this big brawl in the middle of the street. Tom's bashing this guy on the head with a vodka bottle, and they ended up chasing them away.

Gary Owens: You could bring your own beer in there. It was crazy. There'd be a lot of fights in there, man, and it got kinda rowdy at certain points. Some of the other people who weren't into music would go in there and get wasted and be, like, "Look at all of these fucking weirdos—let's beat 'em up!" That kind of shit. You had to watch your back a little bit.

One time, the Kalani High football team came in there, brought their own beer, and decided to fuck with everyone. All the punks fuckin' joined together and beat up a few. We'd defend each other, stick up for each other. It was good and it was bad too, you know? It brought in some people who just did not handle their liquor, basically. Then somewhere in late '80, maybe '81, they got their license and a bartender and then it kinda became legit. That's when it started happening.

George Kail: You know, in those days, the drinking age was eighteen, and shit, there were people going to 3-D who were fifteen and sixteen. We tried our best to run the place by the law, but in those days it was almost impossible because everybody had a fake ID and everybody knew how to look older, especially the girls.

WAVE WAIKIKI

Jack Law: I noticed that this bar down the street called Lava Lava was for sale. It was on the market for a long time, and it kept going down in price. Finally, I said, "You know, Bob, we better buy this bar or somebody's going to buy it and compete against us." And so we did. That became Wave Waikiki.

Right before we took possession of it, Hula's caught on fire. I get this call in the middle of the night saying Hula's is on fire, and I run down there. It was an old house converted for business over the years and a short circuit in the crawlspace between the ceiling and the roof started it. The fire department was able to put it out quickly, but it still did so much damage and the structure was so weak anyhow that we basically had to rebuild the whole thing.

I moved my whole staff over to the Wave, and our customers went there while we were rebuilding Hula's. It was really dark and dingy because we didn't have much money to do anything with the interior, but it had a dance floor and a DJ booth. It had three floors. There was a mezzanine that overlooked the main floor and a third floor.

The guy who owned Lava Lava was a gay man from Switzerland, I think, and he had gay baths on the third floor, and he had all these little rooms up there with showers and stuff that I had to have torn out. It was a separate operation where you went up the back staircase. The third floor is where I installed dressing rooms and my office, bookkeepers for both Hula's and the Wave, and a video editing bay for our music videos.

At the time, nightclubs with cabaret licenses had to have live music, and the Wave, which had one of those four o'clock liquor licenses, really took off. Then right before New Year's we were able to get Hula's open again and so all our customers went back to Hula's. So before two o'clock, when Hula's closed, I had no customers at the Wave. I thought, *What can I do to get more customers and not scare away the after-two o'clock, gay, mixed crowd?* That's when I decided to go with The Squids.

THE SQUIDS

Beano Shots: I used to hang out at China Sea Tattoo shop in Chinatown. The owner's name was Mike Malone, and he introduced me to Kit Ebersbach, 'cause Kit was hanging out there too, and so was my future brother-in-law, Michael Corcoran, who later wrote for the *Austin Chronicle*. He's an awesome writer. I eventually married his sister Bridget.

At the time, Kit had a gigging band called The Tourists. We used to go see them. They were at Pirate Bully Hayes in Pearl City, playing Talking Heads and more new wave stuff. Kit wanted to start a new band, and he wanted me to be in it. The Squids was my first real working band.

Kit Ebersbach: I had to browbeat some of my friends who were musicians to form a group called The Tourists. It was started so I could do original music, but it never really panned out. We did a lot of new wave

The Squids were one of the first bands in Hawaii to embrace new wave and punk. From left to right: Gerry Ebersbach, Frank Orrall, Kit Ebersbach, Rudy Trubitt, Beano Shots. *Courtesy of Kit Ebersbach*

stuff. It was a combination of songs nobody knew at the time, but also things that were more approachable, like the Rolling Stones and Cheap Trick. The Tourists lasted for about a year and then it kind of had its time. To their credit, they went along with my fiendish plans and were terrific players, but these were professional musicians, and I needed guys who were a little more hungry, more in the underground.

My wife, who is a classical pianist, said she would learn bass and play it, so that made two. And then I played a lounge gig at a place called Quinton's Wharf, out in Hawaii Kai, with a bass player who was the only other professional guy in town that did new wave. His name was Dave Rorick—now Dave Roe—and he could sing "Take Me to the River," and when we played the song, this busboy comes up and says, "Can I sit in?" He sat in on drums, I talked with him, and I came home and said, "Well, we got a drummer!" and that was Frank Orrall. He was eighteen years old.

After that, I was looking for another gig that was really based on original music, and I found it with the two Daves—David Sumida and David Trubitt—who were looking for a band and had original material.

Dave Roe: Kit and I took a lot of shit from the local jazz scene. One guy walked up to us—I'll never forget it—we were standing outside the gig, and he looked at us and said, "You guys have deteriorated so much. What happened to you?" It was hilarious, man. Kit and I just egged each other on the whole time.

Kit and I were really getting into the songwriting scene then. I was writing songs and Kit was writing songs and starting up The Squids at the time. It coalesced around The Pretenders for us, who became the first kinda punk band that had real songs. A couple years ago, it came full circle for me because I got to play on a Pretenders record. That was sort of a pinnacle for me, hanging out with Chrissie Hynde.

I loved Hawaii and I really didn't want to leave, but I knew that if I was going to go national and do anything of any substance, I had to get out of there. LA was out of the question, and I had a cousin out here in Nashville who was a ventriloquist and comedian who performed at the Grand Ole Opry. He offered me a place to stay, so I just took off for Nashville.

Beano Shots: I brought in my friend David Trubitt. He was one of my young friends that were from Manoa. Both of us played guitar. Kit knew a drummer named Frank Orrall, and Kit's wife, Gerry Ebersbach, played bass. We got together at Frank's house, and everything just came together really fast.

Gerry Ebersbach: Kit couldn't find a bass player. He had Beano, he had Rudy, he had Frank, but he had no bass player. He couldn't find anybody, and I said, "I'll learn it." How hard could it be, right? Mostly you play the root of the chord, you have to play on the beat, and there's only four strings on the bass. I know my theory, you know; this is not going to be that hard.

So he bought me a bass, I started learning it, and two weeks later we did our first show in Hawaii Kai. I'd never played a stringed instrument before. That was the time I realized that if you're going to pluck a string, it better be the same string you're fretting on your left hand.

David "Rudy" Trubitt: The first night we met Frank and jammed with him, we drove out to Hawaii Kai to his dad's house and waited around the living room 'cause he was practicing with another band that was like a trio, and I remember they were playing "My Generation." That band's rehearsal finished and the other two guys left, and we all piled into his little bedroom space and played. I think right away, it gelled pretty quick. I don't think anyone had any question about it. It was like, "Oh yeah, this sounds great—let's go!"

Peter Bond: The Squids had a gig once, someplace in Hawaii Kai, and there were all these people, all these kids, and everyone was there to see this brand-new band. I mean, there was nothing like it prior to The Squids. There was no other band that I knew of that was doing anything remotely like them. The Squids were the first band to come along and be weird. Suddenly, I didn't have to be six-foot-two, coke spoon around my neck, and all that stupid shit, you know? I could be some weird, skinny haole kid who didn't know how to dance, and immediately there was a group of people, and it was a small enough scene that everybody knew everybody.

David "Rudy" Trubitt: We ate a bunch of pizza, and I was pretty nervous. We were playing the gig, and I started to feel nauseous. I kind of turned my back on the audience for a second, barfed up my pizza onto my PA, turned around and kept playing.

Frank Orrall: Rudy, before shows, got a lot of butterflies. He couldn't help it, but he threw up on his amp 'cause he didn't want to throw up on stage and have somebody clean it up. That gives you a feeling of how green we were that we would be nervous playing inside of a pizza parlor with probably fifteen people in there.

Byron Lai: Frankie Orrall, I mean, he was the first thing you'd notice about that band, like, "Wow, that kid can play the drums!"

Kit Ebersbach: New wave drumming isn't all that intricate, but you gotta have the groove or people can't dance, and he was right on top of it. Frank was just so talented. He was so much fun to play with. Totally positive energy.

Frank Orrall: I wrote my first song while I was in The Squids, and I just made up some story. It was me trying to write songs by listening to the radio: *I remember that morning I heard you leave, and I heard the car door slam...*None of this happened to me, but it rhymed, it had verse-chorus-verse-chorus, and Kit, very gently, looked at it and goes, "Yeah, it's good. I see a structure there...Now try and write from actual experience," and that was *huge* for me. I was kind of embarrassed when he said it. I was going, "Wow, you're right! What was I thinking?" But that's the kind of thing they instilled in me. I was the youngest member and the greenest, and I learned a huge amount from those guys.

Kit and Beano and Rudy were the songwriting trifecta. Beano brought that New York vibe, like, he loved all the Television, Tom Verlaine stuff. Kit loves John Cage and classical music as well as Hawaiian music, and he's got a very experimental, ready-to-try-anything kind of thing. Rudy, he was informed by Rockpile and The Jam and The Who. In other words, they all brought these different things to The Squids.

Beano also used to write a lot with Rollo Banks, who's actually Mike Malone, the tattoo artist who owned China Sea Tattoo. They used to enjoy writing songs together, and they would hang out all the time and shoot the shit down at the shop. I think that's where a lot of the songs were born. We'd go down there too. It was like going to visit a pirate. He would do artwork for us too. Beano would have him make posters for us. Yeah, I used to love going down there and listen to Rollo tell stories 'cause he really was like a pirate.

Kit lived in public housing down there, him and Gerry. They worked there, his studio was there. I remember going to Kit's house for dinner and sleeping over and coming out and all the cables were ripped out of my car. It was wild. I didn't spend a lot of time down there, but whenever we'd drive through, it'd be exciting.

Beano Shots: Kit Ebersbach was our leader, you know? Whatever he suggested, we would follow. He was always trying to do fun things. So one day Kit said, "These punk rock musicians, they all have fictitious names, so let's come up with our names." I think I was the first one to come up with an idea.

I was at the tattoo shop, in line to get a tattoo. There were two big Filipino *blalahs* in front of me. One guy had his name tattooed on his back: Bino. B-I-N-O. It gave me an idea to call myself Beano, like in the British comics, B-E-A-N-O. Then I was at a store one day and saw BB shots at the cashier counter and I said, "Okay, that's gonna be my last name, 'Shots.'"

Kit Ebersbach: When I was an undergraduate, I took a degree in Japanese, but I wasn't a very good student. I tried to find how close I could come to "Ebersbach" in Japanese, and I came up with *Ebisu-baku*. "Ebisu" was kind of like an aboriginal or a barbarian, and "baku" means "vague." So I was "Vague Barbarian" and no one liked that, so I just said I'll stick with something cute. I called myself "Kit Ebisu" and then it got to be "Kit Ebi." "Ebi" means "shrimp."

George Kail: We opened, actually, before Wave Waikiki, if you're looking for a timeline. The Wave opened up, I think, a few months after we opened. They had some bands that started out with us. Remember The Squids? They started out at my club, at 3-D.

Kit Ebersbach: The best thing that can happen to a band is to have a steady gig because you really learn how to play your songs, and you gel as a band. The gig at 3-D itself wasn't much of anything—we were making chump change—but it's where the band really came together.

Frank was like a high school hero, and his personality's never changed since I've known him. He was always smiling and friendly and genuine, and he had a lot of good friends who supported us. When we got our first steady gig, it was his friends who first came to see us and then it grew from there.

Gerry Ebersbach: Kit said, "You and the drummer have to be one." So I made sure I really listened to Frank. Frank and I were like twins. We became really tight in our playing, and I felt more like brother and sister with him. It was really interesting. Playing in a band broke all my rules. I hate playing with other people; I like being a soloist. But I found playing with other people in this kind of music, there's a lot of energy coming off the stage going out, which is a really amazing feeling. You have the guitars, the drummer, and the bass, and this power goes off the stage into the people. It's just amazing.

ANYTHING GOES

Beano Shots: There were two really good bands at the time that I thought stood out at 3-D. One was Obscene Routine and the other was Collision. Both those bands were getting gigs. I got to know the singer of Obscene Routine, Frank Abreu. Before he put together Obscene Routine, Frank would play at 3-D as a trio, and I thought, *Man, the guy has a lot of talent. He's a really good songwriter too.* When he started Obscene Routine, I got to know the other guys too. They were really good.

Frank Abreu (guitarist/vocalist: Obscene Routine): Kail let me live in 3-D. He didn't have money for an alarm system, so he would let me sleep on the pool table, and I was the security at 3-D. He would lock up, I would be locked in. I couldn't get out. If there was a fire, I probably would've had to climb down the fire escape.

3-D became a hangout for me. I'd go over there any chance I had. I'd go hang out with Kail and bring my guitar. He didn't know how to read music or play a bass, but he bought a bass and said, "Let's start a band." So me and Kail used to sit there and write songs. This is how I met Steve Kendall, who became the drummer of Obscene Routine. He would come by the club, and because Kail owned the club, we could play any time we wanted. So Kail goes, "Let's learn three songs, and we'll play them this weekend, Friday and Saturday, live at the club, and we'll see what people think." The Squids came around, and they would share the gigs with us.

The actual band formed when we had to fire Kail because he sucked at playing bass. But he knew, he knew. He said, "Man, I'm just gonna be a club owner."

I said, "Yeah, you should just own clubs."

Gerry Ebersbach: I remember playing at 3-D one time and I heard somebody had thrown someone off the balcony.

"Oh my God, is he alive?"

"Yeah, he's fine."

"But it's the third floor, and that's a cement sidewalk down there!"

My kids had an interesting time because they went to all these places, and the bartenders would take care of them and sneak them sodas and stuff.

Frank Orrall: 3-D definitely felt like an "anything goes" place, like our own Studio 54. Kim and Kail, they loved to fuel that place the way Andy Warhol would have, and so it got the attention of Jack Law.

Jack Law had the two best gay clubs in town. He had Hula's and he had Wave Waikiki, but everybody preferred Hula's, so nobody was at the Wave until 2 a.m., when Hula's closed. So he came to 3-D to court us to come over there to play from nine until one to bring in the punk and new wave crowd there.

Jack Law: I had an empty club before two o'clock, and it occurred to me that, yeah, this punk rock crowd, they're revolutionary anyhow, and they'll get along with gays, and they did.

Beano Shots: I remember Jack Law came to 3-D to check us out and he talked to us and asked if we could be the house band at the Wave. We were the first band to play there because they just opened.

Frank Orrall: Jack said, "I'll walk you over to check out my club." So we finished our set and packed up, and by the time we got to the Wave, it was, like, 2:30 and that place was *going off*. I mean, there were guys shirtless on top of speakers and amyl nitrite in the air, and it was pretty exciting. I remember thinking we just came from a punk club, but I was all intimidated because they were way rougher than us.

Gerry Ebersbach: The first day we went there, I was like, "Wow, they really want us?" because there was a big stage and everything. Then one of the guys went up the stairs and came running back down: "Two guys are making out up there!" and I'm like, "Oh my God, where are we? Where are the kids?"

Peter Bond: Oh my God, I loved the Wave when it opened. I was there every night. If you got there at 9:00 to 9:30, they let you in free. We didn't have any money and were broke as shit, so we would go early, maybe get a drink, and we would dance all night. Then The Squids would play, and the DJs would play all the latest, coolest music.

Beano Shots: The transition from 3-D to the Wave was a little bit rocky because by then we had a lot of fans from 3-D who were too young to get into the Wave. So we lost some of our fans, but going from 3-D to the Wave was a really big step. They had a full-service bar and a DJ.

Peter Bond: The best club you could play at was the Wave. They had the best sound, the best lights. They really dialed it in. You had a sound man who'd really pay attention to your whole set; you'd have a guy on lights; you'd have a fog machine and an incredible sound system. It was awesome to play there.

Frank Abreu: The Wave was different. That's where we really thought we were legit because we got paid with a check. There was no cash; there was a contract. It was night and day from the way Kail operated. It was just a handshake before.

Gary Owens: If you were more into the underground stuff, you probably went to 3-D. If you wanted to go somewhere that was packed late at night, you went to the Wave. The Wave back then, after 2 a.m., it turned completely gay, pretty much. Once Hula's closed, everybody would come down to the Wave, and the whole crowd would kinda change. You'd be out dancing and there'd be nobody with shirts on. All the people who weren't really into that were like, "Ooh, I gotta go."

Later on, though, the Wave got more and more straight as time went on. By the '90s, girls who got off from work at strip bars came in there, and all the dudes would follow, so that kinda turned it straight.

Jack Law: When Hula's opened up, there were other gay dance bars in Waikiki, and it was cool for straight and gay people to go to dance clubs and dance with each other and have a good time. That continued until AIDS happened; When AIDS happened, all of a sudden, that stopped. Nobody knew where you got it or that it was a sexually transmitted disease. You didn't know if you could catch it by someone sweating on you on the dance floor. People were dying. It was awful. It's not like if you got it you might die—no, if you got AIDS, *you were dead.* It changed the world.

Frank Orrall: I'll put the Wave up there as one of the super pivotal nightclubs because it brought the gay and the straight cultures together, and it went until four o'clock, so things went deep. They would play New York disco in there, they would play punk rock. It was the place where everybody ended up.

SONYA & REVOLUÇION

Sonya Mendez: For a whole year I was unemployed. It was one of the best years of my life because it came to shape what became Sonya & Revoluçion. I was full of angst, pissed off from being fired from my previous gig, and I had no money. I needed to do something fun and exciting.

Somebody told me about the Wave, which was a new place that just opened up, and that they might be looking for new bands. I called Jack Law up and said, "Hi, my name is Sonya Mendez, and I have a trio that I put together, and we'd like to audition for you." Here I am thinking we're going to play three or four, maybe five songs, and he says, "Okay, I want you to play the whole night Sunday, 9 p.m. to 1 a.m." I thought, *Oh, shit...four hours of music?* So we rehearsed and learned a ton of music. You know, when you're unemployed you've got a lot of time.

Sonya & Revolucion in 1982. From left to right: Chris Bovard, Billy Mendoza, Sonya Mendez, Greg Hickey, Mimi Connor. *Courtesy of Sonya Mendez*

Then I thought, *Oh God, I gotta tell everyone I know!* We invited all of our friends. I sent a little flier to every person I thought would come out to the Wave. That was eighty people. We didn't even have a name. Half of them knew me from singing lounge music at the Hilton and were there out of curiosity, and I jokingly say the other half were there to see me fail.

I remember the first night, Jack Law comes walking in, and it's about 11:30 on a Sunday night and the club is busy. All of a sudden my heart starts beating really fast, like, "Oh my God, oh my God, he's not gonna like us, he's gonna fire us, we're never gonna work here again!" He stands there, casually leaning against the bar, and I see him looking around, looking upstairs, looking around the club, but he doesn't say anything. The end of the night comes, and we're allowed to have a *pau hana* drink, so we're at the bar and he looks at me and goes, "Wanna play next Sunday?" We were ecstatic, like, "Oh my God, we're gonna play next Sunday!" This went on for about six Sundays in a row. We kept the same flier, and we kept X-ing out the date and adding new dates.

Jack Law: It basically came down to how many people walked in the door. Sonya's band was a great—and I mean *great*—cover band. Sonya was fantastic and everybody in the band was talented, and they could play anything and people would get up and dance.

Sonya Mendez: I would watch to see which songs the DJ played that would make people rush the dance floor and then add all of those songs to our sets because in my mind, if you're going to play live music, then you gotta play the music that makes people want to dance. We picked all the winners.

John Andreoni (drummer: Fallen Angel, Sonya & Revoluçion, Passion, etc.): I was playing with Fallen Angel at the Rock and Roll Clinic, doing whatever was new on the radio: ZZ Top, Bryan Adams, Eddie Money, John Cougar, stuff like that. The whole time, we'd hear stories about the Wave and how well Jack treated everybody and how fun and successful that club was, and so we all wanted to play at the Wave. Well, suddenly,

I found myself being offered a job with Sonya, so I quit my band and joined her band.

Bands would rehearse maybe once a week and might be lucky to learn one new song a week. That kept them popular. Sonya took that to the next level, all right? We learned two or three songs every week.

We're still good friends, but I wanted to kill her, and she wanted to kill me when I played in her band. She hired a full-blown coliseum rock drummer to play songs half of which were made by a drum machine. She'd pick a Eurythmics song, right? I mean, they don't have a real drummer in that band—it's a computer. We just butted heads all the time, but it was so pleasant and so fun to play at that club. I never took it for granted. The Wave valued and stuck with live music right up until the last day, and for that I'll be eternally grateful to Jack.

Sonya Mendez: In addition to our Sunday night gig at the Wave, we were working four nights a week, directly across the street at the Rock & Roll Clinic, doing hard rock songs. One night, I'm on my break, sitting outside, and Kit Ebersbach from The Squids comes walking over and I say, "Hi, how are you doing?"

He goes, "Well, not so good. We just got our notice."

I look at him and I go, "Not! Really?"

He says, "Yeah, Jack found another band."

"Who?"

He looks at me and goes, "You!"

Jack Law: It's called paying the bills. You had to give people a reason to go to the ass end of Waikiki where we were, and the band was always important because you could go anywhere and listen to recorded music. The band was the reason for people to come out, and it was that way for the whole twenty-five years at the Wave.

One of the things I'm most proud about is that I've met payroll twice a month for almost fifty years. Sometimes I had as many as 150 employees, and believe me, that's not easy. If you want to be successful, you've got to pay the bills.

Beano Shots: The Squids broke up in 1982. That's when Bridget and I got married and I came back to the farm to work.

David "Rudy" Trubitt: Ten months, six nights a week at the Wave, four sets a night, and when we finally burned out on that and gave up that gig, it was time for it to be done. But what the heck do you do after that? The only thing left to do, in my mind, was to try and move to the mainland. Kit and Gerry had two young kids, and we were in very different places in our lives, so it was not possible for the band to pick up and move.

Gerry Ebersbach: The very reasons that made it easy for me to learn this kind of music were the very reasons Kit got tired of it. After a few years, he had done as much of it as he wanted to, but he really got to explore its energy and the feeling of a change in culture, because that's what music does, right? When there's a change in music, there's a change in culture. It was the most collaborative, creative, amazing group of people. Really supportive of each other. It was an experience I keep striving for.

Kit Ebersbach: The Squids changed everything for me. It enabled me to write songs and have people take them seriously. That was really important, but the biggest thing other than that was that it was the first band I was ever in where everybody was having a great time and enjoyed each other's company. There was no rivalry or any kind of weird vibe happening between any of the band members. We just came together and made music and had a great time.

Frank Orrall: I learned a lot from those guys. That was a profound experience for me, playing in that band. It gave me my creative wings. I remember it ended super fast, and I was like, "Let's keep going! What do you mean? This is fun!" because all of a sudden it was like, "Yeah, we're going to do our last shows." But I think it was kind of like buttoning it up, wrapping it up: *That was good. We did good work. All right, let's move on.* And those guys were like that. They were artists first.

5

REVOLUTION ROCK

Though The Squids may well have been the first working band in Hawaii to perform original new wave and punk rock, other progressive-minded outfits joined the party soon after. Some, like Collision and Obscene Routine, paid their dues at 3-D Ballroom before graduating to special attraction status at Wave Waikiki. Other notable but short-lived acts were forged from the ashes of The Squids, including Fun and Profit, featuring Rudy Trubitt and Gerry Ebersbach; as well as Kit and Gerry Ebersbach's synth-centric Pacific Ethno Techno. Still other novel and exotic sounds began to emerge on the scene.

Bob Marley, in 1979, performed before an enlightened but smallish audience of about 5,000 at the Waikiki Shell. If he'd lived to play the Islands a decade later, he could have certainly sold out Aloha Stadium and played to a crowd at least ten times as large. It was more like a slow, steady burn than wildfire, but once reggae caught on in Hawaii, it forever left its brand on local culture.

By the early '80s, several Hawaiian acts like Billy Kaui, Na Mele Kane, and Brother Noland had begun to dabble in reggae, though authentic roots bands were still a rarity if they existed at all. "There didn't seem to be any dedicated reggae bands until Cool Runnings started up," notes guitarist Chris Planas, who helped found the pioneering reggae troupe in 1981. "If there were, I didn't know about 'em."

Once, after Cool Runnings held a free show at Kapiolani Park, Planas remembers meeting Butch Helemano, years before Helemano would grow into a Hawaiian reggae star. Thrilled to encounter a real live, local reggae ensemble, Helemano practically begged to join the group. Cool Runnings, however, was already plenty large, having incorporated a number of local and transplanted musicians and a pair of cocksure instrumentalists of Jamaican origin who were harboring notions of fronting their own bands.

With reggae still on the periphery, Cool Runnings played wherever it could: Kojack's Place, the Young Street watering hole that featured everything from Hawaiian music to comedy to new wave; and 3-D in Waikiki, where some of the rough-and-tumble nightclub's punk rock clientele put up with their music as long as the DJ played the latest ska platters in between sets. Some of Cool Runnings' punk rock contemporaries connected with reggae's themes of protest and revolution and began adding reggae tunes to their repertoire. Politically motivated bands like Collision and Fallout fell in with the island's communist activists.

In time, Planas and drummer James Ganeko departed Cool Runnings for nouvelle vague rockers Nuclear Tan, then Pagan Babies; Maacho went on to head his own reggae combo, Maacho and Cool Connection; Scroo formed Ranking Scroo and Crucial Youth; and percussionist Sluggo, along with Collision's keyboard player-slash-guitarist Dave Tokuda, joined a new high-powered ska outfit featuring Frank Orrall called Mumbo Jumbo.

Just as Cool Runnings took up the mantle for reggae, Mumbo Jumbo was an early proponent of second wave ska. In year two of their venture, following the departure of Orrall, Mumbo Jumbo invited the ebullient and overflowing Robert Scott to man the microphone and share vocal duties with local stage veteran Naomi Summers. Though an admittedly limited crooner, Scott gave the group an offbeat comedic touch and turned Mumbo Jumbo into the scene's premier party ensemble. "I was notoriously flat through all of my bands," concedes Scott. "But I was a really good frontman."

Audiences were occasionally treated to appearances by Scott in costume, like when he dressed up as a superhero in an opening slot for A Flock of Seagulls at UH's Campus Center Ballroom, and as a pirate for a now-legendary seven-band boat party aboard the four-masted, 100-plus-year-old Falls of Clyde sailing ship in Honolulu Harbor.

Formerly the lead vocalist with Bad Posture and Castration Anxiety, Scott was generally the center of attention wherever he went, recalls former bandmate and UH classmate Arnie Saiki. "Robert would roller-skate on campus, and he had a very straight, very colorful, and very tall mohawk," Saiki remembers. "And he had these glasses which were a little bit like bottle glasses, but they had all kinds of knickknacks glued to them."

Another favored accessory worn by Scott in those days was the skull of a monkey, roughly the size of a human fist, gifted to him by Tokuda, who Scott says worked at an animal laboratory at UH. When the primate passed away from natural causes, its head was boiled for three days until all that remained was smooth off-white bone. It hung from Scott's neck from a chain. "Robert always stood out," says Saiki. "Like, famously stood out."

COLLISION

Ronnie Ravelo: My brother was a very good singer, and when Widow was done and I came back to Hawaii from LA, I said, "Let's do something together. Make me a list of what you wanna do." So he got back to me and showed me all these albums from Styx, Journey, Supertramp, and all that. I looked at those albums and I tossed 'em. I said, "No, we're not doing that. We're gonna do punk and we're gonna do ska."

It was very surprising how quickly everything came together. I wanted to play guitar, so we got another guy to play keyboards and guitar, and a bass player, and they worked really well together. Tom Hamasu was a jazz bass player, but he was totally into this new music. He and Dave Tokuda were already playing punk and new wave and ska. They actually belonged to the communist party, and they were very rebellious. That was the beginning of Collision.

We had a gig at 3-D for a while. We did the Wave for a while too. Tommy and Dave were really into The Clash, so we did some of that, some Gang of Four and some originals my brother wrote. They invited us to play some of their communist functions and I go, "We're not political!" But their crowds loved what we did and they danced. I just wanted to play music.

James Ganeko (drummer: Cool Runnings, Nuclear Tan, Pagan Babies, etc.): I remember seeing Collision for the first time. They used to have an off night at the Wave. Adam, the singer, had a doll around his neck, and he was biting the head off, and it was like, "Wow, man, this is heavy!"

John Dahlin: Collision did some reggae, but they also played Clash songs, and they were super, super-talented musicians. The funny thing that brought Collision together is they were Maoist communists. I saw them several times at 3-D. They had this singer and he was really, really good, but for some reason, he always fought with them, and they sacked him, and I sang for Collision for a while.

We used to practice in some garage near downtown, and they had a fake wall that you would move over, and it was their communist literature book room, and we would practice in this place. They loved The

Clash 'cause with *Sandinista!* and all that, they were sure The Clash were communists.

I played a few shows with them, and honestly, I think that I just wasn't the caliber of singer they were looking for, so we kind of parted, but we stayed friends.

Patrick Donegan (KTUH Monday Night Live director; Progressive Arts founding member; soundman): The RCP was the Revolutionary Communist Party, and they were the guys who handed out a paper called the *Revolutionary Worker.* They knew to hang out with the punky people and reggae people to do what they call "struggle," which is to talk about Maoist philosophies and what's wrong with mainstream society. There were a handful of bands that were RCPers, and they were always saying, "Man, I just read in the *Revolutionary Worker* last week this thing—here, you should buy a copy for fifty cents." So we'd hear about Steve Biko and Nelson Mandela. There were lots of marches that were organized by RCPers.

Cool Runnings was the reggae band with members living on top of the Haleiwa Theater for a couple years until they tore it down to put up a McDonald's. That was another "people's struggle."

COOL RUNNINGS

Craig Okino (bassist/vocalist: Cool Runnings, Pagan Babies): After I moved back to Hawaii from the Bay Area in 1976, reggae was still not easy to find, but more and more American labels were starting to release reggae albums. So I would go to Records Hawaii a lot, which was in a large, warehouse-like building on Pi'ikoi Street, and I made friends with a clerk there who saw me buying reggae LPs and was curious about the music. It turns out he had a large studio space upstairs from the record store. He played some guitar and knew other guys who were interested in jamming. So we started having reggae jam sessions in his studio. That's how I met some of the players who would later be in Cool Runnings and the Pagan Babies, like Chris Planas and Nelson Hiu. It was fun, but it didn't sound that great at first because we didn't have a drummer.

Chris Planas: Records Hawaii used to be at 404 Pi'ikoi, and these friends of mine worked there. On Sunday nights it became this thing where, "Oh, let's get together, listen to some reggae and drink beer and smoke pot and start playing." I got turned on to reggae as well in the late '70s because the record stores that carried punk rock music also carried Jamaican imports.

We were all local Asian American guys, college educated; a good number of us went away for school and came back. We got it to be kind of cohesive, but we didn't really have a drummer.

There was a reggae radio show on KTUH hosted by Daniel Warner, and people who listened to reggae listened to his show. He said, "I got this guy who plays drums; he plays like Sly Dunbar," and that turns out to be James Ganeko. So James shows up with his drum kit, and that whole sound just kind of fell into place.

James Ganeko: I knew Daniel Warner from living in Japan. My father was in the military, so I was born and raised in Japan, and we moved around and ended up coming to Hawaii in the very late '70s. Daniel also moved to Hawaii and became a DJ at KTUH. We were both big record collectors. His collection was unreal. He got a lot of his records straight from Jamaica. He said, "Hey, go check out Records Hawaii. There's some guys who work there and they're jamming reggae." So I went over there and got to meet some of the guys.

I wasn't really familiar with reggae drumming. I mean, I'd hear the beats on the recordings and try to play what I heard: the one drop, rock steady, all different types of rhythms.

Chris Planas: Some of us wanted to play out because we saw the potential with James, and again, Daniel Warner said, "I know these Jamaican guys. A couple of them are in the military, and one of them lives on the North Shore. Maybe I can hook you guys up with them." And so that happened. We drove up to a house in Haleiwa, set up, and we all played. That became Cool Runnings with Maacho and Sluggo and Ranking Scroo. It was 1981.

Craig Okino: Back then, Maacho was known as Egy, because his real name was Egland. Egy and Scroo were from Jamaica and were in the Army. Sluggo said he was from St. Thomas, but we found out later he was from Cincinnati, and Bongo the sax player was from Philly. Well, that did it. We were a real band with actual dreads, and we called ourselves Cool Runnings.

James Ganeko: It was the first time I actually met guys from Jamaica and so they were the real deal. They showed me how to play the beats. Cool Runnings lasted, I'm guessing, probably a couple of years. We started connecting with the punk scene because bands like The Clash were doing some reggae stuff, and we were doing some early 2 Tone. We were doing an off night at the Wave for a while.

Craig Okino: We started playing Sundays at the Wave and other nights at 3-D and put on a few of our own shows at the late, great Haleiwa Theater.

We were a pretty motley crew—a few dreads and some local guys—but the music was good, and we had a loyal following. Gradually, though, the egos started clashing. Maacho and Bongo were increasingly at odds with Sluggo, who they said was a poseur and wasn't a real dread. They quit and then Chris, Nelson, and James quit to form a band with Collision's bass player, Tommy Hamasu, called Nuclear Tan. We tried to carry on with some replacement musicians who had never played reggae before, but it wasn't the same and Cool Runnings fell apart.

Chris Planas: I left Cool Runnings to join this band, Nuclear Tan, with James Ganeko on drums; our keyboard player was Nelson Hiu, and we had a Berklee School of Music-trained bass player named Tommy Hamasu. Anybody who went to school with him will tell you he was a monster on bass and was already playing with name musicians before he moved back to Hawaii. Nuclear Tan did stuff like The Police, Grace Jones, and some originals that were edgier than your regular new wave stuff.

MUMBO JUMBO

Jim Rossi a.k.a. Goopy Rossi (bassist: Mumbo Jumbo, Hat Makes the Man): My parents split up in '77 or '78, and my mom wound up moving from California to Hawaii. In August of '81, my dad passed away and a week later, I was in Honolulu, starting at Kaiser High. Within a month or so, I met the cool haole rock-and-roll kids and got into one of their bands, playing terrible three-chord rock like "867-5309/Jenny."

Then I met this guy Renarde. Renarde Clerx was this Dutch kid who lived in Hawaii Kai. I don't remember what his dad did, but he had this pretty bigshot job. Then there was John Dahlin, who blew me away because he was the most punk rock person I'd ever met in my life. He had that John Lydon look and that kind of sneer and that attitude and swagger. He was like the cool punk rock kid in school. He had a band with Tom Clerx, Renarde's brother.

Tom would ask me for bass lessons, and he was really a Sid Vicious kind of character where I don't think he ever held an instrument before.

Mumbo Jumbo at the Blaisdell Exhibition Hall, 1984. *Courtesy of Goopy Rossi*

He looked amazing with it, though. He was this buff, six-foot-something, scary Dutch guy, while Renarde was super skinny and anemic-looking and played the clarinet.

And so Renarde was like, "Hey, I wanna start a ska band, and I have these guys that want to do it. Do you wanna play bass?" When we first got together, it was Frank Orrall on drums, Renarde on clarinet, me on bass, and Ronnie Ravelo from Collision playing guitar. January or February of '82 is when I think Mumbo started. I was still fifteen.

Ronnie Ravelo: I remember Frankie calling me up, wanting to do a ska band and saying, "You're the guy!" because we'd always talk ska. When I was in LA, I saw The Specials and I would talk to Frank about how much we loved ska and liked this band and that band. Our first gig was at 3-D.

Peter Bond: Mumbo Jumbo played English Beat, Madness, maybe a little bit of 2 Tone. They were great, a lot of movement. They were so fun. Goopy was really moving. He had those big glasses and would wear these real goofy aloha shirts, but once you plugged him in, man, he was just *goin'* the whole time.

Goopy Rossi: I remember when we didn't have anything happening on the weekend, we would just drive into Waikiki and walk around. We'd get propositioned by prostitutes and run into the religious fanatics and watch the tourists. It was kind of teeming late into the night. There were just people out wandering around, so it wasn't weird for us to be hanging out on the sidewalk in front of 3-D.

One of those Japanese gun ranges was downstairs. I didn't understand what that was all about, and somebody explained you can't shoot a gun in Japan, so that's like a fun thing to do while you're in Hawaii: go into the basement of a punk club and shoot guns.

Gary Owens: Every summer, Rodney Bingenheimer used to come out for Rodney on the ROQ's Hawaiian Summer Vacation. He'd take over and deejay at 3-D. That was pretty cool because in the early '80s, KROQ was the station to listen to in LA, man. All these hot little chicks from LA would come out too, and we'd be like, "Yeah! Who did he bring this year?" He'd play like it was his show, pretty much; some stuff that was popular, but then he'd throw in underground LA bands on that new wave, modern music tip that didn't have any airplay.

George Kail: Because of my background in LA, I got to know Rodney Bingenheimer, who was a well-known DJ, and he opened up his own club there on Sunset Boulevard in the '70s. He had everybody and their mother involved, from Joan Jett, David Bowie, and so on. I always stayed friends with him, and when I opened 3-D, because of my communication with Rodney Bingenheimer, we were bringing in acts from the mainland, bands like Agent Orange and Circle Jerks. I didn't know those guys from Adam, but Rodney would call me: "Kail, Kail—Agent Orange would like to come over!" So he was my link. He was sending bands left and right, and I don't remember all the bands. We were scheduled to have Black Flag play once and something happened and they canceled.

The bands that would come in from LA, it was pretty funny because they didn't have a place to stay, and they'd sleep in the club. They had keys, we trusted them. I'm sure they delved into our alcohol, but in those days we didn't care. The attraction for these bands from LA was not necessarily the money. We would pay for their airfare, and we would not pay them very much. I mean, if the whole band got $500 for the whole week, they were lucky. It was a vacation getaway for them. I can't even remember how they showered, but I gotta tell you, it was definitely an underground scene. It doesn't get any more underground than that.

Gary Owens: We walk into 3-D, a weeknight, and Siouxsie Sioux's in there and I didn't think it was her. I turn to my friends. I'm like, "Look at this girl, she thinks she's Siouxsie!" She just looks at me and she's like, "I *am* Siouxsie, you idiot." Later on, she had an album out as The Creatures, which was recorded in Hawaii with Hawaiian singers. I didn't know about that until after the album came out. She had come down to 3-D, I guess, to hang out with her drummer—what's his name, Budgie? And we were all calling her a poseur. I wish I'd have known it was actually her. I would've hung out with her, but of course, I was a kook about it.

Another time, I'd gotten into a fight the week before, so Kim and Kail kicked me out of 3-D. I remember hanging out in front of the club, just being out of control, and the chick from Berlin went in there, and I'm like, "Ha!" So I went to the back where the power box was, and I turned off the power. My friends were in there, and they were like, "Yeah, she grabbed her bodyguard—she was all scared!"

I think I turned off the power a few times. I remember one time Kim was chasing me down the alley because I turned it off, and I'm all, "Well, let me back in and you won't get the power turned off!"

COMMIE VIBES

Goopy Rossi: For me, Fallout was my favorite band. In terms of playing ability and energy, I thought they were one of the best bands. I think the punk rockers were confused because on the one hand, punk is all about being rebellious, but Fallout were *really* outsiders because I think people were kind of turned off by the whole commie vibe.

They did a bunch of Clash covers, they did The Jam, and then they'd do weird stuff like Bowie's "Modern Love," and the thing that drove my brother Hozy nuts—because he became their drummer—was they spent more time trying to figure out if the song's message was in line with their RCP agenda. It would drive Hozy crazy because they spent three hours talking about the lyrics to a song and, like, an hour practicing.

James Ganeko: We would have deep discussions when we were in Nuclear Tan. Chris and all those guys were very intelligent and had these heavy, heavy conversations. We would always tell Tommy, "Tom, if you call yourselves communists, it's a guarantee people are going to be put off right away. Call yourself something else and say what you want to say, and people will probably listen to you more openly."

Gary Owens: I don't want to get political or anything, but I grew up in a military family and I used to get into fights with some of those guys. There was the RCYB, the Revolutionary Communist Youth Brigade, and me and my friends, we weren't into that. I mean, it's cool, though; you can play your music, but it just got to the point where me and a couple of my friends were like, "Fuck this!"

Ronnie Ravelo: 3-D had that great divey atmosphere, and you never knew when a fight was gonna break out. When I was still with Collision, we were playing there once, and guys were taking the records glued to the wall and throwing them at us. We would say, "Guys, could you stop that? You're gonna hurt someone…" *Whoosh.* They'd throw another one. So I threw off my guitar and went into the audience. "COME ON!" Next thing I knew, someone swung at me, and my brother went out there. Tommy was out there. You never knew what was gonna happen at that place.

Gary Owens: I remember getting in a fight, not with a communist, but with some dickhead, and I just flattened him. I'll never forget that. The guy was trying to throw me around or something, and I just looked at him like, "What's your problem?" He was only fucking with me, and I'm like, "You're gonna go down!" and fucking clotheslined him. He left after that. Nobody knew him. He was fucking with the wrong guy. That was at the Falls of Clyde, over by Aloha Tower.

I remember I jumped into the water and had all the harbor police chasing me around. They didn't like that too much. They didn't get me, though. Those Falls of Clyde shows were fun.

Robert Scott (vocalist: Dervishes, Mumbo Jumbo, Bad Posture, etc.): Gary Owens jumped up on the rail of the Falls of Clyde and he goes, "Party hearty, mates!" and he dives off the rail and swims under the keel in pitch-black, nasty Honolulu Harbor and comes out on the other side. Everybody's freaking out; his brother Chris is like, "What the fuck? Somebody save my brother!" That was insane. That was the craziest place to play.

George Kail: There was a lot of chaos. You know, I gotta tell ya, I've been shot at, I've been spit on, I've been punched. When I had 3-D, I was sitting in the front talking with my doorman, and my crazy partner, who was a total drunk, pissed off the wrong person a couple weeks earlier, and that person proceeded to come up the back steps of 3-D on the second landing—we know who he is; he was never arrested. He opened fire and shot my doorman right in front of my eyes. I saw the doorman try to run, and his legs collapsed under him. The leg had severed to where his foot was dangling from his leg, and the guy had just missed shooting me. The guy who did the shooting got away with it.

It's a very unique city over here in Honolulu, where sometimes you have family that is on one side of the law and you have family that's on the opposite side of the law. I don't know if you know that, but it's true. So again, I had to get away from Kim, and that's what led me to open up Pink Cadillac.

6

HARDCORE RULES

When Talking Heads and Blondie—two of the more accessible groups of the New York punk scene—appeared on the pop charts at the close of the 1970s, a quandary arose. Radio had given punk rock a broader audience, though its standing as a refuge for outcasts and dissenters was quickly called into question. "Punk Is Dead" became a recurring declaration of writers, critics, and naysayers quick to convey a would-be insider's grasp of all things current and trendy.

As if on cue, a particularly ornery sub-brand of punk rock, intent on wresting punk from the mainstream once and for all, emerged. This sound, more unruly than anything that had come before, was played at breakneck pace and reveled in chaos. Hardcore, they called it. First seen in Los Angeles, it quickly cropped up in San Francisco, New York, Boston, and Washington, D.C., threatening other cities with infection.

A brash new breed of punks from LA's neighboring suburbs, with little regard for what came before, quickly moved in on the original Hollywood scene's lively and creative commonwealth. Warlike packs of juveniles with testosterone-fueled rituals like slam dancing and stage diving rejected the art- and fashion-inspired elements of LA's first wave in favor of a much more physical, ultra-masculine variant of punk, alienating much of the scene's female membership in the process.

Kailua's Jeff Dahl was already entrenched in LA's punk community when he joined hardcore outfit Angry Samoans in 1980. Though he'd advocated for this louder, more aggressive sound, Dahl thoroughly renounced the new scene's predilection for violence. "There were a bunch of jocks and bullies and racists that were showing up and starting these big slam pits and beating the shit out of little kids," attests Dahl. "I turned my back on that shit. That was not anything I was part of, or into, or anything like that."

In like manner, Honolulu's earliest scenesters were soon eclipsed by a younger crop of punks who found greater resonance with Black Flag, Dead Kennedys, and Fear than Television, Patti Smith, or Richard Hell. By the time Penelope Spheeris's punk rock feature *The Decline of Western Civilization* showed in Hawaii in April of 1982 at the University of Hawaii at Manoa's Physical Sciences Auditorium, attendees were already staunch converts to hardcore. "Everybody was slamming in the aisles of the theater," testifies John Dahlin, the Kaiser High graduate who fronted some of Honolulu's earliest hardcore bands before hooking up with Seattle-area standouts The Accüsed, an eventual player on the national scene.

A heavily distorted reworking of The Chantays' 1960s surf rock opus, "Pipeline," was the B-side to a single by Agent Orange that earned serious spins on Honolulu FM powerhouse 98 Rock. A smash nowhere else but Hawaii, it gave many local listeners their first taste of punk rock and merited a thank you from the Southern California band on the back cover of their 1982 *Bitchin' Summer* EP. The following year, Agent Orange was flown in for a nine-night engagement at 3-D Ballroom, marking the first time a hardcore band from the outside world played in the Islands.

Hawaii's punks, eager to keep pace with their mainland counterparts, all but apologized to Agent Orange frontman Mike Palm for Hawaii's backcountry status and lack of hipness, though Palm says it was never warranted. "Really, I don't understand it because Hawaii is not behind," expressed Palm in a 1983 interview with Honolulu music mag *Novus*, conducted on the roof of 3-D Ballroom overlooking Kuhio Avenue. "This is exactly what it's like on the mainland. If they want to go over there and see, it's the same thing. This 3-D club could be in the middle of LA."

Still, mainland hardcore acts were a rare treat throughout the 1980s: Circle Jerks played at 3-D in February of 1984, just before the venerable punk club closed its doors; The Vandals performed in '86 and The Brigade (shortened at the time from Youth Brigade) in '87 at the same location as 3-D, though by then known as Odyssey. Also in 1987, MDC played Queen Theater, which for a brief time began to feature live music after police pressured its owner to cease its screening of X-rated films. This scarcity of name-brand punk rock shows left Hawaii scenesters no option but to stage their own gigs at various nightclubs, house parties, and rental halls. Their rough-and-ready exhibitions satisfied a growing demand, and inceptive punk combos like The Sharx, SRO, and The Efekt were seen as pioneers of hardcore in the Islands.

When they played, SRO—short for Something Really Offensive—induced mosh pits quite readily with "The Mokes Are Coming Out Tonight," a rampageous ode to local brutes who relished administering beatings to anyone unlucky enough to cross their path. Sporting a punk look was usually reason enough to earn a generous bashing. The all-too-real song quickly became a scene favorite; an oft-requested hit on college station KTUH and a notorious anthem of the Honolulu underground.

John Dahlin: That was the transition in, like, late '80, '81, when Black Flag and Adolescents and Circle Jerks and all those hardcore bands were becoming more widely known. That was the big changeover, and that was when we started ADMS Family. It stood for Anarchy Doesn't Make Sense and then it became Another Dumb Music Scene and whatever you could think up. I remember all of a sudden, all of these Kaneohe and Kailua guys started showing up too. They had a couple of little bands, and they were more hardcore. There were no other bands from anywhere else to go see, so we just kind of had to invent them as we went, taking cues from what we heard and saw.

Jon Lange (bassist: The Efekt): ADMS Family was my first punk rock show at 3-D. When I walked in, that was my first time there, and I was like, "Holy shit, this is cool!" It was so cool it was scary. I didn't know anybody at the show, and it was a tense fucking scene. I was like a deer in the headlights. I must've been fourteen or so.

The Efekt live at Kojack's. *Courtesy of Jon Lange*

John Dahlin: Dana Collins, the drummer for The Accüsed, had been on vacation in Hawaii with his mom and his sister. I was passing out fliers for a Cool Runnings show at 3-D, down in Waikiki, and this punk kid comes up and says, "Hey, man, what's going on? There's an actual punk scene here?" He pretty much abandoned his mom and his sister for the rest of the week and hung out with me.

He was an amazing drummer. We had an ADMS Family show at 3-D, and he sat in and played "Red Tape" by the Circle Jerks and nailed it. He's like, "Yeah, I got this hardcore band back on Whidbey Island in Washington, and we need a singer, man. You're coming back, aren't you?"

My family kept our house in Vancouver, Washington, when we came to Hawaii, and we were renting it out, and so the plan was to move back after my dad retired and I graduated high school. I mean, within a week of moving back to Washington, I bought a car, went up to Whidbey Island, and joined The Accüsed. They weren't anything then. They were just three kids. Dana was fourteen at the time. Whidbey Island's like an hour north of Seattle and it's really remote. We practiced in a well pump house.

Gary Owens: There was Red Lion Pizza Parlor in Waikiki, and they also had a Red Lion Spaghetti House with a DJ in there. That's when I first discovered punk rock in Hawaii. Dougan Dimmitt, who was the first real punk rocker that I knew, he was in there. It was a punk rock dance contest. They didn't know what they were getting into. Dougan fuckin' started moshing in there, and everybody's like, "What the fuck is this?" He's just knocking people over. They kicked him out of the place: "You're out of here!" and it's like, "What? You guys wanted punk rock, and punk rockers dance like this, so what the fuck?"

John Dahlin: I knew Dougan really well back then. We were kind of neighbors in Hawaii Kai. He lived across the highway and on the ocean. He was from a really, really well-off family, something to do with Pennzoil, I think. It was just him and his parents in this giant, giant house, and he kind of took over the guest house by the pool. We would sneak firewater out to the guest house, where Dougan had a VCR. I saw the Sex Pistols at the Longhorn Ballroom video back in 1980 at Dougan's house. He had some other crazy documentaries, footage of The Slits and stuff like that.

He was just this lonely guy who had been into Kiss and then got into punk. He was alternately really abrasive—and I think a lot of that came from the fact that he came from a family that could afford to be that way—and yet, at the same time, he was just like anybody else and just wanted to have friends. He was an interesting guy.

Johnee Kop (pro skateboarder; drummer: SRO, The Sharx, Dana Lynn/ Chokebore, etc.): When I was about fifteen or sixteen, I went to the mainland a couple of times. There was a guy named Don Hoffman. He was the son of the owner of the Pipeline, which was a very famous skate-park in Upland, California. One day, I called them up long distance and I said, "I'm from Hawaii and I skated your skatepark. I just want a place to stay the next time I visit. Do you know of any place I can stay?" and he said, "Oh, you can just stay here!" So I stayed, I don't know, maybe a month. I lived at the skatepark owner's house. As I think about it, that was pretty crazy. They even picked me up at the airport.

I was introduced to these guys, Steve Alba and Micke Alba. They're famous skaters who lived in the area, and they took me around too. Steve introduced me to, like, the Sex Pistols and punk rock in LA, the spiked hair and the boots and stuff like that. I even went to a couple of shows with him. After the summer hanging out in Los Angeles, my skating improved, and I came back with a punk rock look. I would dye my hair yellow or whatever and skate around like that.

John Dahlin: Down in Kahala, you know, those big houses out at Black Point and Diamond Head, there would be these huge parties at these giant mansions. And they would have multiple bands, and kegs, and just hundreds and hundreds of kids from all around the island would go to these things. It was so amazing. It was like that movie *Dazed and Confused*, where they would have these massive parties. That's where I met John Kop. You know, Johnee Kop. I remember he had a leopard skin vest on and orange spiky hair, like, "Who's this guy? I gotta be friends with him!"

Jon Lange: I went to a party at Black Point. I was maybe fourteen, I think. This was a fucking monster party; it was giant. I couldn't even tell you how many people were there, but there were kegs of beer and people just fucking *trashed*, you know, just out of their minds fucked up. They would happen every year for a couple of years. That's the beauty of growing up in that scene: it's an island, it's isolated, and with word-of-mouth people knew shit quick.

Barry Oshiro a.k.a. DJ Barry Freeze (vocalist: The Sharx, Hypo-Depression; DJ: Odyssey, Sub Club): The first punk bands I heard were Black Flag and all the early hardcore bands: Circle Jerks, Fear, TSOL, The Germs. I used to see some punks around with homemade Black Flag shirts, spray-painted T-shirts, so I was just curious. I found Black Flag stuff at Tower Records and then Bad Religion's first album. When I bought it, the lady behind the counter shook her head in disapproval. That was shocking back then. There was a handful of students at Kalani

Barry of The Sharx. *Courstesy of Jon Lange*

into that stuff, like John Kop. We had our own spot that we'd always go sit down at for lunch.

I did a lot of mail order, and a lot of times I wrote to the bands, and they used to write me back. Like, Crass wrote me back and sent me stickers; Mike Muir from Suicidal Tendencies, he wrote me back and sent me stickers; Glenn Danzig used to handwrite stuff 'cause I used to order stuff in the Fiend Club—singles, T-shirts, and stuff like that.

Johnee Kop: Frank Orrall taught me how to play drums. I had a Sonar drum set. He came over to my house a couple of times and showed me how to do a beat and stuff. He was a friendly guy, and I just started talking to him, maybe at 3-D or something. I was in high school and he was a little older than I was. From there I just learned on my own. I was stoked. I was saying to myself, "Holy God, this guy's a star, and he's in my house teaching me how to do a beat!"

Frank Orrall: Kop used to stand there, right on the side of the stage just watching me, and I'm going, "This kid's totally studying me, man." But I loved him because he was so forthright. He's like, "So when you do that thing with the drums, are you doing this?"

I go, "Yeah."

"Okay." And then he would leave.

Then he would come back the next week and he would go, "So when you do this, do you do this?"

And I go, "Yeah." Then I said, "You know what? I'll come to your house and give you lessons."

He was so bold, you know? He's so great. He lays it on the line: "I want you to show me how to do *this*."

Gardner Pope a.k.a. Gardner Maxam (bassist: The Sharx, The Vacuum, J-Church; vocalist/bassist: Cringer): I remember seeing Johnee Kop around. You couldn't miss him. He was like my punk rock crush, my first one. I just thought he was so fucking cool. And he was such a dick. I mean, he was a friendly dick, but he would always just fuck with you. I saw him wearing a shirt that he had obviously made with the Black Flag bars and it said "Rise Above," and I went home and I made one too.

For me, there were a bunch of these slightly older kids, and I thought they were so cool, and I felt like a loser and they pretty much confirmed that. They were nice enough, but I always felt like a Johnny-come-lately poseur, wannabe punk. I still carry that with me, and I don't know why.

Brian Walls and I were friends from quite young and were already in a rock band. It didn't even have a name. He bought a guitar and took guitar lessons and learned how to do solos and stuff. At the same time, he got into Iron Maiden, and I liked some of their stuff, but in general, I wasn't a metal fan. I remember at the time being kinda like, "I don't know about this." I felt a little weird about that. And at some point, we started a punk band.

Barry Oshiro: The Sharx used to play at parties. First it was John Kop, Gardner Pope, and Brian Walls, and whoever wanted to sing could sing because they just played covers at that time. They were kind of metal-punk because Brian was totally into Iron Maiden and Black Sabbath, so he did all of these amazing solos and all this real metal stuff. We used to all hang out and drink and listen to my boombox, and Gardner heard me sing and asked me if I wanted to sing for The Sharx, so I said, "Yeah, I can sing!"

Gardner Pope: Barry looked like he was thirty from the time he was fifteen, so he could go anywhere; he could buy liquor at any time. He was our ringer, like, "Barry, go buy some beer." We played parties, we played Anna Bannana's a couple of times, we played a couple of small festival-type things, but there was no regular club where we could go to play because most clubs didn't want anything to do with punk, and I don't blame them. A lot of the Hawaii punks were fairly belligerent at times.

Raoul Vehill (vocalist: Devil Dog, Battery Club, The Beasts): I went to this high school that was the second worst high school in Denver, and three or four liberal arts colleges were trying to get me to go to their schools. I'm Latino plus I'm lower middle class, and for whatever reason, I was precocious in terms of reading and writing, so there were a lot of financial aid packages and student loans available to me.

In the end, I decided to go to a small liberal arts college called Hawaii Loa. I was like, "Well, hell, Hawaii? I'll go to Hawaii!" It appealed to my sense of adventure then, and it was the most exotic place that I could get to when I was eighteen. I could have ended up in a lot worse places.

There were these two guys, Erik Mori and Chris North, who I formed Battery Club with. It was basically three-chord, power pop, proto-punk. We were more or less the only guys in my college who would listen to the Sex Pistols and punk or whatever, and I think that maybe I was kind of naturally theatrical, but I remember Battery Club never got very popular with the scene. We had a punk edge, but maybe because we were a little bit older and not from Hawaii, my perception at that time was, "Nobody really likes us, so fuck it—we'll just do what we want anyway." We played in Waikiki at 3-D sometimes.

Robert Scott: Battery Club was incredible. Raoul was singing songs like "I'm a Spy for the CIA," and I think there was a song called "You Owe Me a Fuck." They were punk, but more on the art side. It was radical and intense, but Raoul had this existential, poetic edge.

Raoul Vehill: Hawaii Loa had a basketball team, and I remember Battery Club played one time at a basketball game, and strangely enough, the coach wanted us to be the team band whenever they had sporting events. Erik and Chris were like, "Yeah, let's do it!" and I was like, "No way." We broke up before we all graduated, so I was starting to look for people to do my next band with because I was writing songs.

John Dahlin: Early on, there were no punk clothing stores. There was a catalog you could get from LA from Poseur, and you could buy stuff by mail order. Dougan Dimmitt had those catalogs.

I remember going to Ala Moana and stealing dog collars from the pet shop and taking the studs off of 'em. On Kuhio Avenue, there was a bondage shop that opened up. It was like this sex toy shop right by Hula's, and it had this real gay theme to it, and they had all this cool leather and all this stuff, but it was so expensive. We couldn't afford it.

One time, I found a dead mongoose in a trap, and the bugs had eaten off all the meat so that all that was left were these awesome dried, bleached bones. So I made this mongoose bone necklace, and I used to wear that all the time.

The first store I remember actually ever carrying stuff like punk rock buttons and sleeveless leopard-skin shirts and stuff was in the Ward Warehouse, which is knocked down now. It was kind of like a girly surf shop, and we'd go there all the time and steal Buzzcocks buttons and stuff like that. I don't even think the people who worked there knew what they were selling. They just had a smart owner who knew this was what's coming, so we'd better start carrying it.

Barry Oshiro: You could take silk screening in high school, so a lot of us made Black Flag and Circle Jerks shirts that way or just with marsh pen. Back then it was secret when you found cool stuff. There was one of those women's stores in Ward Warehouse, and they had wristbands: "You can get spikes at this store…Don't tell anybody!" And then, "At Holiday Mart, you can get steel toe boots…Don't tell anybody!" And you could get spurs and bandanas at Paniolo Trading. The LA punk look back then was steel toe boots, bandanas, and spurs, just like the Circle Jerks skanking logo guy.

Gardner Pope: When I was fourteen, probably, I went to Tower Records with a friend of mine and we saw Lance Hahn. He was wearing a Sex Pistols T-shirt, and he had a chain and a lock around his neck except it wasn't the Sid Vicious kind; it was an actual chain that you would use to lock up a parking lot and a padlock like you would lock your locker at school. He looked ridiculous. He came up and talked to us, and we were nice to him and then we went away and we made fun of it. I'm sure I looked just as ridiculous, but I didn't have an actual chain and padlock around my neck, just for the record.

Matthew Grim: My friends and I discovered Dungeons & Dragons in the ninth grade. We were the biggest *Napoleon Dynamite* fuckin' doofuses. I can remember the feeling of a new dungeon quest and being so lathered up. Like, we were not fuckin' cool. There wasn't one fuckin' cool bone in our bodies. Look at my ninth grade picture. We were the dumbest, geekiest, fuckin' no pussy-gettin' people, guaranteed.

John Kop was infamous then. He was the O.G. punk rocker who spray-painted "Rise Above" and Black Flag's logo on the steps of my school or something. I just heard this legend of this punk rock guy who came in and did this at our school and "Fuck those punk rock people!" Then I saw some punk documentary or something and I was like, "These guys are fucking cool, man." Something kicked in and I started thinking, "I think I like this—I wanna be a punker!"

My friend Allan Schlemmer was one year younger than me, I think, and everybody made fun of him 'cause he was so small back then, and I kind of took him under my wing. He looked up to me and respected me as this old-school punk when I was probably ten minutes more punk than him. He was down to do crazy shit, and me and him really got along.

I remember I saw fliers for 3-D, and I was like, "Let's go to this thing!" I went to the thrift store and bought a generic polo shirt and then I painted an upside-down dead alligator on it, thinking that was punk to have, like, this anti-Izod shirt. Then I diced up the sleeves and fringed them out, and it just looked so fucking gay, so I cut the shirt up with a razor blade, and it was so fucking lame it was hilarious.

We start going to 3-D and trying to hang out, and we're just the nerdiest dumb fucks who don't have any idea about punk, trying to fit in. We walk by and some of the 3-D regulars are sitting outside, super fuckin' punk. We knew we had no idea what punk was, but we wanted to be part of it. Some legit punk—I think it was Tom Clerx—finally acknowledged us and made some small talk and drank some beer with us. Once we got that little acknowledgment, we were hooked on punk and immersed ourselves in it. Dead Kennedys this, Black Flag that, fuck the system, question authority, and all this fucking shit. We were getting suspended from school and catching hassles. We went down that punk trail big time. That was our identity.

Lloyd Veerman (drummer: The Efekt): Music was changing and the look was changing. You walk around with a yellow mohawk and you're gonna get stared at from police, grunts, and mokes, and you better be ready because you'd get it from all sides, even from your parents. The boys would come to my house with spider hairdos; John Bopp, our singer, would have a new weird look; Allan Schlemmer would have a mohawk, but my father would look at us and just laugh because he knew we were just having fun.

We'd go shopping at Salvation Army and just kind of make our own fashions. Plaid outfits that looked like pajamas with belt buckle things that made you look like you were in Adam & the Ants or Bow Wow Wow. Anything checkered would be new wave-ish. It was like Halloween every day.

Raoul Vehill: I hooked up with some guys who were communists and were in a band called Fallout. They were more politically conscious than I was, and there was always that dynamic. I think they just liked punk and that energy and that cultural expression because it was against society or against the prevailing culture.

When we were brainstorming band names, somebody noticed that Devil Dog was "God Lived" spelled backward, so we were like, "Okay, *that*." The difference between Battery Club and Devil Dog was basically going from punk to hardcore, but I didn't always want to use that speed rock formula. I thought I wanted to go in the direction of maybe Flipper or Birthday Party.

When I heard SRO was opening for Agent Orange, I remember feeling jealous because Devil Dog was playing around too. At a certain point, though, SRO started to wear Devil Dog T-shirts, and directly after that, people started to slam during our gigs, and that was kind of like the turning point. We got pits going just as big as SRO and The Sharx, and it was like, "Okay, we've arrived."

Kalea Chapman (guitarist: Poi Dog Pondering, Love Crabs, Food): Raoul was amazing. He was a great frontman. What I knew him as was this kind of cocky, kind of macho, but super self-deprecating, funny-as-hell guy. His lyrics were so damn funny. Battery Club was great, but Devil Dog is when he really hit his stride. He was like a punk rock god with eye shadow. I mean, in my circle, we were like, "Man, this guy's the real deal!"

Kit Grant (KTUH DJ): Sometimes there's a character you play when you're on stage, like a persona, and for Raoul, I mean, it really was kind of real. He had swagger and charisma and stage presence and a bit of danger, although in his quiet moments, he was just kind of a normal, quiet guy. We were roommates for years, and although all the girls would be drooling over the Godfather of Hawaii Punk Rock, it'd be like, "Yeah, but he doesn't put the toilet seat down."

They're like, "I don't care! I wouldn't care!"

Yes, you would.

Raoul Vehill: I end up writing songs and performing them because I have things inside of me that I want to say, and getting up in front of people and saying them is kind of addicting, you know? At first, people weren't thrashing to us, so I knew we needed to stand out, so I would take a lot of my clothes off and take some fake blood or body paint and—hey, I saw someone spit fire on TV—so I'd do that and whatever else I could think of to put on a show.

Robert Scott: Raoul is really a genius poet and an incredible performer. I would rent an auditorium at UH and call our friends' bands, whoever wanted to play, put up fliers, set up the door, figure out whose drum set we were gonna use, whose PA we were gonna use, and set up our own gigs. It was a crazy wide range of music from The Dervishes and Devil Dog, and toward the end of that era, there were these incredible speed metal bands that would play and just melt your whole reality with their set. It was mind-blowing stuff.

It got a little bit out of control. Some of the punks just trashed the joint. I remember seeing a guy rip the water fountain off the wall, and I rented the room, so I'm responsible for it. I was going, "I don't know how much longer I can do this."

Raoul Vehill: I don't remember how the last version of Devil Dog fell apart. I think it was because I fell apart with booze and drugs. I was drinking so much, the other guys were like, "You're scaring us, dude."

My girlfriend left me for another guy. She left me for some guy in SRO. Not to make a total soap opera out of it, but she was a big source of my identity, I think. Plus I was in love with her. She was really sexy. I first saw her stripping at Saigon Passion, I guess, and I was like, "Wow."

I remember a friend of hers asked me if I could get her some drugs. I was like, "I don't know where to get any drugs."

Then one night, I'm in front of the Wave, trying to get in after coming from 3-D, and they both roll up in a cab, and they get out and go right to the front of the line, and she starts talking to me, I start talking to her, and she's like, "You wanna go in?" So I went in with them.

I changed her name in *Hawaii Punk*, the book I wrote, and I'm so sorry I ever wrote that book. It's fictionalized enough to be fiction, but it's basically my experience in the bands I was in and the women I was with in those days. I kind of wish I had never written about those women because I violated something that should have been secret. I wrote it when I got locked up, when I was in prison.

Even though I had more than a handful of girlfriends after her, I didn't really get over her 'til I wrote that book. *Hawaii Punk* was also how I got over my attachment to singing in a punk rock band and the affection, attention, and affirmation that being a punk rock singer in Honolulu gave me.

7

A HATFUL OF DREAMS

In the spring of 1981, when Boomtown Rats promptly sold out their lone Hawaii performance at Wave Waikiki, it suggested a growing appetite for more innovative, forward-looking sounds in the Islands. "They were one of the first alternative bands to play in Hawaii," remembers Peter Bond, who would later preside over adoring crowds on that very stage with a band of his own. "Everybody went just to see what was going on outside of Hawaii."

It wouldn't be long before Honolulu got its fill of "new rock," as the city's concert wars of the 1980s were just heating up. Promoter Ken Rosene, newly hip to the new wave, flew in Grace Jones to play Wave Waikiki in early 1982. Rival concert man Greg Mundy, eager to get in on the action, presented Bow Wow Wow only weeks later at the same venue. For Obscene Routine's Frank Abreu, whose band opened for several eminent acts at the Wave, the era conjures flashbacks of indulgence and excess. "Grace Jones, she wouldn't get on stage until she had an ounce of blow in her dressing room," he tells. "Cheap Trick, same thing. They just wouldn't go on stage, and so I got a call from the promoter 'cause I was dealing back then, supplementing my income."

Also in 1982, Rosene announced a partnership with a mainland Realtor to open a new concert venue opposite Ala Moana Beach Park called Coconut Grove. Formerly a 600-seat Polynesian showroom known as the House of Lono, it gave local audiences an opportunity to catch ascending acts like Missing Persons and Berlin as well as artists with cult followings such as Sparks and Warren Zevon. Notably, Rosene also secured a five-night stand with San Francisco post-punk sensation Romeo Void at Wave Waikiki in January of 1983.

The big money, however, was in straight-ahead arena rock. Over the next couple of years, it was ZZ Top, 38 Special, Jefferson Starship, Quiet Riot, and Night Ranger for Mundy; Pat

Benatar, Def Leppard, Aldo Nova, Blue Oyster Cult, and Huey Lewis & the News for Rosene, all at the Neal Blaisdell Center Arena.

Back at the Wave, Jack Law settled on a new headliner in Sonya and Revoluçion, a talent-laden combo much more suited to the rigors of steady gigging—four sets a night, five nights a week—than those quirky art rockers The Squids, who they replaced. Fronted by Sonya Mendez, the Waikiki lounge singer who'd been serenading tourists at the Hilton Hawaiian Village's Garden Bar, Sonya and Revoluçion were constructed as a working band for the times: part new wave pop, part rock and roll. Scenesters of the day decried Sonya's endless repertoire of cover songs yet grudgingly conceded her band's professional sheen and top-rate musicianship. So skilled was her bassist Benny Rietveld, in fact, that after he left the Islands in 1982 for the Bay Area, Rietveld found success working and touring with such luminaries as Santana, Sheila E., and Miles Davis. Revoluçion guitarist Chris Bovard's virtuosity, meanwhile, is spoken of with great reverence to this day.

With a resonant sound system and a live band belting out hits they could dance to once the party drugs kicked in, tourists and Waikiki nightlifers cared little for original material. As more dancing meant more drinks sold and vice versa in perpetuity, Law saw great value in Sonya and Revoluçion and named them Wave Waikiki's house band, a much-coveted title they held for four years. "It wasn't like we needed a different band every day," says Law. "No one ever got tired of them. It was really amazing."

Meanwhile, ex-Squids drummer Frank Orrall bounced around a number of fondly remembered bands, but until he found major label success with Poi Dog Pondering, his most promising group, and the one Wave regulars will swear "should have made it big" was Hat Makes the Man.

An ambitious crew of musicians blessed with camera-ready looks and an ear for the latest tuneful, guitar-based British and American alternative sounds, Hat Makes the Man quickly earned the endorsement of Greg Mundy, who provided them prized opening slots for major rock concerts in Honolulu. The surging band and their exhilarating originals caught the ear of "Mr. Bill" Mims, 98 Rock afternoon jock and program director, who added Hat tracks "I Never Said" and "Winds of Time" to the station's playlist. It was a major coup for Hat Makes the Man as airplay was scarce for homegrown rockers, and it had been years since anyone on the local rock circuit had a hit on commercial radio. "Bill Mims really liked us and respected our music a lot," asserts Hat vocalist Marti Kerton. "He would not have put us on the air—he would not—if he didn't feel like we could hold our own on the radio."

So while Sonya and Revoluçion enjoyed their perch atop the metaphorical Wave Waikiki marquee, in many ways, of all the local bands to strut the Wave's stage, Hat Makes the

Man's star burned brightest. With the advantage of radio play, opportunities to showcase their dazzling stage show at local festivals, block parties, and arena shows abounded, and Hat cultivated a strong following that extended beyond the bounds of the Waikiki nightclub scene. Mundy, convinced he could take Hat Makes the Man to loftier heights, made it his mission to introduce the music world to the next big thing from Hawaii.

HAT MAKES THE MAN

Peter Bond: Hat Makes the Man was actually my first real band. The whole thing started because I was friends with Rudy from The Squids. We were high school-age buddies who went to different high schools, and he was a year behind me. He was a musician, and there were a bunch of other friends who were musicians. We'd jammed a little bit until he got into The Squids.

Then a friend of mine said, "Hey, I know this guy that likes the same kind of music as you and plays guitar. His name's Byron. You should

Hat Makes the Man at Liberty House, 1986. *Courtesy of Matthew Miller*

get together with him." So I talked to Byron and both of us were into bands like The Records and really power-poppy new wave, I guess you could call it. The Pretenders too. We got together and played music, and we'd go to his house and learn songs; he'd play the lead parts, and I played the rhythm.

Byron Lai: The Squids definitely inspired us to do something. I think Peter and I kinda looked at each other and thought, *Oh, we should start a band too.* I know I felt left out, like, "They're having fun, and we're not having fun."

Peter Bond: Once The Squids broke up, I think Byron kind of asked Frank and Rubella if they would jam with us. We had really good chemistry, and we got a gig right away at the UH Campus Center Ballroom—but not the ballroom—we played the actual cafeteria. But everybody came down because Frank was kinda famous. The word got out, everybody showed up. Club owners like Kail came down. Greg Mundy came down. We did our set and everybody was really, really excited about my band. Greg immediately started to mentor us. Kail was like, "Come play my club!" Girls talked to me. That was new. So, yeah, it was awesome.

But The Squids had a lot of success, and I was just starting a band, and we were playing 3-D for probably a hundred bucks a night or something stupid like that, so Rubella left and we hired Matt Miller. The thing that was so cool about Matt's bass playing is it's very busy and very melodic. He wasn't just playing the root; he was playing hooks on his bass. Matt actually went to school with Rudy, and he'd been in a few small bands. I remember Matt's band played things like Dave Edmunds, which was, for the time, kind of like, "Ooh, I never heard these guys before!"

Byron Lai: The mods liked us, but the more punk crowd probably didn't like us. There were some tough girls in that punk crowd, and I remember one of them saying, "I don't think I like Frankie's new band." It was kind of a mixed reception at 3-D.

Peter Bond: Hat Makes the Man, very early on, we were just a band with four sets of new wave music that we were playing at 3-D, and some guy hired us to play on one of the military bases. When we got there, we pulled up and the sign above the door said, "Annual Formal Officers' Ball."

So we set up, we could hear them singing their songs and everything, the curtains came up, and the guy was like, "We got this band for y'all—Hat Makes the Man!" So we started playing and they fucking hated us. They hated us, and with every breath they drew, they hated us more. They were crying out, "Zeppelin!" and I was just a cocky asshole. I was like, "Here's a Led Zeppelin song," and we'd play something by Madness, and they were just infuriated. They hated us but they were all dressed up, their wives were in their prom dresses, and they had their sabers and white gloves, and they couldn't do anything.

So 300 guys were in there. We went backstage after our first set, took a fifteen-minute break, came out, and 293 of them had left. There were seven people who were thrilled with what we were playing. We played two more sets for those seven people; then they let us go.

Marti Kerton (vocalist/violinist: Hat Makes the Man, Electric Lunch Band, Henry Kapono, etc.): Peter and I would sing individually and everything, but our thing was a blend of our voices. People seemed to like that combination of two singers. That was our sound.

In the beginning, to be honest, I really didn't think it was going to lead to much. To me, it was just kind of fun. I didn't actually harbor any ambitions of becoming part of this band or anything. That discussion never took place. I did come in and sang some songs, and I just never left.

Peter Bond: Marti and I worked at Tower Records together, and she was also interested in the newest of the new music that was coming out, and she would come down to the gigs all the time. She was from New York, and she was super hot, and she had a great voice, and we'd get her up on stage and sing a few songs and everybody loved it. They'd be like, "Holy shit, that girl can sing!" So over time, we brought her into the band, and she became the star that she is.

Marti Kerton: It didn't take long, once we started playing, before Greg Mundy became our manager. I've never met anyone like him. He's one of these people that's immediately all in and does not have any regrets. When he says, "I want to work with you guys, and I'm going to make you all stars," it's not just bullshit. I mean, he actually does believe it himself. He had high hopes for us.

Jack Law: I was friends with Greg Mundy and his wife. Greg was a great promoter, and he was his own worst enemy too, because he would get into these bidding wars against Tom Moffatt and Ken Rosene. He'd want a group so badly and didn't want another promoter to get them that he'd end up not making much money or even losing money, and he didn't have deep pockets.

Peter Bond: We were playing the Wave, and Greg Mundy was our manager at the time. He brought U2 here and talked Bono into coming down and seeing his pet band. So Bono came to the Wave and watched us play a set.

Afterwards, I went up to say hi to him, you know, and he said, "Your band is great, but I gotta ask you, why are you playing so many covers?"

Marti Kerton leads Hat Makes the Man in song, 1986. *Courtesy of Shawn Lopes*

I was like, "Well, you know, the owner kind of expects us to play covers. They want us to get people to dance…" and he stops me. He's like, "Listen, fuck the covers and fuck the club owners and fuck getting people to dance. The thing that's going to change your life is a three-minute song that you write. If you don't write that three-minute song, you'll never amount to anything; you'll just burn out in clubs."

And so I talked to Frank, and Frank was just *frothing* to do originals, of course. So we just started doing our own music and it worked. Greg Mundy was behind us, he had a bit of money, and he got our album done. He was able to get our name out there enough so that people heard us, and we got "I Never Said" played on 98 Rock. We had a little bit of buzz going.

Frank Orrall: I remember Greg taking us to some beach park between Aina Haina and Kahala, and the Edge was there with his wife and his daughter, and Bono was there having an outdoor picnic. Bono was swimming, wearing a shirt, and I remember thinking that was the weirdest thing I ever saw. He was probably trying not to get burned with his Irish skin.

Marti Kerton: Although we never opened for U2, we spent a day at the beach with them and went to dinner, and Bono gave us his opinion of our band. I remember him telling me—and he was really earnest about it too— "And you should always wear white on stage. I can just tell that's part of your personality." He suggested that the violin be used a lot more in our music. They were all very nice.

You'd always see a celebrity dining at Keo's, and I actually remember we were exiting the restaurant and I was already on a high like, "Oh my God, I'm with U2!" and Tina Turner was coming in as we were going out, and she recognized everybody and stopped to chat. That was just a surreal moment.

Byron Lai: There was a time we jammed with Iggy Pop. That was cool. I think he did a show at Coconut Grove on Ala Moana Boulevard. So he came to the Wave one night when he wasn't doing his gig, and we played "Louie, Louie" and "Gloria."

Peter Bond: When Hat Makes the Man got the call to open for The Pretenders, we were so excited. It was a huge deal. We opened for INXS, who were super cool. They brought beer to our dressing room and hung out with us. We opened for John Waite. Romeo Void was a cool band to open for.

Byron Lai: We did The Romantics and Robert Palmer shows at Andrews Amphitheater, The Busboys at Campus Center, and the Rockmania show that Greg Mundy put on at Aloha Stadium. It was Cheap Trick, Aerosmith, and REO Speedwagon with us opening. My cynical view of it was "Well, Greg didn't have to hire an opening band since he had us." We were playing and all these grunts in the first row were flipping us off. We felt a little out of place at that show.

Matthew Miller: We'd done a lot of shopping center gigs. There was one show at Liberty House in Ala Moana. That was at sort of our height, and we had all of these young teenagers wanting us to sign their arms with pens. So many of these younger kids couldn't come see us at the Wave, so they'd come see us play whenever we'd play outside. Those were always super fun. I was never one to let it get to my head. I always thought it was more amusing and cute, you know? It was always sweet.

Byron Lai: We went to LA to get some exposure. Greg Mundy had booked us a few clubs in the Los Angeles area. It had to have been at least four days because we played four gigs: the FM Station, Music Machine, and both Madame Wong's—Madame Wong's West and the original Madame Wong's. Madame Wong's West, I don't know if you've ever been there, but it's a multi-level building with three separate floors. I remember it went pretty well. We had a good reaction.

Marti Kerton: Greg had his fingers in a lot of pies, and Rodney Bingenheimer was one of his friends. He wanted us to interview with Rodney on the ROQ, so we met up with Rodney and we did one of our songs live in the studio. I think Greg wanted us to feel what it was like to be on the road. If we were going to be a working band, this is what our future would look like, basically. I loved it. I was like, "Yeah, I'll sign up for this for the rest of my life!"

Peter Bond: So Mundy had this in with a guy at a major record label. It's in California, the round building…Capitol Records? Greg's like, "We're gonna get signed to Capitol!" So we go. This guy's got this huge office; it's the full record exec office. It's got all these cool records on the wall, and you sit down on these uncomfortable little chairs, and he's got the big desk. He and Mundy exchange pleasantries. I think Mundy gave him a bump and then he says, "Okay, guys, I'm going to do for you what I never do, but this is what you're going to get." And so he puts our cassette on and listens to our first three songs for about twenty seconds each. He stops and goes, "Yeah, I think you guys have a good sound. But here's the reality…" and he pulls out this box, and it's filled with cassettes. And he says, "This is all the unsolicited stuff I get *every week.*"

He says, "I know Mundy, so therefore, I'm going to pay a little more attention to you guys. I'm going to see what happens. I'm going to see how you guys do, if you guys can get a following going," etcetera, etcetera, etcetera. "And I'll keep an eye on you guys. Thanks a lot. I'll see you later!" And that was it. We were so crestfallen.

Marti Kerton: It was definitely a letdown. The way that the A&R person left it was kind of like, "Well, yeah, all you need to do is get a keyboardist in there and you're home free!" which was kind of bullshit, but that's what they're used to doing, is giving you hope, but the hope isn't realistic. And we were forced with this "get a keyboard" mentality for a long, long time. We got so tired of it. Like, why the fuck do we need to get a keyboardist? We're who we are, and you either hear it or you don't.

Frank Orrall: I don't remember being disappointed that something didn't happen because I didn't expect anything to really happen. It was super exciting going out there and playing, but Kit Ebersbach had already instilled in me the idea of making it yourself. It was as though he were saying, "The record company's not going to be the one that touches me on the shoulder with a sword and says, 'You can make a record.'"

Matthew Miller: It seemed like a big jump. Here we are, this big fish in this little pond and then you go to a bigger place and you're nobody. That was intimidating, a little bit. It was all very interesting, but I wasn't drawn to the idea of moving to LA and trying to make it. I think Greg Mundy really believed it would work, but he couldn't necessarily convince everybody that there was more than just Hawaii for the band. I wasn't necessarily convinced. I could never get a good sense of what it would take to really make it, but it didn't seem we could make the next step staying in Hawaii.

Byron Lai: We were all talking about "So where do we go from here?" and it seemed like, well, we have to move to the mainland. Not just take a trip but actually relocate. That's where I had to ask myself, "Do I really want to continue with this?" I remember talking to Frank about it, and after talking, I think he made his decision too, because he was wanting to do his own thing.

It turned out really bad because Frank, myself, and Matt decided to leave together, and it wasn't my intention to do that. I was the oldest one in the band, feeling the pressure of being in my thirties already and thinking, *Okay, do I keep on doing this rock band thing or do I get a real job?* I didn't like the way it looked, because it seemed like the three of us conspired to drop out of the band and leave Peter and Marti holding the bag, and it wasn't like that. We all had our individual things that we were dealing with.

Peter Bond: I was crushed, to be honest. I was really sad. We were sick of each other. We spent two years, five nights a week together, playing the Wave. Visions were changing. It wasn't working. It wasn't happening. Nobody was too pleased with each other at that point. It wasn't like we hated each other or anything, but nobody was really getting along. We weren't hanging out together anymore, you know. Frank already had his own side project, we had our friends, Byron had friends, Matt had friends. There's that time when the band does everything together, and those first few years are the magic times, and as time and tide move on, it's what happens.

Matthew Miller: It was a hard ending. It was definitely like a crash and burn at the end, in a way. I was sparring with Peter and Marti, and we weren't all getting along all that well. There were different ideas on what we wanted to do. Like typical bands, you get five fucking people together, and no one communicates; no one speaks to each other. You hear from someone else that someone said this, someone said that.

It was really kind of pivoting on Frank because Frank, to me, was one of the main creative powerhouses of the band, and he really wanted to do his own thing with his original stuff. There was a push to keep us alive in Honolulu playing at the Wave, and that really went against Frank's ideas, 'cause playing the Wave was a grind and didn't really allow him to get out there and explore his new music, play different places, travel, and do all those things he likes to do. I think when I felt like he wasn't going to stick with it, I wasn't probably going to stick either. I think Marti and Peter were really hurt that we didn't want to keep going with it. That was the really shitty bit. It was a tough time.

Frank Orrall: Sometimes there's just this feeling that maybe the wind has gone out of the sails a little bit. I was starting to get into other music. I was following The Pogues a lot, and I started to play more acoustically, playing on the street in Waikiki, and there started to be this little collective of people from the Whirling Dervishes and some of the other bands around town like the Love Crabs, who I fell in love with and basically recruited to be in Poi Dog Pondering.

Jack Law: I was very disappointed when Frank left. You know, Frank started playing at the Wave when he was a teenager with The Squids, and his musicality was quite amazing for somebody his age. He'd be sitting behind the drum set, and his smile would just beam right to the back of the room. He just had that kind of charisma. Even now when I see him, he has that same little boy charm.

Peter Bond: Greg Mundy was pissed because we'd signed contracts. And Frank was just sort of like, "Well, sue me." So Mundy was making all this noise and rattling sabers, so I was like, "Well, I tell you what—I got these guys, and we'll start Hat Makes the Man up again, and we'll keep going."

HAT 2.0

Beano Shots: In 1986, I was asked to join Hat Makes the Man. I asked my friends, the Rossi brothers, Goopy and Hozy Rossi, who played with Mumbo Jumbo, if they wanted to join Hat Makes the Man with me. We fit in really nicely, but we never released anything because we weren't together for very long.

Peter Bond: So we got Beano; he was into it. Beano was a more edgy guitar player than Byron, who had more of a jangle, and I got these two brothers—a guy named Hozy and a guy named Goopy—and they were like this rhythm powerhouse. They were fucking *amazing*. Drummer and bass player. Like, Jaco Pastorius-level bass playing, and the drummer was tight as a drum.

Those guys were great musicians and really nice guys, and they were good on stage, but everybody loved Frank, and once Frank left the band, we could not continue that magic that Frank brought. He had star power and it's not even anything that he carries; he just has it. That level of personality was no longer in the band. It lasted for, like, several months, and we just gave up on it.

Marti Kerton: When our second incarnation happened, I really enjoyed it. I really, really did. Goopy and Hozy were a great rhythm section. I really respect the hell out of them and wish that I'd had more time playing with them. And I always thought Beano was a very charismatic player, a very soulful player, and an original player, and to be able to collaborate with someone like that was beyond my expectations.

In retrospect, however, I do feel like we should have changed the name, but Greg wouldn't let us. He was like, "We've already come this far on the name," and we just went along with him, but after listening to some of the stuff we'd do together, it was painfully apparent that this band was not Hat Makes the Man. We should have named it something completely different. We should have just jumped in and done our own thing. I don't think change is a bad thing at all.

Goopy Rossi: I think that band, when we were good, we kicked ass, but Jack Law was not into it at all. I think the first night playing the Wave after we joined the band, Jack Law pulled Peter aside and told him, "Your drummer is way too loud." It was fun, but we weren't drawing the same amount of people, and our nights at the Wave kept getting reduced. Our last show was at Queen Theater. We opened up for Gene Loves Jezebel. It was probably December of '86.

ORIENTAL LOVE RING

Beano Shots: Eventually, I had to quit because my mother had cancer and I had to take care of her. The next year, 1987, was really crucial because my mother passed away from cancer, my first son, Nick, was two years old, and my second son, Matty, was just maybe a week old when my mom died, and I had to do something quick because I didn't want to get depressed. So I asked Peter if he wanted to start a new band, like a brand-new band, and he said, "Yeah, sure, okay." Peter knew a bassist, Chad Ikezawa, and a drummer, Bryan Brundell. Chad went to Bryan and said, "Hey, man, you gotta join this band—I mean, look, you got Peter and Beano in this band. How can you pass it up?" That's how Oriental Love Ring got started.

Peter Bond: Beano called me up and he said, "You know what, I got some songs. You wanna come by and listen to 'em?" So I went over to his house. He played me some of his songs, and we were having fun, and I said, "You know, I know a bass player." Chad would always come up to me during Hat Makes the Man and say, "If you ever need a bass player, man, I play bass…" and I'd always be like, "Yeah, sure, man." I knew he worked at Tower, so I called him up, and he was a little starstruck, like, "Oh my God—I know a drummer!"

Beano Shots: I remember one night at the Wave when Hat Makes the Man was on a break, Goopy came up to me and said, "You know, if I ever start a new band, I'm gonna call it Oriental Love Ring," which was choice number three in the condom machine in the men's bathroom.

Oriental Love Ring. Clockwise from top left: Chad Ikezawa, Bryan Brundell, Beano Shots, Peter Bond. *Courtesy of Peter Bond*

So that was my first answer when it came to, "Oh, what are we going to call ourselves?"

Peter Bond: We already had a gig. We were going to open for Camper van Beethoven, so we learned seven songs, and that was one of those bands that just clicked. The four of us were inseparable for like two years, man. We did everything together. As far as decadent rock and roll—drinkin', druggin', having a blast—that was that band. And it lasted exactly three years. It was very rock and roll.

Beano Shots: The Replacements was probably our main influence, and all these other bands coming out of Minneapolis; they were like pre-grunge. We went from 1987 to around 1990. During that time, we sure did a lot. We were the first band from Hawaii to be in South by Southwest.

We were in South by Southwest '90. Poi Dog Pondering played the year before, but by then, they were considered Austin residents.

I had these great connections. My tattoo artist friend Mike Malone had married Margaret Moser, who worked with the *Austin Chronicle,* and she was one of the organizers for South by Southwest. She and Mike came to the Wave one night to see Oriental Love Ring, and she was blown away. Through her influence, we were treated like kings over there. I mean, it was just amazing. She got us Saturday night, which was the last and best night, at the Ritz, right there on Sixth Street. Probably the best place to play at South by Southwest. A real happening place. I couldn't believe it.

I met one of my idols, Lenny Kaye. Lenny Kaye was a guitar player for Patti Smith, and he was there. I was with Margaret Moser, and she pushed me towards him and said, "Go introduce yourself!" So I did and he was the nicest guy. The first thing I said was "I learned all of your solos," and he just smiled and said, "I bet that wasn't very hard." I saw him the next day at the South by Southwest barbecue, and he said, "I watched your band at the Ritz—you guys eat Poi Dog Pondering for breakfast!"

Peter Bond: We got all these write-ups in newspapers when we did our Austin set. People were raving about us. We had all this buzz, and we had all these record guys come down and see our set and talk to us, but it was the same thing: "You guys need to come here. We can't do a long-distance love affair with you from Hawaii." Fuck, you know, Beano was a farmer. I, again, wasn't leaving Hawaii and neither was Chad. We came back and immediately lost our gig at the Wave.

8

HAWAII'S ONLY ALTERNATIVE

From Suite 206 in the stately, pillared edifice known as Hawaii Hall, the oldest of all major structures on the University of Hawaii campus, KTUH-FM went live in the summer of 1969. It was a landmark occasion.

Just three years earlier, UH students Fred Barbaria and Ken Kuniyuki had convinced school authorities to dust off and recommission a roomful of radio equipment that had been locked away on the second floor of Hawaii Hall. These were relics of KUOH, an FM station established in 1955 as part of the University of Hawaii's Speech Communications Department. For several years, it featured a part-time lineup of classical music, jazz, and BBC dramas weekdays from 6-10 p.m. until it was defunded in 1961 by the state legislature.

Once resurrected as KTUH in 1966, it operated by AM carrier current—a closed-circuit system that utilized cables strung across campus—delivering content to Hemenway Hall's student lounge and the UH dormitories along Dole Street.

With approval from the Board of Regents, KTUH went public on the FM dial on July 7, 1969, as an "educational station." Its special non-profit status meant no adherence to a bottom line, which allowed for a liberal, broad-minded array of programming. Song selections were left to KTUH's student-run staff of volunteer DJs, and its late-night, anything-goes freeform explorations gave listeners a reprieve from the stodginess of Top 40 radio. The on-air talent then, as today, was strictly amateur yet refreshingly bereft of overtrained, slick-talking jocks. To get the word out, program guides were printed twice a month and distributed around town at record shops and other places students and potential listeners were thought to frequent.

At a paltry ten watts, however, the station could only be heard in portions of Honolulu, and it would take nearly five decades of incremental gains to obtain island-wide coverage. Compounding matters, funding was a constant source of frustration for its staff. "KTUH's budget was probably only a few thousand dollars a year," says Barbaria, who served as station manager from 1966 to 1973. "A lot of the DJs would bring in their own records to play in the early days."

By the time the station moved its studios across Campus Road to Hemenway Hall in 1979, the folk, garage rock, prog-rock, and acid rock favored by some of its staff in its formative years had given way to the trends of the coming age. A diehard bloc of DJs sworn to such hard-rocking, pre-metal outfits as Montrose, Robin Trower, Frank Marino & Mahogany Rush, and UFO had developed a solid following at KTUH and considered the station an important stronghold of heavy rock in Honolulu. Meanwhile, a checkered pack of young interlopers, keen on the latest punk and post-punk clatter, edged their way into this domain, setting off a rivalrous, sometimes humorous tug-of-war between camps. "When I first applied to KTUH, I wrote on my application that I liked punk," recalls longtime KTUH staffer James Kneubuhl. "This led to an interview with the program director where, right in front of me, he said to another staff member in a complaining, condescending tone, 'This is the second applicant this week who wants to play punk.' Wow, talk about welcoming. That was my first inkling that the then-powers-that-be at KTUH considered punk some kind of threat."

In the end, it could be said this new wave of DJs ultimately prevailed, as KTUH, like many college radio stations across the country, became a bastion of "college rock" or "alternative" sounds of the 1980s, exemplified by adventurous subsurface artists such as Laurie Anderson, Burning Sensations, The Nails, Kate Bush, Mojo Nixon & Skid Roper, and Butthole Surfers, to name but a handful. The station's slogan through much of the decade and beyond was "Hawaii's Only Alternative."

A once-in-a-while live music showcase from the 1970s called "The Pakalolo Patch" was recast in the '80s as "Monday Night Live," which became a popular weekly feature at KTUH. It was through re-aired snippets of these live recording sessions that local underground bands of the day like Devil Dog, SRO, Cringer, The Vacuum, and Saud would enjoy repeated radio play, a feat that once seemed far-fetched for homegrown acts without professionally produced recordings.

In 1984, the school's Board of Regents approved a modest but much-appreciated increase to 100 watts, and by the time KTUH was boosted to 3,000 watts in 2001 (raised again to 7,000 watts in 2016), it had already cemented its place as a great beacon of alternative culture in Hawaii. "KTUH is important because it's always offered programming other stations don't offer," ventures Barbaria, who notes that while the focus for commercial stations is to draw as large an audience as possible and maximize profits, KTUH was only interested in entertaining and informing. Much of its music was unlikely to be the sort heard on commercial stations, ratings be damned. It's a formula that has served the station well over the years. "What I'm probably most proud of," he says, more than five decades later, "is the fact that KTUH is still on the air."

Robert Scott: Growing up in Hawaii, you're just so thirsty for any kind of information about an alternative viewpoint, and KTUH was a hotbed for that. I would hang around a little bit, sitting in on some shows, and they had this incredible library. It was as big as a bedroom with floor-to-ceiling racks and shelves of records in this meticulously alphabetized collection that included everything.

I was a communications major at the time, so getting up on the decks and going live on a radio show, and just the fact that you could get on the mic and talk to people out there was amazing to me. I think that's the beauty of college radio, you know? It's young people kind of learning about the world and putting it out there, and you never know what you're going to get. A lot of it centered around the group at the "Manoa Hilton" with Kit Grant, Jai Mansson, and folks like that. They were DJs and they kind of ran the house at KTUH in the '80s.

Charlie Palumbo (drummer: SRO, Elvis '77, Travel Light, etc.; KTUH DJ): The Manoa Hilton was the punk rock version of a hippie flophouse. The coffee table in front of the old ratty sofa always had a bong with nasty water in it, ashtrays filled with cigarette butts, beer cans pretty much everywhere, and posters all over the walls. There was a major KTUH faction, and Dave Moffat from SRO and Raoul from Devil Dog also lived there.

Kit Grant: It was a house up on a *pu'u* behind what used to be a haunted house where University Avenue and East Manoa Road come together, maybe a ten- or fifteen-minute walk from campus, so it was perfect for students. It was a six-bedroom house, three baths. The first time I went

Charlie Palumbo began DJing at KTUH in 1979. *Courtesy of Charlie Palumbo*

there, I got invited to a toga party, and it wasn't even Halloween. It was pretty lawless. I started coming over to the house, and eventually they needed a roommate.

There was lots of adventure, lots of drama, lots of people having sex with other people. It was a pretty crazy time. People from the radio world, people from the video world, and people in punk rock bands were living together, and we'd never have a shortage of musicians who would come over and play. We'd take the mattresses out of all of our rooms and put them up against the wall facing our mean neighbor to kind of muffle the sound.

Once, Frank Orrall brought over some band, and they were performing "Jesus Walking on the Water" just before the party got too crazy, and here come the cops, up to the back of the house. I happened to be walking out, and they were like, "We got a noise complaint—what's going on?" and I was like, "Oh my gosh, I'm so sorry, Officer. We're having a church revival." They just looked at each other and said, "Never mind," and they left and never came back. We just had a raging party after that.

Patrick Donegan: The first year I went to UH-Manoa, I saw there was a student-run radio station and thought, *How about if I go check that out?* They had an amazing record library, and everybody was super knowledgeable about specific types of music.

I remember there was a little bit of tension between the older rock people and a bunch of us kids who were listening to new wave and punk stuff. We didn't have a history of, like, Rainbow or 13th Floor Elevators or Hawkwind. We didn't know who they were. We had never heard their names. But we knew The Cars and we knew Devo.

Kit Grant: When I first started, there was this sort of punk rock/classic rock divide. Rock music was all just taking itself way too seriously, and of course, punks don't take themselves very seriously at all, and there were a lot of accusations of being sniveling young brats and not knowing what good music is, and "Oh, that's not how you end a song."

DJs who were on before the punk shows would apologize to their listeners: "Well it's been really great to be with you, and I'm really sorry about what's coming next..." It was all good-natured rivalry, mostly, but the transition was a little more abrupt than some of the old guard would have liked.

There were also DJs like Suzy Creamcheese, who loved any kind of manic music: Alvin & the Chipmunks, the Fleshtones, anything that was high energy, kind of absurd music you could dance to. H'lane had a show where she played a lot of early prog rock and psychedelic rock bands, things like Tangerine Dream and Can and space music stuff. Not a lot of identifiable songs came out of her show, but it was fascinating. It was a wall of hippie noise that would go on and on and on. She would have two turntables going in the air room, and she would also patch in the newsroom, which had two more turntables. She was so stoned, she would sometimes have four records going on at the same time, fading each one in and out obsessively. It was hilarious. She was great.

At KTUH we used to say, "If you don't like what's on, just wait four minutes, and if you do like what's on, just wait four minutes."

Jim Kneubuhl (KTUH DJ): By far the most eccentric DJ I can recall was a woman who went by the name of H'lane. She was a hardcore hippie who carried on as if it was still the '60s. She lived in the cane fields of Haleiwa, and her show consisted of spacey, new age records that record stores like Jelly's would let her borrow. She carried her I Ching book around with her, and anytime she had to make a decision about anything, out would come the coins. She also felt like it was her inalienable right to smoke pot anywhere and anytime she felt like it, and the production room would often smell like a bong after she'd been in there.

It turned out that before she relocated from California to Hawaii, H'lane was the mother to a couple of love children who were given up for adoption. One grew up to live a fairly straight life and later wrote a book about the period where she was separated from her mother. That book was the basis of *Lane 1974*, which was an independent film that came out a few years ago, and I must say, the actress who played a younger H'lane did a pretty convincing job. To the best of my knowledge, H'lane is the only KTUH-related person to ever have a film made about them.

Patrick Donegan: The station had a show called Monday Night Live, where bands could get on the air and play their music live. It was, I think, '83 or something when I became the Monday Night Live director. We were booked all the time and had lots of bands come through. I was there every Monday night for the almost ten years I was at KTUH.

Scott Mackenzie (KTUH DJ/music director): I went over to apply to be a DJ at KTUH, but they were like, "Oh no, all the slots are all filled, but you can help out with Monday Night Live." I did that just to get my foot in the door, but actually, that was a great way to meet everybody because we had every band in town wanting to play on Monday nights.

You'd toss around cords and plug them here and there, and it was Dave Tong and Pat Donegan who showed me what to do; every once in a while, there'd be a band that wouldn't need too much extra attention, and it was like, "Scott, why don't you do it? Just put on some headphones and twist the knobs until it sounds good."

Raoul Vehill: KTUH helped bands get recorded too, because you could go there and play live on the air and get a tape of it. That became at least one of Devil Dog's demos, if not two, and we would sell copies of those at stores like Jelly's. It was a way to get your music to people who went to your gigs.

Kit Grant: It was a great way for bands who wouldn't ordinarily have access to a real studio with decent engineers to get a good, basic demo tape. It was also great experience for the staff to learn how to set up and mic everything in the live studio and on remote broadcasts. We'd keep our own tapes of the bands and if a song was popular, it could get airplay throughout the day on different shows whereas otherwise it would've never gotten on the radio.

Scott Mackenzie: My younger sister was going to high school, I think at Kalani, and that's how we ended up getting people like Cringer, SRO, and Hypo-Depression to come by, and other bands from the local punk scene. We'd record them on Monday Night Live and I'd play them on my show. I did Cringer and Devil Dog's first demo cassettes.

Every time we did Monday Night Live and it went well, I'd make recordings of one or two of the best songs and make them available to the DJs to play on air. Devil Dog was probably played the most during that time, offensive lyrics and all. We had to report to the record trades and give them our top fifty songs, and they'd always be in our top five.

Jim Kneubuhl: Monday Night Live was definitely one of the coolest things KTUH did. In my mind, though, I think it's really a shame that so many of the Monday Night Live tapes went missing from the station. Even while I was at KTUH, those tapes were disappearing. They were in a locked room, so it had to be people involved who were doing this. One time, George Winston played on Monday Night Live, and the next day the tape was gone. In terms of documenting an evolving music scene, can you imagine how historically valuable all those missing tapes would be today? Monday Night Live gave a lot of local bands something to strive for.

Scott Mackenzie: I did end up getting a freeform show from 3 to 6 a.m., then a better slot from midnight to three, and finally, a prime-time show from nine to midnight called "Scott's Soundz From the Scene." The station was only about 100 watts then. There wasn't much power to it. There were certain dorms you could get it best and other dorms you wouldn't get it very well at all.

I was also music director, so different people and bands would sometimes call me up and ask me where they could play in town. I remember I became good friends with Youth Brigade when they came over from California. I helped bring them and had them come up to KTUH, and one of the guys even stayed at my condo in Waikiki one of the nights they played in town. They had made it pretty big in the punk world, and we all looked up to them, and they were super cool people.

Franchon Luke (DJ at KTUH, Radio Free Hawaii): I was taking Journalism 150 at UH, and I got into KTUH's news department because it was the only open position they had. As far as an air shift, everyone starts out with an overnight freeform show, so I was doing Wednesday mornings 3 to 6 a.m. for a while.

At one point, I was filling in temporarily for another DJ's Tuesday night rock slot from nine to midnight, and when it became open, everyone applied and I got it. A lot of people were really, really mad because I was an outsider, the girl from the news department who'd been doing a freeform shift, and all of a sudden I get this prime-time rock show. I took a lot of flak for it and so did the program director who put me in that slot. I think it was Jai Mansson. There were so many angry people.

Kit Grant: There was a bit of a formula in deciding who got the good slots, and part of that meant showing up to staff meetings and volunteering for as much as you could, paying your dues and contributing in other ways. If you show that kind of hustle and you help the station by filling in other positions that maybe aren't as sexy, like with Franchon doing the news, it always gets you extra points for getting a prime slot.

Franchon Luke: Sometimes things happen for a reason, and my show actually got to be really popular with people who listened to KTUH. Part of it is because I really wanted it to be accessible to everyone and appealing to every ear, because a lot of the rock shows at the time were very eclectic and probably too weird for most listeners. There was a lot of Frank Zappa, things like that. Sorry, but it's true.

At the same time, all this new music was coming out, this postmodern, new rock, whatever you want to call it. Bands like Sisters of Mercy were being signed to major labels, and it was all getting bigger and more accessible. The station had a couple of power increases, and KTUH was starting to reach more of the island, so when I would pick new records for my show, I wanted to make sure the songs were catchy and interesting and what more people could get into; I wanted everybody to tune in to KTUH and not just keep it exclusive and obscure. Maybe playing things that were a little more commercial was uncool, but it's probably what made KTUH a little more listened to at the time.

Scott Mackenzie: Franchon's was my favorite of all the shows I listened to. She actually got the most phone calls of anybody at the station. Franchon was always super friendly to everyone, and even though sometimes DJs wouldn't answer the phone, she always answered and played people's requests, and she had a good ear for new music. Franchon could really get those phones ringing.

Mohammad Rouf (DJ at KTUH, Radio Free Hawaii): I was born in a village in Bangladesh. Name of the village is Abalpur. In the '70s, of course, in the homes, no TV. When I was fifteen or sixteen, the university close to where I lived gave some entertainment once a week to different high schools—it was a field trip—and the entertainment was a one-hour black-and-white TV show. That TV show was *Hawaii Five-0*. I give credit to Steve McGarrett. Without him I probably wouldn't know what Hawaii was. So I always have to be thankful to Steve McGarrett and Danno and Chin Ho and Kono. I still miss Kono, the Hawaiian man.

From very young, I always wanted to go to college. So then I thought it would be a good idea to go to college in Hawaii, where Kono lived. I did not do research, anything like that. It was in the Pacific, and it was part of the USA. Good enough for me. It took me four years to do the paperwork and come to the University of Hawaii.

Immediately after I arrived here, I realized that I had to learn the language. I used to learn English from watching Eddie Murphy. *Saturday*

Night Live was my all-time TV show, and another show called MTV. That's where I would get my news. Also George Carlin. You know the old guy? Bald-headed George. That's another guy. The only thing I didn't like about George: He used profanity too much, but that's his problem, not mine. Another source was the graffiti in the bathroom, the classroom.

One day, I learned there was a radio station on campus for students. I just couldn't believe that you could have a show and talk to people. Unbelievable! I said, "I want to get a radio show!"

Charlie Palumbo: I was doing the noon-to-three afternoon rock slot right before Mohammad came on to do his country music show from three to six. Now, Mohammad in those days had a very limited English vocabulary, so I would introduce him and say, "All right, ladies, hold on to your panties, 'cause Mr. Mohammad is here and he's gonna make you *sweat!*" That was the beginning of our friendship.

Mohammad Rouf: You had to choose a time slot. I chose three to six in the afternoon, Thursday. That was the country show. What do I know about country music? Music from the country! Tammy Wynette, Willie Nelson, Merle Haggard. Oh my goodness. This was an eye-opener to me. I remember looking at that microphone the first day, and my T-shirt was completely wet. That's how nervous I was.

Charlie Palumbo: KTUH was huge for Mohammad's Americanization. He probably didn't know shit about music, but it allowed him to talk to people and develop his sense of humor. Between his accent and limited vocabulary, there was a lot of material to be had. We would do skits for his show where I played President Reagan and other characters, and we would go back and forth with each other. It just caught fire. People were like, "Who is this fuckin' kook on the radio?"

Kit Grant: Oh, Charlie and Mohammad. They were incorrigible together.

Mohammad Rouf: Yeah, that "Ronnie Reagan" used to call up all the time. I think he loved our radio show. Also, this other guy, Reverend Fixation, used to get on the air and tell us all about the Holy Bible and baptize people live on my radio show. He used to bring heathens to the studio and yell and scream and baptize them right there on the radio. I don't know where all these people came from. Every time, the studio had ten to twenty people in there for my show. They just showed up. I couldn't figure that out. It was like party time for three hours. So then I switched my time slot to nine to twelve Sunday morning, and I changed my show to "Mohammad's Sunday Morning Service."

Darius Amjadi (KTUH DJ): I appeared as several characters on Mohammad's show. Basically whoever he introduced me as, I played that character. I had an uncomfortable turn when he introduced me as Jesus and asked me how I planned to take Oral Roberts home to heaven, with Mohammad offering increasingly violent ways. We got a few death threats called in and had to make sure that the station doors were locked.

Mohammad Rouf: We never had any guidelines. We just broadcast, that's all. College radio is a free thinker's radio. You're allowed to think freely. But I will never forget one incident. A Southern Baptist minister in this town wrote a special complaint to the president of the University of Hawaii that I said something bad about his specific religion. And when I was called by the president's office about that, I just said, "I did not say anything to offend anybody. What did I say that was not allowed to be said on the radio? I want to know that."

I was afraid that I would lose my radio show, but in the end, they did not put a muzzle on my face because I did nothing wrong. That was my happiness. I will never forget that.

Jim Kneubuhl: My lasting impression of Mohammad was how likable he was. To me, it was valuable to have an on-air personality from his part of the world who could express himself without coming across as deadly serious. Even before 9/11, a lot of Americans viewed people from Muslim countries as Koran-crazed zealots out to undermine the Free World.

Mohammad could be silly or go off on a tangent you didn't agree with, but he never came across as arrogant or dismissive of the beliefs of others. His humor wore a little thin for me, but I never had any misgivings about what Mohammad was doing. I think there was a compassion informing his presentation. He could make fun of things without it sounding like gratuitous mocking.

Darius Amjadi: I see Mohammad as a kind of brilliant radio version of Andy Kaufman. I remember him asking the UH president, Al Simone, why we always got finger sandwiches at official events: "We are hungry university students and we deserve full-sized sandwiches!"

Charlie Palumbo: Then there were the Bobos, who were a group of guys that hung out on campus at Manoa Gardens, where you could buy nachos and pitchers of beer. It was kind of a party place, right below KTUH at the Hemenway Hall courtyard. The Bobos occupied one or two tables there every single day, basically throughout the entire '80s. We would hang out, smoke weed all day and night, from six o'clock in the morning.

Patrick Donegan: At one point in the mid-'80s, I was houseless and slept outside at Andrews Amphitheater. There were a handful of people at that time who would come and sleep there. A couple of the Bobos were in the UH maintenance department. One guy worked from midnight to 8 a.m., so he would turn on the sprinklers at six in the morning to give us a warning. We'd get wet and wake up.

Charlie Palumbo: We'd have Bobo parties where we'd walk down to Star Market and get a couple boxes of Tyson Chicken thighs, microwave 'em in the fast-food kiosk near Kuykendall Hall, throw some oyster sauce on 'em for a quick marinade, and start barbecuing at Bilger Hall and different places on campus.

More and more people came to these Bobo parties, and one day The Sharx showed up with all these punks, and in a building that should have been empty at the time, there were literally hundreds of people.

I can still see the faces of the security guys walking through the door and down the hallway, like, "What the fuck is going on here?" There was a carnivorous orgy of barbecued chicken with no cooking or eating utensils, people eating partially cooked sizzling chicken thighs right off the grill, a punk rock band playing, and kids skateboarding everywhere. Totally nuts.

SRO was one of KTUH's most requested bands of the 1980s, local or otherwise. *Courtesy of Gardner Pope*

Scott Mackenzie: I managed SRO for a while. I'm pretty sure Ed Moya called me up to see if I was interested because he knew me through Charlie Palumbo, who became their drummer at one point, and they knew I was hanging out with Youth Brigade and played local punk and a lot of mainland West Coast punk on KTUH. They thought it was a good match, and I said, "Sure, let's give it a go." They were quite talented, and it seemed like that was the next step. I liked how "The Mokes Are Coming Out Tonight" was super catchy, and it still gets caught in my brain once in a while.

I thought SRO sounded just as good if not better than a lot of the bands we were playing on the air. We were going to go on a West Coast tour and follow Youth Brigade around, at least to start. I passed on a couple of SRO's tapes to Youth Brigade, and they were sharing it with their friends on the West Coast. I don't know how close it was to actually happening, but it seemed as if we were getting close to signing with the label they had. It felt like we were right there, ready to go bigger.

When Agent Orange came to play at Queen Theater, we had SRO open for them. I did that show with a guy I knew named Mike Evans.

He was on KPOI and before that he was on KROQ in LA, and he did the mornings there. He would play "Smoke Two Joints" by The Toyes, and Agent Orange's "Pipeline" on KPOI, stuff most people hadn't heard before and made them popular. He knew Agent Orange from the KROQ days, and that's how we hooked up the deal to bring them back to Hawaii. We gave them a Hawaiian vacation and maybe a little money for playing. I remember we had them staying in Waikiki, and I had to bring them some food every once in a while as part of the deal.

One day SRO had an internal fight, and since I hadn't gotten them to the West Coast yet, it was "We don't think you're doing much for the band." And then I'm like, "Wait, wait, let me just try one more time to get us to the mainland." In the meantime, they disbanded. They had a lot of drama, I guess you'd call it. I really saw a lot of potential in that band.

9

WEEKEND NIGHTS, PAGAN RITES

When a number of records by Adam & the Ants, Bow Wow Wow, and Talking Heads were released at the fore of the 1980s, their exotic palpitations seemed the product of radical new wave invention. To anyone familiar with Nigerian juju, Ghanaian highlife, or the hypnotic throb of the Royal Drummers of Burundi, however, they suggested something more lineal. Enchanting melodies and polyrhythms of West and Central Africa had found their way into the works of some of rock's more adventurous bands, suggesting the onset of a new era of multiculturalism in popular music.

At the time, renowned musician and activist Peter Gabriel, co-founder of the culture-bridging WOMAD (World of Music, Arts, and Dance) festival, had just delivered the haunting anthem "Biko," which, for many, first brought to light issues of institutionalized racism in South Africa. It preceded international anti-Apartheid hit singles like "Free Nelson Mandela" by the Special AKA and Artists United Against Apartheid's "Sun City" by several years, as well as Paul Simon's *Graceland*, the 1987 Grammy Album of the Year, which introduced a number of Black South African singers and musicians to a global audience.

There was increased experimentation with non-Western sounds in the world of pop, and by the end of the decade, a new popular term, "worldbeat," would be used to describe the fusing of traditional ethnic and contemporary forms of music.

In Honolulu, few were as wise to the growing inventory of international sounds as Craig Okino. Already immersed in reggae as the bassist for Cool Runnings, Okino expanded his search for exciting, out-of-the-way musical offerings to Africa and the Black Atlantic. "The very first African album I ever got was by Prince Nico Mbarga & Rocafil Jazz, and that blew my mind once again, like reggae had done years earlier," relates Okino. The sharing of his

WEEKEND NIGHTS, PAGAN RITES | 119

new musical discoveries with friends led to the formation of the Pagan Babies, a long-lived, well-loved ensemble of the Honolulu scene. For more than a decade, the group deftly rode the world music wave to acclaim and even earned notice nationally as semifinalists in *Musician* magazine's Best Unsigned Band Contest in 1990.

Whirling Dervishes (later shortened to Dervishes), featuring local scenesters Arnie Saiki and Robert Scott, was another ambitious and unconventional project: a curious, anything-goes '80s alt-rock take on klezmer, or Jewish folk music of old Europe. Lesa Griffith, an avowed fan, dug into the Dervishes' funky musical goulash straight away.

Through her father's employment with a major airline, Griffith had spent a good portion of her childhood in fascinating, far-off locales like Accra, Ghana; Kinshasa, Zaire; Amman, Jordan; and Jakarta, Indonesia. Naturally, she says, those experiences informed her tastes in music and, in later years, her work as a writer. "I got into food writing at some point, and I like to think it's my international background that opened up my world to different kinds of cuisines, but also, I think, different kinds of sounds," posits Griffith. "I have a lot of aural associations, like, I love Arabic music from living in Jordan. These experiences opened up my palate in different ways."

A return to the Islands to study at the University of Hawaii in the early '80s saw Griffith author a music column for the student newspaper, *Ka Leo O Hawaii*, which in turn led to a stint with a locally produced music magazine called *Novus*.

At the time, Burt Lum, founder of *Novus*, had sought to document all the quickly moving musical developments in the Islands. This was a full decade before the introduction of the Internet to the public, and a small-run periodical seemed the way to go. "I was kind of tracking the local alternative music scene, and I got exposed to a bunch of bands that were playing around town," he remembers. "The core of my passion was to spread the word."

Among *Novus'* offerings were exclusive interviews with visiting musicians like R.E.M., Sly & Robbie, Wynton Marsalis, and His Master's Voice, the New York-based art rock troupe featuring former University of Hawaii students Mark Abramson and Keiko Bonk. Having recently signed to PVC Records, which also featured such notables as The Cure, Bad Brains, Angry Samoans, Siouxsie & the Banshees, and The Plasmatics, His Master's Voice made a tour stop in Hawaii in 1983, and another in 1985, performing both times at Wave Waikiki. "We were probably unlike much of what was going on in Hawaii at the time," reckons Abramson.

Delighted by the growing array of fascinating bands both touring the Islands and roaming the local circuit, Lum, along with friend and editor Gary Chun, recruited a crew of young writers to produce a magazine unrivaled in its chronicling of the vibrant and increasingly diverse Hawaii music scene of the 1980s.

PAGAN BABIES

Chris Planas: When Cool Runnings started to wind down, that's when a lot of guitar-based African music compilations started to be released in the United States. Craig Okino would bring those records around and make me tapes; then I began to look for that stuff, and that's what we started playing for fun.

Frank Orrall was our original drummer, along with Craig, myself, and Nelson Hiu. We were jamming this stuff in somebody's garage in Kalihi, just kind of fooling around with it, and finally somebody said, "I can get you a gig with this stuff since there's not much going on right now at Anna Bannana's. What's the band called?" We had all these names, and I said, "Why don't we call it Pagan Babies?" If you went to Catholic school at a certain time period, they'd ask you to donate money to the Pagan Baby Fund to help children in Africa. That's kind of where the name came from.

Craig Okino: Chris, Nelson, and I started jamming with Frank Orrall, who at the time was drumming in several different bands. The four of us were the original Pagan Babies. I thought we should try playing African music as well as the reggae and ska we were used to. Somehow we got a gig at Anna Bannana's, and I was amazed at the reception we got. When we started playing "Aki Special" by Prince Nico, everyone in the audience—all of whom I'm sure had never heard a note of African music before—jumped up and started dancing. We all thought, *Hmmm, maybe we've got something here.*

Frank Orrall: Craig was always collecting world music and making these fantastic mix cassettes that were loaded with treasures from Nigeria, Senegal, the Caribbean, Mali, Zimbabwe, New Orleans second line music, and so on. Those mixes blew my mind. I never heard music like that before. In particular, it was the Nigerian stuff that really bowled me over.

I had a little drum kit with a kick drum, snare drum, hi-hat, a wood block, and a frying pan for a cowbell, and that was my setup. I put the kick drum up—like a bucket—on the backseat of my scooter with bungee cords and filled it with all the drums and percussion and drove to

One particularly popular Pagan Babies lineup included
(from left to right): Craig Okino, John Nelson, Elyce Tajima,
Jon Walman, and Chris Planas. *Courtesy of Charley Myers*

the gig at Anna Bannana's every week. Pagan Babies was so important
for my development as a musician.

Robert Scott: Pagan Babies ruled Anna Bannana's. Those gigs were so
much fun. Their spirit and their musicianship were just amazing. Chris
Planas is incredible.

Chris Planas: I thought it was just going to be a one-off gig. It seemed
everybody who was not mainstream showed up. College students who
were African, punk rockers, just such a range of people showed up that
first night. That was in February of '83. The first time we played there,
we packed the place, so they gave us another gig the following month.
Then it became every other week, then it became every Friday, and then
it became every Friday and Saturday. We just kept drawing people. It

was every Friday and Saturday for a really long time. The band had a lifespan of about twelve years: '83 to about '95.

Lesa Griffith (writer/editor: *Novus, Time Out New York, Honolulu Weekly, Honolulu Advertiser, Honolulu Magazine,* etc.): I lived in Africa as a kid, and certain African artists were big in the UK, so if you were reading *NME*, you were reading not just about The Clash, but you were reading about Fela Kuti and King Sunny Ade. I had actually gotten into African music through following the British music press. In Hawaii, Pagan Babies were totally at the vanguard.

Burt Lum (founder/publisher: *Novus, Brouhaha;* co-host of KTUH's *Rough Take*): I was doing radio at KZSU. That's the Stanford University radio station. This is, like, between '79 and '81. While I was doing that, I was following the Bay Area jazz music scene and getting exposed to some of the bands that were playing over there. But at the same time, there was this whole punk scene happening there too, and it was a really vibrant time. So when I graduated in '81 and came back to Hawaii, I was thinking, *Man, there's gotta be stuff happening here too, right?* So I looked into the local underground scene, and I was able to connect with folks who were already in bands. I'd go check out Nueva Vida, a jazz band playing at a pretty nondescript place called Kojack's.

There were also a bunch of reggae bands. I remember Cool Runnings was playing in Waimanalo once, and I drove out there to see them. From there, I'd hang out at Anna Bannana's, where I met the Pagan Babies, who were a cool synthesis of afro-reggae and this upbeat ethno sound. I'd go seek out the interesting bands that were playing at the time.

WHIRLING DERVISHES

Robert Scott: We had a band called Bad Posture that had a steady gig because we were cheap and played three-chord rock and roll for tourists to dance to. So we ended up getting gigs at Kojack's, which was some dive bar on Young Street, and Keone's Brauhaus in Waikiki, playing four sets a night on weekends. Our drummer was literally playing on a trashcan. I think we only had one original, so when Bad Posture broke up, Arnie and I wanted to do something different. He had the idea of doing a psychedelic klezmer band, and he knew a guy who played clarinet.

Arnie Saiki (guitarist: Dervishes, Bad Posture, Castration Anxiety): Whirling Dervishes grew out of Bad Posture, and I thought it was time for us to do another band in another context. What we wanted to do was to add all kinds of fun and color and culturally appropriate as many things

Whirling Dervishes' Robert Scott, left, and Arnie Saiki, right.
Courtesy of Gardner Pope

as we could, because in some ways that's what Hawaii felt like at the time. There are so many different cultures that make up Hawaii, whether it's Japanese or Puerto Rican or native Hawaiian, but we were looking at cultures that were not represented. There wasn't a lot of klezmer music or, like, Sufi dance traditions in Hawaii, which is already an exotic place, but what would Hawaii exoticize? So we had an eclectic and somewhat psychedelic sound.

Lesa Griffith: My favorite band to listen to and dance to was Whirling Dervishes. I'd never heard of klezmer music before they started, and I just thought it was the most wonderful thing. Robert Scott was such a great frontman.

Arnie Saiki: The inventiveness of it all was so engaging, and Robert was very daring, but I think he would get frustrated by the sheer wackiness of my demands. He would do these backflips on stage and thrash around, and the performances were fantastic, but he would end up hurting himself sometimes. Of course, it was terrible of me to recommend things like, "Oh, if your back hurts the next day, you should have an aspirin." You know, I didn't care as long as we put on a good show. I was kind of an asshole.

WORLD MUSIC, WORLD TRAVELS

Craig Okino: In the early years, Pagan Babies went through numerous members. Frankie eventually quit to start Poi Dog Pondering, and we got Jon Walman, the drummer from Mumbo Jumbo, to replace him. Nelson Hiu, ever the restless musician, quit too. Then a friend of the band recommended Elyce Tajima as a singer, and she really added to our sound. John Nelson also joined as a percussionist and occasional vocalist. Both of them played a little keyboard as well.

Elyce Tajima (keyboardist/vocalist: Pagan Babies): I worked at a vegetarian restaurant called Laulima on King Street, not too far from Isenberg Street. The guy who owned it was Alan Young. He's a New York-born

Chinese guy, fascinating and moody and amazing. He could make a souffle out of almost nothing out of your fridge. He's that person. Alan is the one who talked to Nelson Hiu, who was the original keyboard player from the Pagan Babies and told me the band was looking for a female vocalist.

I went to see Pagan Babies play at Anna's, and I'd never been there before. The music was unusual to me, but it kinda made you want to dance. They were not what I would go see, but they were interesting.

I met with Craig and Chris and had an audition, and I started singing background. It was a slow process of growing into a full-time member.

Craig Okino: At some point the band's repertoire began to include not only reggae and African but other music of the African diaspora like calypso and soca from Trinidad, zouk from the French Antilles, and a little Latin, Haitian, and Brazilian too, with a few New Orleans tunes thrown in for good measure. All those styles were gaining popularity globally under the blanket term "world music," which basically meant non-white, non-American music.

James Ganeko: Playing drums for Pagan Babies was very challenging. They would play everything from African to calypso, Latin stuff, and reggae.

First, they had Frank Orrall drumming, then there was Jon Walman, and then I replaced him. That was when John Nelson was in the band. He left to go play with Frank and Poi Dog Pondering, and I quit to go play the Korean bars, where you play from 10 p.m. to 4 a.m., you get paid under the table, and you don't get any nights off, but it was a good-paying job. That's the only reason I did it. I hated leaving the Pagan Babies, but it was time to do something else.

Elyce Tajima: It was fascinating doing these other types of music. I especially loved the reggae songs, and the African music was such a pleasure to hear and play. Of the whole group, though, I was the least of the musicians in terms of musicianship, I have to be honest. I felt like my priority was to engage with the audience, because when I first went to see them, they were great musicians, but it was Frank Orrall who engaged the crowd. He had that shining smile, and he just oozed personality, and he had a way of pulling people in. He really, really was an amazing drummer, oh my God. I think Pagan Babies were way more the live band than a recording one, and I felt like it was my job to whip up the band and the crowd into a mood.

Craig Okino: Bill Danos joined on drums and Mike Muldoon on percussion in 1986, but the band really gelled when Bailey Matsuda came on board as keyboardist. Bailey had music degrees and was an accomplished jazz musician, and his tasty playing made everything work and elevated the quality of our music. Plus he played some guitar too, which made the two-guitar African songs sound better. That made three songwriters in Pagan Babies: myself, Planas, and Bailey, and it was definitely the best Pagan Babies lineup. It was also the longest lasting at around six years by my count, which is an eternity for a band.

Elyce Tajima: Papua New Guinea was incredibly fascinating. We played in Port Moresby for a big fair. We got to do this gig through an Australian woman who lived in Papua New Guinea. She was at the University of Hawaii, and there was an important person there from Papua New Guinea, and they came to see us at Anna's and got us over there. I remember a lot of fires because there were tribes that lived in the hills, and it felt like there were fires going on all over, but that's how they would cook.

Another place we went to was Thailand, for a month. We were in Bangkok. We were the house band every night for, like, six nights a week or something, at a really nice hotel. I remember we played at Slim's in San Francisco. We opened for a lot of big reggae bands in Honolulu too, like Black Uhuru, Third World, UB40.

NOVUS

Burt Lum: I was trying to figure out how to get the word out on the local scene, and I thought print media would be a cool thing to do because I had already learned about fanzines and how you could just put together your own magazine without a lot of money. There was one I remember in the Bay Area called *BravEar* that was really well-written and covered a lot of bands that I really liked then, like Pearl Harbor and the Explosions and Translator. There was also one in Hawaii called *Honolulu Babylon*. They made me think the print format could be a cool thing.

Gary Chun: My cousin who became a doctor graduated from Stanford the same time as Burt, and when he found out Burt was going to start up *Novus*, my cousin called me and said, "Hey, you should work with this guy I know, Burt Lum. You should get together." So I thank my cousin for introducing me to Burt.

Novus started off basically as kind of a jazz magazine because I think that was a mutual interest; then when things started popping in terms of national bands coming here to do shows, we gathered a little staff like Lesa Griffith, Jay Junker, and Victor Sam because we all had an interest in music. Jay, who wrote under the name Ras Manu, would do reggae and Hawaiian; Lesa would do more new wavey-type stuff; Victor was an early hip-hop head, definitely.

It was essentially Burt's dream of documenting the local scene. We did interviews with visiting bands like R.E.M., Sly & Robbie, and the like. R.E.M. did a show at Aloha Tower, which became a venue for a brief while.

Victor Sam (writer: *Novus*; nightclub DJ): I first met Burt and Gary hanging out at the Daniel in the Lion's Den reggae show at KTUH with Dan Warner. They told me about this publication that they were doing called *Novus*. Burt had a good job with Hawaiian Tel, and that's what was supporting it, but they did hope that someday it would make enough money to at least more than pay for itself. I offered to write an article for them on Bill Laswell's first album, *Baselines*, because that's where my head was at—really abstract New York City stuff. I didn't know if there was really going to be an audience in Hawaii for avant-garde material like James Blood Ulmer or Ronald Shannon Jackson.

Gary and Burt, though, always impressed me with how much they knew. Burt told me, "Gary knows a little bit about everything in terms of music." Whenever I'd talk about wanting to hear something, Gary was always the first one to say, "Yeah, I read about them—they're supposed to sound like *this*," and "Oh yeah, that's on such-and-such label."

There was that indie magazine that had all those reviews of mostly obscure music called *Option*. Whereas *Creem* or *Rolling Stone* would have maybe fifteen, twenty reviews at the very most, this one had a hundred. That's pretty much all that it was, and Gary had a subscription to that. He'd knock out articles in, like, twenty minutes that would take me a couple of hours. I'd get discouraged and say, "You know, Gary, I can't crank it out like you," and he was very encouraging in saying, "If you don't write about this stuff, no one else will, and if you're enthusiastic about it, you'll reach someone that needs to hear it."

Lesa Griffith: It was such a nurturing, inclusive environment. *Novus* was such a mishmash, but Burt somehow brought together people from all different avenues of music. People like Jay and Gary are serious music people with all kinds of knowledge from all different angles of music. They could cover anything. It was pretty amazing how he got that stable of people together.

Then there was the Pacific New Music Festival. A couple of them, actually, where a bunch of local bands would play. I'd write about them and try to offer some real critiquing in my own unskilled way at the time, but I was just a snarky kid, and I'd be talking more about their haircuts than the music. I regret it now. A couple of people super hated me at the time, but I was just trying to develop my chops. What an opportunity, though. I was able to interview the singer from Circle Jerks, being nineteen or twenty, then got to hang out in a hotel room with Icicle Works, things like that.

At the time, I could still fly for free because of my dad, and I would make these summer pilgrimages to London by myself, stay in a hostel, and go to as many gigs and concerts as I could: Alien Sex Fiend, The Cramps, Sisters of Mercy. I'd go to the 100 Club and see whoever was there. There was a store called Kensington Market on Kensington High Street, and I'd go there, buy as many clothes as I could afford to show off when I got back to Hawaii, and suffer in the heat with jackets and stuff.

Burt Lum: Lesa Griffith was really into the new British sounds that were happening at the time. She was in the local scene too, and she introduced me to bands. Chris Planas, of course, playing in Pagan Babies and other bands, he was always kind of a rootsy, bluesy guy, and he wrote reviews in *Novus* as well. Neal Izumi's a graphic designer by trade, but he's always been on the leading edge of music and art and even did a comic strip for us. Victor was a full-on DJ with lots of musical knowledge, and so when you come in contact with these folks with this energy, this sort of vibrance, it's really fun.

We'd print anywhere between 500 and 1,000, maybe up to 2,000 copies, and we'd get them distributed in various stores, from Hungry Ear to Jelly's to Tower Records. To be honest, I wasn't really that interested in selling subscriptions because I think we, in essence, gave it away. A lot of it was motivated by the excitement, the energy, and just feeling you were part of a scene. I think that's what drove us.

Kit Grant: Burt was always so creative and so DIY. He was a little older than us, but he was just super interested and enthusiastic about things, and it was always easy to work with him because he was open to all kinds of ideas. He was very active at KTUH as well as the 'zine world, for sure.

Gary Chun: Because we were getting all these promos, we wanted to play them for people. Burt and I started, I think, late Fridays on KTUH; then it became Saturday afternoons. *Rough Take* was the name of the show, and we'd have our playlists printed in *Novus*.

Our theme song was Afrika Bambaataa's "Looking For the Perfect Beat." We'd pride ourselves on playing some of the early hip-hop that was coming out of the East Coast and a lot of alternative, independent rock with a smattering of major label stuff. We were probably the first people to play twelve-inch hip-hop singles on KTUH.

There's a track from the Athens, Georgia, band Love Tractor that Burt still uses on his current Hawaii Public Radio tech show that used to be our outro music.

HIS MASTER'S VOICE

Burt Lum: His Master's Voice was a group with Hawaii roots that signed to an indie label and were based in New York City. They had an album out in the early '80s. I remember going to one of their performances when they came out to Hawaii and it was great. Kinda visceral. I thought at the time it was very New York.

Keiko Bonk (vocalist: His Master's Voice, Cosmic Oven): When we were living in New York, we used to go to LA a lot, not just for music, but Mark's family is from LA, so we'd go there, and His Master's Voice started to gig there more. We'd do gigs in LA just to get back to Hawaii. Some guy saw us at some LA show, and he wanted to take us to do this demo in Burbank somewhere. We didn't know whether to trust him, but we did a three-song demo, and he called some friend of his in New Jersey who was associated with this record label. It was probably a mistake because we were not a good fit with this producer guy. Out of that came our album *Missionary*.

Mark Abramson (guitarist: His Master's Voice, Cosmic Oven): Keiko and I had issues with the producer because that record, we felt, was not representative of our sound. We were basically a power trio with a singer. Anyway, when we finally got to play Oahu, we'd do Anna's and Wave Waikiki, and we even played a couple of places on the Big Island just to make money so we could get back to New York. We always loved coming to Hawaii. You can't take the locals out of us.

BROUHAHA

Burt Lum: There was a lot of fascinating music happening around Oahu then, but over the years, *Novus* became kind of a production. It got to be a glossy print, staple-bound format with ads and a masthead, and it was a lot of work. I got to the point where I was like, "Man, this is like working for the printer!" I mean, you're not making a lot of money. A lot of the smaller fanzine kind of magazines are passion-driven, and at a certain point, *Novus* just sort of outlived its passion. In our case, we morphed it into something else called *Brouhaha*.

What I decided was, if printing was the most expensive piece of the equation, what if I were to eliminate printing and have each contributor xerox their own page? So I told everybody they could still be a part of the project, but instead of giving everything to me and having me lay it all out and pay a printer, why not everybody produce their own page? Just say and do whatever you want, however you want to design it, then xerox both sides of your page, and that would become a page in *Brouhaha*. It went in the opposite direction of *Novus* in that *Brouhaha* was a much more freeform publication, more like a traditional fanzine.

It turns out that I had a coworker at Hawaiian Tel who told me her dad owned Club Hubba Hubba, and I nearly fell off my seat because it was the most infamous strip club around, and she was just this regular local Japanese girl. So I brainstormed this idea that we could do a *Brouhaha* concert there. She said yeah, she could help set that up, so she got me connected, and that's all it took. We had Pagan Babies, Hat Makes the Man, and a bunch of local bands play. We didn't serve drinks so that we could do it all ages. There weren't many clubs that we could go to that would be open to the stuff we wanted to do.

Gary Chun: We tried to mix the bands as best we could. We'd do some punk and other types of rock and roll. It all fell together pretty easily. I think our main concern was the venue itself, but they were actually pretty cool.

Robert Scott: I remember I emceed a show at Club Hubba Hubba. I think it was a fundraiser for the *Novus* guys, and I sat in with Hat Makes the Man for a song. Playing Hubba Hubba was fantastic because it was a classic Hotel Street venue. They had that giant runway, like a *hanamichi*. It was crazy fun just to be in that space.

Peter Bond: Club Hubba Hubba. Man, that was a strange gig. The dressing room was the girls' dressing room, and one of the strippers was in there, and she was really annoyed that we were actually there, like, "Why are you guys here?"

"Well, fuck, we're just here to play music, you know?" It was cramping her style.

Gary Chun: For some reason, we thought it would be more edgy if we had one of their strippers get up on stage, and I know we got some blowback from some young feminists. They were not happy with that. I remember it was all pretty innocent, but it was like, "Oh my God, this is a big political statement to allow a stripper to perform!" But...*ehhh.*

Burt Lum: Some of the strippers were asking, "Do you want us to strip?" and we told them, "Uhhh...maybe not." So at least one came out in little pasties instead. She was used to completely stripping down to these old geezer types, so she was a little uncomfortable just dancing around in her outfit for a younger, mixed crowd. We were probably being a little insensitive, and to be honest, if I had to do it again, maybe I'd be more sensitive to it now, but no one really turned against us.

Raoul Vehill: I crawled on my belly down the gangway where the strippers would prance and parade. My girl was a stripper too, so I brought some props, like stuff she would wear on stage, I would wear on my head. Or I would wear her jacket and take all her glam stripper clothing to a punk rock show, because when you're looking at bands like Devo and stuff, it's like, "Okay, what can you throw in there to make it...different?"

MOVING ON

Burt Lum: After a certain point in time, I ended *Brouhaha.* I came to the realization that we could just do it for fun, but at some point, you gotta make money, you gotta focus on priorities. We did what we wanted to do, and everyone kinda moved on. Chris Planas moved to the Bay Area, Victor Sam moved to the Bay Area, the other writers moved, respectively, to whatever job or career they had.

Lesa Griffith: I graduated from UH and did a publishing course. These days, it's at Columbia, but back then, it was called the Radcliffe Publishing

Procedures Course in Cambridge. Then I moved to New York, because if you want to be in publishing, that's where you gotta go.

Elyce Tajima: Some of us wanted to move somewhere and some of us didn't. That's when I think a bolt of reality hit me and said, "Look, you aren't twenty, you're headed for thirty, and what are you doing?" I think that started nagging at me more and more. Did I want to be a part of Pagan Babies if we weren't going to take it to the next level?

I went on my own trip to Europe and missed a couple of weekends, and I didn't have a fantastic experience. I know my mood changed considerably when I came back, and I think that affected the vibe of our performances a bit and the dynamic within the group.

Chris Planas: The real end of the band was Craig Okino's decision to leave in early '94. He was the engine. He sang lead while playing these ridiculously syncopated bass lines; he ran merch, including T-shirts with his graphics; he found funding for our recordings, wrote setlists—all the stuff that was essential to a successful band. Since then, I've led bands and played for band leaders, and I've come to appreciate Craig's work ethic. When he left he was fine with us keeping the name going, where others I've played with would have taken their marbles and gone home.

We decided to call it a day with one final performance at Anna's in February 1995. It was twelve years to the month of our first gig there in '83. I figured we'd get a decent showing, but I wasn't prepared for the massive crowd that turned up. Later on, friends told me they waited in line for an hour and never got in because the whole dance floor was packed with people. Aging punks, preppies, locals, foreign students, friends, all laughing, sweating, moving like it was when we started. Past and present members showed up, including Craig and Elyce, and for me, that put an exclamation point on the end of a beautiful story.

Craig Okino: So the Pagan Babies broke up for the same reason all bands do—personality clashes. But hey, we had a really good run, longer than most. We ruled Anna's for years, a medium-sized fish in a small pond. It was a little disappointing that we couldn't seem to break onto the national scene.

Being in a band ain't easy. Musicians can have huge egos, and keeping a group of strong personalities together is no mean feat. But it's all worth it when you're on stage, the music's grooving, and everything's clicking. We had many, many moments like that over the years.

Burt Lum: Endings are always bittersweet. You've gone through this whole period of creation, bringing people together and having the ability to produce something meaningful. And then there's this point when you come to this realization that maybe its time has come and it's time to either end it or do something else. It became a choice between continuing to do *Brouhaha* as a labor of love or just kind of moving on, and I think that's a natural transition that occurs in any endeavor. You recognize it, accept it, and move on.

10

THE AGE OF METAL

By the dawn of the 1980s, Honolulu was primed for heavy rock and roll. An exceedingly young, testosterone-driven market, it figured in the top 5 percent nationally in ratio of males eighteen to twenty-four. When KDUK-FM switched from a dying disco format to album-oriented rock in 1980, its ascendancy was dramatic. By 1982, it had become the first station on the FM band to claim the number one spot in the Honolulu market's radio ratings.

Branded 98 Rock, its brilliantly marketed logo T-shirts, stickers, board shorts, Ripper wallets, visors, and assorted accessories were ubiquitous. The station sponsored a steady stream of concerts, including massive summer shows at Aloha Stadium featuring the likes of Black Sabbath, Blue Oyster Cult, Molly Hatchet, Heart, Foreigner, Joan Jett, and others, which helped cement rock's hold on the local market. Up-and-coming musicians had begun to look to homegrown bands like Shnazz and Teazer and their polished stage shows at Waikiki's Rock & Roll Clinic and the 23rd Step in Kailua with aspiration.

By the time 98 Rock reverted to its legacy call letters KPOI in 1983, rockers and metalheads were a common sight in Honolulu. With their long hair, concert tees and blue jeans, they seemed innocuous enough, like a uniformly dressed-down version of the post-hippie crowd of a decade earlier. Far less alien than the haphazardly shaven punk rock misfits outfitted in dog collars and combat boots.

The punk scene, though, was the more active subset, partly due to its staunch DIY ideology. Convinced no popular nightclub or radio outlet would ever be interested in their brand of entertainment, punks often banded together, created communities and support systems, played each others' parti es, and booked their own shows at any venue that would let them. A tiny show was better than none at all, and holding a gig at a small bar or rented space was a hardcore outfit's greatest ambition—it was fairly easy to pull off, and bands did it regularly, often inviting their friends' groups to share the bill.

By comparison, heavy metal combos might employ a more conventional approach. When a particularly determined band felt it was ready for the bright lights, it might hire a manager and send out demos in hopes of signing with an established label or opening for big-name acts at the Neal Blaisdell Center Arena. It could be a lonely proposition, though. Competition for coveted slots at high-profile events and local nightclubs was fierce, and hard rock acts sometimes saw their peers not as allies but more like rivals. A group's fan base could be equally territorial, viewing other bands and their fans with suspicion or hostility. This is not to say the early metal scene was without camaraderie, but it certainly lacked the level of cooperation seen in the punk community. So while the number of metal and heavy rock groups starting up in garages and bedrooms across the Islands likely dwarfed the number of hardcore punk bands, shows for punks were much more plentiful throughout the '80s due to their emphasis on unity and coaction.

Still, it could be argued that Hawaiian metal enjoyed greater reach beyond the Islands. Long before joining Megadeth and achieving guitar god status on the world metal scene, local virtuoso Marty Friedman spearheaded a number of visionary and prescient speed metal and power metal outfits in the Islands, and by the mid-1980s, the most acclaimed of his bands, Hawaii, along with fellow homegrown rockers Aaronsrod and Sacred Rite, boasted albums with international distribution that helped amass legions of fans across Europe, Asia, and the Americas.

Jimmy Dee Caterine (guitarist: Sacred Rite, Sabre): I would go and spend the night over at my friend Tim's house when we were eleven or twelve years old. Frank Orrall had a band that did all these Rolling Stones songs when he was in high school, and we'd go over to watch his rehearsals. What Frank would do is, he'd let us drink beer, but before he sent us home after he had his rehearsal, he'd make us eat two or three mangoes to get the beer smell off our breath.

I wanted to play in a band too. I took one guitar lesson at Harry's Music and learned "Cat Scratch Fever" and that same week learned stuff on my own off *Powerage* 'cause that was the record AC/DC had out at that time. I had the Rush live album and learned "Bastille Day."

My first year of high school at St. Louis, my friend who I would go to Frank Orrall's house with went to school at Iolani because his mother was a teacher there. He had met this other kid there, Kevin Lum, and said to me, "This kid's a great drummer. He doesn't have a drum set yet, but he goes into the music room and just jams on those drums. You really should talk to him."

I invited Kevin up to my house to jam, and he got his parents to buy him a little black, five-piece Pearl set. It was just me and him, so we played an instrumental song, "Coast to Coast" off the Scorpions' *Lovedrive* album. We played it all day and had a good old time, and we just decided "Okay, we have to start a band."

For about a year, we went through a ton of musicians. I mean, we tried everyone we knew who could play, and not very many of them lasted more than a day; from the first time we played together, Kevin and I were already so tight and locked in, like two pieces of a machine, and it was hard to find the right people to join us.

Angelo Jensen (vocalist: Aaronsrod; bassist: Kaos): At fourteen, fifteen, sixteen, I already had a moustache, and I would get into clubs all over the place. Back then, eighteen was the drinking age, and they didn't card *anybody*. You looked the age, you got in.

Growing up, I would see the Piranha Brothers, Teazer, Zontrazio, Shnazz. Those guys inspired us. We used to go and sneak into York's right near the university. The Piranha Brothers would always play there, and I would always bribe the owner with a joint. I'd give him a big, fat joint and he'd let us all in.

Back in those days, clubs didn't just book local bands; they'd also hire mainland bands for a month-long or two-month-long residency through an agency. They'd put a band up somewhere, and their literal job, every single day, was to be the house band for a month or two. So you'd get a rotation of these mainland bands coming into Hawaii.

At the time, Hawaii could be kind of isolated, and when you're stuck in that bubble, you don't see what's outside, so it was cool to see other bands come in and play. It really inspired you.

Mark Kaleiwahea (vocalist/guitarist: Sacred Rite, Sabre): My cousin and I and these two seniors at St. Louis decided that we would do the Brown Bags to Stardom thing. That was my ninth grade year. Brown Bags to Stardom was a statewide talent show where all the winners from all the high schools would go to the Waikiki Shell and compete. One of the judges that year was Vernon Sakata, a guitar player who was in a band called Shnazz. Funny thing is we did an Aerosmith song and a Shnazz song.

SABRE

Jimmy Dee Caterine: I'd seen Mark play at a battle of the bands at St. Louis, and not only could he play guitar, but he could sing too. He could sing great. I approached Mark and asked him if he'd be interested in coming up to my house and playing with us, and he agreed, but he was a little standoffish at first. It took a minute, I think, because even though Kevin and I were decent musicians, we were also kind of nerdy, and Mark was a little more cool. I hated that he was a better guitar player than I was, but it was a perfect fit.

Mark Kaleiwahea: I grew up in Ewa Beach, but Kevin grew up in Hawaii Kai, and Jim's house was up in the hills overlooking the Kahala golf course, so these guys had it together, man. They had some money.

First time walking into this upstairs room where they rehearsed, in this A-frame house, there was this huge drum set and, like, two Marshall half stacks. They had *stuff*, you know? Jim and Kevin had these massive record collections of these bands I had never heard of. Back in the day, nobody knew who Saxon was or Armored Saint or any of those obscure metal groups.

Jimmy Dee Caterine: Kevin and I, like I said, we were nerds. My mom gave me twenty bucks a week to spend however I wanted. You could go to Vinyl Donut when all the new records would come out, and they were four dollars and I could buy three or four of them and have lunch.

Kevin had diabetes and his parents took care of him and bought him anything he wanted. If he needed money or whatnot, he could always have it. We'd go into Tower Records and hit the import section for records that might've been big in Germany or France at the time, collecting all this music from bands like Samson, Saxon, Riot, Y&T, or UFO. We were getting deep into all that stuff.

Mark Kaleiwahea: We didn't have a bass player yet, so just two guitars and drums; nobody was singing. But we jam together and there's something there; a sound in your head and a feel that you're going for, and we had it. It was exciting.

As we started to write songs, we all clicked on Iron Maiden. Like, I really liked Van Halen; those guys didn't. Later on, I really liked stuff like Ratt and that kind of California rock where the guitar players are rippin' and the singers are singing real high. That's the kind of stuff I really liked, and those guys, not so much. They were more into the whole new wave of British heavy metal, but we discovered that Iron Maiden was our common ground.

I remember we played our first gig as Sabre. I was maybe fifteen or sixteen years old, and there was another kid at St. Louis who wanted to have a party at his parents' house at Black Point. We go there in the afternoon and set up in this one room, and he says we can start whenever people start coming in. Pretty soon there'd be, like, 500 people from all around the island milling through this house, man. You could barely walk through the place, it was so packed. There were people spilling out into the neighbors' yards. It was nuts.

So now, the next time some other rich kid is having a party, maybe in Kailua, guess what? "Oh, I saw this band at a party named Sabre… We gotta find them!" So that's what we started doing, man. We started playing house parties.

Jimmy Dee Caterine: I'm not kidding you, once we played that Black Point party, every weekend there was a party to play, so we started asking people for a hundred bucks to go play at their party. We started doing parties out in Haleiwa and Hawaii Kai, all over the island.

Our first bassist got his bass taken away from his stepdad for bringing home a report card with "Fs" on it, and my buddy Porter Miller filled in, but he left for college. Then Kevin lived across the street from this kid who played with this bass player named Peter Crane who was supposed to be really good but was really young. We watched him play once and he was so good, we got him to play for us. We gave him the hardest stuff to learn. We said, "Hey, we listen to this band Iron Maiden a lot. Can you play this?" and he just killed everything. It was like a dream come true.

Angelo Jensen: I remember the first time I ever saw Sacred Rite, they were called Sabre. And they were playing at the very top of Tantalus. There's that pavilion there at the very top, and bands would show up and plug in all their gear to a light socket and put on a show right then and there. They were awesome.

Mark Kaleiwahea stood out because he was a shredder. Mark Kaleiwahea and Brian Spalding are two perfect examples of Hawaiians who don't have to only play Hawaiian slack key music and wear aloha shirts. We've got Hawaiians who can play rock and roll as well as the white guys and they kick ass.

KAOS

Brian Spalding (guitarist: Aaronsrod, Kaos): My mom played ukulele, and my cousins all played guitar and ukulele, and my dad had jazz and Hawaiian albums, so I copied the music off his albums and off the TV. I really wasn't into any rock music, but if I heard a commercial on TV and the song sounded good, I tried playing that on the ukulele. Or the theme music from nighttime dramas like *Barnaby Jones*.

I never started playing guitar until I was sixteen or seventeen. By then it was a happening time for jazz fusion and that's what I was listening to. I liked George Benson and Larry Carlton and Al Di Meola. I had albums from Roy Buchanan, Les Paul and Mary Ford, and this guitar player named David Spinozza. I just tried to copy it all. That was my training before I got exposed to the rock stuff.

To tell you the truth, when I would go to my friend's house and he would play the Scorpions' *Tokyo Tapes* album, I thought that music was evil. I used to think it was the work of the devil.

Angelo Jensen: Me and a buddy of mine, Barry Lasit, who was in a lot of bands as well, were auditioning guitar players, and Brian Spalding showed up with a little Fender Twin Reverb amp and a Fender Strat, and he had the goofiest haircut. He was just a nerd, total nerd. I thought, *Oh my God, really?* But he plugged in his guitar, dude, and he scared the shit out of us. The first song he played was Triumph's "Rock 'N' Roll Machine," and if you listen to that song, there's a guitar solo in it, and he played it note for note. And we're just looking at him, going "What...the...fuck...?"

Brian Spalding: At first, I wasn't into heavy rock, but after a while I got into it. Whatever guitar player was melodic and exciting to me was what I was into. Right around that time, I got exposed to some friends who had UFO albums and Judas Priest and Iron Maiden records. I didn't even have any of that stuff, but I borrowed their albums and started learning those songs. It wasn't that hard for me because years before, I had ear-trained myself at home, so I had an easy time figuring out songs. I didn't even know that many rock songs, but the reason why I wanted to tackle "Rock 'N' Roll Machine" was because I thought, *This sounds pretty difficult; I wonder if I can do it.*

Angelo Jensen: When we got together, we learned the whole Ozzy Osbourne *Diary of a Madman* album, and it was pretty mind-blowing that Brian was pulling off all the Randy Rhoads shit without even trying. That band turned into Kaos.

Ken Rosene and Greg Mundy were the two big concert promoters in Honolulu at the time. Any major concert in the '80s was either a Greg Mundy or Ken Rosene show. Ken Rosene had a modeling agency on the side, and it just so happens my cousin did all the girls' makeup, so I got to know Ken. He asked Kaos to open for Hawaii. It was a heavy metal festival with a "Miss Metal" contest, a headbanging contest, and all that corny crap.

Barry Lasit (vocalist/guitarist: Kaos, X-Chaser, Martial Law, Widow-maker, etc.): I was working at Cosmic Airbrush, where we'd always have the radio on. We were listening to 98 Rock, and all of a sudden, here comes Hawaii; they're on the radio. One of the guys in the band, I think it was Gary St. Pierre, says, "We're gonna have this showdown this weekend with Kaos and we're gonna kick their ass!" He was talking about doing degrading things to us, and I'm working down the street, grubby from doing motorcycle parts. He said something personal about me and it was like, "Wow, brah! You like say dat kine stuff?" So I just got on my bike and rode over to the station, which was on Bishop Street. I went inside and stood outside the studio, like, "Come outside, brah!" I was fuming.

Marty Friedman comes out and he's like, "Hey, man, hey, man, it's just for publicity. Don't do anything crazy!"

I said, "This guy's history!"

He's like, "It's just PR."

I told him, "If it's just PR, you gotta let the people you're talking about know beforehand. If someone talks shit about you, you're gonna react. Plus, I'm a local guy. Come on, Marty!" I calmed down after that. I said, "Okay, it's just PR, it's just PR." I let that slide. We got along after that, but we didn't win the showdown.

AARONSROD

Angelo Jensen: After the show was over, we were backstage, and Greg Mundy was there hanging out. Even though he and Ken were rival promoters, they all used to hang out because everybody had the same coke dealer. He goes, "You guys were amazing. Get rid of the singer."

We're all looking at him like, "Excuse me?"

He says, "You guys were really, really good. Get rid of the singer."

Mind you, Barry Lasit was the lead singer of the band, and I would sing one or two songs in the whole set. I remember we would play "Desert Plains" by Judas Priest, and Barry would pick up his electric guitar and I sang the lead. And every time I sang that song, people would come

Angelo Jensen and Gerard Gonsalves of Aaronsrod.
Courtesy of Gerard Gonsalves

up to me and go, "Dude, you gotta fuckin' sing!" Everybody kept saying that. "You should be the singer, you should be the singer," and I'm like, "Fuck that, I don't want to be the singer; I'm the bass player!"

I think that night opening for Hawaii was the final straw. Brian pulled me aside and said, "We need to move on from Barry. You're going to sing, and I'm bringing in a bass player that's better than you." So he brought in Ed Dysarz. He and Brian went to Aiea High School together. That's how Aaronsrod was born. Barry didn't like it. Our friendship went into the toilet right after that. It was kinda rough for me because he was my next-door neighbor.

Brian Spalding: That's the hard part. Any time any of our band members changed it was difficult. We had several people who came and went, and we had to tell them we had to move on because we needed to elevate the group. You have to make those hard decisions. Sometimes it's because of skill and sometimes it's personality. Some of them we were really close with.

Barry Lasit: I did have some feelings about that. I did. I didn't think I was better or worse than any of the other guys, just different. I thought we had the potential to do something if we'd just continued on, but I probably was wrong because that kind of style went out with the dinosaurs. You gotta evolve or else you're gonna go the way of the T-Rex. Bye. I went on to join other bands. It's like having a girlfriend; these things come and go.

Angelo Jensen: Aaronsrod got the attention of Rick Keefer at Sea-West Studios. Rick Keefer produced Heart, Aerosmith, Adam Bomb, TKO out of Seattle, and so on. All these great records. We bugged the shit out of Rick Keefer. We must've given him a hundred demo tapes.

Finally, we had a meeting with Rick. He had this beautiful studio out in Hau'ula, beautiful house. He listened to all of our stuff and goes, "You guys are great but you gotta get rid of the drummer." Here we go again. Son of a bitch. If we wanted this deal with Rick Keefer, we needed to get a new drummer. Gerard Gonsalves came into the group, and that's what made the band that you hear on the record. He's a hard rock drummer, but he's very funky, very groovy. The minute he started playing with us, you could feel it.

Rick reached out to Roadrunner Records and went, "Hey, I got this great band out in Hawaii named Aaronsrod. I'm producing their record, sign them." And they did. We were in our twenties, we didn't know any better, so when we signed our contract, we signed to Rick Keefer and Sea-West Studios. We signed over all of our rights to our music publishing, everything to Rick Keefer, not knowing any of this. We didn't know anything about business. So basically, Rick Keefer now owned all of our material, and he's the one who signed a contract to Roadrunner as if those were all of his songs. He's the one getting all the money. Our album is out there, and everything is going to Roadrunner and Rick Keefer.

SACRED RITE

Mark Kaleiwahea: I was probably seventeen or eighteen when we recorded our first album under the name Sacred Rite. Then you start getting a little bit more popular and start playing bigger places. I think most of us had become of age already, so we could play Coconut Grove, and we opened a lot of shows at the Blaisdell.

At that point, there was a definite shift because we were old enough to play the clubs. By the time I graduated high school, we were already pretty well established. We did a lot of recording and opening for bands at the Blaisdell and Aloha Tower. We opened for Ozzy twice, if not three times; Quiet Riot twice; Triumph twice.

When we opened for Ozzy on their *Bark at the Moon* tour at the Blaisdell, they invited us up to the Ilikai Hotel, where they were staying. Ozzy was there, Bob Daisley was there, Don Airey was there, and Tommy Aldridge was there. We're all sitting around the pool deck, it's dark as shit, no pool lights on, no nothing. We're having drinks, just shooting the shit, and frickin' Ozzy is off in the corner. He's got on a Dracula cape and he's running around chasing cockroaches. You know

Sacred Rite. From left to right: Peter Crane, Mark Kaleiwahea, Kevin Lum, Jimmy Dee Caterine. *Courtesy of Jimmy Caterine*

the big cockroaches we have in Hawaii? I guess he's never seen those before because he's running around the pool deck trying to stomp on these cockroaches, and we're just laughing at him.

Jimmy Dee Caterine: We had seen Queensryche release their first EP, and it just took off. I said, "That's what we gotta do. Let's not look for a label; we'll just release it ourselves." I took some of the money we made from our gigs and pressed a thousand records. After a week or two of calling distributors to see if they would distribute our record, I got a call from Dutch East India Trading. So I sent them 900 Sacred Rite records, and they were calling me within two weeks, saying, "Okay, we need some more." So we pressed up 3,000 more records with a new cover and everything.

I remember when Sacred Rite was starting to hit, there was kind of a scene with bands like Hawaii, Sacred Rite, and Aaronsrod. That's when it really came alive because you had several good bands that could kind of lead the way. Rex Havok was another band that got popular around town, and I remember we played with them at Coconut Grove.

Angelo Jensen: We knew Neil Delaforce from Rex Havok. He showed up at one of our shows, and I asked him to join Aaronsrod. Rex Havok had just broken up, so he was a free agent. I was surprised he said yes. He was older than us and way cooler.

Over time, we opened for Ratt, we opened for Priest. Dio and Dokken came into town, and our job was to play an after-party for them at the Rock & Roll Clinic. That was amazing. Both bands came to the Rock & Roll Clinic, and Ronnie James Dio's sitting there checking you out while you're playing. No pressure, right? We did one for Rush. Whenever hard rock bands would come in for vacation, Rick Keefer was in touch with a lot of labels at the time and he would send Aaronsrod out to meet them and show them around.

Loudness was blowing through town one night, headed back home to Japan from the mainland, and all they wanted to do was meet girls and eat spaghetti. We were looking at them, like, "Meet girls and eat spaghetti?" They were in love with spaghetti. So we went to get spaghetti somewhere, and of course, we made phone calls to our girlfriends' girlfriends: "Hey, we got Loudness in town; we need some female company." We all met at the Jazz Cellar, and then we ended up across the street at the Outrigger Hotel. Loudness was a bunch of fun guys.

Gerard Gonsalves (drummer: Aaronsrod): Loudness was in town, and Angelo and Neil took them for a drive around the island. Neil was driving and Angelo and Loudness' vocalist, Minoru Niihara, were riding in the back, and as they drive through the Pali Tunnel, Minoru yells out, "Be careful, rock star in back!"

Brian Spalding: When you see famous bands like Judas Priest on the albums and in the magazines, you put them on a pedestal. Then when they show up and get out of a van in shorts and T-shirts, the grandeur of it kind of diminishes.

Getting to the backstage area and seeing the crew putting the whole production together and seeing how big all of it is and how much work goes into all, that is what I was more captivated by than meeting the bands. If you go from playing at high schools to that kind of professional environment, it's pretty startling.

Angelo Jensen: My girlfriend at the time was one of the biggest dope dealers in Waikiki, and she obviously had a lot of friends. One of her most important clients was Cliff Williams, the bass player from AC/DC. At that time, Cliff and his wife had a house in Hawaii Kai, and he'd always be at the apartment picking up. And so me and Cliff got to know each other. We'd hang out and we all started going out together. He liked going out with me because I would suck up all the attention in the room by the way I looked. He was a shy guy and didn't like a lot of people coming up to him. Whenever I left the house, I'd change my whole attire to look the part, so when people would say, "The guy from AC/DC is in here," of course, everyone would look at me and think it was me and come up to me instead. Cliff loved that shit.

One night, we all go to the Royal Hawaiian, and I'm sitting at a table with Cliff Williams and Brian Johnson from AC/DC and we're drinking stupid gallons of mai tais, just round after round, getting wasted.

So Brian Johnson leans over to me and goes, "Hey, wanna take one of these?" and he hands me a little Halcion tablet. I'm not going to turn Brian Johnson down, right? So I take it, I don't know what the fuck it is, and ten minutes later, that's it. That's the last thing I remember.

I wake up at home, in my bed; nobody's there. I'm looking for everybody, but I don't know where everybody is—this is before cell phones—so I go over to my best buddy's apartment, and my girlfriend's there. I walk in on 'em screwing. Okay, that's interesting. It doesn't really faze me because it isn't like we're in love or anything. And my friend tells me, "You're a fucking hero!" Well, I totally blacked out, right? So what did I do?

He goes, "You were out of your mind. You jumped on the table, the guys from AC/DC were egging you on, and security finally had to kick us all out." Apparently, I ran away from security, then pulled a driver off his pedicab, stole the pedicab, sped down Kalakaua Avenue with the cops looking for me, and they never got me. So he goes, "I gotta tell you, Brian Johnson and Cliff Williams, they love you, man!"

MARTY FRIEDMAN

Mark Kaleiwahea: I started teaching guitar at Hot Licks, the one that was across the street from Tower Records, right by Ala Moana. Me and Marty Friedman were the guitar teachers there, amongst a couple of other guys. Marty was very unique and definitely did his own thing. He wasn't trying to fit into a scene; he was just Marty, man. I wouldn't say we were friends, but we were friendly because we saw each other only when we were at Hot Licks teaching, and that was only for a second here and there, but I got nothing but respect for that guy. He's definitely a monster player. Marty has a unique style, very different, and that style was not what was happening at the time. The popular guitar players were Eddie Van Halen and Warren DeMartini, all this more bluesy stuff, and he was more from the classical Uli Jon Roth style, which is more difficult to make fit, but he just stuck with it, and then of course Yngwie Malmsteen came along and blew that style wide open.

John Dahlin: There was one local metal band that I really liked, and that was Marty Friedman's first band, Vixen. Tom Clerx and I ran into him at a house party. His band had played and we were trying to talk him into playing with us. I'm like, "Dude, we play in hardcore bands. You'd be so good with us!"

He's like, "Oh, I really like that stuff. There's some really cool bands like Dead Kennedys!"

It never happened, though. It was like an hour of drunken rattling, but you can just imagine if Marty Friedman joined ADMS Family.

Jimmy Dee Caterine: We always knew Marty was great, but until he put together Hawaii, his other bands, Vixen and Aloha, didn't sound super tight to me. They definitely had something going on, but I was never into the speed metal because it was a lot harder to get things tight when you're playing so fast. But watching Marty play, fuck, all the stuff he was doing scale-wise and in terms of theory was pretty amazing.

Revered guitarist Marty Friedman, known for his time with Megadeth, launched his career with several leading-edge metal bands in Hawaii.
Courtesy of Pat Ohta

Angelo Jensen: Brian took guitar lessons from Marty Friedman. Marty Friedman lived in Hawaii Kai. Rich family. You know, very well-off. Killer house. Big, huge house. We'd go to his house all the time, and Marty would be in the corner, guitar in his lap, shredding while talking to you. Dirty fingernails, he'd never change his guitar strings on his guitar; his guitar strings were disgusting. His room was all *pilau*, you know? Who's this frickin' weirdo? And then he would play and you're like, "Holy shit!" I never really saw Marty out in the scene. I don't think he hung out, and that's why I didn't know who he was at first, like, "Who's this kid?"

Brian Spalding: Marty was teaching guitar, and he was into Uli Jon Roth, and I was just getting into Uli's music. A friend of mine said, "You should check out this guy Marty." That was 1981. His parents had a house up on the hill in Hawaii Kai that had an addition connected to the garage. That's where he lived. He would show me a lick, and I would do the lick right after he did it. So I was catching on really quick, and it wasn't anything like "Put your finger here" and "Put this finger there." Before you knew it, we were harmonizing, and it happened super fast.

The lessons didn't really happen. Marty didn't see any sense in teaching me anything. He said, "Screw it, let's just jam." Eventually he and I would get together and jam once in a while.

Barry Lasit: I got to know Hawaii's manager pretty well. Norm Dale owned a heavy metal shop called the Cavern on Ward Avenue, near the Blaisdell. He was quite a character, like a P.T. Barnum carnival barker kind of dude. I was a graphic artist, and he talked to me about doing an album cover for Hawaii. I took it with a grain of salt, but he actually did pull through and even put my name on the credits for *Loud, Wild and Heavy*.

Personality-wise, Marty was a trippy kind of guy, but he was always nice to me, and he invited me to his house one day. His house was the biggest, most incredible house in the area. I go up to his house and he's got all these guitars all over the place. I see at the front door he's got two guitars: a BC Rich Bich and some kind of Ibanez Iceman. So I go into his house and it's a *wreck*. He's like, "Yeah, the maid hasn't been here in about a week." Then he said, "I really dig the album cover. That was so cool. This is from me. Go ahead and pick out a guitar. Any guitar you want, man." There was that beautiful red BC Rich Bich, but I'd always wanted a Gibson Explorer and that's the one I picked. They'd already paid me pretty well for the album cover, so I felt weird about taking the guitar, but he had a million of 'em.

ROCK AT QUEEN THEATER

Jimmy Dee Caterine: My dad was kind of a hoodlum, I'd say, and he had some problems and had to go away for a while, so when we moved to Hawaii, my dad put people in place to kind of watch over his family, you know? So there was Jimmy James, who we used to call my brother, because I'd known him my whole life and he was always around, but we're not really related. He was probably eighteen, nineteen years older than me. He started building a sound, lighting, and stage company where he would provide equipment for shows, so he would get us all sorts of gigs.

Mark Kaleiwahea: Jim's mom got the lease for the Queen Theater in order for us to have a place to play 'cause we couldn't do anything. Most clubs wouldn't have us because nobody wants to hear that stuff in a nightclub.

Jimmy Dee Caterine: Jimmy James was trying to start a live music venue, so we pulled in some bands to do some metal shows at Queen Theater and also some national acts like Megadeth. We did punk shows and I even brought in Gene Loves Jezebel, and we did a Hat Makes the Man show too, which went really well. My mom and Jimmy handled all the details, and Jimmy had the sound and lighting covered.

Mark Kaleiwahea: Maybe in the punk scene, everybody was a little more accepting of each other, but I know in the metal scene, it was competitive. You could just feel it at shows. Take the Queen Theater, for instance. You got three bands playing, and backstage, nobody's talking to each other. It was like being at a wrestling match or martial arts competition or something. It was super weird, man. I mean, I'm friends with all the guys in Aaronsrod on Facebook, super friendly, bruddah-bruddah, the whole thing, right? But back in the day, to me, it didn't feel that way. It was very "spandex standoff," man. It was funny.

Angelo Jensen: Sacred Rite, they were the big one. They were the main competition. We're all brothers, we're all kinsmen, and we all came up together, but at the time, there was a lot of competition going on.

We did a show with Sacred Rite at Queen Theater, and I think that night we broke attendance there; 800 people came to that show. Think about that for a second: 800 people in Hawaii showed up to hear two local metal bands play their own music. It was basically a sold-out show.

Jimmy Dee Caterine: We had left for the mainland just before the Megadeth show at Queen Theater, and at some point, the whole Queen Theater situation was abandoned because there was no one like me, on the street level, to tell my mom and Jimmy what concerts would be good and what would actually work. For about two years we'd given it new life, and it could have been great, but any improvements to the place would have been put on us, and with the electrical problems and everything, the owner and Jimmy couldn't work things out.

BIG STEPS

Mark Kaleiwahea: When we finally left Hawaii in '87, we went to Oklahoma 'cause that's where Jim's dad was, and we knew if we went to LA or New York, we would get eaten up. Like, we just didn't know what we were doing. We would've been fed to the wolves. So it was like, "Well, let's go to Oklahoma so if something really goes bad, at least we got a roof over our heads, and it's halfway between New York and California."

There's a place called Rockers just down the street from where we were staying. So we're like, "Okay, we're badasses. Let's go in there and show this town what's up." I walk in and some Dio song is playing and

I'm like, "Wow, cool. They play good music here. This oughta be awesome."

We all get a drink and go through the second set of doors, and I think they're playing the Dio CD, but it's actually a live band covering a Dio song and it sounds like the frickin' record. I was blown away. My first thought was, "Holy shit, we're in trouble, man. We don't sound *nothing* like that." Jim started talking to the guys like, "Well, who's your booking agent?" That's how Jim was. Like, if I wanna get where you're going, just tell me how you got there, and I'll do the same thing, basically.

It turned out that their booking agent had an office in the same building, upstairs. The agent had us play Easter Sunday night, and afterward he was like, "Man, you guys did great. I'm gonna shoot your name to the next closest place that I book, but you gotta ditch your originals. Nobody wants to hear that stuff." It was one of those things, man. If we wanted work, that's what we were going to have to do.

So we go play a week in Nebraska, then come back to Tulsa for two weeks. We play a week in Dallas, come back for two weeks. Play a week in Missouri somewhere, come back for two weeks. So the circle got bigger and bigger, and we ended up in the Rockies circuit, which was Tucson, Arizona; Colorado Springs, Colorado; Denver, Colorado; Cheyenne, Wyoming. You could spend five months doing that. We were playing the "A" circuit, which, in Hawaii terms, would be the bigger clubs like Gussie L'Amour's and the Wave. The "B" circuit would maybe be the kind of places back home like the Jazz Cellar, 23rd Step, and Bully Hayes. Then the "C" circuit would be like some karaoke bar next to Liliha Bakery, you know what I mean? We did that for two years, as the working band version of Sacred Rite. We started writing what we thought people wanted to hear, and that was a mistake. That wasn't our forte at all.

Angelo Jensen: In 1986, after Aaronsrod opened for Judas Priest in Hawaii on their *Turbo* tour, we all decided we were going to move to California. We had a record contract under our belt, we had our first record out, so we were already better off than most bands. We thought we could go to LA and start playing and make shit happen.

We flew to Los Angeles in '86, and four days after getting there, our drummer and our bass player quit and flew back to Hawaii, leaving me, Brian, and Neil there in Hollywood on our own with no rhythm section.

Gerard Gonsalves: It became apparent real quick that we had moved up too soon without properly planning things out. We had a band account that was quickly evaporating, none of us could find jobs, and rent was coming up. Edward and I honestly felt that we needed to come back home, and we really thought the rest of the guys would eventually follow us.

I actually did look back on the situation with regret a couple years after we came home, but I believe everything happens for a reason.

Angelo Jensen: Me and Brian already made a commitment to stick it out, so we hired guys and started playing the Sunset Strip within a year of landing there. So considering we had lost almost half the band, that was pretty good.

We started playing Gazzarri's and the Whiskey and the Roxy and Troubadour, Coconut Teazer, FM Station, all the great Hollywood and Sunset Strip clubs. And we were pretty damn fucking good. Most bands started playing Tuesday nights, and we immediately started getting weekends.

But let me tell you something. Talk about a different scene. In Hawaii, I stood out, I was different. But when I went to the mainland, we were all a dime a dozen. Even the guy at baggage claim at the airport had big hair. The janitors looked like Nikki Sixx.

When we got there, Guns N' Roses was getting really big, and all the bands were that sleazy, LA glam kinda rock, and although we dressed kind of funny here and there, we stuck to our guns. We kept it power metal. Classic metal. And that genre wasn't really hittin' it there in Hollywood. But throughout the rest of the '80s and into the early '90s, we played and played and played, and suddenly it was over. It was all done. One month after Nirvana's big record came out, all the labels that had hair metal bands or hard rock bands on their roster were dropped. If you were already signed, you got a letter in the mail: "You're done, thank you."

The Hollywood scene in general became less and less focused on that genre. Punk music started to come in more on the Strip and then you started to have alternative rock, and it was the '90s, so a lot of that grunge came in, indie kind of stuff. It got to be where anyone who walked into a bar dressed like Motley Crue was a joke. People would start laughing and make fun of you. Our crowd was gone. It was immediate. I could even tell you the year: It was 1992. One minute, everyone's got leather pants on and hairspray in their hair, and literally the next week, it's over. It happened like that.

11

EXTREME NOISE

To suffer the indignity of a blindside sacking and watch his former band's rise in the world of rock was a matter of frustration for Barry Lasit. If there was any resentment, however, it was short-lived. As Kaos pushed on without him as Aaronsrod, Lasit fell in with a younger set of musicians keenly attuned to the faster, heavier brands of metal in emergence. The timing, he says, was significant. "After Kaos, I'm glad I went in another direction because I was right there at the moment when change happened," contends Lasit. "I got to actually experience the big transition right before my eyes."

To be sure, there were several sweeping and far-reaching developments in heavy metal in the 1980s. As MTV and FM radio helped turn metal into a major force in popular music, mainstream acceptance also led to its dilution and commercialization. Hard rock groups eager for widespread success began courting new audiences with radio-friendly power ballads and glitzier styles. Pushback, however, came from metal's most hardened and devoted wing. This growing faction, bound to the more cabalistic and cacophonous components of metal, doubled down with a harder-faster-louder philosophy that gave rise to speed metal, then thrash metal, two of the many proliferating subgenres that shattered the limits of the heaviest rock around.

Punk rockers, who had always found themselves at odds with the shallow posturing and puerile male fantasies of hard rock, gradually found common ground with metal's more radical devotees in chasing a more potent and powerful sound. A mutual admiration developed between the two camps, which slowly, perhaps cautiously, warmed to one another.

Record shops began to set up special heavy metal and hardcore punk sections in their bins to meet growing demand, and it wasn't rare for diehards of one style to occasionally dip into the offerings of the other for an ear-ringing fix. Bootlegging and homemade tape trading among fans around the world helped both prominent and obscure metal and punk bands reach far-flung regions of the globe via mail. Even fanzines, those low-rent, xeroxed, cut-and-paste publications, which had been almost exclusively the domain of punk rock, supported the new underground version of metal in breaking away from its more mainstream forms.

Galvanized by this unholy convergence of hardcore punk and heavy metal, Pat Ohta, a high schooler at Mid-Pacific Institute, produced *Iron Cross*, one of the Islands' most widely distributed fanzines of the mid- to late '80s. Though fully committed to metal, he quickly became a convert of hardcore as well. "If I saw a metal band wearing someone else's T-shirt, I'd start wondering who that band was. Sometimes they'd be punk bands," Ohta recalls. "Once I discovered Metallica, Anthrax, and all those groups, it didn't take long before I discovered bands like Minor Threat. I liked the rawness of punk, but they also talked about social issues, and that resonated with me. I just got really into it."

Inevitably, a new, up-and-coming crop of musicians, equally inspired by the unbounded aggression of hardcore punk and the bombastic power of heavy metal, began to hybridize these sounds into deafening amalgamations that would soon take local underground rock to previously unknown extremes.

X-CHASER

Woody Soueira (bassist: X-Chaser, Optimum Fury, Ciguatera): My friend Danny Obenario didn't have a band, but he was playing guitar, doing Van Halen, all that kind of stuff in high school, at Campbell. I don't know why, but for some reason he asked me, "Why don't we start a band?" So I took the bus to Chinatown to my uncle's pawn shop, and my uncle took a bass off the wall and gave it to me. Somehow, Danny got a hold of Barry Lasit, who was in a bunch of bands.

Barry Lasit: I don't know if their band even had a name yet, but Danny and Alex Locquiao, their other guitarist, had this cool dual harmony thing, kind of like how Thin Lizzy or Judas Priest used to do. It wasn't shredding but just simple harmonies that really make a song pop, man. When I saw them play, I was like, "Wow, these guys are pretty good!" I heard they fired their singer, and I kind of made it known I was

X-Chaser's Danny Obenario (left) and Woody Soueira (center) with Brian Spalding of Aaronsrod backstage at Queen Theater. *Courtesy of Elwood Soueira*

interested, so I got invited out to this place in Ewa, this community hall out there where you were allowed to jam, and that's what we did. I could tell they'd been rehearsing a lot.

Woody Soueira: We called our band X-Chaser, and Barry brought a couple of his girlfriends to some gigs—he was kind of a stud muffin—and we'd be playing and they would be on the left and right side, go-go dancing. Nobody did that. He had the vision. Then at this battle of the bands, Barry had a tie on and a suit, but it was all a setup. We knew this one guy from Ewa, this big dude, and just before we played, this guy pushed the crowd away, and he went up to Barry, fucking grabbed his clothes, and ripped it. The clothes tore off, and Barry had his rock-and-roll outfit underneath. Shit like that. Barry was ahead of his time, that guy. He was a showman.

Barry Lasit: The one advantage X-Chaser had over everybody else was our following. The band had so many followers from Ewa, dude. It's a tight community out there, and they would always come out in force for their brothers. They really supported us.

SCARRED 4 LIFE

Rich Tarantino (guitarist/vocalist: Scarred 4 Life; bassist: Saud, Stage Dive): After I graduated high school, June of '82, our family moved from the San Francisco Bay Area to Hawaii. My dad got a teaching job out there in the Waianae school district and so we lived in Makaha. We were cool with the locals right away, I think, because our family spent some time living in Indonesia, and we knew how to blend in pretty easily. We respected people and didn't act out of sorts.

My brother Ed and I were fully immersed in hardcore by that time. We'd seen a lot of shows in the Bay. Our first show was Dead Kennedys and Flipper in some old warehouse, and it was the scariest experience ever. I was seventeen and Ed was fifteen. In those days—1980, 1981— there were a lot of freaks and weirdos who adopted punk rock and would go to shows. And it wasn't like they were punk rockers; they were just weirdos and outcasts, and it was real dangerous. You didn't know what kind of psychos were gonna show up.

Ed Tarantino (bassist: Scarred 4 Life, Cringer, Broken Man): Skateboarding almost had the same kind of free-thinking attitude as punk. Building ramps in backyards and finding places to skate, it had that same DIY feel. We had a tight skate scene in Hawaii, and the punk rock thing was integrated with skating.

One of the guys who skated with us was a UH marching band guy, so he was a good drummer. My brother could play guitar pretty good, and because he was better than me, it was natural for me to play bass. One of our skater friends became our first singer, and we started our band that way. That was our first band. We called it Scarred 4 Life. Those first gigs, our singer would have his knee pads around his ankles because we'd play shows right after going skating.

My brother and I also had a skate music fanzine called *Thrash 'N' Tool* with skate photographs, record reviews, stuff like that. It got written up in *Thrasher* magazine. They liked it. We had massive correspondence with the whole DIY punk rock scene across the world and exchanged fanzines with all kinds of people from Europe and all over.

At the same time, we had a record store that operated out of the back of my brother's trunk called Thrash 'N' Scratch. As we got exposed to more stuff, we were ordering it as well. So we'd show up at shows, pop open the trunk, and sell records.

Rich Tarantino: Living in Makaha, we had to order our music from ads in the 'zines that we brought with us from San Francisco. One in particular was called *Ripper*. There was also *Maximum Rocknroll*. We saw an ad that Rough Trade put out for wholesale ordering, and we inquired about that and even went downtown to apply for a general excise tax license to purchase wholesale. We would get mailed lists of what was out, and a lot of the stuff we didn't even know, so we had to read the descriptions of the records; if it was hardcore or sounded like it would be hardcore, then we would order it: SSD, The Freeze, Negative Approach's first EP, S.O.A., Minor Threat, of course. We would put prices on the records, stick them in milk crates, and sell them at the places we'd skate at.

Ed and I first heard "Straight Edge" by Minor Threat when we mail-ordered their first EP, and even though we'd had beers and stuff at punk shows or whatever, drinking was never something that we were really into or sought after. So we latched onto the idea behind straight edge, and the group of skaters we hung out with didn't partake in alcohol or smoking, and straight edge became an identity we all subscribed to.

Ed Tarantino: There were a few of us who were full-on straight edge: no drinking, no drugs, and no fraternizing with women, basically. No sex. I was full-on into that mindset. There was something about that aesthetic that we liked. That kind of "masculine monk" bravado thing.

The thing is, I started dating this girl named Heather. Heather Hahn. I met her skating. She was hanging out at a skate ramp or something like that. I realized I had seen her before 'cause when the Circle Jerks were playing at 3-D, which was a significant event—a real hardcore band was playing Hawaii—my brother and I were interviewing them for our fanzine, and there was this chick sitting with the guitarist, Greg Hetson. That was Heather Hahn, who became my girlfriend later on. We kind of became inseparable in some ways.

Rich Tarantino: I started lifting weights and started to grow my hair out long, and I noticed that I was being noticed by women, and that was a first for me. I liked it. I liked the attention.

There was a personal issue I had that went deeper than the straight edge ideal that Ed was breaking. He and I were always tight together. It was always me and him. We moved around a lot and only had each other growing up, ultimately, as friends. And when Heather came into the picture, that broke it up, and so I went through some shit and did something that was kind of lame. I tried to hit on her and…well, let's just say these things came back to haunt me. The things you do sometimes get done to you later in life. Then you realize how lame it was what you did. I did have a reconciliation with my brother not too long after that happened, and I apologized for trying to stir up shit and break them up.

But really, I'm the one who broke the whole straight edge pact because when Christian Hosoi, the pro skater, came to town, I would smoke weed with him. I had totally broken from straight edge at that point.

Ed Tarantino: My brother and I did a gig out at the rec center in Hawaii Kai, and some of the guys at the show got into an altercation with Job Corps just up the hill. Those guys from Job Corps came down and just started fucking pounding people, basically, and they came out with crowbars and started smashing cars. They smashed our car pretty badly. People were running and shit because they were coming after everyone. A lot of those Job Corps guys were ex-cons, you know?

Jon Lange: A bunch of bands were going to play. What happened was all the guys at Job Corps didn't like us being there, and they fucking attacked everyone. It was fucking nuts. I was waiting for the rest of our band to show up, drinking beer in the car, shooting the shit, and I see one guy come flying by, and there's a big moke chasing him. I'm like,

"What the fuck's going on?" All of a sudden, I just see people running everywhere, and some of these dudes have sticks. Turns out some big fuckin' mokes said they didn't like us, and during the show they threw something through the plate glass window and jumped in and just started beating the shit out of people. I walk in while all this chaos is happening—shit's breaking, glass is fucking flying, windows are smashing—and I grab my bass, go back to the car, stick it in the back seat, and the rest of the band shows up and I'm all, "It's a riot, let's go!" We went to Foodland in Koko Marina, got beer, and went to the beach instead.

Rich Tarantino: We were all inside the hall, and we heard that there were a bunch of locals who were pissed and they were coming for us. I don't know what happened to anybody else, but I got chased by two guys—one of them had a hammer and it was *scary*. I ran for my life, and I remember I fell and the guy was over me with the hammer, and I'm, like, yelling things and he's yelling, "Rock rules! Rock rules!" like there's some kind of competition between punk rock and the kind of rock he knows. I'm all, "Yes, I know, rock rules! I love rock too! Black Sabbath, man, that's what I listen to!" And I guess he just ran off to chase another person or something, but I was so relieved I didn't get hit. I was cowering, down on the ground, professing my love for rock too. It was weird.

Ed Tarantino: My brother's Toyota Corolla was smashed up, and my dad went to talk to Job Corps, and they did a full body and paint job on the car because they trained people to do that kind of work. So the same guys that smashed the car had to fix it.

Rich Tarantino: They asked me what color I wanted it painted, and I chose this hideous blue, I don't know why.

Ed Tarantino: Hanging out at Heather's house in Nanakuli, I could hear her brother playing guitar in his room, and he was playing The Clash and shit like that. I asked her about him. Lance went to school at Kamehameha, and I said, "Hey, ask him if he wants to play in our band." So we brought him in, and my brother started singing.

Lance had a shitload of songs he'd already written. We'd already had our own songs that were short and fast and sometimes kind of moronic. Some of my brother's lyrics were misogynistic while Lance's stuff wasn't maybe as hardcore, but it was better written in some ways. His lyrics were far more thoughtful and political.

From playing with us he got exposed to the rest of the punk scene in Hawaii and started collaborating with other people, and at that same juncture, my brother and I started getting into the new thrash metal that was coming out, stuff like Celtic Frost and Slayer and Voivod, and it really opened our ears, like, "Holy shit, metal's now the heaviest thing!"

Rich Tarantino: We were reading about punk bands that were starting to go the metal route and getting chastised for it. But me and Ed were always into Black Sabbath, so it was our roots. One day Ed and I went into the Cavern and saw Slayer's *Haunting the Chapel* on cassette, and we bought it and we're all, "Holy shit, this is exactly what we love!" It was so rad. We were blown away. And that's what I started to write, exactly that style. Some of the old-school haole punks from the North Shore accused me of being "Motley Crue" now. It really bummed me out because I respected these guys as old-school, hardcore skaters and I thought the music I was playing was still raw and aggressive, but they probably didn't hear it that way because my hair was long and bleached blond and I wore a bullet belt and a spiked bracelet.

Ed Tarantino: We'd started chasing this heavier sound, and it morphed the band again. It's not that Lance wasn't exposed to metal or didn't have an appreciation for it, but he wasn't really that kind of player, so we started seeking out more of a metal guitarist. Ironically, we found this other guy from Kamehameha who was more of a metal player, and we kind of morphed from being a hardcore band to being more thrash metal-ish. We didn't necessarily push Lance out, because he was already starting to collaborate with other people in the punk scene like the Kroll Brothers, who we knew through skating, and people like Gardner Pope and Dave Carr.

Rich Tarantino: The feeling I got from Lance was that he didn't really like me because I would say things flippantly and wasn't very politically correct, probably. The way I tried to manipulate his sister bummed him out towards me, and ideologically, he was on his track and it wasn't the same as mine. Musically, I think there was a difference as well. He didn't play much hard, fast, as-fast-as-you-can hardcore. He was more into bands like The Clash and The Proletariat. Musically and lyrically, we weren't a good fit.

IRON CROSS

Pat Ohta (promoter; activist; *Iron Cross* publisher): I always had this understanding that we're in Hawaii and most things are never going to happen unless we make them happen. I think I had that attitude shift when I started learning about the whole do-it-yourself movement in punk rock.

I put out four issues of *Iron Cross*, which was sold locally and in parts of the mainland to promote heavy metal and punk rock music and our local bands. The articles were done by classmates and anybody who wanted to contribute. The first issue had Sacred Rite and a little article on KTUH.

My dad worked at HonFed Bank and had a small staff at his office, and one day he sat them down to take our handwritten things and type them out into columns, tape them onto pieces of paper, and we photocopied everything. By the time Issue Four came out, it was free and had worldwide distribution. I used to get letters from different countries saying, "I just picked up your magazine in our local record store here." What I discovered was that when you do your own fanzine, you get so much shit for free. Although I had to write to the bands, I would get boxes of records, pictures, bios, and it became really easy to interview bands.

As far as music I was listening to, I just liked it all by that time. At school, there was a small group of people who liked new wave, metal, and punk. Whether one person liked The Smiths or Slayer or the Dead Kennedys, we were all friends. I got into all forms of music.

SAUD

Jaime Ikeda (guitarist: Saud, Stage Dive, Broken Man, etc.): Most of us met in school, at Mid-Pac. I played guitar in Saud, with Matt Dale singing, Rob Cribley on drums, and Lloyd Orsino on guitar. We went through a bunch of bassists, but the one that stuck out was Rich Tarantino, who used to be the singer for Scarred 4 Life.

I have to give Rob's older brother Jim Cribley props because he was the one who introduced us to Metallica. Metallica just came out with *Kill 'Em All*. You know back then, brah, there was so much static, yeah? People were playing records backwards and saying it was devil music. But as a kid, you don't care. That made some kids like that stuff even more.

Rob Cribley (drummer: Saud, Stage Dive, The Wrong, etc.): Pretty much all my friends at Mid-Pac were punks, and those who weren't were tied to the skateboarding scene. Saud's singer, Matt Dale, was going there. Jaime Ikeda was going there.

Jaime's a fucking machine. That guy's just an insane player. He totally schooled me. He can play beautiful slack key, he can play metal, he can play everything. When Metallica's *Master of Puppets* record came out, he said, "Yeah, I just got the new album," and he'd already taught himself to play almost everything off the fucking record. He's like, "Oh, let me show you." Like, *what*? He's just so talented.

Jaime Ikeda: We were just kids who were exposed to Slayer, Black Flag, and Metallica, doing the kind of music we wanted to the best way we knew how: 50-50 metal and hardcore. I wish I could go back to that time when you don't know any better and you just go for it. Sometimes that's the best way to approach life. You just go with what feels right.

Ed Tarantino: I could see that Saud was influenced by both punk and the new thrash metal scene, and they really nailed that sound. That's where we had gone too, so it was really cool to see a younger band that liked bands like Hirax as well as Bad Brains.

It wasn't just us as punks getting influenced by the metal sound; it was other bands across the globe turning to metal. You started hearing straight-up hardcore bands sounding more metal, like Corrosion of Conformity. There were a bunch of bands that did that.

For me, there was a sound and a heaviness there that was awesome. What I didn't like about it was how lame the lyrics were. In some ways, I was more in the Lance Hahn camp of being kind of political and progressive and true anarchists while metal was kind of regressive in that way, being more about toxic masculinity, you could say. I didn't care for a lot of the lyrics of some of the thrash bands. I thought they were goofy and neanderthal.

Pat Ohta: The mother of one of the guitarists in Sacred Rite wanted to do shows at Queen Theater, and since I did *Iron Cross*, I was contacted for leads. I submitted a whole list of bands I thought should come here, and the first one chosen, for whatever reason, was Millions of Dead Cops. I was in the ninth or tenth grade, and I had no money to bring a band, so she agreed to help finance it. But by the time the fliers got out and everything got squared away, it was one week or so before the show and there was no time to promote it, and so the show tanked. The second show was supposed to be D.R.I., but too much money was lost on MDC, so D.R.I. never happened.

Jaime Ikeda: One of my good friends was Pat Ohta. He was so involved in the world metal scene, just being pen pals with everybody and tape trading. This was before the Internet, basically. He was very DIY. He went to Mid-Pac too, but he didn't play music. There were unseen guys like that, and unless you knew what was up, you would never hear of these people. If you played in a band, your name might get out there, but there were so many other people in the background like Pat who kept the scene going.

Pat Ohta: I would help with local band shows with friends. People like Lance Hahn or whoever, at Coffeeline, Church of the Crossroads, those kinds of places. There was always a crew that would let you know about shows and you could just help out.

A KINETIC AND AGGRESSIVE ENERGY

Jaime Ikeda: There was this one X-Chaser show at Queen Theater. Me and Lloyd Orsino, our other guitarist in Saud, tried to start a pit. This is when metalheads only headbanged or threw their horns up, so we got up on stage and said "Okay, we're gonna stage dive!" People didn't know what we were doing, so when we dove off, people moved out of the way. Lloyd landed on his head and got knocked out. EMS came and the ambulance took him away. Dave Murray from Iron Maiden was there, and he was concerned. I think he lived in Hawaii at that time, from what I heard.

Angelo Jensen: Yeah, Dave Murray, the guitar player from Iron Maiden, married Tamar, who was a bartender who lived in Hawaii. We all kind of traveled in the same little circle, and Dave Murray would come to Aaronsrod's shows and hang out. He was really just a regular joe. He barely spoke. He's a quiet cat. You'd never know he was a rock star. Dave Murray looked like some haole surfer guy with long hair.

Woody Soueira: Aaronsrod played at Queen Theater, and we opened up for them. They were pretty big at the time. The stage was high, and I remember being on the end and a couple of younger guys came up and one goes, "Yeah!" and stage dived and people would catch him. This other kid comes up, goes, "Yeah!" and I guess he mistimed it because I remember him jumping off and nobody caught him, and he hit his head and was kind of knocked out. I'm watching the bouncer pulling him up between the seats, and the show goes on.

Years later, talking to Lloyd Orsino, I found out it was him. We just started laughing. Lloyd tells me they drag him up and take him outside. He starts to open his eyes, he's coming awake, and he sees Dave Murray from Iron Maiden looking down on him: "Hey, man, are you all right?"

Barry Lasit: There was one guy who jumped up onstage, dancing, "Yeah, yeah!" and looking at his friends, "Yeah, yeah!" and I had this water pistol machine gun filled with Jack Daniel's, and I would squirt it in this guy's mouth. He was just about to jump, and I assisted his jump, grabbing him by his belt right as he was jumping, and flipped him. He flew high, brah, but there wasn't enough crowd to catch him. They stepped back, in other words. He hit the floor pretty hard and had a concussion.

Jimmy James was telling us, "You guys might get sued." Someone had it on video and showed it to me, and like, oh my God, I'm flipping the guy, but in the moment, I didn't purposely or maliciously flip him over. He was jumping already and I just assisted him. I mean, I wouldn't do it again, or at least I would make sure there was a crowd that was thick enough to catch the homie. I didn't even know what stage diving was, but you could tell there was a new energy to the music—a kinetic and aggressive energy. Things were changing.

Jaime Ikeda: I got more into the hardcore side of things. When Matt left Saud, we needed a singer. Michael Penrose was a super cool punk rocker, and he stepped in. He was pretty rad on vocals. That became Stage Dive, which turned into Broken Man when Michael left for the mainland.

Rich Tarantino: With Stage Dive, Jaime wanted to do a hardcore band like Scarred 4 Life was in the beginning, with short, fast songs. We were at his house, and he was trying to get me to write songs like I used to write, and I couldn't produce any. I think it's because I had outgrown it and I wasn't in that place anymore. I remember him really wanting me to and he was like, "Come on, Rich! You can do it!" It's such a weird feeling, trying something you used to do, and you just can't do it anymore, like you're trying to be something that was in the past.

DARKER AND HEAVIER

Barry Lasit: Music Mac was opening its first big store across from Waimalu Shopping Center, and they asked X-Chaser to play outside in the parking lot for the big grand opening. We liked the owner, Larry. He hooked us up and stuff, so we said, "Shoots, we'll play, yeah!"

Earlier that day, there had been a fight, and as we were playing, one kid had gotten beaten up, and this kid lived across the way in the apartments upstairs from the shopping center. He went and told his dad, and his dad was enraged that his kid got beat up, and he came over with a hunting knife; as we're playing, we're watching this happen. It's a weird perspective to have when you're looking down on all these people and really see everything that's happening. I'm thinking to myself, *I gotta stop this—something bad's going to happen right now.*

Sure enough, this guy shanked this kid—he was a kid, you know—and he gutted him, full on, like where your six-pack would be; he just split him wide open, and I'm like, "Oh my God!" Everybody just stopped playing, like, "Whoa, whoa, whoa, what's going on?" I knew this kid, right? And the kid walked over to me, and he was holding his stomach, and the man—he was a man—who did this to him had left already. The kid came up to me and looked down at his stomach and then his guts just fell out. The ambulance came and they put him in this suit they have when that kind of wound occurs, and I thought, *My God, this kid's gonna die right in front of me.*

Years later, I'm in Waikiki and a guy walks up to me and says, "Hey, man, do you remember me?" I'm like, "No, who are you?" He opens his shirt and shows me this big, long scar, right in the middle of his stomach, and I'm like, "I remember you now, dude!"

There was this belief that we were inciting all this violence, and we were doing it purposely, riling these kids up to committing violence. There was no such thing happening, but there were these rumors going around to the point where these Christian rock guys I knew would give me the sign of the cross every time I walked by. It was kind of funny to me because I'm not like that, but it was that transitional time when mosh pits started happening at metal shows, and there were still people who weren't getting it.

Woody Soueira: The music was turning even heavier. What was turning me off playing the heavier stuff was when they started the growling vocals and all that, but Danny kinda liked it and started going towards that sound. Danny turned me on to bands like Celtic Frost, and we would go to Choice Cuts and collect all these import albums. I liked the energy and the power of the music.

Barry Lasit: I thought the energy was good at the beginning, but after a while it started getting too dark with the lyrical content. I remember the band had a meeting and the other guys were like, "Okay, here's some music we're thinking of doing," and it was King Diamond and shit like that and I'm like, "Are you fucking kidding me? You think I'm gonna sing like that? It's not my style, dude, that's not my style." I knew they got offended because I was laughing at their musical choices, but to me it was funny because they thought I was gonna sing like King fucking Diamond!

Woody Soueira: Within our band, Danny and Barry were the main guys. Danny wanted to go heavier, and Barry had his own ideas about what he wanted to do. Barry knew a lot of well-known musicians, and he started playing in the clubs with bands like Widowmaker, and we went on as Optimum Fury.

Barry Lasit: I thought X-Chaser would get back together at some point but we didn't. Me and Danny have two totally different personalities, and as far as the musical direction of the band and orchestrating all of the arrangements, he was the man, for sure. He was a shredder, and he had a talent for harmonies.

I could tell they wanted to go heavier, and yeah, I like the heaviness of Metallica and Megadeth, but not the kind of music that's so heavy that it's unrecognizable from rock. I think I'm more of a hard rocker. So after X-Chaser dissolved, I went on to play in some of the house bands at C5 and Rock Cellar. I was in Martial Law and Widowmaker, who were more straightforward rock-and-roll bands. More Guns N' Roses than Metallica.

We were also playing in the military clubs and everything and we had a lot of gigs. In those years, we were playing so much that I bought myself a brand-new truck in cash, like, "Here you go." Things were great at that point and it was fun, especially on nights like New Year's Eve or Halloween, but performing in those bands was like being a human jukebox. We played all the standards so many times, like "Paranoid" or "Crazy Train" or "Living After Midnight," for example, that I just have a mental block on those songs to this day. I can't even remember the lyrics.

Chris Esteron (vocalist: Devil Kine Music, Days/Weeks/Months): I ran into Pat Ohta once at Tower Records and I was like, "Dude, what the fuck ever happened to *Iron Cross*? I loved that 'zine!" The story he told me was he interviewed Quorthon from Bathory, and he called Sweden and got in trouble with his parents because it was like a three-hundred-dollar telephone bill. They cut him off and he wasn't allowed to call anybody ever again. That was it.

12

THE KNAVE OF CLUBS

On December 2, 1983, fifty photojournalists from *National Geographic, Time, Newsweek,* and other eminent publications descended on the Islands for *A Day in the Life of Hawaii,* the latest in a series of best-selling photography books by Rick Smolan and David Cohen. The concept was a novel one: Invite a select group of photographers to capture life in a particular international destination, in one 24-hour period, with the best images constituting a full-color, oversized tabletop book.

There was considerable buzz leading up to its release in July of 1984, and a behind-the-scenes TV special surrounding the book's production aired on PBS stations around the country with a sprightly Sonya Mendez in one scene, frolicking outside of Wave Waikiki. *A Day in the Life of Hawaii* sold out on the first day it was made available, and tens of thousands of copies were eventually purchased across the island chain. For the remainder of the year, it was displayed prominently in bookshops statewide.

One striking image, spread across pages 204 and 205, is of a clique of punk-chic youngsters seated along a dimly lit edge of 3-D Ballroom at night. As they share some gossip and a light, off to one side is a young Matthew Grim, outfitted in a Sid Vicious T-shirt, looking at the other kids with anticipation, half his figure cut out of the action. It's among the last photos taken in Hawaii of teenage Matthew, the piteous sap the current Matt Grim is glad to have long left behind.

When he departed Honolulu for Northern California in the fall of '84 to attend De Anza College, Grim, eager to embark on a new phase of his life, began exploring the music scene of San Jose. There, he befriended several key figures, including influential DJs and musicians, and through these affiliations, enjoyed a swift and unlikely ascension in popularity. "I went from nowhere in Hawaii, where I was a dork, to rolling in the pussy," discloses Grim, who presented himself as a suave out-of-towner answering to the name of GQ. It was a complete reinvention of identity. "I didn't have all my Hawaii baggage of being this nerdy Dungeons & Dragons dumbfuck. Like, I was a cool punk rock dude there and people respected me. It was awesome, actually."

Imbued with confidence, he learned to deejay and began organizing dance events at local halls and youth centers with the attitude and inclusivity of the underground shindigs he knew back home. "I wanted to bring everybody together, from goths to new wavers to neuros," explains Grim. "My goal was to basically bring 3-D to San Jose."

By carefully weaving danceable club tracks in and around a moody death rock playlist, he crafted a distinctive soiree that quickly amassed a loyal and enthusiastic coed following. He then quit his job and dropped out of school to try his hand at event promotions.

By the time Grim brought his brash and intrepid little brother Michael into the fold, live concerts seemed the next logical step. The younger Grim wasted no time tendering lowball offers for touring punk and metal bands. "Mike was very weird, and he didn't have any shame in anything that he did," recalls Matt. "He ended up calling Gary Tovar, the owner of Goldenvoice, who did all the big punk shows in LA. We don't know this guy from Adam, and Mike is a fuckin' talker. He's pretty good at schmoozing people, and, dude, Gary Tovar fuckin' *loved* Mike. He was like, 'I can't believe some fucking kid from San Jose had the fucking gall to call me and ask me to give him Suicidal Tendencies!'"

Remarkably, Tovar passed along such acts as The Exploited, Necros, GBH, King Diamond, and Megadeth to their fledgling operation to fill existing holes in the bands' tour schedules. It was an unbelievable endowment for the new teen party kings of San Jose, and an indication that there could be greater success on the horizon for Grim Family Entertainment, their growing promotion company. "Our goal was to move to Los Angeles and do underground clubs and blow up in LA just like we did in San Jose," reveals the older Grim.

The original plan called for Michael to head to LA first with a mutual friend, find them all a decent place to stay, and have Matthew join them after he took a quick jaunt back to Honolulu. It never materialized in quite the way they envisioned, and while in Los Angeles, Michael established himself in the good graces of hardcore giants Wasted Youth at a crucial juncture in the band's evolution. "Somehow he weaseled his way in, and he was managing them," remembers Matt Grim. "I was like, 'Fuck, he's living the high life!' But I was stuck in Hawaii."

For the time being, Grim decided, he would make the most of his stay on Oahu and get reacquainted with the local nightlife, though this time as an accomplished DJ and promoter.

In an odd twist of fate, a grand opportunity to make a name for himself in the Honolulu club scene would surface at the very spot that set him on his path of self-discovery years earlier.

Jack Law: When Wave Waikiki opened, nothing had ever worked at that location. It was Lava Lava, Fast Eddie's, and the Dragon Lady before that. And then when the Wave took off, we were *the* place, the big club in town, and all of a sudden we had a lot of competition.

There was Pink Cadillac, then Masquerade, which was a huge place across the street, built from the ground up by a local developer to directly compete against us. They even took away our parking because we had a big parking lot across the street, and that's where they built their nightclub. The competition's business plan was simply to get the Wave's business.

Gillian Gilbert and Peter Hook of New Order onstage at
Wave Waikiki in 1985. *Courtesy of David Carr*

Along Ala Moana Boulevard, Restaurant Row opened up with places like Black Orchid and Studebaker's; then more bars and restaurants opened up around Aloha Tower, and the center of nightlife moved away from Waikiki.

So it was important to have live music, because otherwise people would go to every other club and then only when those places closed at two o'clock would they come to the Wave. That's the problem a lot of four o'clock clubs had, and so I had to make sure there was a reason for people to come before two o'clock, and live music was the key.

Gary Owens: I saw Bow Wow Wow at the Wave, I saw X there, I even saw Icicle Works, which I liked a lot. Romeo Void played there, and I remember being bummed out 'cause I thought the singer would be super hot. I was like, "That's her?"

For a hot second, Limelight opened up next door to the Wave, and that's where I saw Specimen. There were a few years after 3-D closed, in, like, '85, '86, '87, where that whole area around the Wave was just booming with nightclubs. You had Pink Cadillac, the Wave, Limelight, Masquerade, Phaze. That whole area was fucking happening.

PINK CADILLAC

George Kail: We sold 3-D and I forced the sale, to be honest with you. I didn't get along with my partner anymore and I said, "Look, I gotta get away from this—we gotta stop it." We sold it and I got some money, but it wasn't very much. I think I walked away with twenty-five grand.

Gary Owens: Pink Cadillac was a place that Kail found because my brother's band did a show there. When Mama's Mexican Kitchen closed down, they let us do something there for one night. We had a bunch of bands play, and Kail came out and he's like, "How did you guys get this place?" I hooked him up with Ed Moya, the guitar player, and I go, "Ed's parents own it." So I introduced Kail to Ed, and Pink Cadillac got going there.

Before that, it was a game room. I remember when I was a kid, like in intermediate school, we used to cut out of school and go down there. They had foosball and pool. It was a pool hall and we used to go play pinball machines. Waikiki was a completely different place, man. There were these little hole-in-the-wall bars that were hidden behind places. Now it's so sterile and expensive, and there's not much fun to be had there unless you got a lot of money.

George Kail: I never had a lot of money, and I never knew shit about opening nightclubs, but I did it out of curiosity and the excitement of getting into the field. I'm extremely artistic and the reason my nightclubs were a success were the amazing ideas that would come to me.

When I built Pink Cadillac, I had a Cadillac going through the roof. We took an old '60 Lincoln convertible, put the whole car inside the club,

Pink Cadillac was among the most popular Honolulu nightspots of the '80s and '90s. *Courtesy of David Carr*

and it was a DJ booth. The DJ would stand where the steering wheel was, with the two turntables, and the records were in the back seat. The headlights and everything worked on that car. It was pretty cool. We even built a stainless steel dance floor. Pink Cadillac was pretty much a huge hit. We were around the corner from the Wave.

SODA POPS

John Friend a.k.a. DJ John John (DJ at Soda Pops, Odyssey, Sub Club, etc.): I started deejaying at Soda Pops, which was a teen club, in '84. That's the same year 3-D closed, so all those punks would go to this teen club and pour booze into their sodas. Private and public high school kids would go there, and you'd even have over-eighteens going to this club. It was weird. We'd play "Jam On It," "Din Daa Daa," and a lot of Sisters of Mercy. It was all over the place.

Waikiki was a disco playground then because tourists wanted to go to the disco, and students came out to party for spring or summer break because the drinking age was still eighteen.

I remember meeting Matt Grim at Soda Pops when he had a curly mohawk. Not a good look. Never a good look.

ODYSSEY

Matthew Grim: There was a little burger joint in Waikiki in the early '80s, and me and Alan Schlemmer would always go there to get fifty-cent burgers when we were poor teenagers, flying on acid. The guy that owned the place was named Jay Jay, and he was always cool to me.

Jay Jay was, like, a Pakistani or Indian guy. Older guy, way older. I would periodically see him around Waikiki, and he was always interested in what I was up to. I ran into him when I came back to Hawaii in '87, and I told him about my nightclubs. He said, "Hey, I took over this nightclub called Systems—you say you do nightclub?"

I'm like, "Dude, let me come by sometime and tell you what I'd like to do there."

He said, "Okay, do it. Don't worry for it." He would always say, "Don't worry for it," and so I opened Odyssey there on the third floor, and Systems was on the second floor.

Odyssey fuckin' took off pretty much right off the bat, I remember. I was doing the same thing I was doing in San Jose: goth and this kind of alternative, modern music. Dude, all the chicks from Hawaii School for Girls would come because we were all ages and it was fuckin' HSG *chick-o-rama* at Odyssey.

For all intents and purposes, Odyssey was my club, but I was getting screwed out of all the money, basically. It was all my idea, I had all the keys to it and everything, but I wasn't handling any of the liquor shit. Jay Jay's people were handling all of that. I was making a few hundred bucks a night, like 250, 300, 400 bucks a night, and they were making all the bar sales.

Odyssey was on the top floor, in the exact same spot 3-D was, and right below it was Systems, which was just a regular bar on the second floor. It was like a weird watering hole that never caught on. It was shitty. There'd be, like, fifteen alcoholics in there.

But Odyssey took off for me. It was packed with wall-to-wall people on Fridays and Saturdays. It was fuckin' excellent, man. There were so many hot bitches there. I had go-go cages and I would do crazy fuckin' live art exhibits. I hired this Black homeless lady who you'd always see in Waikiki to sit in this mirrored room. It was this one-way mirror where you could see in, but she couldn't see out. I just paid her to sit in there and do whatever she wanted, and everybody would look in there like it was a museum exhibit, and she'd be reading the paper or taking a nap or whatever.

Another time I went to the pet store and got all these mice, and I painted them fluorescent colors and called them "The Crazy Psycho Mice" like some Barnum & Bailey shit or whatever, and I painted them—not spray painted—theoretically, it was shit that wouldn't kill them, but I'm sure it wasn't pleasant for them. Some animal people got all fuckin' pissed and were gonna call the SPCA and the Health Department, and

Jay Jay was like, "No more animals!" I would do random, weird shit, like, every weekend.

Raoul Vehill: The property owners were probably happy to see 3-D close with all the thrashing and chaos and underage drinking. Then to see another club open up in the same spot and find out punk bands played there too, the landlords probably had a hard-on to evict Matt Grim.

By the late '80s, Raoul Vehill's bandmates grew
concerned with his substance use. *Courtesy of Gardner Pope*

Matthew Grim: I even brought bands over to Odyssey. I brought Agent Orange twice, Youth Brigade played there, and the Vandals. The local punk bands like SRO and Devil Dog would play there too.

Actually, I thought Devil Dog was a good band, but when they would go on stage, Raoul would fuck shit up, like, "Dude, what are you doing?" I remember I 86'ed Raoul from the club lots of times. I liked him, though. He was just like one of those dogs that seems to get kicked all the time. He'd get beat up, but he'd usually deserve it.

Sometimes I would get so irritated because there'd be a bunch of shows where he didn't even sing, or he'd spit up some fuckin' puke or fake blood or whatever, and Jay Jay's like, "Why the fuck is this guy here?"

You could tell Raoul was trying to be a performance artist, but it was like, "Dude, when you go over the top and fuck my shit up, we ain't having that!" So he'd beg me, "Let me please play here again!" and then he'd fuck up the sound system and blow some speakers, and I wouldn't let him back. I'm like, "Fuck no! If you rent your own sound system..." and then I think one time he did rent his own sound system and I said, "Okay, you guys can play." And then he got so drunk and took all his clothes off and got punched in the face. Just stupid shit.

Raoul Vehill: I spit fire and flipped off the stage before, and I may have gotten in a fight or two, but not while performing. I did hit a guy on the head with a beer bottle one time, but again, not onstage. I honestly can't say for sure specifically what I may have done to get kicked out of Matt's club because my alcohol and substance abuse was beginning to scare even my bandmates.

SUB CLUB

Matthew Grim: I closed Odyssey because the management was fucking me over. They only wanted to give me a hundred bucks a night or something. I was like, "Are you kidding me? Fuck this!"

With Jay Jay, everything was an amalgamation of shit he would throw on the wall to see what would stick for as cheap as possible. He was a weird guy who had his hands in everything where you're like, "What in the fuck? How did that happen?" He even had some deal where he took over a whole building a block or two from Odyssey on Nahua Street where there was some scary underground after hours called Secret. Secret opened at fuckin' four in the morning, and it was all hush-hush, a locked door thing, where all the bar people would go after work. I was like, "Let me have the club during the evening before it turns into Secret," and he agreed because he was all about making money. I started doing Sub Club there.

I copied a popular underground club in San Francisco called Sub Club. My version was in a normal lounge kind of bar with some koa wood trim, but we turned off the lights and I had some videotapes of goth-y, kind of dark shit: Throbbing Gristle, Skinny Puppy, Psychic TV, Foetus, Wiseblood, Ministry. That's when I really started getting into industrial music. Basically non-danceable crap. Revolting Cocks, that kind of noisy shit. Way more B-sides and dark music. I made it way more underground.

I had John John come deejay and Barry from The Sharx—DJ Barry Freeze. He had a record store and had gotten into dark, post-punk death rock stuff. Then there was a guy named Tony, who I think was Crazy George's roommate. He was an expert on industrial. He was really into it. It was him and Crazy George that first brought industrial music to Hawaii at this one record shop called A New World's Record that was under a staircase in a two-story building on Beretania Street. It was the size of a janitor's closet, and they sold only imports. They were into all kinds of crazy shit, and they even started an industrial band called Fester.

Barry Oshiro: Around '86 or '87, I started deejaying. I think it was Matt Grim who invited me into the DJ booth and asked me if I wanted to try deejaying, first at Odyssey and then at Sub Club.

I used to go to clubs in LA when glam rock was really big in the '80s and I kind of took their format where some clubs would sometimes play glam stuff like T. Rex and Hanoi Rocks and The Sweet, and I would mix that in with, like, what we used to call death rock: Siouxsie, Alien Sex Fiend, that kind of thing.

John Friend: Matt would let me stretch out. I could play album cuts of Front 242 or Cabaret Voltaire or I could play Nina Hagen. I could play Cream, I could play Iggy Pop, I could play Test Dept., I could play Psychic TV. I could play just about anything, and people were listening because it was a good sound system. It might've been drunk teenagers listening, but they were listening.

Matthew Grim: Somehow I also got fucked over at Sub Club, and I started working at Pink Cadillac, where I got fired five different times for coming in late. I worked at the Wave for a couple of years, and they fired me for working at Pink Cadillac, and I'm like, "Well, fuck, you guys are only giving me two nights a week, and it's not the weekend. I can't survive on two nights." I was getting paid only $8.50 an hour at the Wave, and Pink Cadillac was paying me 150 or 250 bucks a night, and I was like, "Fuck you guys, then."

At the Wave, the hours were way longer, like 9 p.m. to 4 a.m., and it was like a hardcore job. At Pink Cadillac it was fuckin' cool. It was way less hours. The Wave banned me over that for a month or two. I liked everybody over at the Wave too. I remember I was super pissed about that.

LIKE A CAT WITH NINE LIVES

George Kail: At Pink Cadillac, my doorman was shot. I remember one night I was in Pink Cadillac along with my best friend, who was Maurice Damien. We were both from Pittsburgh. Maurice was a celebrity over here. I heard *BANG-BANG-BANG-BANG,* and everybody was running from the front door, and I'm thinking, *The son of a bitch, somebody's firing off firecrackers.* I was upset. Then I see all these people rushing through the front door, going, "He's got a gun! He's got a gun!" and I'm thinking, *Oh my God, what's going on?* Maurice was hiding in the goddamn walk-in freezer. It turns out it was the doorman's own roommate who shot him. The doorman was named Kaz. The sad thing was Kaz was paralyzed from the waist down.

About three months later, Maurice came to see me at Pink Cadillac, and after we shut down, I said, "Come on, let's go to the Wave; let's go have a drink. There's a girl over there who wants to meet you." I talked him into going over.

Prior to going in, we were hanging out front, deciding whether we were going to go in, and I remember this guy, a local moke, hanging out front. He was so drunk it was unbelievable, and I remember he was harassing everybody, going over to people, "You fucka!" What had happened was he came over to me and Maurice, and he started shit with me. He says, "You fucka, you da one. You own that Pink Cadillac! You responsible for my friend, he paralyzed!" I go over to the door guy, who tells me, "I can't do nothing because he's not on our property."

Jack Law: This was a guy that we had 86'd hours earlier who had come back. One of the things about the Wave, which is why the Wave was so successful, is people always felt safe there. We would have retired police officers come in and do seminars. So many places similar to the Wave would open and close very quickly because safety was the last thing on their agenda, and their security would cause more problems than the customers. We had very few problems, but unfortunately, there were exceptions over twenty-five years.

George Kail: No sooner do I turn around than the guy punches Maurice in the throat. How about that? Three hours later, Maurice is dead. Maurice had just opened a second salon in the Honolulu Club. He had just signed the lease, bought all the furniture, had a lovely daughter. He was the most sweetest, handsome, cool, kind person in the world who did nothing but calm the guy down: "Calm down, buddy…Everything's okay…Don't worry, relax…" *BOOM*. Punched him right in the fucking throat. Horror story. All I could concentrate on was following the asshole. The police were on the scene pretty fast. I do remember getting the police on the guy, saying, "That's the guy! Get him now!" They did a good job. He ended up getting six years for killing Maurice.

The Wave was sued. Jack Law hated me forever. It was a vintage war between me and Jack Law over Maurice. He felt like because I was in the nightclub business, I turned on him. I lost my best friend in life who was like my brother.

I have to knock on wood, the fact that I'm still here. I'm like a cat with nine lives, my friend.

13

THE KIDS ARE AOK

It was in 1980 that Kalani High School earned a grand total of two victories in Oahu Interscholastic Association football. Though it was a dismal campaign, it turned out to be the most successful season of the next decade. For the perpetually woeful Falcons, who sometimes struggled to even field a proper team, there were multiple winless seasons in the '80s and an abysmal thirty-four-game losing streak that began in 1982. When Kalani finally broke the hex four years later with a 13-10 decision over crosstown competitors McKinley High, the team's fortunes improved, though just barely, as they recorded one regular season win a year for the remainder of the 1980s.

What Kalani High School lacked in gridiron greatness, however, it made up for in rebel style and nihilist cool. While the majority of its students adhered to a conventional sense of fashion, it was not uncommon then to spy custom-made punk band T-shirts, studded leather jackets, and purposely torn clothing at pep rallies and assorted school functions. Equally so with Kaiser High, their more distinguished football rival (and 1979 Prep Bowl champs) six miles to the east. Both public high schools, which served the largely desirable and well-to-do neighborhoods of Kahala, Aina Haina, Niu Valley, and Hawaii Kai, produced a number of prominent scenesters and musicians, replete with partially shaved heads and wildly colored hair.

There were other high schools, both private and public, as well as various colleges and universities around the state that also became important incubators as punk rock and its myriad offshoots—new wave, hardcore, and death rock among them—began to spread across the island. By the mid-1980s, the intertwined communities of punk rock and skateboarding allowed youngsters of divergent neighborhoods, schools, and backgrounds to connect and join forces. Steadily over time, Oahu's punk gigs and favored skate spots began to more closely resemble the kaleidoscopic cultural makeup of the Islands. Meanwhile, a lively network of independent music shops, local fanzine publishers, and college station KTUH championed the underground sounds of Honolulu.

One particularly enterprising circle of adolescents formed a colorful and creative coalition that helped define the local DIY punk scene of the mid- to late '80s. Comprising forward-thinking bands of assorted musical subgenres, this crew circulated hand-stapled 'zines and crudely recorded cassettes of their strident and uncompromising music around Oahu. By decade's end, a small congregation of these young artists and musicians cut across the Pacific in search of adventure and musical fortune in that great, golden promised land of punk rock called California.

David Carr (drummer: Cringer; vocalist/guitarist: The Vacuum, The Wrong, etc.; Hawaii Punk Museum creator): My entry point into the local music scene was through my older brother Kevin. He, Rudy Trubitt, and Matt Miller went to high school at University Lab School. They were in a lot of rock bands. I remember at some point Rudy and some of the other guys shedding their old rock stuff and just going more for new wave. I was hanging out with this one guy who was heavily into rock and lived across the street, so we were playing more of the classics, but that's where I got my chops up.

Dave Derby (bassist/vocalist: The Dambuilders, The Exactones, Communiqué, etc.): Dave Carr and I took guitar lessons together at the Yamaha Guitar Center in Aina Haina. This must've been seventh, eighth grade. This would've been '78 or something. We had this one teacher who was kind of a dick, actually, but he was like, "So, you're friends with Dave Carr? Man, you should really learn to play guitar from him because he's way better than you are!"

I'm like, "Yeah, no shit." Dave was kind of like a musical genius, even at a young age.

Dave Carr's house was a fifteen-minute walk from where I lived, and he had this little side area where he and his brother would record stuff. I remember listening to what he was recording and being like, "How are you doing all this? It's amazing!"

Barry Oshiro: Dave Carr was into classic rock back then, and he had long hair, like, down to his ass. It was weird that he would hang out with punks, but we had the same sense of humor, I think. At school, we had this corner in front of the cafeteria where we always hung out, and so you would see all these punk rock kids with this one hippie.

David Carr: Really, through Barry, I got to meet some of the cooler people. He told me, "When I first saw you getting on the bus and you were barefoot with hair down your back, I was like, 'Who is this fucking hippie idiot?'" Then he met me and he was like, "Oh wait, you're funny!" and "Oh, you know punk bands?"

One night, when I was a junior or senior at Kalani, so '83 or '84, I came home from a party, and I'd been drinking, and I kind of looked at my room and it was all these classic rock posters like Yes and Led Zeppelin and Aerosmith, all this stuff I loved, and I'm like, "*Ehhh*, I'm just gonna take these down." It was partly because I had met the Kalani punks, and I was gonna commit to being into what's happening now. I had a small record collection, and I just took it and started selling it to kids at school, like old Ted Nugent albums, and I started buying anything from ska to rockabilly to punk. My brother probably had about fifty good punk and new wave albums already, and I started taking those records and learning those songs.

By my senior year, I had a band called The Start, and we played mostly mod stuff. A handful of people in Hawaii had started riding Vespas, and there was a mod thing, so we played a ton of The Jam and Sham 69, The Saints and other punk and post-punk stuff.

ACTION SUNDRIES

Barry Oshiro: I was seventeen when I had a record store. My grandma used to have a store that I would work for, delivering candies. It was a wholesale-retail business near Ala Moana, and her main customer was—this is really weird—Philippine Airlines. They would buy a lot; like, thirty cases of KitKat, twenty cases of Nestle Crunch, twenty cases of Cadbury.

I dropped out of high school to get my GED instead. I was failing already because I would cut class so much. So she said, "Well, if you're not going to go to school, you gotta do something." So she opened up a store for me. I had this little 7-Eleven-type store. Business was really, really slow. We sold ice cream and my mom and my grandma wanted me to sell shave ice. I said, "Okay, I guess. You're paying for everything, so…"

Sometimes it would just be hours and hours and then someone would buy a pack of gum. I was just sitting there all day, so I brought in my turntable and speakers. Francis Sipin from Free Will would keep me company and watch the store for me sometimes. I had a little black-and-white TV, and we would watch *Twilight Zone* in the morning.

We weren't making much money, so I used to just order records for myself because now I could get 'em for wholesale. I started selling punk records and indie records in there, and that sort of paid the bills 'cause candy was, like, twenty-five cents and the rent was over a thousand bucks or something. The store was called Action Sundries, and it was in Kapahulu, the next driveway from where KC Drive-In used to be. The property owners had a travel agency that was right upstairs, and I got into a little trouble because they noticed that a lot of punk kids would come by and ended up hanging out and skating outside.

I would do mainland buying trips too. I would bring back a whole bunch of records, crazy colored hair dye, and cool posters you couldn't find in Hawaii at the time: Siouxsie & the Banshees, The Smiths, The Cure. I met people like Lance Hahn, who would come in to check out records and order records, and we would hang out. But after about a year, it was losing too much money and my grandma told me, "Yeah, it's time to close it already." I was just too young and not responsible enough to do anything with it.

Gardner Pope: I went to Action Sundries all the time. That was kind of a hangout place for us, and that's why the store didn't do very well. There were all these punks hanging out there, and I would have Barry make

Barry Oshiro behind the counter at Action Sundries. *Courtesy of Gardner Pope*

me shave ice with ice cream in it, and we'd all stand around and talk. But Barry was very knowledgeable about records, and there were a few serious record collectors who would come regularly into his shop to buy records because he had Sisters of Mercy twelve-inch records and all that kind of stuff you had to import. There was Tower Records, Jelly's, Hungry Ear Records, and Barry's shop. Those were the places to get import records.

THE VACUUM, HYPO-DEPRESSION, AND CRINGER

Barry Oshiro: We all liked punk, but I started listening to Joy Division, then Bauhaus, The Cure, and Sisters of Mercy, and I guess Dave and Lance got into it because I started selling those records in my store. I think Lance wanted to do, like, a side project, and he was totally into Christian Death, who were from that early LA death rock scene. So Hypo-Depression was me, Lance, Dave, and Dave's brother Kevin. We used to practice at Dave's house. Kevin wrote a lot of the lyrics. Dave wrote most of the music. Lance wrote some too. It was really cool because I loved Lance's guitar. It just had more of a heavy rock sound to it.

Gardner Pope: Dave and Kevin were well into music before all of us and actually had musical knowledge. They were very talented. Dave was already playing around on his four-track and was in a band before I was in a band with him. He had a house that you could practice at, and he and his brother had all of this musical equipment. From that house was where a lot of these bands spawned.

Lance was already in Scarred 4 Life, who were a pretty straightforward hardcore skate band except Lance didn't skate. One day, Lance just called me up and said he was starting a new band and wanted to know if I wanted to sing for it. Dave already had a drum kit and said, "I can play drums." That was the beginning of Cringer. I was already in The Vacuum, a death rock band, with Dave, playing at his house, and from there, other bands happened because we had this group of people, we had a space, and things were starting to come together.

The first Cringer lineup included Gardner Pope as vocalist, Lance Hahn on guitar, Ed Tarantino on bass, and Dave Carr on drums.
Courtesy of Gardner Pope

Frank Orrall: I felt like the young kid in The Squids, but when I was playing in Hat Makes the Man, I was twenty-something and there was this younger crop of bands in '84-ish, like Cringer and The Vacuum and Whirling Dervishes, and I was seen as the old guard, even though there was only a few years' age difference. Some of them had more contact with the early goth stuff that I didn't know so much about but enjoyed the vibe. Dave Carr had these beautiful songs; super captivating and full of mood.

David Carr: The Vacuum was, I guess, the year I graduated high school. I was already hanging out with a lot of the hardcore punk kids, and I knew the Sharx had already broken up, so I asked Gardner to play in this band. I knew him as this cool, kinda mellow hardcore dude who also liked other kinds of music. I'd also been hanging out with Frank Orrall through the older kids like The Squids and Hat Makes the Man and knew him fairly well from drinking, playing Dungeons & Dragons, or listening to music at other people's houses.

Kevin Carr and Barry Oshiro of Hypo-Depression. *Courtesy of Gardner Pope*

One night in Waikiki—it was 1984, I guess, or early '85—and this club I was at was pretty empty but Frank was there. We had a few drinks and started talking and I go, "Would you ever want to play drums with us?" I had a drum set, I had a bass, and I had a guitar and a microphone, and I played him a couple of home recordings I made with a half-track reel-to-reel that you could bounce tracks on, and he was like, "Whoa, this is really good!" We started playing. We played at Anna's. We'd played two UH gigs at the geophysics building, and then we played the United Puerto Rican Association hall.

U.P.R.A.H.

Rob Cribley: There was that Puerto Rican hall in Kalihi that was rad. You just had to be careful not to get your ass kicked. It was one of those places. There was some Samoan bar right across the street, and those guys would be pretty hammered and then they'd want to beat up on the punk kids for being little troublemakers.

David Carr: The first Puerto Rican Association was a conservative group and then some of them broke off and started the new United Puerto Rican Association of Hawaii, and many times my mom was president of that group. I'm half Puerto Rican and also Italian and Irish, and my parents met in New York, but my mom, when she came over to Hawaii, was pretty quickly doing things with the Puerto Rican community here.

They would have a Three Kings' Day parade every January 6 over in Kalihi, from one of the churches there to the Puerto Rican hall. I asked my mom, "Could you ask if we can have a gig there?" and they said yes. So The Vacuum's last gig was the first-ever show at that venue.

We headlined over these mostly hardcore bands. Scarred 4 Life and Cringer played and a bunch of other bands. Everyone sat down when The Vacuum played, and my parents were there too. I could see them in the audience, and it was just this really awesome moment. Later, there were more gigs there by other people, totally separate from us, which was great. It's always good to have a place to play. That was a fun place for shows, for sure.

Gardner Pope: Somebody set off a fire extinguisher at the hall and we had to clean it up. I got into an argument with the person who did it and he's like, "Well, what the fuck do you care?" and I'm like, "We're the ones who rented it, dumbshit! We're the ones responsible for this now." But whatever. That was such a part of the ethos of the whole thing, you know, "Fuck shit up!" People are trying to do something for the scene, and you just want to get drunk and fuck everything up. It's like, well, can't you get drunk and have fun?

David Carr: My dad was printing up The Vacuum cassette, a hundred at a time, and they kept selling out at Jelly's. They sold, like, 500 of those. I never expected to even sell ten of 'em, so it was a huge success in my eyes, and it didn't hurt to have Frank in the band, obviously. Eventually, Frank was like, "Yeah, you gotta weed me out of the band 'cause I'm gonna focus on Hat and what we're doing." They were trying to hustle and get a major label deal.

AOK

Gardner Pope: We pretty much got into a positive punk attitude at some point, and that was our jam. There was definitely a more positive movement that was happening with certain bands on the mainland like 7 Seconds, which we were all really into. It felt good. We did a bunch of stuff; we put together all these bands, we made 'zines, and it was fun.

David Carr: It was probably late '85, early '86 that *AOK* started. *AOK* was a 'zine put together by Lance Hahn; his sister Heather Hahn, who was super nice and a Kalani punk who had become a bass player for Free Will; Francis; Gardner; Jackie Arrisgado, who did a lot of the photographs; Raya Miller; and the Krolls, James and Jon, who went to Kaiser.

The Kroll Brothers were outgoing, super creative, comedian-level funny guys who made their own banners, jacket patches, and band

T-shirts for Just In Fun and Free Will. They were always willing to jump into projects, start bands, work on *AOK*, whatever was happening. They were nice, nerdy, funny kids who were super expressive and kind of hyper in their own ways and just wanted to be part of a scene.

Ed Tarantino: Lance and Heather were living with their mother and stepfather way out in Nanakuli. Lance went to Kamehameha, and I'm guessing because their mother worked in town at Chaminade University, Heather went to Kalani, which isn't too far from there. Heather was, in many ways, more integrated into the punk scene than Lance was, because a lot of those scene people were going to Kalani, like Dave Carr and all of those kids. It's kind of funny that she was way ahead of him in that regard. We introduced Lance to this punk world that he was external from. He was almost on his own path up until then.

David Carr: We were good friends and we were seriously into music, going to gigs and partying. Some of it was more political too: not liking Reagan and war and racism and poverty and just basic shit that built on moving forward and developing political ideas as we went. That's part of the beauty of the DIY ethic, like, "Yeah, we can do this, and we can actually stand for things too."

Lance in particular had a strong work ethic and knew how to connect with people. Even when he was living out in the Waianae area, he had pen pals all over the world, pre-Internet. Lance knew all these bands, listened to all their music, and got these demo tapes from all around the world. He just knew a lot about the global underground scene and would review and interview a ton of obscure bands. He was so into it.

GOLDEN (STATE) OPPORTUNITIES

Gardner Pope: In the fall of '85 I went to Los Angeles for college. I did sound recording, music recording, and unfortunately, what I learned about it was that I hated it.

David Carr: After Frank left The Vacuum, I was like, "I wanna go and be a part of the punk scene somewhere on the mainland." Gardner was moving to LA to go to Loyola Marymount for college, so I moved with him and I was just like, "Yeah, can I stay in your dorm room, you think?" So that was kind of a bad idea. I mean, it was really fun and I made good friends, but I was putting way too much stress on Gardner and his roommate. They were even nice about it, but finally they decided to put their foot down and say, "Look, just find a place. You've gotta do it." I was there maybe two months or something and using other people's food cards to eat at the cafeteria, and you could just eat as much as you wanted every time you went, so I guess I was being a freeloader.

Gardner Pope: I ended up working at the radio station at my college, and through that I got tickets to go to a lot of shows for free. It was intense. Unfortunately at that time, the shows in Los Angeles were huge and violent. I would go to these places, and there would be at least three big fights every time. I'd go to see Suicidal Tendencies at the Balboa Theater, which was not in a good part of town, and I remember thinking, *I'm going to be killed here.* It's funny to think back on it because in a lot of ways it seems very traumatizing, but it was something you put up with to see all these bands you'd been listening to for so long. I got to go see 7 Seconds and SNFU, bands that were in their heyday and really meant something to me at the time.

I saw the Dead Kennedys at the Olympic Auditorium, and that was terrifying. It was huge and there was a shit-ton of people there. Fishbone opened for the Dead Kennedys, and they didn't go over well with the all-white hardcore idiots. One of the Fishbone guys ended up jumping in the crowd to fight somebody, and he got stabbed and there was all this drama, whether or not the show was going to go on. It doesn't sound fun but literally, when it's over, you're like, "Wow, we survived."

David Carr: We would go to Fender's Ballroom in Long Beach, and we saw The Adicts and Discharge and Bad Brains, and one of the singers from Black Flag had his own band. We saw a lot of shows, Descendents and all kinds of shit there. But the big sucky thing about it was that there were these skinheads—and not the good kind of skinheads or the anti-racist, anti-fascist kind of skinheads that I'm fine with—but the skinheads that were involved with white supremacists like Tom Metzger. This was in 1986, and they would literally be selling or handing out their White Aryan Resistance newspaper. It was the fucking stupidest bullshit, but it was scary because there was a lot of violence in that era of the scene in LA. I remember being in Fender's Ballroom watching a band, and I'd see some kid running, and there'd be twenty skinheads chasing after him. Usually they caught him, they'd beat him, and then it would just be over. What the hell could I do? I was helpless to stop it.

One night, me and Gardner were walking to a gig, and these WAR guys pull up in a kind of a Repo Man-type car and they're like, "Are you Jewish?" and we're like, "Ah, fuck. Keep walking, keep walking." But I guess I'm lucky I never got punched, knocked down or seriously assaulted by anyone.

Gardner Pope: A lot of people in our crew ended up moving to Los Angeles the year after I got there and decided we were going to continue our bands. It was a good excuse for everyone to try and do something after high school. Dave came, Lance came, the Kroll Brothers, Francis came, Heather came, later on Raya came. My friend Derek Imose was also living with us and played drums with Cringer. Ed Tarantino, who played bass for Cringer, and his brother Rich also came. We ended up with two townhome apartments near the airport, basically. I lived in a two-bedroom apartment, and we had at least five people living there, sometimes seven. It was grim. It wasn't a good time.

The Vacuum never really did anything in LA, maybe one party, and Cringer didn't either for a very long time, and when we did, our shows were few and far between. That kind of smaller, inclusive punk rock scene did not exist in Los Angeles when we were there. It was bigger and more corporate, I would say, and more business-oriented, and small bands wouldn't really get shows.

Ed Tarantino: The culture of the scene in LA was far more rigid and venue-oriented and less DIY than we were used to. Getting to play the clubs was a big barrier. Questions of draw come into play where these clubs look at either door sales or bar sales. So it took us a while to even get some traction there, and part of why we finally did was Lance Hahn was an amazing networker. It was in the peace punk scene that we started to kind of get some attention. Those DIY events we started getting invited to. But it was hard. We didn't get many gigs when we were up there.

We played a gig in East LA that was in a rec center or something, and it was sketchy and in a dangerous neighborhood, but that's an example of how there were so few gigs that we had to go all the way across the city to find a place we could do a show at. So when we'd see punk shows, it would usually be big bills with big headliners thrown by big promoters, and we'd go down to Long Beach to Fender's or the Roxy and I'd see Rollins Band or Bad Brains. In fact, there's a Bad Brains live record with HR on the cover, and if you look at the crowd, you'll see both Lance and myself.

Gardner Pope: I did my four years in college, but we all kind of started drifting apart there. Los Angeles sucked. Some of the people went back home to Hawaii, and Lance went up to San Francisco and moved into the *Maximum Rocknroll* house and started working there.

David Carr: Lance had so many pen pals and friends and when Cringer eventually moved up to the Bay Area, he was working at *Maximum Rocknroll* as a volunteer shitworker. He put in a lot of work and just embedded himself in the heart of the scene. The band got a lot of gigs and became a staple of that Gilman/Bay Area scene. Everyone knew who they were. In that sense, I think it paid off in being able to put out vinyl, tour and play with other bands.

Gardner Pope: In San Francisco, a lot of times you'll have a large house that gets broken up into flats, but Tim Yohannon from *Maximum Rocknroll* had an entire house, so there were a bunch of bedrooms where people lived and then he had a large living room-type space that was an office with all of these computers. That's where they put together the magazine. When I moved up there, I started working there too, and that's how I learned to use a computer.

While we were still in LA, Cringer and Free Will had actually gone up there and played at Gilman, and that's probably what pulled us there because that was the kind of scene that we were into. It was smaller, and shows were actually put on by fans. There was a regular place to play, and they would have shows all the time. It was way more DIY, and bands like us started moving there to be part of it. If you went to a Gilman Street show, it was very unlikely that there would be a fight, and if there was a fight, the people there broke it up immediately. I can't stress enough how awesome that was. It was totally different from LA.

THE WRONG

David Carr: I moved back to Hawaii to join The Wrong, which my brother had started with Jim and Rob Cribley. I heard their demo and asked to join their band. We put out an album on a label with some guys I had met in LA, and that was Flux Records. *College Music Journal* added us as their Jackpot pick as the best thing that was released that week, but for the most part, not many people heard about it. We didn't know how to promote it or anything, but in Hawaii, people liked us. We put out great music and got some vinyl out, got some good reviews and played some great shows.

Rob Cribley: The Wrong started out in '86 as me and my brother Jim and Kevin Carr, with mostly Kevin's songs. Then Dave ended up coming home from LA, and we drafted him into the band.

I think I was desperate to get out of Hawaii, and in '89, The Wrong moved to San Francisco. We did a lot of shows for about two years. We played with Green Day and a bunch of bands. Econochrist was one, Crimpshrine, Operation Ivy. We were trying to get into that scene when we got there, and we put out a record and got put onto a couple of compilation records. There was a point where we felt like we could actually maybe do this, but we kind of gave up too soon.

J-CHURCH

Gardner Pope: Cringer ended up touring with Citizen Fish, which was awesome. We had never done anything like that, and it was a huge undertaking. Crowd-wise and everything, it was very successful because of Citizen Fish being ex-Subhumans.

We bought a fucking $400 Ford van from the Libido Boyz and drove across the country in that and an old pickup truck, and that was hard living, you could say. It was a great tour but when we got home, Lance was just like, "I don't wanna be Cringer anymore. I just want to start a new band." He wanted to do something different, and he didn't want to be stuck with having to do Cringer songs. That's how he explained it to me.

In the '90s, as J-Church, we played more regularly, and it felt like we were a real band. Going to Europe was a whole different thing. It was more real. You had more real places to play, and they treated you like a real band, and oftentimes there'd be a place to stay and they'd feed you. Once in a while they'd even put you up in a hotel, and by "hotel," I don't mean a fancy hotel, but like a small, independent, family-run, six-room *pensión*. To some extent, at that point, we had missed the European heyday for American bands, but there was still some hangover from that, and people would come to see you just because you were an American band.

J-Church got to the point where we started to tour more regularly. We did that for a while and I just got tired of it. I'd been broke for so long. I was never poor, but broke. You leave and the life that you have is on hold for you because you're gone but you come home and everybody else's life has moved on. So there's something about that that's off-putting, and it was kind of depressing. I just got to the point where it wasn't going anywhere exciting for me. I was in a band from the time I was thirteen and I quit when I was thirty because I just felt like I didn't want to do it anymore.

Most people would consider J-Church to have been Lance's band, so it was much more his project, and he had a lot more invested in it, but he was in horrible shape. He was overweight and would get winded easily.

None of us were athletes, but Lance was in bad shape physically and never did anything to combat that. He didn't eat well and wouldn't pay attention to his diet at all. We were all vegetarians, so it wasn't fast-food, but he would make a huge plate of spaghetti and put some store-bought sauce on it and that's what he would eat. That was it. I'm amazed that he could play guitar and sing at the same time because that's not easy.

We'd usually be sleeping on the floor together, and he had pretty bad sleep apnea, and I didn't know what that was back then. I just knew we'd be lying there and all of a sudden he would stop breathing. I remember that distinctly and feeling distressed about it. There was no going to the doctor, and nothing was known at the time. My understanding of it was that some of what happened to him was genetic. I'm not even totally clear on what happened to him other than his kidneys failed at the end.

Once I left the band, we basically didn't speak again. I had heard a couple times that he was in the hospital. Someone would call me and tell me, and that had actually happened several times, and so the last time I had a friend call me, it was like, "Lance isn't doing well; he's in the hospital." My feeling at the time was, "Okay, this happens periodically and I'm sure he'll be fine." One morning a friend of ours called up. I hadn't spoken to him in a long time and so as soon as I heard his voice on the phone early in the morning, I was like, "Oh, this isn't good." And he told me.

14

THE EDGE OF HONOLULU

Outsiders would be forgiven for not having ever heard of Kalihi. Quite literally, in Hawai-ian, Kalihi means "the edge." It's a section of Honolulu that's never appeared in a travel brochure or TV ad, though unsuspecting visitors flying into Hawaii's capital have come to know it as the point in which they suddenly second-guessed their vacations. If Waikiki's sun-kissed tangle of hotels is your destination, there is no convenient way to bypass Kalihi. A tour van or shuttle would likely try to whiz you past it on the freeway.

It begins just after the airport, with homeless encampments as the H1 freeway meets Nimitz Highway. To the south of Nimitz is the industrial waterfront, to the north and up a block, Oahu Community Correctional Center—the state prison—along with rows of warehouses, auto repair shops, aging homes, and housing projects. Kalihi is an old neighborhood and among the few in ever-changing Honolulu to be routinely sidestepped by gentrification.

Six blocks up from the docks fronting Nimitz Highway, on Waiakamilo Road, is Ka'ahumanu Homes, a cluster of two-story concrete dwellings built in 1959 to address a shortage of low-income housing on Oahu. Even by public housing standards, it's modest in design. Among its inhabitants are working-class locals, immigrants, single mothers and their brood, the elderly, and at least when I lived there, a few welfare cheats. For the first fifteen years of my life, it was home.

As youngsters in the 1980s, we cruised Kalihi's industrial backstreets on our bikes, exploring rooftop parking lots and vacant buildings and frequenting video game parlors. On longer excursions, we might bring along a boom box, but just a small one, since a larger model might invite attention from some dickhead high schoolers or a bigger, brawnier pack of weekend riders looking to jack our sounds.

As the kid with the largest cassette collection in Ka'ahumanu Homes, I would often supply the music, usually a tape in each front pocket. Some of these artists I knew from the radio (AC/DC, Missing Persons, Grandmaster Flash & the Furious Five, Stray Cats), while other more obscure bands (Girlschool, Dream Syndicate, Boomtown Rats, Bush Tetras) I might have read about in *Creem* or *Novus* or seen on TV once. There were many times I took a chance on an album just because I liked the cover.

When punk rock first penetrated the public consciousness, right before hardcore took hold, it came across as a freaky, artsy scene for misfits and weirdos. I can recall seeing a feature on the TV show *Real People* of a punk party in which attendees danced like lunatics, and doll heads and assorted limbs were served encased in Jell-O as some sort of absurd dessert. Punk rock seemed humorous and campy to a grade-schooler.

Several years later, at about age twelve, I caught a snippet of a Circle Jerks performance on a special "Parents of Punkers" episode of the *Donahue* show. For the uninitiated, *Donahue* was a daily afternoon television fixture of the 1980s in which host Phil Donahue introduced controversial social topics to a studio audience while a panel of guests, seated on stage, would be fed to the bristly, opinionated crowd of mostly middle-aged housewives. This time, an audience member barked, "Listen, kids—get with it, clean yourselves up, and go to work!" to an assemblage of young punk rockers. While most days the topics were dull and unrelatable, this episode had me glued to the television.

As video snippets of *The Decline of Western Civilization* flashed across the screen, I realized there was a fury and urgency to this new version of punk, which no longer seemed kooky or offbeat. I had never seen slam dancing before, and the turbulent vortex it generated left me transfixed. It was dangerous, compelling, and fascinating. It also proved frustrating for me, ultimately. You see, in the early 1980s, if you saw something on TV that piqued your interest, you weren't likely to see that clip ever again. You simply stored it away in your memory bank and played it over in your mind from time to time. Unless you were lucky enough to own a VCR then, you could only hunt for more of it—somewhere, anywhere—or hope for another chance occurrence somewhere down the line.

I chose to dive headlong into hardcore, purchasing a cassette of Circle Jerks' *Wild in the Streets* at Tower Records on Ke'eaumoku Street with my allowance money soon after. As far as I knew, there were no other kids in Kalihi into that stuff back then. None whatsoever. For years, I had to enjoy my hardcore records and tapes—Black Flag's *Everything Went Black*; Angry Samoans' *Back from Samoa*; Bad Brains' *Rock for Light*; *The Decline of Western Civilization* soundtrack—by myself, pretty much. Whenever I was left alone at home,

I'd crank up the volume on the family stereo, strip off my T-shirt, and celebrate my burgeoning supply of testosterone with a sweaty, lonesome slam dance party in my living room.

Facing the west end of my housing project, on Kaiwi'ula Street, is the back entrance to King David Kalakaua Middle School. It was in the ninth grade, at what was then known as Kalakaua Intermediate, that I met Michael Silva, a fellow student who attracted attention wherever he went. His lustrous locks—the envy of female classmates—grew past his shoulders over the course of the school year. He kept his flourishing mane parted down the middle and accessorized by a Motley Crue headband. On occasion, he sported mirrored aviators for effect.

Even on warm days, he rocked a black windbreaker emblazoned with a large Black Sabbath back patch. If feeling particularly provocative, he might apply eyeliner he found lying around his bathroom that morning or write "OZZY" on his knuckles before heading off to school.

The crew of adolescent rockers to which he belonged included his capricious identical twin, Gabriel, and their brooding classmate Raymond Bala, but of all the shaggy-haired, denim- and flannel-clad thirteen- and fourteen-year-olds, Michael, with his affinity for the phantasmagorical and flair for dark theatrics, cut a particularly striking figure. I couldn't have known it then, but I would at long last meet other neighborhood kids who, though thoroughly immersed in the sounds and symbolism of heavy metal, would eventually embrace hardcore punk as I had.

Gabe Silva (guitarist: M.U.G., Pongoids): We were all into metal, especially Ray and I. Then my brother started getting into it because he started hanging out with us. There's a period where we all had long hair, but he wore all that leather and spikes and stuff. He presented himself and carried himself as a metalhead.

Mike Silva (vocalist/bassist/guitarist: M.U.G., The Pugilist, Pongoids, Freak Hunt, etc.): I started the year listening to Ozzy; then it progressed to Iron Maiden, Dio, Judas Priest, bands like Accept. I was being inundated with all of this stuff, people coming left and right, going, "Here, listen to this." But once the Cavern opened, that's when I started discovering the really heavy stuff.

Ray Bala (drummer: M.U.G., The Pugilist, Pongoids, etc.): The Cavern was a huge deal. It was this independent record shop that carried the stuff you wouldn't normally find in Tower Records or Hungry Ear. They brought in every genre of heavy metal from around the world—magazines, accessories, stuff like that. We used to go there pretty religiously and just hang out after school. It was like heavy metal school. The owner was pretty knowledgeable. He would tell us about all these bands he was trying to get recordings of. The thing is, he and his sons didn't even look like they listened to metal. They looked like your typical Midwestern white folk.

Mike Silva: Me, Ray, and Gabe were at the Cavern almost every day and for sure on weekends. There was a situation where the owner and his sons would let me get behind the counter and help people pick out stuff, like, "Oh, check out this spiked wristband" or "Look at this studded belt." I wasn't getting paid but I didn't care. I got to listen to whatever records were in the store, and it's where I got most of my music.

Gabe Silva: At the time, we'd go to the 50th State Fair, and there'd be all these metal bands playing. And not like AC/DC-type bands. These guys were cool, like real heavy metal and early thrash metal. Bands like Hawaii and Aaronsrod and Sacred Rite. Norm Dale, the owner of the Cavern, was also the manager of Hawaii, so we and some of our older friends ended up hanging out and following Hawaii around. When Hawaii would play shows, we'd be there, carrying their instruments, breaking down their instruments. We would even show up at their band practices sometimes. They were super cool.

Mike Silva: We were trading tapes with people from around the mainland. That's what metalheads did in the '80s. You would trade bootleg cassettes of demos or live bootleg concerts of bands. That was our thing. We would write to pen pals around the world through these metal magazines and be like, "What do you got? I got this cassette of this local heavy metal band, and I'll trade you for your live Metallica in San Francisco." That was how the music got disseminated.

People don't know that a lot of the Hawaii metalheads were hearing bands like Slayer and Venom before their albums even came out. Ray was really, really big into tape trading. He had this huge collection in

M.U.G. often practiced in Ray Bala's Kalihi Valley garage.
Courtesy of Shawn Lopes

his closet, almost half the size of the closet wall, of tapes that he traded or bought.

Ray Bala: I had a shit ton of demo tapes, live tapes, interviews, all this bootleg shit. I don't think anybody had anything original. They just dubbed it off their copy, so sometimes you'd get super good recordings and other times you'd be like, "Fuck, did you record this in your bathroom or some shit?"

Mike Silva: I discovered the Satanic Bible when I was in the ninth grade. My mom and my sister drove me down the street and made me throw the book in the trash because they didn't want it in the house and I was like, "But it's nothing like what you think it is!"

I was hated in school, man. People would destroy my artwork because I was drawing Eddie, the mascot from Iron Maiden, or Ozzy Osbourne, or this devil stuff. I even got sent to the principal's office. One of my teachers saw my artwork, sent it to the principal's office, and I got lectured by her and him about Satan being in my house while I watched the horror movies I liked to watch. They were like, "You're gonna get possessed if you keep listening to this music," and I challenged them. I was antagonistic. I was like, "You have no right to take away my art!" So I was starting to get frustrated with institutions like school and society and being judged by other kids.

Gabe Silva: The thing with my brother is he takes a lot of shit, he absorbs it, holds it in, and it affects the way he thinks. He'll keep himself closed off and he won't say anything back. He's not like me or Ray, you know. We're like, "No, fuck *you!*" So he wore what he wore, he would draw what he would draw and took a lot of shit, but when we started making music, all that shit came out. All those years of frustration. That's why we sounded the way we sounded, and that's the sound we liked.

Mike Silva: Eventually, the Cavern started bringing in a bunch of punk rock records. I was already aware of punk rock like the Ramones and The Clash from MTV, but when I saw the first Suicidal Tendencies album, I was like, "Whoa." You got all these guys on the cover wearing these button-up shirts, but they all had "Suicidal" drawn on them in Sharpie. And in the middle was the band, hanging from their feet from a jungle gym, and I was like, "What is that?"

So I go home that day, one of my brothers or sisters is watching MTV, and I hear the opening drum beat to "Institutionalized" and I watch the video. I'm like, "Holy shit, if this is real punk rock, I like this!"

At the time, I was getting disillusioned with the whole heavy metal thing, you know? Venom and all these guys singing about the devil, it's like, you can't take that stuff seriously. But what Mike Muir was saying in that video, I was like, "You know what? That's exactly how I feel."

Shawn "Speedy" Lopes (writer/columnist: *Honolulu Star-Bulletin, Honolulu Advertiser,* etc.; documentarian; DJ: Radio Free Hawaii, KTUH): Mike Silva and I had this one art class together, and that's where we got to be friends. I could see he was obviously really into metal and I knew we could relate. I was definitely more into punk rock than metal, but I could still rap with him about bands we both liked. By the time the year was over, though, his knowledge of metal grew, like, exponentially. I couldn't keep up. He knew all those obscure European bands in *Kerrang!* and all the subgenres—black metal, power metal, speed metal—and yeah, I was fascinated by all of it, but I was never able to convert him to any of the hardcore or post-punk shit I listened to. In fact, I remember in class one time, he drew a metalhead impaling a punk rocker with a spear.

Mike Silva: Shawn was the only guy in Kalihi who listened to punk at the time. I remember he liked all that stuff. I think we became friends because he wasn't like everyone else in school. He wasn't like us, the metalhead kids, but he was kinda like "the other." Nobody sat next to us in the ninth or tenth grade. That's why I thought it was cool when we started hanging out that he understood what I was going through and what it's like to be really into something and to be the only one. He never cared what other people did or thought. That is an individual. He gets it.

Shawn "Speedy" Lopes: When we were all in the tenth grade, Hawaii played the Farrington High School auditorium. Probably because Mike, Gabe, and Ray had the connections. I remember word spread pretty quick that there was a free concert after lunch, and this huge mob of students started to grow in front of the auditorium. I made sure I was at the very front of the pack near the entrance.

At some point, school security started to get overwhelmed, and this one guard shoved both of his hands into the middle of my chest and pushed back against the crowd with all his might, straight into my heart area. I thought I was gonna get crushed and die, like, right there. Then when the show started, the audience just lost their fucking minds, even the ones who didn't even like loud or heavy music. It's like they never heard anything like it. This one Samoan kid jumped up on stage and started doing this hard, spastic, body jerk dance while the band was playing, and the audience went apeshit. Security tackled him to get him off stage, and the crowd got even louder. It was on the brink of pandemonium.

Ray Bala: When that guy got up on stage, I don't know if he was really into it or just trying to be funny. There were some mentally challenged kids too, up front, just going off. It was like, "This is so fucking weird."

Mike Silva: By the time we got to Farrington, I was getting picked on a lot and bullied. Football guys would try to mess with me in the cafeteria and try to throw forks at my head, or trays. It was like, "See, I'm the oppositionist. I'm the guy that makes you uncomfortable. I'm a threat just by being me. I'm an individual while you're all sheep." And that's why I gravitated to the punk rock thing, 'cause it was like you could be whoever you wanted to be and nobody cares. You're a total individual.

Gabe Silva: I found out this one guy was slapping my brother, bullying my brother in class or whatever. Then I saw that guy in school, and I was like "Eh, you fucka!" He saw me and started running down the stairs. Another day or so, I'm in class, and I get called into the office. Fuck, I just yelled at this dude, I didn't hit him. What the hell? So I get there, my brother's sitting there crying, my mom's fucking yelling at the principal, the other kid is crying, and his mom is apologizing to me. She's like, "We're sending him back to Samoa to live with his uncle." I never saw that kid again.

Mike Silva: A lot of metal bands picked up on the speed of punk. Eventually, we started becoming aware of punk rock bands. Around 1984, my dad bought Gabe a guitar and me a bass. We actually called ourselves Rigor Mortis. I think we covered Metallica's "The Four Horsemen" and some Slayer, and we had a few of our own songs. Then we found out maybe a week later there was a band from Texas called Rigor Mortis, so I said, "Let's call the band Evilspeak," after one of my favorite horror movies.

By the end of '84, going into '85, after we started getting into the whole skateboarding thing, we started incorporating more punk to our music, and we changed our name to M.U.G. If you listen to our first M.U.G. recording at KTUH and you listen to the speed that we played at, that's early black metal.

Gabe Silva: We were metalheads, but we started meeting a lot of other people because we skated. My brother actually rode a Suicidal board. It was a huge fucking board. You could fit two people on it. Suicidal Tendencies was definitely one of our main influences. I rode a Dogtown board with a Mug root beer sticker on it and I said, "How about we just call the band M.U.G., Mean Ugly Guys?" I was kind of joking.

Ray Bala: In the beginning, we didn't know how to play for shit. If you listen to what we were doing early on, you'd be like, "This is just straight-out noise punk." Chaos. It was just how fast can we play, basically.

Our first show was at Coffeeline, near UH at the YWCA. They had a little coffee shop in there and a little stage. That was New Year's Eve, '85, going into '86. There were people lighting fireworks outside. We had Matt Dale from Saud on vocals, who we met through our skateboarding contacts, to fill in temporarily because we didn't have anybody singing.

Jaime Ikeda: I was stoked to meet M.U.G. I remember the first time I saw them, they played "Subliminal" from Suicidal and "Necrophiliac" by Slayer, but they played it faster, more aggressive. It was hardcore. Cool guys. From Kalihi, of all places.

Mike Silva: There was a group called No Business As Usual. They were political activists and really anti-war. That's how I came to know Mari Matsuoka. I owe her a lot. She was a hardcore M.U.G. fan and she helped a lot of the local bands in a lot of ways. A lot of people write her off as "She's a communist," and "She's with that commie bookstore, Revolution Books," blah, blah, blah, but don't realize that all the concerts they went to, she was the one who helped put them on.

We were playing at UH this one time and a fight broke out during M.U.G.'s set. I turned to everybody in the band and said, "Cut the fucking music!" So everybody stopped and I turned around and laid into the guys who started it. I said, "You know what? This is a fucking free gig, and we have a hard time finding anywhere to play, and it's this kind of bullshit why we don't get to play. Fights break out, shit gets ruined." I said, "If you guys wanna fight, take that shit outside. If not, I'm pulling the plug, M.U.G. is done, and I'm getting off the stage." I don't know if they made up or whatever, but after a few minutes, somebody told me everything was cool, so I turned to the band and said "Okay, start it back up."

After we were done with our set, Mari comes up and says, "I want to introduce you to somebody" and she takes me to meet Jello Biafra. I'm like, "Oh, whoa, cool!" He's got this big smile on his face and he's like, "Nice meeting you," and this and that, and he goes, "Okay, first thing I wanna say is you did an excellent job at handling that situation by stopping that fight. And second, you're really good at acting like a madman on stage."

Gabe Silva: Jello turned around to me and said, "You should play punk rock ukulele!" I was just staring at him like, "That would never take off." But if you listen to Flogging Molly, Dropkick, The Tossers, all these groups, The Rumjacks—they're playing instruments from their culture. I just totally missed the boat.

Mike Silva: A while later, we were playing on KTUH again and in between one of our songs, the guy in the booth comes in the room and says "We just got a call from Jello, and he says M.U.G. could go national if they wanted to," and we just sat there like, "Holy shit, Jello frickin' said that?"

Randy Szucs (vocalist: Broken Man): Broken Man's first show was opening up for Jello Biafra's spoken word show at UH, where M.U.G. also played, and I remember M.U.G. just killed it. Some of the Suicidal crew came over from LA like Aaron Murray, the professional skateboarder—probably for some skating—and my guess is they saw there was a show in town that weekend. Some of them got into a fight with the Hawaii skinheads. There was a big brawl there.

Mike Silva: M.U.G. spent most of '88, like, done. We had to break up because I started having all these issues with mental illness. It's been a lifelong thing that no one really diagnosed in a proper way, but for the first time in my life, I'm actually seeing somebody for it.

The first time I blacked out from it was at the Sub Club. We had just started our set and I don't know if I fell into the drums or whatever, but I had a full-blown panic attack, and the older scene guys were like, "Oh shit!" They grabbed me and carted me off to the bathroom, and they're splashing my face with cold water and they're like "You need to breathe!" Everybody was like, "What the hell just happened?"

Gabe Silva: There was one time my brother was gonna get sent to the Hawaii State Hospital and I stopped 'em. I said, "You're gonna try and take him, *you're* going to the hospital. Don't even touch him 'cause I will break your ass."

"Oh, but here's the ambulance."

I was like, "No, fuckin' leave!"

And I stopped them from taking him.

Mike Silva: I wrote "Snap" trying to explain what I feel. "Suicidal Run" was just about suicide, then later became an anti-suicide song directed at myself. I was feeling all these negative things and at times felt I shouldn't be here, and I changed the lyrics because actually, there is a reason to be here, and you gotta stop that shit.

Ray Bala: I was gradually getting more into oi and stuff like that through guys in the scene. Right after we graduated high school, I started gravitating more towards skinhead music and adopting that look.

Mike Silva: We were hanging out in Waikiki near Pink Cadillac and 7-Eleven with all the skinheads, who were the old punk rockers, and eventually M.U.G. had this huge skinhead following. Ray had these oi records and I was like, "Yeah, this is kinda cool." There was this whole mindset of having a job and being a responsible individual, so I kind of embraced that working-class pride identity. I do remember calling up Ray and saying, "You know, I think I'll get into the skinhead thing."

Gabe Silva: Curt Swanson, he's an older skinhead. He introduced us to the Cro-Mags' music. What I learned from him was that the bass player and the vocalist from the Cro-Mags studied the Vedic scriptures. So I wanted to know what this band's connection to Hare Krishna was all about. I kinda started to read up on it, but I didn't really take to it until '93 or so when the whole Krishnacore thing was happening.

Jesse Perrin (HARSH Co-Founder): As I understood it, Curt and all the older hardcore guys got turned on to skinhead culture from military guys who were originally from punk scenes in other places before being transplanted to Hawaii. There were guys who came out from the East Coast who were stationed in the Marine Corps or the Army and realized, "Hey, there's a scene out here." We're like, "Fuck, let's meet these guys." Next thing you know, the first generation of hardcore guys who wore leather jackets all of a sudden had flight jackets and Doc Martens. The younger guys like me, Ray, and Mike were right behind them, getting into the skinhead lifestyle.

Mike Silva: I've actually had confrontations with police about being a skinhead. I'd be roaming around Ala Moana before work to kill time, and security would follow me into Liberty House. Next thing you know, I got vice cops going, "Hey, hey, come here. We need to talk to you!"

I'm like, "Oh no, what?"

They're like, "What are you doing here?"

"Well, I work over there at Orson's Chowderette."

"You're a skinhead, you're a Nazi. You can't be a skinhead because skinheads are Nazis," blah blah.

I'm like, "What do you know? You watch television and believe all that stuff. You don't know anything about us. You don't know where the whole thing came from." But I never tried to explain it to them because I realized they wouldn't understand. They just wanna believe you're a bad seed.

Shawn "Speedy" Lopes: A little bit after we graduated from Farrington, Mike helped me land a job working with him at Orson's in the food court of Ala Moana. McKinley was the nearby high school, and there would always be a pack of young punks, skinheads, and metalheads—even a few glammies—hanging out in front of Orson's in the afternoon, probably because they recognized Mike from his band. Mall security wasn't sure what to do.

It was that era when Nazi skins were making the rounds on talk shows and people began equating all skinheads with racists. I remember there was a regular customer, nice guy, who picked up his order from Mike and asked him, kind of in fun, "Hey, you're not one of those skinheads, are you?" Mike just looked at him and answered, "Yeah, I am. I'm a skin." The guy was confused, I guess, because Mike's brown. I always wanted to jump in and set the record straight in those situations, but how do you educate someone on the entire history of skinhead culture, Jamaican influences and all, to a stranger in passing?

Ray Bala: The Hawaii Anti-Racist Skinheads was a reaction to that media bullshit that was going on in the late '80s, early '90s. Just the mention of the word "skinhead," the reaction of everybody and their brother who didn't know jack shit about it was "Nazi." Yeah, take a look at the color of my skin, fuckwit. That's why I don't trust the fuckin' media. It's their account of something they don't understand. Or their scapegoat. They weren't searching for the truth. The airtime they gave to the Nazis was way more than what they gave to the anti-racist or traditional skins. So HARSH was a reaction to that. I believe the organizers were Jesse Perrin and Chris Smith.

Jesse Perrin: I first met Chris Smith through common friends in Palo Alto, California, before he moved down to Hawaii. Chris was a punk rocker. It started with Chris, me, Ray, and Mike, pretty much. The original firm that we put together was called HARSH, for Hawaii Anti-Racist Skinheads, "Punks and Skins United." SHARP had already come out of New York at the time—Skinheads Against Racial Prejudice—and we went off of that kind of model.

About a year after the infamous riot broke out on the Geraldo Rivera TV show with John Metzger, people were coming down on anyone with a flight jacket and bald head. They didn't understand that skinhead culture didn't actually originate with racists. It originally came from the West Indies' rude boy scene, and it got so tiring explaining that to people. You just wanted to get into a fight already. You're like, "I don't care, let's just scrap because you don't like me anyhow. I don't give a fuck."

HARSH was put on a gang task force list by HPD and military police because we would jump military guys who called us out. When we got arrested they took pictures of our patches and all that bullshit. We were probably thirty to forty strong at one point.

Mike Silva: When we got back together in '89, Gabe didn't rejoin the band. He kinda did his own thing. I think he didn't like the direction the music was going 'cause it was different. We already had James Kroll on bass, who used to be in Just in Fun, with his brother Jon on guitar. They both played with us, and we started getting more melodic. The music wasn't as fast anymore. Then Warren Young and Troy Miller joined the band, and we added Ryan Kunimura on trombone for our ska song, "Working Man," which changed our direction a little bit.

Ray Bala: Yeah, our music was different, but we were also getting better at our instruments and we got tighter. And M.U.G.'s popularity grew really fast with Jon and James in the band. Now we were making day trips out to Hawaii Kai and plastering our fliers all over the telephone poles, especially near the high schools like Kaiser and Kalani. Jon and James were from that area, so they had friends, and their friends told their friends.

Earl Crawford (guitarist/drummer: Luau Guys, Friend of the Family, Ciguatera, Devil Kine Music, etc.): What struck me about that version of M.U.G. was there were two tall white guys and a couple of smaller skinhead dudes and I'm like, "What the fuck is this about?" But it was really melodic and musical, and what was different was suddenly there was a shitload of hot white chicks, all in the front. Nobody had chicks like them. I'm from Waianae, so back then I was like, "Where the fuck do all these hot chicks come from?" Now I know the girls were from Hawaii Kai. I was inspired. I started making punk songs after watching M.U.G. for the first time.

Gabe Silva: It all started when the Red Hot Chili Peppers came out with that song "Fight Like a Brave." I remember it clearly because that's when our music started to change. James wanted to play more slap bass because he wanted to be like Flea, and we had instrumentals that sounded like a shitty punk version of a Red Hots song. My brother actually has some recordings of that, and you can hear *BOM-BOM-BAAAAYYYYMMM*!!! *BOM-BOM-BAAAAYYYYMMM*!!! I was like, "Great. Fuck this shit." Even our ska stuff wasn't that cool because we weren't a ska band, and to do ska songs right, you needed all the instruments, which we didn't have.

Mike Silva: I didn't like the direction it was going. It was getting weird. It didn't sound like punk anymore. When I listen back to a lot of that music, it sounds okay, but it's not what M.U.G. was about initially. At some point, I dissolved the band. I'm like, "We gotta stop."

15

THE CROSSOVER

At the bottom of a crudely sloped parking lot in Kalihi, in the basement of an old Puerto Rican tavern, a sanctuary for local punks and metalheads was established in August of 1985. By arranging a one-off, multi-band gig here, Dave Carr unwittingly recast the United Puerto Rican Association of Hawaii's rental hall as a vital gathering place for the scene's coming generation.

In short order, similar venues in some of Honolulu's sootiest corners were secured by key benefactors like indie superstore Jelly's as well as Progressive Arts, a small but dedicated collective that included culture-junkie-turned-activist Mari Matsuoka and KTUH soundman Pat Donegan. "We weren't in touch with the underground music scene so much at the start, but we knew it existed and that it needed a lot of help," explains Donegan. "We were the responsible adults who would book places for the kids, and Mari would get out there and do the promotion, basically. At some point, Mari got on the radar of Jelly's."

Jelly's, by the mid-1980s, was a popular shop for specialty comics, used books, sports cards, and hard-to-find recorded music. It was a well-known hub and hangout for nerds and nonconformists. As business grew, Jelly's relocated from a modest nook it shared with a lighting fixture shop on the corner of Kapiolani and Ke'eaumoku to a cavernous property on Pi'ikoi Street. There, several ambitious projects were launched for the benefit of its underserved clientele.

In 1988, in the offices above its main floor, Jelly's began publishing a community newspaper covering art, music, entertainment, and social issues called *Scrawling Wall*. That same year, Jelly's released *No Place to Play*, a cassette-only compilation of fifteen unsung bands toiling in the local underground.

Also of significance was its sponsorship of a no-alcohol club it christened the Backdoor in an airport-area catering hall operated by the reputed Luau King of Hawaii, Chuck Machado. The all-ages nightspot occasionally featured reggae and worldbeat acts like Wisdom Tree, Pagan Babies, and Maacho & Cool Connection, though most weekends it was overrun by the island's hardcore kids, whose ranks had recently swelled with the incorporation of a thriving thrash metal scene and a growing cadre of newly organized anti-racist skinheads looking to blow off steam.

Both locally and nationally, the metal-hardcore crossover had reached its zenith, and Honolulu's once-provincial punk scene, now fortified with inveterate headbangers and skins, routinely drew hundreds of young malcontents from across Oahu to its loud and unruly shows. By 1989, this new, expanding crossbreed had achieved full-scale evolution.

Jason Reece (vocalist/multi-instrumentalist: …And You Will Know Us By the Trail of Dead, Ifany, Mukilteo Fairies, etc.): I was born in Huntington Beach, California, and I moved to the Big Island, on the Hilo side, when I was about four or five. My folks were kind of weird, hippie sort of parents and wanted to live in the jungle, so I think I was about ten when we went to the rainforests in Mountain View, where we lived with no electricity. We used generators and a water catchment system. It was really off the grid, and I was super bored because the kids nearest to me were, like, a mile or two miles away. After a while, my mom was just getting fed up with living in the boonies out in the middle of nowhere, and when I was about sixteen, we moved over to Oahu.

I started getting into music because of skateboarding and reading *Thrasher,* which turned me on to some punk. It was hard to get music on the Big Island at that time. It's so different from Oahu. But before moving to Oahu, I was definitely reading about the scene there. I had found some kind of 'zine that had Cringer in it and talked about Lance Hahn and what was it—Club 3-D? To me, Oahu seemed like the mecca, like, "I gotta get over to Honolulu!"

Willie Fruean (guitarist/vocalist: B.Y.K., North American Bush Band, Rootonics, etc.): As far as playing music, I was really accelerated for my age. When I was six years old, my dad taught me to play guitar, and

I picked it up quickly. It was easy for me. But the thing is, I couldn't do much with it because my sisters danced hula and my parents would make me go to their practices after school.

I was Hawaii's youngest Polynesian drummer for the longest time, playing Tahitian and Samoan stuff, and I frickin' hated that shit so much. I *hated* it. I always wanted to play drums and bang on shit, but my parents would never buy me a drum set. They were like, "Play this *toere*." I was thinking, *Fuck this—I don't want to play this stupid fucking log!* but it was easy. *BAH-DAMP BAH-DAMP!!!* I think it's just that I'm Samoan, man. You gotta have rhythm.

Guy Takaki (bassist: Luau Guys; vocalist: Nocturnal Fear): Willie can play anything. I've seen him pick up brass instruments and just start playing. He's just that kind of guy.

Willie Fruean: It was our freshman year of high school, in '87, when Scott Akana and I met Dave Samford, and he was the only bass player around, so we started playing. He liked the same music as me and a little bit of punk, but he wanted to learn more. We would always skate and hang out every day. He was like my brother. We were inseparable.

Another guy that went to school with us at Mililani was Guy Takaki. Guy was like, "Hey, you guys, check out my band at the Makakilo bunker." There was an old military bunker up on the hill in Makakilo, and that was the first show I ever went to. There was just one light in there, and it was super dark. I remember being scared, like, "We're just kids—are we gonna get beat up?" People were drinking beer, smoking pot, but nobody really gave us shit. There was no too-cool vibe or anything like that, nobody trying to punk you. It was just like, "Hey, we're all here, let's party!"

Guy Takaki: It was an old bunker that was owned by a church that would rent the space out on weekends for birthday parties or whatever. We would rent it, have two or three bands play, and charge people five dollars for a cup if they wanted to drink from our kegs. That's how we would fund the shows, and we'd use the money to pay for the next one.

It was usually a bad idea, though, because it never really paid itself off. It just got people drunk and stupid.

The bands that would play there were Infection, Luau Guys, and the band that I was with before I joined Luau Guys called Nocturnal Fear, which was kind of a black metal, Slayer-type band, mostly military kids who went to school at Radford. I was the only one from Mililani. We also had Optimum Fury play at the bunker. They were these Filipino guys from Ewa Beach, and they had really good equipment, so we would always invite them to play so we could borrow their stacks and stuff.

Willie Fruean: I decided this was a scene I liked, and when we got back to Mililani, Dave, Scott, and I started B.Y.K.—Beat Your Kids. We were all classically trained musicians and could read and write music and all that shit. It was just a couple of months before we were playing the Backdoor.

Now, I don't know if Chuck Machado's famous luaus actually happened at the Backdoor or if they just made the food there, but that would've been some ghetto-ass luau to be in this industrial area near the airport. I have to say, though, Chuck Machado was a cool-ass motherfucker. He was cool. If you got to the Backdoor early, Chuck would be there, and he'd always have leftovers from his luaus, so we'd always get a couple of 40s from the liquor store and eat his food. He was a nice guy. A man of very few words.

You hear these stories in every scene, and there's always one cool old guy who owns a place and just lets shit happen. I mean, that place was laid to waste every weekend. The kids would leave the parking lot trashed, and the place couldn't have been making that much money when it was two or three dollars to get in.

Earl Crawford: Back when Luau Guys was just starting, I went with some friends, these three chicks, to a UH show. I was like fourteen or fifteen. I had on my leather jacket, and I used to wear biker rings on every single finger.

This one band came on, and I'll never forget it: The lights went down, the crowd went away, and all of a sudden it was dark and there was a circle pit—literally the old school-style circle pit—and the girl I kinda liked at the time, she was like, "Oh, you should go!" So I took my glasses off, and I couldn't see shit. I have horrible fucking vision. She grabs my glasses, pushes me into this pit, and I don't wanna seem weak or anything, so I do some rounds, sweating my ass off with my leather jacket on.

Next thing you know, the lights come on, the circle pit disperses—it was like a movie—and I'm standing there in the middle of all these people. There was this line of skinheads looking at me, holding their mouths, talking to each other; they're pointing, like, "Yeah, that's the guy. That's him." Then the leader of the skins walks straight up to me and goes, "I know it was you. Don't even think of going anywhere. We're gonna figure this out."

And I was like, "What? What happened? I don't even know what you're talking about."

There was this one big, fat skinhead dude who kept saying, "It was him! I know it was him! He did it! I saw him do it!"

I'm starting to get scared, like, "Do what?" There were, like, ten or eleven of 'em basically indicating that they were gonna beat the shit outta me, and the girls I was with were getting worried.

After they talked and pointed some more, I noticed the skins had a weird look on their faces. What I didn't know was behind me were all these Waipahu death metal Filipinos, maybe twelve of 'em, and they all had that stereotypical "I carry a knife" look, right? One of them tapped my shoulder and he goes, "Brah, any time you like go fuckin' lick dese haoles, let us know. We be right ovah deah," and he pointed to these guys standing there in the dark, leaning against the wall with their arms crossed. Then the leader of the skins is like, "We know you did it, man." And he goes, "We're gonna remember you." And then they left.

I guess what happened was one of the skins got his head cut, and there was blood all over the place. And they started saying that I did it on purpose, that I punched him in the head and caused all this blood to gush out, and he had to get rushed out in an ambulance. It was the first time I'd ever seen a skinhead, and so I was fearful of all skins at this point.

Jesse Perrin: He fucking coldcocked me right in the fucking face. Why, I don't know. I was pissed. I thought he was trying to single me out.

Earl Crawford: Next thing you know, the Backdoor is happening. Our first show, we show up, I see M.U.G. and all these skinhead dudes, and I'm like, "Oh no—ahhh, fuck..." They all had "HARSH" on their jackets. I didn't feel good about it at all. They see me and they start pointing and talking again.

My brother Dave comes up, and they're all like, "Hey, Dave, what's going on?" and he goes, "Hey, what's up? Did you guys meet my little brother?" He pointed to me, and all their jaws just dropped. Turns out, my brother was going to Pink Cadillac all the time and hanging outside with all these skinhead dudes. They all became his friends. So it became one of those unspoken things, like, "Just let it go."

Guy Takaki: Earl and Dave Crawford's family lived in this really small house in Waianae. They shared a room and it wasn't bigger than half a garage, but they made it work. Dave had to put one of those footlockers at the end of his bed so his feet wouldn't hang off the edge. At 6'8" and 300 pounds, Dave Crawford was the biggest guy in the scene but also the kindest. He'd do anything for anybody that he could. He had a heart of gold. He was also the most musically skilled of any of us.

Earl Crawford: So many shows or months into the Backdoor scene, I finally see Jesse, the guy they said I cut, by himself, and I said, "Hey, man, I need to talk to you. Between me and you, I have no idea what happened. Did I do something and cut your head open?"

He goes, "Yeah, you did."

I was like, "Dude, I'm so sorry, I had no idea. I don't see very well without my glasses, and I have all these stupid rings on, and I probably did it without even knowing. How can I make it up to you?" and he goes, "How about you get me a twelve-pack and we'll call it even?" There was this place on Nimitz I would go to and they never carded, so I bought a twelve-pack, gave it to him, and that was it. We never talked, though, after that.

A VOICE FOR EVERY BAND

Guy Takaki: I started working for Jelly's, I think it was '88 or '89, and got to meet Mari Matsuoka, who was one of the promoters for Norm Winter from Jelly's. Mari wanted to make sure that every band had a voice. She knew where to find the right venues, how to fund the shows, how to find graphic artists to design good fliers. Somebody had to put down a deposit for those gigs at the Backdoor, and that was pretty much Mari.

Matt Yoshihara (guitarist: Tarrasque, Travel Light, etc.): As far as putting on shows, Mari was the one who led the way. Without her, I don't know how they could've even happened. It was through her contributions and her influence that bands got connected, and we had shows galore for years after. That woman had so much to do with all of it.

Norm Winter (owner of Jelly's Music and Books, founder of Radio Free Hawaii): It started with Mari coming to me and asking for help with concerts for local bands. They were these garage bands—some reggae, some punk. We had a hell of a hard time because every place we tried, we had noise complaints and had to shut down. There was a church in the University area; we did one in an abandoned spot somewhere by Salt Lake; we did one near Kapiolani and McCully, sometimes in these garage-type places.

Guy Takaki: Norm was really supportive of the bands, and those shows would bring a lot of customers to his stores. This led to the Backdoor being a new venue for a bunch of bands at the time. No money was made by Mari or Norm for any of the gigs Jelly's sponsored. They just rented the PA, and whatever money was made would go to the bands.

THE METAL EDGE

Mike Silva: The Backdoor is really significant because it's where it all culminated into something really different and diverse. When we first came on the scene, it was us, Scarred 4 Life, and Saud that were influenced by metal, and everybody else was just punk rock. We eventually lost that metal sound, but Saud turned into Stage Dive and then morphed into Broken Man, who became *the* metal band of the day. When Luau Guys, Tarrasque, and Optimum Fury came along, they didn't even play in the metal scene; they chose to play in the punk scene. That's when you started to see metalheads come to the punk shows.

Matt Yoshihara: It was the intersection of everything. We never had shit for years and all of a sudden we had the Backdoor, which became the one spot where we could be as real and crazy as we wanted.

BROKEN MAN

Kili Kaohu (drummer: Broken Man): The whole crossover thing just exploded. The metal and punk rock crowds started blending; the bands started blending their sound. You could go see full-on heavy metal bands like Pestilence and Saphyre Syn, but then you also had the punk scene, and that's where I was like, "Ho, shit—this is all *raw!*" Everybody going all frickin' aggro, in your face and pissed off as hell. The pits would go insane, especially when M.U.G. would play. Damn, people were losing their shit. That was proof positive that we were not the only crazy motherfuckers listening to this demented music. That's when we got into it. It was like crossing the river Rubicon. There was no going back.

Guy Takaki: You could say Broken Man kind of led the charge. They were professional and they had a full, clean sound and a tight stage show. They also had the best equipment. We'd use borrowed stuff and all this ghetto equipment with recycled parts, but frickin' Broken Man, they came with half-stacks and full Marshalls, man. They were at eleven when everyone else was at, like, seven on the volume scale.

Willie Fruean: Broken Man really had their shit together. Every other band seemed like they were fucking around, having fun, because we knew we weren't going anywhere. But they *wanted* it. It seemed like they practiced all the time because they never fucked up. They got up on stage, no fucking around, no talking to the crowd, like, "Hey, guys, how you doin' tonight?" Just song after song. They were like a machine.

Randy Szucs: Broken Man wasn't really metal, and we weren't your typical punk rock either. That crossover sound was always up my alley. I dug it. It was real aggressive, hard music. I was like, "This is the kind of band I want to be."

Ed Tarantino: When I got the call to join Broken Man, it was like Scarred 4 Life again where I felt like I was the weak link. These guys could play, man. Jaime, Kili, Rodney, they were all so fucking solid and so good and so tight. It was way beyond what I could play, really. Randy had a

Broken Man, 1989. From left to right: Kili Kaohu, Rodney Bagcal, Jaime Ikeda, Ed Tarantino, Randy Szucs. *Courtesy of Shawn Lopes*

big presence and powerful voice that really worked with a metal sound; that huge, shouting vocal with a full-on, tight thrash backing. I was just stoked that they brought me in.

Guy Takaki: I would get scared sometimes listening to Randy's voice. I mean, it was *threatening*.

Randy Szucs: I think I've just always been an angry guy. Growing up in LA, I was always the kid that got into fights on my football team or at school. Maybe I had something to prove. I just didn't like taking shit. The vocals had to be kinda gnarly because those guys in my band, for as young as they were, were shredders, and Kili beat the shit out of his drums, so it had to be heavy.

As far as what I wore, that cholo hat with the flannel on and bandanas and shit, like a cross between Social Distortion and Suicidal Tendencies, I loved that look because of where I grew up. I went to school with all those kinds of guys. I always thought it was a cool look.

Earl Crawford: The Backdoor was a blending of everyone's scene. I had my friends in Waianae, and they had their friends in Maili and Nanakuli. All it took was one or two people to go to a show and talk about this thing called the Backdoor that had pits and live bands to people who never heard of shit like that, and then they start carpooling to go out there.

Then the Mililani guys would show up with B.Y.K., the Infection guys from Aiea would be there, and Radford and Moanalua High had their own punk rock skate kids, not to mention the town side, which I had zero knowledge of. So when everyone pooled their friends together from all parts of the island, it worked out great, in my opinion, because the Backdoor was centrally located.

Jason Reece: The Backdoor was where I felt I was at home in a lot of ways, even though I was a Windward-side kid at the time. All the city kids who hung out there, like M.U.G., were kinda like rock stars in their own right. They were the fuckin' coolest. Going to a Mean Ugly Guys show, there was so much energy. The pit was always fun. Tarrasque, Luau Guys, Broken Man—those were all the bands I'd go see.

I met our singer, Damien Tolentino, when he put up a flier at Coconut Grove Music in Kailua, looking for a band. It said he played guitar and liked Verbal Assault and Agression, bands like that. He turned me on to all of this obscure punk shit. He was twenty-two or something, maybe twenty-three, and he was this older dude who'd served in the military and could drink and buy booze. I was seventeen and taking classes at Windward Community College, which is where Beau George, our bassist, and I connected. That›s kind of how Ifany started happening.

I was probably a year into drumming and I was terrible. Our songs were super fast and ridiculous and about being bored and having unity in the scene or whatever. Every cliche, we hit it. I didn't have any aspirations of becoming a rock star or anything ridiculous like that. I think the goal was to make songs and then after that maybe play at the Backdoor. That was definitely the biggest goal for that band. If we could play a show on the Honolulu side, we succeeded.

Having kids at the Backdoor going off to our music really gave me that energy to keep at it. I didn't know it at the time, but it helped shape what I would do in the future, like good building blocks, you know?

WE WERE ALL OUTCASTS

Earl Crawford: The Backdoor was self-governed, man. Lord of the Flies all the way. There was no security.

Chris Esteron: There were no bouncers. The scene policed itself. And even though people talk about the aggro, the violence—and yeah, it definitely happened—nobody talks about the camaraderie, man. If you found your way to the Backdoor, if you found out this existed, you were a fucking weirdo and you found your fellow weirdos.

Willie Fruean: The Backdoor is where I started to see all kinds of people at a show: Here's a skinhead, here's a metalhead, here's a guy with dreads, just whatever, you know? Nowadays, that's just a normal night out, but back then, we were all outcasts. People looked at us weird. If you went to a 7-Eleven, they automatically thought you were there to steal shit. It's hard to explain to young people today that tattoos used to make people think you were a delinquent. They think it's normal now because their grandma has one.

Woody Soueira: I remember doing gigs at the Backdoor, and there would be this array of people like the skinheads, the goth people, the heavy metal rockers, and we all had our own thing, but we all came together under one roof. I remember going, "Wow, these goth chicks are pretty hot!" but they scared me.

Matt Yoshihara: The pits at the Backdoor were incredible. The best thing I ever saw was an all-girl circle pit egged on by Randy and Broken Man. It was a fucking sight to behold. Amazing.

Randy Szucs: I did that a couple times, and I would tell the crowd, "If any guy goes in there, I want you all to kick his ass." I just felt like there were times when these girls really wanted to go off, but they would just get smashed in the pit by these metalheads and dirty punk rockers. The biggest all-girl pit I saw had at least a hundred girls in it. It was fun but those pits could get dangerous too.

I remember one show we played, and this one kid came up to me and he's like, "I'm gonna get in so much trouble, but I don't care 'cause this is the best show I've ever been to!" His braces were ripped off his face, and they were sticking out of his mouth, and I had Rodney cut them out because he carried pliers with him for his guitar strings.

Rich Tarantino: I think it was the end of '89 and the beginning of 1990 when I returned to Hawaii with a wife and kid. What blew me away was how the music scene exploded. It was pretty amazing to see how many people were seeing live bands that never would have come to Hawaii before. All these kids were coming out and it's like, where were they years ago?

I was blown away at how huge it had gotten in Hawaii. I guess I'm not sure what happened and why the locals were into this music that they used to hate back then. Now they were coming to the shows. That just blew me away.

THE RIOT

Willie Fruean: I remember one time it was unusually crowded at the Backdoor because word was out that any show could be the last show there, and it was coming to an end. Mari and Jelly's were already out of the picture and Chuck wasn't even around anymore, but the shows kept getting bigger and bigger.

One night, there were hundreds of people inside and at least another 200 people outside, just drinking and partying. I come out to have a beer and I hear a bottle break and then I see bottles start fucking flying. Shit started happening. Basically, some local guys started scrapping with the Backdoor regulars, but they were getting their asses kicked. Everybody chased those motherfuckers down the street, and somehow they got away, but they left their Volkswagen Bug there.

Earl Crawford: I remember there were three guys on one side of the car trying to turn it over, then spinning it around and around, upside down in the parking lot. At that point, me and Willie ran away like, "Fuck, I'm getting out of here!" It was the wrong fucking car too. That's the worst part.

A melee at the Backdoor led to an overturned VW Beetle.
Courtesy of Holly MacGregor

Jesse Perrin: Basically, we flipped over their Bug, and they all had to climb into one car, and to make a long story short, they got fucked up good.

A couple of months later, they show up with more people. No one was ready for it, and they sort of slipped into the crowd and just started beating the piss out of people. A friend of mine got hit by one of their cars and she flipped over it. I saw her smack onto the pavement, and the next thing you know, I felt a knife go into my back. It didn't even hurt at that moment. You feel like a walking stick of butter because of the adrenaline. You know it, though.

I looked at Ray Bala and I'm like, "Dude, I've been stabbed..." and he passes me a fucking baseball bat. He's like, "I know."

Mike Silva: I remember somebody whacking this one big dude with one of those baby Louisville Sluggers, busted it over his head, and the guy just got madder. He picked up Dave Suzuki, and I was trying to get to Dave. I was like, "Oh shit!"

Jesse Perrin: Dave Suzuki, one of my best friends, was a little Japanese guy and he had a lot of heart, but he was already knocked out and being dragged around unconscious by this big, local dude who was built like a tank. Dave had his jaw broken in two places.

My friend Pete Jordan was trying to clamber underneath a car because this guy was going to beat the piss out of him next. I went behind the dude, broke the baseball bat on his head; it splintered and the end went flipping over, down the parking lot, and the guy just turns around and goes, "FUCKA!!!" All I could do was grab the splintered end of the base-ball bat and lean forward like, "Come on, dude!" I was going to shove it into him. He got my body language. I fucking buried my foot in the ground and got ready to fuckin' pike him. That's when all the cops filled the parking lot, and he opened up the trunk of his car like he was getting something, then saw the cops and took off.

I remember a cop was trying to stop people in the parking lot, and I walked right by him. I made it a block up the street stumbling, col-lapsed, and my friend Pete, whose ass I'd just saved, found me and commandeered a car full of teenage girls and dragged my bleeding ass into the back seat and said, "Drive him to the fucking hospital right now!"

A couple of people got injured really bad, and there were people standing around in fear to fight or back us up. That's what kind of ruined HARSH. It was one fight, one night. I knew who my friends truly were, in a way. On one hand, I don't want to be that dramatic because I get it: The guys who were scared to fight were kids, but it was like, "Well, fuck you." Eventually we just created FCS—Fist City Skins—and we all got that tattoo. But yeah, the Backdoor had some legendary scraps in that parking lot. It was as epic and crazy as any legendary punk rock spot that people talk about in any other city or other place.

C5

Willie Fruean: The Backdoor was great, but I kind of liked C5 even better than the Backdoor. A lot of people don't give C5 props, but that place was the shit. I loved that place. It was on Hotel Street, in a basement, so you had to walk down some stairs. Inside, it looked like a typical Korean hostess bar with red velvet booths and white tables, with a stage that was maybe a foot high. We'd go there after the Backdoor closed down.

The owner, Min, was a crazy-ass Korean lady who always seemed mad, yelling all the time, but once you got to know her, you realized that's just how she was. She had a white husband—I guess he was retired military—and since she always liked rock and roll, when she came to Hawaii, she wanted to open a rock-and-roll bar.

Guy Takaki: C5 was this really dingy, hole-in-the-wall club on Hotel Street. The owner, Min, catered to the military guys who wanted to hear old heavy metal like Judas Priest and stuff. If you were a working hard rock band then, you either played the Jazz Cellar, C5, or both.

Once in a while, though, when there were no other bands scheduled, she might do a punk night with one or two bands, but the problem was the punk crowd would never spend any money, and they destroyed the place. Tables would be broken, bathrooms would be demolished. For those shows, she would have to hire extra security.

Min also had her Rockfests, which were two- or three-day events. The first one was at Aloha Tower, where all kinds of bands played, like us and B.Y.K.

Willie Fruean: She didn't like our music at all, but she realized we could bring people in, so she let us play. I don't think she ever knew we weren't old enough to drink because she would just give us drinks all night long.

This one time, we had a gig set up at the Backdoor and when we showed up it was fucking closed. This might have been when they actually closed for good. What are we gonna do? So after about 200 or 300 people show up, I'm like, "All right, everybody, follow me… The gig's gonna go on—it's at C5!" So we all get there, it's a slow Sunday night, and I tell the guy behind the bar, "Eh brah, we're gonna have a show tonight." This mob of people just walks in and packs the place. We were all underage, but everybody was drinking; it was just a free-for-all, everybody partying. I think somehow Min found out because she showed up later and we're like, "What, you don't like this shit? You made a lot of money tonight!" She just shook her head.

TO THE BAY AND BACK

Kili Kaohu: We talked about moving to the Bay Area for a good year before we actually left. That was my senior year of high school, 1989. Hawaii was kind of limited as far as places to play. Moving to the mainland, we might have a little more success spreading the Broken Man gospel. I wasn't worried. We knew eventually we would have to work for a living and do the band thing on the side.

Everybody was on board with the idea, but Randy just got his life together. He was a roughneck in the hood for a couple of years, living on the streets. At the time, he got a steady, good paying job; a solid apartment; solid girlfriend. We understood he had his own life to live. So in Randy's place we brought in Alton Takata. He had a strong voice too.

Randy Szucs: My life was a mess. I'd been homeless for, like, at least a year. I was living in cars, abandoned houses, and in buildings that were still under construction. I always had a job, but for some reason I could never earn enough money to get my own place. I'd also been in and out of jail a couple times. After I'd finally gotten a decent job and a place to live, they were like, "We're all moving to San Francisco. Do you wanna go?" Back then they were just kids. Everybody lived at home except Ed.

Ed Tarantino: I'd already lived in the Bay Area, so it wasn't as much of a transition for me, but I don't think Rodney or Kili had even been off the island before. I remember I picked them up, and there were these massive trucks barreling down the 880, and I was weaving in and out of traffic, and they were in the back of my pickup truck, just fuckin' tripping on everything.

Kili got a job at Burger King, and the first night he worked there, they got held up at gunpoint and locked in the freezer.

Kili Kaohu: We lived in San Leandro, and our place had three bedrooms, but I think it was cheap because it was in the hood. There were shootings all the time and shit. We just needed the basic necessities of life and a jam room. We were getting gigs maybe once or twice a month. I remember we opened for D.R.I. and Death Angel at the Omni in Oakland.

Ed Tarantino: I think the band was motivated by Aftershock, who were a really good, really tight thrash band from Hawaii that moved up to the Bay Area to make it. We kind of followed in their footsteps, and our apartment wasn't far from where the Aftershock guys were.

For good or bad, it was a mecca for metal because there were a ton of bands, and venues were booking that stuff, so there was an audience for it, that's for sure. But there was also more competition, and one of the bigger venues, the Omni, got to the point where they told the bands they had a minimum amount of tickets they had to sell on their own to get on the bill. It was basically a pay-to-play model.

Kili Kaohu: We came back to Hawaii to play a couple shows. Matt Yoshihara from Tarrasque set it up and paid for our plane tickets and everything. That whole thing came out of Matt's pocket. While we were away, that's when we got jacked.

We just came back from the airport, and we were pulling in to our apartment, and our front door was wide open—*what the fuck?* Jaime, he got out of the car, walks in. "FUCK!" He starts snapping. We walked into a nightmare. We had no TV, no stereo, and they trashed the place. It's like somebody went in there and used it as a crash pad or something. The refrigerator and freezer doors were wide open, and it was stinking because the electricity was turned off. They fuckin' trashed the place, man. They left holes in the wall. It reeked of…Yeah, there was no way we were staying there. We bailed. That was '91. Alton didn't come back with us. He decided to stay there.

Ed Tarantino: Jaime's car was stolen 'cause they found the keys in the apartment. They ran off with it and dumped it somewhere. I think that shook them up pretty badly. I'd moved out of the band apartment by that time, but they didn't want to stay there anymore. They were totally devastated by it. So that kind of drove the band back to Hawaii.

Randy Szucs: They were only up there for a year, but that year to me felt like an eternity. They were making a name for themselves, and I'd go to Jelly's and get their new album with Alton singing for the band. Broken Man meant a lot to me. That whole "broken man" thing was kinda true, I felt, 'cause I was pretty broken for a while.

Kili Kaohu: When we got back home, our friends encouraged us to call Randy, and it turned out, yeah, he wanted to do the band thing again. Within a few months we put Broken Man back together and we were doing solid.

Rico Lago, the promoter, got us a lot of shows, and we got help from Mari Matsuoka too, doing a bunch of shows: Helmet, D.R.I., Sepultura, Ministry. After Ed left in '92 or '93, Casey Honma from Tarrasque stepped in on bass, and we recorded our EP in '95.

Chris Esteron: Later on in the '90s, when Pat Ohta was working for Goldenvoice, he would sometimes hire me as extra security for shows. This one time, when Broken Man opened up for Suicidal Tendencies at After Dark, I was backstage watching the show, and this dude came up and stood next to me, just watching Kili play drums, and I realized it was the drummer from Suicidal. He's like, "You know that guy?"

"Yeah."

And he goes, all excited: "He's fucking *amazing*. Top ten drummers in my life!"

A few months later, Sepultura played here, and I remember I was asked to take them to a bar next to the venue to get some food, and same thing. The drummer for Sepultura, Igor, was like, "You know this drummer?"

And I was like, "Yeah."

He goes, "Favorite drummers, number one: Bill Ward. Number two: Dave Lombardo. Number three, your friend."

Dude, Igor Cavalera is a *beast* on drums. For him to say that about Kili is no joke. That's high fucking praise.

Randy Szucs: Kili was awesome and always so aggro on the drums. And he was really young too, just ahead of his time. We used to have to borrow drums in the beginning, but when he invested in a real kit and just focused on it, that Hawaiian talent really came through. Kili's drumming was always one of the best aspects of the band. He was so dope.

Kili Kaohu: My full first name is Hekiliokalani, which means "The thunders of the heavens." My mom named me that. I don't think she could've known that I would end up playing drums in a heavy metal band, but it's an appropriate name. Right on, Mom. Good call.

Randy Szucs: Broken Man did have a little bit of hype. When they went to the Bay Area, they got a buzz because they were different. What they did was they pressed our album, *Absolution*. I gave them artwork and they made this marbled vinyl with this weird insert that wasn't even a real album sleeve. It was just this weird thing this guy put together. He might've sent us, like, fifty copies of it. I'd recently found a bunch of our shit on eBay and I just bought it all. We never got any distribution. We signed a contract and that was it, man. It was kind of dumb. We probably needed some kind of guidance from a manager or somebody who had it more together and could guide us through the business.

Kili Kaohu: Rodney was about to get his registered nurse degree that he was working on for five or six years, and at that point his final semester was coming up, and with all that studying, it was gonna be hard to jam. I was training as a cook and there was a lot to learn. Randy went to computer school and when he earned his degree, he got a job in Seattle. We all had shit that took us away from our music. The last show we played was with Testament in August of 2000.

Randy Szucs: When Rodney told me he didn't know how much time he would have to commit to the band, I was like, "Fuck, I'm gone then." Jaime had already left and we were a four-piece by then. I always felt like Rodney was the band's foundation. He was always our most solid guy, and he'd been writing a lot of the music. What was I going to stay in Hawaii for? I didn't have any family there, a lot of my friends had already left for the mainland, and one of the main reasons, if not the only reason I was staying was because of Broken Man. I really believed we could do something great.

We probably should've tried to tour years earlier, but maybe that's where that local mentality comes in where playing with major bands in your hometown seems like enough at the time. We got to open for Ozzy Osbourne and Marilyn Manson. We got to play with Slayer and Red Hot Chili Peppers, Danzig, Pantera, bands like that. That right there is a pretty decent list of bands to play with.

NOTHING'S FOREVER

Jason Reece: Something changed in me. I wanted to take music seriously, I guess. I knew Conrad Keely, my bandmate in Trail of Dead, from going to school at Kalaheo. He was this fuckin' hippie prog dude who was into Rush and Yes, and he lived a block away from me when I first moved to

Kailua. When he moved from Hawaii to Olympia, Washington, he wrote me letters about seeing Fugazi and the Melvins, and the idea of being on the mainland and seeing all these great bands was really attractive. If I really wanted to be in a band that toured and put out records, it was going to be way more difficult to do it from Hawaii. 1990 was when I moved to Olympia.

Earl Crawford: You think those times will last forever, but nothing's forever. You know, when my brother passed, it was fast, it was abrupt, and no one saw it coming. He had a muscle virus that attached itself to his heart, and basically it just slowly killed his heart's ability to be a muscle. It became more of a sponge; it became an enlarged heart. The doctors said he had the largest heart in the state of Hawaii, and at some point it filled his whole chest cavity. That's how he knew something was wrong. He couldn't breathe one night, and I guess his heart expanded so much it was pushing up against his lungs. He went in to check it out on a Friday; the family went to visit on Saturday, we joked around, and he was like "Don't worry about it." What he never told us was they gave him six months to live.

Then Sunday morning he calls me to bring him some clothes, and when I get to the hospital, walking down the hallway, everyone's running into his room; you hear the beeping alarm and I'm like, "Oh no." I walk in, turn my head, and I see him convulsing on the bed with three or four guys on both sides trying to hold him down. I was tripping the fuck out.

They put me in a room and twenty minutes later, some doctor came in and asked, "Did anyone talk to you yet?" and he goes, "They told me your brother passed away."

Yeah, it was kinda nuts. Growing up, playing with him, I always had visions of us playing music together for the rest of our lives, so when he died, I felt lost. I had a really hard time. I had a hard time wanting to play music.

Willie Fruean: I just couldn't go to his funeral. I remember taking a shower and I just couldn't go. I totally freaked out, like, "I can't do this." It scared me 'cause prior to that, I had another friend die, and

I had to be a pallbearer at his funeral. It's just fucking traumatizing. I just thought, *Fuck this, I'm not going to anybody's funeral. They're dead anyway, they understand.* But still. I mean, I think funerals are for you, not the dead person.

Randy Szucs: That was pretty heavy. But growing up, I never really dwelled on those things because I had Peter Pan syndrome. I just thought it would all last forever, to be honest with you. As you grow older you realize we're really only here for a short time, but all the things we experienced, that's embedded in me until I die; it's part of me. I'll never forget it.

16

ALOHA, HONOLULU

It was in 1983, the year following his mother's passing, that Frank Orrall experienced his first bout of wanderlust. With neither a time frame nor the promise of a return, he packed his bags for Los Angeles, where his brother Malcolm had been living, and sent his musical cohorts in Honolulu scrambling to replace him. Just as Robert Scott had been recruited in his stead to be the new face of Mumbo Jumbo, James Ganeko held the drumsticks in Frank's absence from Hat Makes the Man. The move spurred a four-column story in the *Honolulu Advertiser's* entertainment section, emphasizing Orrall's impact on the underground rock community.

It wasn't long before Frank found work as a runner on several Hollywood movie sets, though most of the motion pictures he jobbed for failed to make an impression anywhere. "The only one that saw the light of a projector was *Breakin'*," remembers Orrall, whose graffiti-style handiwork can be seen on the jackets of the film's villainous crew, Electro Rock, as well as on the main stage of Radiotron, the club where the movie's most pivotal dance battles took place.

In the film's opening sequence, a young street dancer poplocks atop a cement wall with the words "Palolo Boys" spray-painted beneath him. For decades, this curious detail has elicited gasps of wonder from Oahuans, dumbstruck as to how a Honolulu neighborhood's namesake could have appeared in a major motion picture. "I used to live in Palolo for a while," shares Orrall with a chuckle. "So I did that as a wink to Hawaii."

As he began experimenting with his brother's Tascam four-track recorder, ideas and possibilities danced in Frank's head. Though an ace drummer, he was adept on several other instruments, and a process of recording a rudimentary guitar line, then another, then bass and vocals began to take shape. Soon, ideas and lyrics came rushing forth. "As soon as I started writing songs, I knew that's what I wanted to do," he reveals. "I wanted to be in that seat of writing songs and playing them and singing them."

This solo project, which he dubbed Poi Dog Pondering, resulted in a new arsenal of songs for Orrall, who would eventually record five homespun Poi Dog cassette-only releases in four years. Upon his return to the Islands the following year, a number of his inspired compositions were absorbed by Hat Makes the Man and gave the band's setlist greater diversity and punching power. One particular song, "Searching for the Fertile Fields," became the title track to their second and final release in 1985, an exquisitely recorded live LP that perfectly captures Hat Makes the Man at peak potential, all cylinders firing.

For Orrall, however, it was only the beginning. In 1986, a jumbled crew of Honolulu musicians assembled under the Poi Dog Pondering banner and embarked on a freewheeling busking expedition of North America, eventually settling in Austin, Texas, where more musicians were added to the fold. Orrall and two members of his earliest ensemble, Abra Moore and Sean Coffey, even landed roles in Richard Linklater's Austin-based, generation-defining cult film dramedy, *Slacker*. In little time, Poi Dog Pondering joined the short list of Hawaii-born bands to have earned a recording deal with a major label, delivering albums for Columbia Records into the early 1990s.

In 1997, under the mentorship of industry executive and music impresario Clive Davis, who founded Arista Records, Moore also tasted national success as a solo artist, charting Billboard's Hot 100 with "Four Leaf Clover" and earning a Grammy nomination in 1998 for Best Female Rock Vocal Performance. "What luck to fall in with Frank and that crew and just having a positive influence on my creative path," says Moore, recalling the formative friendships and musical ties made in her late teens in Honolulu. "I was super fortunate."

Kalea Chapman: Almost every weekend, I would be at the Wave just to check out Hat Makes the Man. They were so good. I worked at a sandwich store in Ala Moana, and I would go see Hat Makes the Man after work. I just reeked of sprouts and I had a horrible uniform on, but they were awesome. They were such a good band. It was like going to a concert because the sound system at the Wave was amazing. Peter Bond was such a rock star, and Frank just exuded charisma from behind the drum kit. That was always kind of amazing to me: how can you front a band from the drum kit, you know? It was extremely impressive.

Robert Scott: I don't know if you've ever seen Frank perform, but his energy is like a bright, shining star wherever he goes, and his smile is so genuine and just lights up the whole room. When he plays, he's got a really infectious spirit, and it really touches people. You just never forget it.

Abra Moore (vocalist/guitarist: Poi Dog Pondering; solo artist): When I was sixteen, I started dating this musician named Bobby who was twenty-three or twenty-four and was from Oahu but was going to UH-Hilo. I met him at a gig at a restaurant in Pahoa, and he was in this band called Deviant Sheep. My parents let me date him, and when they played at Wave Waikiki, I would fly to Oahu, and he would smuggle me into the Wave, and that's where I met people like Frank, who was playing in Hat Makes the Man, and John Nelson from the Pagan Babies.

    I graduated from Pahoa High School, brah—home of the Daggers—and I moved to Oahu for college. I had some college friends who were

Poi Dog Pondering on the road in Seattle, August 1986.
Courtesy of Helen McQueen

friends with Frank. He was super fun and encouraging and supportive, creatively and musically, and we all connected through this community of artists, musicians, poets, writers, and friends who moved in those circles. I just naturally fell in with them. It was like we all spoke the same language.

Sean Coffey (drummer: Poi Dog Pondering, Food, Love Crabs, etc.): I would go see Hat Makes the Man shows just to watch Frank and try to learn to play drums. I used to ride the bus over to Waikiki at fifteen with my fake ID to watch him play, then sleep under a hedge or a garage roof somewhere if I missed the last bus back. That happened often.

I saw Kalea Chapman sing a couple songs with Hat Makes the Man at the Wave, and I was already following Frank Orrall around like a puppy, so for Kalea to be brought up there by Frank to sing made him a star in my eyes. I insisted we start a band, and Kalea brought Ted Cho and Cliff Kamida along right away. Cliff came up with the name Love Crabs. Then came Alan Sinton on bass, and in our first practice I thought we were already pretty good.

We played a gig at, I believe, the YWCA across from UH, and Frank was there and he raved about us. The next time I saw him, he was wearing a T-shirt that said, "I'm in love with the Love Crabs."

When Frank quit Hat, the Love Crabs were slated to take their slot at the Wave, but Frank asked a group of us if anyone wanted to go on the road with him and busk, and I immediately said yes; then Kalea followed about a week later, and that was the end of the Crabs. I was seventeen when Poi Dog went on the road.

Kalea Chapman: Love Crabs played the Manoa coffeehouse at the YWCA right off campus from UH; we played at Anna Bannana's, and we actually played a gig at the Wave, which we felt was the biggest thing ever. Frank was playing there and he loved us.

It was through Ted Cho, our guitarist, who seemed to know everyone, that we ended up playing on the street with Frank, and to me, that was like playing music with God. He was so charismatic and just the coolest guy on earth. Robert Scott joined us, and collectively, we played as Food. We'd play some of Frank's songs and also do these acoustic cover songs.

Food was a fun group 'cause people would come and go and we'd play out in public, on sidewalks.

Frank Orrall: A bunch of us, as a group, would end up down in Waikiki to play on the street. It was super loose and we'd play whatever we wanted to play. That whole experience was really fun for me, and I wanted to leave the island and travel across the States. Hat Makes the Man wasn't ready or into uprooting and getting into a car and just driving around and figuring something out on the continent, but these guys I was playing with in this street band, they were all into it. They were like, "Yeah, let's go to the mainland—let's just go travel around and play in the street!"

Kalea Chapman: We probably would not have played on the street by ourselves, but with Frank there sort of legitimizing the activity, he got us doing things we would not have done. It's super fun to play with Frank. He has so much energy and really quickly, he can draw a crowd.

Me, Frank, and Sean got arrested one night 'cause we were performing in front of Woolworth in Waikiki. We saw the cops coming and we had a guitar case open for money, and Frank kind of kicked it shut, and the cop was like, "Too late, bruddah." They charged us with pedestrian congestion. It was very silly, but they did put us in the back of a car and cuff us. My dad had to come pick me up.

Abra Moore: Frank was like, "Be quiet, Abra!" and I was all *tita* at the time, trying to be confrontational with the cops."Abra, don't talk!"

They didn't want me to get arrested too, and I was just running my mouth. I grew up in Puna, out there in Opihikao on the Big Island, and all my friends were Hawaiian and local, and I could switch to pidgin as fast as anybody.

Frank Orrall: We talked to the whole group of people who were playing on the street—there were probably fifteen people in that circle—and said, "Anyone who wants to go, we're going to meet at the airport on this day. We're going to fly to LA." Nine people showed up, man. Blew my mind. We literally just sold everything and came over to the mainland.

Some of them were Love Crabs guys: Kalea Chapman; Ted Cho; Abra Moore, who wasn't in Love Crabs but she knew all those folks;

Sean Coffey; Matt Miller from Hat; Jean Francois Berneron, who's a photographer friend of mine, a French guy and also a singer who I wrote songs with; and a couple of friends who weren't musicians but were down for the adventure.

Kalea Chapman: Frank was always super enthusiastic about *On the Road*, the Kerouac book. I had read it as well. So there was kind of a vague notion of how we were going to be living our lives out on the road. It was all very romantic.

Frank Orrall: We flew over. I had a car there that I bought from my brother, and we bought a GMC Suburban. I had some friends who had a spare garage, and they let us sleep there and use it as a staging area.

We started driving up the western seaboard. All we knew is we wanted to travel and just adventure and there was no destination, but we hoped to get all the way across the States, and we hoped to get to Europe. It was a freeform trip. We went all the way up to Canada and played on the street for food and gas money. We came back down, went down through the South, and made it all the way to New York, and at that point, it was eight months later. We were pretty beat up. A lot of people left along the way.

Matthew Miller: I was already the bass player in Poi Dog, and when Hat Makes the Man came to an end and Frank decided he was going to do his road tour, I was ready to make the jump. I was kind of tired of Hawaii at that point and wanted to check out the mainland.

It was fun. We went to LA, got our vehicles together. It was a fun group of people. We were sleeping at rest stops and traveling, and we went into Canada and played at his girlfriend's place up in Hinton, Alberta, which is beautiful. It was a really fun road experience, and I think I was on it for three months before I was like, "Get me an apartment!" I needed to have a shower and a warm bed to sleep in. I was tired of sleeping at rest stops and busking for money and being cold, but Frank *thrives* on it. That guy loves that kind of stuff. Oftentimes the trickiest thing was finding where we were going to sleep.

We had two cars: a GMC long-bed truck that we had all our instruments in, and then Frank had his 1965 Mustang. Four people could sit in that car. The Mustang broke down in California, in Bakersfield. So we were stuck in Bakersfield, and we were like, "Where are we gonna sleep?" We ended up going to an elementary school. It was summertime, so it was closed, and we slept underneath the eaves of this elementary school the whole night, thinking that we were gonna be busted by the police at any moment.

Frank Orrall: So we get into San Francisco and go down to Market Street and play. We really didn't make very much money there, maybe twelve dollars from businesspeople throwing us change, so we'd go to Fisherman's Wharf and then we'd play some more. But then at night, you couldn't go sleep in the park because you'd get run off, so you'd have to drive out to Sonoma or Napa and sleep on top of haystacks and then come back into the city to play again.

We started finding a rhythm with it. What worked was playing in front of college coffeehouses, you know, 'cause they were more like our age, our peer group, and they would always invite us over: "Oh, you can stay at our house." So that became kind of like a thing; we'd just play out in front of college coffeehouses all across the states. Whatever was gonna happen was gonna happen. We used to have this little saying: "We invited chaos to be the front seat driver of the Poi bus."

Kalea Chapman: There were only a dozen or maybe two dozen nights in over eight or nine months of traveling that we weren't in somebody's house. People just took us in. And again, I think that a lot of that has to do with Frank and his charisma.

We got a fantastic reception at UCLA. We made, like, $300 or something, selling cassette tapes and T-shirts, with a lot of twenty-dollar bills thrown in. We had this cheapo tape duplicating machine, and you could copy one tape to another, and to do them quickly, you would duplicate them at triple speed.

UC Berkeley, we had a great reception there. We actually got booked for a gig on UC Davis's soundstage in front of the campus lawn, which was a really fun place to play as well. We quickly discovered that we were going to do well on college campuses. There was no question that was our audience.

Sean Coffey: We kept going somehow, and things got better. We were busking every day to feed ourselves, and Frank's sister sent him some money. Eventually, we really became this tight, kind of guerilla band that swept through college towns and ended up on college radio stations. That, I think, laid the foundation for the bidding war later for Frank's music. College radio was already aware of Poi Dog Pondering.

The Poi crew at UC Berkeley, 1986. *Courtesy of Helen McQueen*

Matthew Miller: It was just fun and free. I wish I'd had more of an ability to kind of hang with it and enjoy the feeling of going from Point A to Point B and not knowing what you're going to see, what you're going to do, how you're going to eat, where you're going to sleep, and not caring about it, but it came to be too much of a taxing thing in my head after a while. My girlfriend went on the trip with us too, and we both got out in San Francisco. The band kept going.

Kalea Chapman: Once, we slept underneath this restaurant, and we made a fire and cooked beans in a can. We ate *a lot* of bean burritos. Our diet was not very good. There were times we were pretty hungry.

Frank Orrall: We were driving to Austin because Michael Corcoran and Rollo were living in Austin, and they were telling me, "Hey, you gotta get out here—the music scene's amazing!" And so we were in El Paso, the westernmost part of Texas, and if you drive a straight line from El Paso, you can get to Austin. Going down the western seaboard, there were lots of college towns everywhere, but as you get into the heart of the West—Phoenix, Las Cruces—they get farther and farther apart. All of a sudden, we were running out of money, and we were pawning instruments, we were pawning cameras, we were pawning jewelry trying to get there.

We thought we were going to pick up hitchhikers and say, "We'll drive you, but you gotta pitch in for gas." That was our new scam. So we pick up this guy and he goes, "Yeah, my truck just died, and I don't have any money, but if you drive me to San Antonio, I'll give you forty bucks." That's way south, but forty bucks is forty bucks, and that would get us up to Austin for sure.

Me and Sean and Jean are sitting up front with this guy, and this guy's teaching us how to draft trucks, where you can spare gas by getting in the back stream of trucks and letting this wind vacuum behind the truck pull you along. He was teaching us about flashing the lights and how you communicate with truckers, and that was fascinating, but this guy also smelled really bad, and Abra was in the back seat going, "No fucking way. This guy's a drifter." It turns out, yeah, he was totally a drifter, and when we got there, he told us, "I'll be right back with your forty bucks" and disappeared into the night.

Abra Moore: I had doubts right away. "Oh, take me there and I'll get you your money." Nope. We just ended up stranded there and busking in some parking lot to get some money to get to Austin.

Frank Orrall: We basically rode into Austin on fumes, and we stopped at the outskirts because we didn't know anything about the town. It was four in the morning, cold as fuck, and we were sleeping in the car and I was freezing, so I got out and slept on the hood because the engine block was still warm. I remember getting woken up by this cop and immediately started explaining myself: "I'm so sorry, I was tired, I was driving and pulled over..." He said, "No, no, no, it's cool. I just wanted to make sure you were still alive. I found a guy out here with four bullet holes in his head last week."

Kalea Chapman: I was impressed with Austin. The people just seemed really cool there, and it seemed like a very hip town with lots of great music happening. It also had this Southern flavor that I didn't really know because I didn't know Southern people, but it kind of fit with our Honolulu kind of vibe. It's laid back and casual and I really liked it there. We were pretty ragged, though. The New Mexico to Texas thing was pretty brutal. One of the first people we met in Austin later described us as looking like we were completely emaciated. It was like he felt it was his moral obligation to take us in.

Abra Moore: Austin was very welcoming. Artists, poets, dancers, the whole community there embraced us. We quickly made all kinds of friends, and that's when the second phase of Poi was born. All of these amazing, incredible musicians started to get involved. They were all in bands and they knew these people and they knew those people, and all of a sudden we had these connections.

Sean Coffey: Our luck had changed. I remember we made friends pretty quick, and it was just an awesome time: cheap rent; smart, loose college girls; and cheap beer. Austin somehow made everywhere else seem square and boring. *Slacker*, which a few of us were a part of, was an accurate depiction of Austin at the time. It really was like the film. All those people were just cast as themselves.

Frank Orrall: We loved Austin so much, we stayed there for two months. But we kept moving on. We went through Louisiana and New Orleans; Athens, Georgia, and stuff; and wound up in New York, where there was a whole expat crew. Lesa Griffith was there, Arnie was there, Robert Scott was there; there was a whole Hawaii contingent.

Lesa Griffith: I wasn't sure if I wanted to go into book publishing or magazine publishing. In the meantime, Arnie had moved out to New York, and so when I got there, I actually stayed with him first, up on 96th Street or somewhere on the Upper West Side. A small Hawaii crew kind of developed there. I think he got kicked out of the apartment he was subletting, and we found this place on Lexington Avenue and 28th Street. It was a former veterinary building, and our apartment had these super rustic, wide floorboards and a fireplace. It was like being in a farmhouse. I don't remember how much we paid, but there were three of us living there, and I had a view of the Empire State Building from my window.

Arnie Saiki: It was tremendous, on so many different levels, to have Poi Dog Pondering there. Having more people from Hawaii in New York, there was a lot more activity. Instead of being alone or either with Robert or Lesa, now there was a whole group of people to explore the city with. For us, those days were absolutely magical.

Robert Scott: Eventually, Arnie and I got a place on Bleecker Street, where legend has it Janis Joplin stayed. Poi Dog got to New York, and a bunch of them stayed with us, and our New York roommates were all mad at them because they said the Hawaiians sucked up all the cool air.

I would ask, "How was it on the road? How was that experience?" and they would get this glazed-over look. I was expecting a story of how great and fun it was and everything, and they'd have this blank look on their faces.

Kalea Chapman: Robert Scott and Arnie were both living in New York, and some of us were living with them for a little while in a tiny little apartment. We played a few times in Washington Square. I don't think we made a lot of money, but we had a good reception. Robert was there, so he did some songs; he would always come out and sing, like, "Goo Goo Muck" and "Blister in the Sun."

I could have chosen to continue, but my mindset was, "I just want a roof over my head and a job, and I just want to live a normal life." I was ready. I stayed in New York and I remember we all kind of scattered. We didn't spend a lot of time with each other. We just needed to recharge. My dreams of life on the road were completely fulfilled for a lifetime.

Frank Orrall: A lot of people went their separate ways from there. Ted went back to Austin right away. I went to San Francisco to track a demo, and I ended up getting a record contract from an LA-based label called Texas Hotel. John Nelson, one of our Poi members, and Matt Miller were there. Me, Matt Miller, and Abra Moore made the first Poi Dog demo out there in the Bay Area. We lived there for a while, but it was kinda hard for a little bit, you know, broke and living in a warehouse in the East Bay. We met a friend of ours, Bruce Hughes. He's a bass player in Austin. We ended up traveling back to Austin with him to drive him home for Christmas and then decided to just make the record in Austin 'cause there were so many good musicians there.

Abra Moore: At that point I was like, "Okay, I'm done." I was done with the chaos of traveling, and I just wanted to settle in Austin. I got a little job working at Whole Foods and started playing in bands around Austin. I just wanted to chill out, but then several years later, I ended up having my own career, and I did more touring than I'd ever wanted to do in my life.

Frank Orrall: When I was a kid growing up in Hawaii Kai, one of my best friends and his older brother had some guy from the mainland renting a room from them, and he had all these rock posters—this is back in the mid-'70s—so we used to sneak in his room and check out all these great rock posters. I didn't know who the guy was. I just knew he was a tenant.

Fast-forward to '84, when I was living in LA, I took my first Poi Dog cassette album to sell at a place called Vinyl Fetish. The record buyer there was the only guy in California to buy these Poi Dog Pondering cassettes with hand-painted covers on consignment, and we got to talking and he's like, "Poi, that's a Hawaii thing, right?"

I go, "Yeah, I grew up in Hawaii."

"Oh yeah, I used to live there for a while." And we figured out that's the guy who was renting the room from those guys. That was Michael Meister from Vinyl Fetish. He and Susan Farrell started a label called Texas Hotel, and they also had a record store. Poi Dog's first gig on the continent was there in the record store; we did an in-store there. Later on, when they started the label, they asked me if I wanted to make records with them.

We made two EPs with Texas Hotel. They were a really good record label. I mean, Henry Rollins was on that record label; Vic Chestnutt was on that record label; Hetch Hetchy, which was Micharl Stipe's sister's band; Downy Mildew... like, a super indie-cred label. We did a label showcase in New York. We played at CBGBs, and we played some other club. I remember meeting Henry Rollins in the basement of CBGBs and meekly going up to him: "Hi Henry, we're on the same label; my name's Frank."

He goes, "Welcome to hell."

It was pretty fantastic to be playing there, and there was a serious buzz surrounding the band. We got offers from all the majors: Warner Brothers, A&M, Capitol, Columbia. Nobody saw that coming. It was like whiplash. I didn't want to leave Texas Hotel, but it's hard to come back to your band and go, "No" when all of a sudden there's the possibility of renting tour buses and taking the band all over the place and having a budget to be able to do that.

I made sure to do a co-deal so that Texas Hotel was still involved and I could still deal with them on a personal basis and make records while Columbia would be the distribution wing. That felt like a pretty sweet compromise to me. So we signed with Columbia for better or for worse. They were the ones that promised the most creative control, and I could also keep our publishing. Everybody else wanted half our publishing. It was a rough-ass experience for me because I was so used to being in that "indie bosom," and the major labels aren't in it for any cultural reasons, so I was glad when we finally got dropped by them.

But it was a great experience. It took us across the States, back and forth, multiple times. We had the budget to swing the bat, where I could direct my own videos for a while, things like that. When all the dust had settled, it also gave me knowledge and fortitude so that when I got out of that contract, we just started our own record label: "Ah, fuck this, we already know how to do this; we'll just do this ourselves." Being around the major label system, we knew how to rent tour buses and put a budget together to make a video; we knew how to look for distributors.

They promised us the world, but it's not necessarily the way things played out. I negotiated an instrumental record and a children's record, but after *Wishing Like a Mountain*, I recorded instrumentals with an experimental artist named Ellen Fullman. Kit Ebersbach also came out, and we made this beautiful instrumental record that was supposed to be Poi Dog's third album. An A&R guy basically came down from New York and said, "Look, contractually, you can release this, but we'll just drop you." It pissed me off because I'm like, "Wait a minute, I thought we agreed on this!" And they said, "We want a vocal record."

The only thing that worked was that they said, "Look, you can just have this record. You already made it, you mixed it. Just make us a vocal record." The instrumental sessions became Palm Fabric Orchestra, and then I went back and recorded *Volo Volo* as their vocal record. That's why I have the boxing gloves on the cover of *Volo Volo*.

Abra Moore: I think Frank gave me this four-track, and I started demoing songs. I was always writing songs because it's just in my nature, I guess, and I signed with this indie singer-songwriter label called Bohemia Beat Records and made my first record, *Sing*. I traveled all over Europe, and it was really wonderful and a lovely introduction into the industry, very mellow. I had a good family around me. Clive Davis got wind of that record and wanted to sign me to Arista.

Everything's an opportunity in a positive way. It's like, wow, you have this amazing crew of people that believe in you, and they want to help you with your creative expression. What a gift, right? "Four Leaf Clover" completely opened doors for me. Can you imagine, this local girl from Opihikao hanging out with Alicia Keys at Clive's house? When he left Arista, he wanted me and Alicia Keys to go with him to his new label, and he flew us up there to his house. Alicia was just coming on the scene and had just made her very first record. I was working on the next record, trying to make Clive a really Top 40 pop record, which wasn't in my wheelhouse, but I was just trying to please everybody at that time.

The cool thing about Clive Davis as a businessman is the business part and the art part are separate. So the artist in him loved my music. I remember when he flew me out to his office, he had the lights down and he was playing this song I wrote called "Happiness," and he was just twirling around in his chair, going, "This is just beautiful, Abra! It's beautiful!" It wasn't a single and it wasn't something that was going to make money. It was just something that he was enjoying. For me, that was like winning a Grammy.

But when it came to making a record and making money, that was a whole different can of worms. I was going into media training to learn how to deal with media and writing with every hitmaker to make that follow-up record to *Strangest Places*. So all of a sudden, I'm cutting singles that I didn't even write; these Top 40 pop songs that are zeroed in and focused on sixteen-year-olds. It just disregarded my whole grassroots foundation, and it kind of left me like, "Ooh, I don't know…" It left all the radio stations and people who supported me scratching their heads.

At the end of the day, it just wasn't feeling right and I said, "I'm not feeling it." Clive apologized and said, "I'm sorry, I'm really good at putting people in a certain box, and you deserve to be on a boutique label where you can be what you want." So we parted ways, and he gave me the record, which was gracious after all that.

I kind of shook the record out, took some of the pop singles off of it and finished it and put it out on another label. It all worked out as it was supposed to. It's such a cool thing to know as opposed to "what if." There's no "what if."

17

DAM NATION

Seated at the base of Honolulu's Manoa Valley—in the shadow of the high-rise enclave of Makiki and a short walk from the University of Hawaii's flagship campus—is Punahou School. The esteemed institution, established in 1841 by American missionaries, ranks among the nation's top prep schools. It's known for its illustrious alumni, which includes Steve Case, billionaire co-founder of America Online; actress Kelly Preston; professional golfer Michelle Wie; and the 44th President of the United States, Barack Obama. In Hawaii, where identity is often tied to one's high school, a connection to Punahou prompts a range of reactions, from admiration to envy to contempt.

Feelings on the beloved Punahou Carnival, however, are much more consistent. For nearly a century, festive throngs from all over Oahu have flocked to the school's campus every first weekend in February for an outing of amusement rides, food booths, games, and live entertainment. Concerts, which have long been among the event's favorite draws, have featured homegrown pop singers, comedians, and Hawaiian music combos, though on occasion, an atypical act might slip through the cracks.

More than a decade before joining Royal Crown Revue, the pioneering Los Angeles ensemble that launched the massive American swing revival movement of the 1990s, Daniel Glass had been the beat-minder for a moderately successful Punahou rock outfit. As Glass recalls, not long after selling his Sonar drum set to local punk rocker Johnee Kop, he was startled to see a ravaged version of his old kit on stage at the carnival with Kop hammering away on it. "I was scared shitless when I saw his band play," admits Glass. "There was a girl with them with ripped-up fishnet stockings and heavy eyeliner, and she was slam dancing with the rest of the band, and she got a bloody nose. It was so violent." The band called itself Anti-Parent, and the capital "A" in their logo was circled to symbolize anarchy. "I was so freaked out by the whole thing," Glass divulges.

It was the early 1980s, and as well as the musical performances, carnival-goers delighted in perusing the event's white elephant tent for bargains on donated books and records. It was at one such sale that Punahou student Dave Derby discovered a trove of twenty-five-cent LPs underscored by a copy of The Jam's *All Mod Cons*. Although a few years belated and 7,000 miles removed from the British mod revival of the late '70s, Derby enjoyed a modicum of glory with a Jam-like trio he formed shortly thereafter called Communiqué. As they gigged about town, the high school juniors quickly gained a loyal fan base of bona fide, parka-wearing, Vespa-riding mods. "We'd be talking to these kinda cute UH girls and their mod friends, and we really thought we'd cracked the code by having these college people following us," Derby confesses. Soon came an invitation to play the inaugural Pacific New Music Festival, a two-day musical event at La Mancha, the Ke'eaumoku Street cabaret, with Hat Makes the Man, Mumbo Jumbo, Battery Club, and a number of Oahu's rising underground bands. "That was the biggest thing I'd done musically at that point," he surmises.

At the time, Communiqué seemed an absolute triumph compared to Derby's previous project, a floundering musical troupe known as The Exactones, who had not yet lived down a dismal performance at a school function the previous year. As class president, Derby had taken charge of entertainment and hired his own band for the sophomore class luau at Sea Life Park. When The Exactones appeared, the crowd groaned. "They were famous for being the worst band," reveals high school chum Eric Friedl. "Everyone liked them personally but dreaded having to sit through their songs at talent shows. They were not universally loved by our classmates."

Though far from headliner material, Derby believed enough in its potential to give The Exactones another go-round once Communiqué had run its course. By late 1984, when most of its membership had begun studying at mainland universities, The Exactones agreed to reconvene in Honolulu every winter, spring, and summer break to play live, record songs, and submit demos to record labels and magazines. In time, the execution became crisper, the hooks sharper, the songs more fluid. It took dedication and some fortuity, but from these efforts came The Dambuilders, the final and most fruitful iteration in a particular line of musical ventures for Derby.

With the colossal alt-rock wave of the 1990s looming, The Dambuilders' ever-sharpening craft for keen and catchy songwriting, and a timely move to Boston, proved to be the difference between another near-hit from Hawaii and an internationally acclaimed indie rock sensation signed to the same label as such heavyweights as AC/DC, Pantera, and Sisters of Mercy.

Eric Friedl a.k.a. Eric Oblivian (vocalist: The Exactones; vocalist/ multi-instrumentalist: the Oblivians, Dutch Masters, etc.; co-owner/ founder of Goner Records): I came to Hawaii when I was twelve. That was right when punk was first happening. You might have heard about punk rock in the early days, but you never actually heard it, at least for me, as a normal kid without cool older brothers or anything. It took a couple years. But I was really excited about that stuff because the media coverage of the Sex Pistols was so over the top. People were so scared of these guys. I thought it was gonna be people playing vacuum cleaners and throwing up on everybody, total mayhem. When I finally heard it, I thought it just sounded like music, and I was totally disappointed.

The weird thing about The Exactones is when I met them, they were really into The Who and Steely Dan, but also The Contortions and James White & the Blacks and all this no-wave stuff. It was this weird mix of popular music and then music by guys who couldn't play at all. The idea was, "If those guys can get a record deal, then we can definitely get a record deal."

I was just kind of a hanger-on, more of a fan than anything, and even though they already had two vocalists, they decided that I should be their singer without actually being able to sing.

Dave Derby: At this time, the band was me, Tryan George, Eric Masunaga, our drummer Keoki Van Orden, and Eric Friedl, who's since gone on to be in this really hugely successful garage band, the Oblivians.

Eric Masunaga was just learning to engineer and produce, and writing and recording just became what a lot of our focus was. From that came the tapes that we'd put out and try to sell at Jelly's and Hungry Ear. We sent them out to a bunch of national magazines and started to get good reviews.

But there was this thing where we really wanted to play live a lot more, and we were just sort of Punahou assholes. We didn't really fit in, but we were trying. Hawaii always had a scene for bands that were really hardcore—bands that we liked—but we just weren't that. We were maybe weirder, more poppy, and kind of all over the place, trying to figure out who we were.

One time we played this show in Kalihi that I think I asked Dave Carr if we could play at. This is when he was in The Vacuum, and there were lots of goth people there, and definitely a lot of the hardcore bad-asses were there too. We showed up and Dave was like, "Hey, you know, maybe just play a short set and…well, you guys might get your asses kicked." He was glad to let us do the gig, but it was like, "Good luck."

Eric Friedl: I just remember sitting there, watching the bands, and going, "Oh my God, I don't know why we're here. This is not our crowd."

Dave Derby: So we decided to play some of our punkier songs and made sure we played everything fast. We also had this kind of faux-cocktail jazz song called "The Golf Course" that Tryan wrote that would speed up at one point and go into this crazy ad-lib thing. There were these skate punk people who were just kind of making fun of us at the beginning, it seemed, doing this circular dance, and when it got to the heavy part, everyone really got into it and started slamming, and we were like, "Fuck, this is amazing!" It went really well, and Dave was like, "Oh my God, that was incredible—people really liked you!"

Eric Friedl: We were just terrified that we were gonna get beaten up, so we were popping Vivarin and drinking beer, and we played about ten million miles an hour, and all the kids with skateboards actually got to run around and skate to our stuff. We went over really well.

Dave Derby: Here I was, back in Hawaii for the summer after my freshman year at Yale, and I kind of got seduced by the idea of going to college, but I didn't really know what the hell I wanted to do, and that night, I was like, "Fuck that, I'm gonna be in a band. This is what I wanna do for the rest of my life. This moment is exactly what I want to live for." From there we got more serious about it.

Eric Friedl: We spent that summer practicing every day. We insulated a shed in the back of Dave's house by putting up carpet all over the place to deaden the sound. We made it through the summer, but the shed eventually collapsed from the weight of the carpet.

Dave Derby: We started recording, and right around that time, we got really great reviews in *Option* and *Sound Choice,* and this dude in Berlin started writing to us and sending faxes. Eric Masunaga was in touch with him, and we were making these serious demos at Rendez-Vous and other studios. This was the stuff that became basically the first Dambuilders record. Our contact in Germany had definitely committed to putting out the record on this indie label, ¡Cuacha!

Keoki's a great drummer and has this really interesting feel. He was kind of like a metalhead dude at the time and liked to play like he was in Judas Priest, which was great, but we wanted more nuance in the drums, so we got Daniel Glass to play for us. Everyone knew that he was this killer drummer. We also hired another badass drummer, John Andreoni, who was in a local hair metal band called Passion, who were really fucking good. We went to go see them somewhere and were like, "This guy's incredible!" So we recorded with him and Daniel.

Daniel Glass (drummer: Royal Crown Revue, Brian Setzer, Mike Ness, etc.): Those guys were more into the punk rock side of things, but they knew me through a band that I was in during high school that performed at the 50th State Fair and Brown Bags to Stardom, doing Selecter, Motels, and Missing Persons songs.

Dave Derby: In the summer of '88, we also met Debbie Fox, who was going to UH at the time. I remember I went to Island Guitars and bought one of those acoustic basses like the one the guy in Violent Femmes uses, and we started playing under the most ridiculous name, Chicken Eats the Worm. We started playing a whole bunch of acoustic songs, and we had this guy, Pete Vidito. Pete was just playing brushes on a snare, and his playing was incredible. It was Debbie, Tryan, me, and Pete. We played KTUH, the UH Campus Center, and even on the street. We wrote a bunch of songs that made it onto the first Dambuilders record.

The Exactones, I still think, is a much better name than The Dambuilders or Chicken Eats the Worm, but in 1988, 1989, it just wasn't that cool.

Pete Vidito (drummer: Chicken Eats the Worm; bassist: Tantra Monsters; DJ at Radio Free Hawaii, KTUH): Chicken Eats the Worm was a super fun, acoustic bridge between The Exactones and The Dambuilders. I guess Dave wanted to do another project after The Exactones, and he and Tryan had these really lovely songs with great hooks. Deb could do this cool John Cale kind of drony violin at times, and I was just playing a snare and a floor tom, doing a Moe Tucker sort of thing. We busked in Waikiki and people were very confused but also very into it. It was fun. Some of those songs are quite beautiful and I hope they're never fully lost.

Dave Derby: It was very, very inspired by Poi Dog Pondering, I would say, 'cause we also started busking around at UH and going down to Waikiki to play and stuff. It's kind of like we saw the seas parting in a way, like maybe this should be The Dambuilders and we should just go to the mainland and do what Poi Dog did, you know—get a van and maybe go to San Francisco or LA or Austin, where the Poi Dog people were.

Eric Friedl: In the end, Tryan and Dave and their violin player Debbie decided to come out and try to be a real band and move to Boston, where both Eric Masunaga and I ended up—kind of on the outskirts of Boston—and I stayed with them for a little bit.

Dave Derby: When we first moved to Boston, it was cold, people were cold, and it was really hard to get a toehold on anything, although the radio station at Tufts University started playing us, and a few people started championing us. It was very competitive with tons of bands. Everyone I knew was in a band, especially then. It seemed there wasn't anything to do in Boston but be in the band. If I met someone who wasn't in a band, they would seem exotic, like, "Wow, what do you do if you're not in a band?"

Daniel Glass: I remember hanging out with them in Boston, and they were like, "You should join our band!" but I was already committed to going to LA to go to music school. I wanted to play jazz and be this super fusion guy and attend the Grove School of Music. Dick Grove was a heavyweight composer, arranger, and major film scorer. In high school and junior high, everyone would play Dick Grove charts.

Dave Derby: We had this Dambuilders record and a tour that was going to be happening at some point, but we didn't have a drummer. Boston was just teeming with really great musicians, so we auditioned a bunch of drummers and found this guy, Stuart Wright, and went on this sprawling, amazing four-month tour of Europe. The first Dambuilders record was really well-received in Europe. Swedish national radio played some of our songs. It was me and Eric Masunaga, Debbie Fox, Tryan George—so four people from Hawaii—and Stuart Wright, who was from Vermont but lived in Boston.

Eric Friedl: When The Dambuilders went on their first big European tour, they decided I was going to be their soundman. I'd never done sound before in my life. Eric said, "Well, you know what we're supposed to sound like, so just sit in with some people and look over their shoulders and you'll be fine."

So the first day was at this place that maybe held like a hundred people, with a tiny board, and you couldn't mess up too bad. I was fine. Then the second day, they opened for Urban Dance Squad at this festival thing in a hockey rink, and the board was, like, twenty feet wide, manned by some German engineer who would not let me get anywhere near the board, and I was just fine with that.

Dave Derby: We actually got nice write-ups on most of our records in places like *Option* and *Trouser Press*. People, I think, found that first Dambuilders record to be charming in a way. We were starting to get something going and then we went to Europe and got really good. You know, you play every night for four months and you get pretty good. The first leg of the tour went through Germany, Austria, and Switzerland. Then we played something like ten shows in Sweden before going to the DDR, right after the Berlin Wall came down but before the currency was unified.

What was cool about playing those shows was that these people had never seen Western bands. It was incredible seeing Leipzig and Dresden, you know, cities that were bombed out from the war and in a state of disrepair. It was fascinating walking on cobblestone streets and seeing

An early version of The Dambuilders in Berlin, 1990. *Imago/Brigani-Art*

people driving around in those really tiny Trabant cars. Apparently, you could blow one up just by using a lighter. So we actually lived in East Berlin for a while, and by the time we went back home, we were a much better band.

The European tour was a long slog and kind of put some tensions within the band. Debbie left the band. Tryan left the band. So there was a brief period when the band was me, Eric Masunaga, Stuart Wright, and Joan Wasser, who we met through mutual friends, and we put out our second record, *Geek Lust*, which started to get some radio airplay. College radio in that city back then in 1992, pre-Internet, was frickin' amazing. All day long you could surf the dial, listening to the MIT station, then tune into the Harvard station, the BU station, the Boston College station, Emerson—they were all good.

Joan Wasser (violinist: The Dambuilders; vocalist/multi-instrumentalist: Joan As Police Woman): When I first got to Boston, my template was New York City—so it's not fair—but I just thought, erroneously, *Oh,* *it's another East Coast city; it's smaller than New York, but it'll just be like a small New York.* I may not have liked it, but I wouldn't have hated it with the venom I ended up hating it with if it wasn't truly the antithesis of New York. It felt incredibly provincial, and it was really hateful, super racist, homophobic, sexist, violent—frat boys trawling around—the Red Sox vibe, oh my God. It was so vitriolic. It was mean and hateful. That's what it felt like. It's not nice, but it had a whole hell of a lot of amazing musicians, and wherever you are, you find your people. You have to respond with creativity.

I got contacted by Dave because they needed a violin player; they were chosen to be in this—oh God, what was it called? It was so silly. Boston had what was called a "Rock and Roll Rumble." Yes, you heard me. It's like, four bands play per night, and one wins per night, and the eventual winner gets money or recording time or something.

I hadn't heard of The Dambuilders, but I learned stuff off their album. My first show was at the Paradise, and I was in the band. But I really wanted to make the violin more of a rhythm instrument and maybe use effects and stuff.

Being in that band was an absolute life changer for me. First of all, Dave and Eric are incredible musicians. Like, *incredible.* Dave's lyrics? Amazing. Also, Dave was a very melodic bass player, which actually left some room for me to do some rhythm stuff.

Dave Derby: Our career arc in Europe was the exact opposite of what it became in the States. Every tour we did after every record we put out didn't quite go over as well, and we kind of lost our audience there. But when we got back to the States, we really connected with the East Coast kind of indie rock scene of the '90s and started putting out our own records. That was a really exciting time when you could just call up the guys in Superchunk and book a show in Chapel Hill, for example.

Eric Friedl: When I moved to Memphis, it was 1990. My buddy who I'd gone to college with opened up a record store in Memphis, so I said, "All right, I'm gonna go to Memphis and see what happens."

I know Memphis is kind of famous for music, but especially at that point, there really wasn't anything going on. No one cared about

Memphis, and it was just like Hawaii, where the people who were doing stuff were doing it for themselves. It wasn't like you were gonna get signed or be famous or anything, but when you're friends with everybody, you go to each other's shows. People were supportive. That's exactly what the scene was like, and it totally reminded me of Hawaii.

Memphis and Nashville were going through the same thing then: Country music was dead; soul music, which was more Memphis' style, was dead. They'd torn down Stax Records, where Booker T & the MGs and Otis Redding and everybody recorded; Sun Studio, where Elvis and Johnny Cash and all of them did their thing, was somehow still there but nobody cared. Graceland was kind of a ghetto, and Memphis was a wasteland, which can be fun because you can do whatever you want and no one cares. You could be in a band, you could open a bar, you could put on shows, and it was wide open.

I was meeting people and I started playing with some guys who could actually play, and our joke band took off. That's how the Oblivians started. I met these guys, Greg Cartwright and Jack Yarber, and they had been in a bunch of bands together. At that point, Greg sang like Glenn Danzig, and Jack sang like Tom Verlaine from Television, and they were kind of working through their influences, but they were both *really* good.

Greg went on tour with some band, and me and Jack were just hanging out. Jack had showed me some chords, and I was like, "Okay, well, what else do I have to do?" and he said, "That's it, man. Don't tell anyone." When Greg came back, we made up some really dumb songs with two guitars and drums, and we switched instruments, taking turns on drums.

The Oblivians were not a serious band, but we were somehow good, I guess. Crypt Records put out our album and got us a European tour for a couple of months with Country Teasers and got us to Japan. We played smaller squats in places like Croatia and Slovenia, and giant halls in Holland and Germany with pretty big crowds. It was a trip to us because no one cared about what we were doing in Memphis or America.

I still cannot play guitar outside of what I play in songs, yet I've gotten to go around the world being a terrible guitar player. It was amazing.

Daniel Glass: When Royal Crown Revue and the whole swing revival started in LA, it was pre-Nirvana and I wasn't in it at the time, but as you can imagine, there was hair metal on the Sunset Strip, and here comes a bunch of punk rockers in old, themed clothes with a horn section and upright bass. It was so out of left field.

All the people in Royal Crown Revue and all the fans who would come to the shows were former punk rockers. As they grew up and began to maybe get more sophisticated, they realized that early styles of American music, whether swing music or rhythm and blues or early rock and roll, were very much like punk rock. They were, in their time, simple and rebellious, and always came with their own sense of fashion. In fact, the original rhythm section in Royal Crown Revue were the guys in the O.G. Southern California punk band Youth Brigade.

These guys had a bebop side project called The Jazz Jury, which I was in before being brought into Royal Crown five years later in '94. The Jazz Jury wound up doing music for the movie *Swingers*. Royal Crown Revue were supposed to actually be featured in *Swingers*, but Warner Brothers wouldn't let us do the fucking movie. Jon Favreau, who's now one of the most famous directors in the world, was our buddy and a swing dancer, and he made this movie on his own for $100,000 or something. He couldn't pay us, but he wanted us to be in it. The whole swing thing was taking off and we all knew it, but Warner Brothers said no. They wanted a ton of money to use our music. We really wanted to be in this movie but couldn't, so another band, Big Bad Voodoo Daddy, which totally ripped us off and in my opinion are the cheesy white bread version of what we were doing, got in the movie and even played the Super Bowl halftime show as a result of that. That made their whole career.

Dave Derby: The Dambuilders started to do some tours of the East Coast, self-booked, just getting into our Ford Econoline, driving down the coast and back. Our drummer Stu was having a rough go of things and quit the band, and within a few days we met Kevin March, and from there it just took off. Around that time, the writing was getting better, and we were really finding our stride, writing the songs that would ultimately be *Encendedor*.

Sonic Youth got signed to DGC and put out *Goo,* and they got Nirvana signed, and from that point on, there were record company people crawling up everybody's butts. That eventually led us to signing a major label deal with EastWest Records.

Joan Wasser: It's pretty hard to imagine, I think, how it was such a different time in the music industry. Not only were major labels signing arty, indie-type bands, but they were giving them proper budgets to make records. It was incredible. It couldn't have been less like how it is now.

Dave Derby: Even though we were very much part of this growing indie rock scene, we didn't quite fit in. Even going back to The Exactones, we were always a little bit different. We were this slightly proggy, punky, poppy mishmash and had a lot of label interest, but for a while, no one really committed, and we knew it was going to be a really good record.

We had two options: One scenario was to put the album that was going to be *Encendedor* on Caroline, who wanted to sign us. The other option that fell into our laps was this EastWest thing. They gave us this deal where they wanted to put out this record, *Encendedor,* which was basically already in the can, and then two records after that. That seemed like a pretty good deal. We thought, *Okay, that's cool; we can quit our day jobs and have enough money to live on, we can tour, and we can really focus on making that next record.* It was kind of a no-brainer.

We did it and we didn't really expect much to happen, but the song "Shrine" got picked up, for whatever reason, by this big station in Atlanta and that was huge. They were maybe the third biggest radio station for alternative rock in America at that point. We had a video that debuted on MTV's 120 Minutes, the same night as Weezer, who we later went on tour with, along with Lush, who headlined. I think a lot of our thinking back then was we just wanted to have a good ride. It felt like a huge vindication.

Joan Wasser: What a boon for us that we were able to make records we loved and set a tiny bit of money aside to live on and tour. There was a magic that we had at that time, and we just played so much together that we sort of found this interesting chemistry. We figured out what we were doing, in a way. It was a special feeling.

Dave Derby: We mixed *Encendedor* in Hawaii with Milan Bertosa, who we had worked with before and is a super talented recording engineer. We flew the band out. Joan stayed at my house and Kevin stayed with Eric. They loved it. It was fun, we had a good trip, we mixed the record and did a photoshoot at Hanauma Bay and ended up walking around to the Toilet Bowl swimming hole.

I remember driving them around to the North Shore and going past Sandy Beach and Makapu'u and through Waimanalo, and Joan was like, "What's wrong with swimming right there? Just park the car, let's go!" Waimanalo is just so amazing.

Joan Wasser: It was like something out of a dream. Being from the East Coast and going to Hawaii, it's like you just took drugs or something. You just can't believe how it's the most outrageously beautiful place ever. And then on top of it, you guys grew up here?

I remember Dave took us to plate lunch places, which as far as I know didn't exist outside of Hawaii, and I remember going to the North Shore. Oh my God, I will never forget seeing forty- or fifty-foot waves and the person on it looked like a tiny speck. I'd never seen anything like it in my life.

Dave Derby: Our next album, *Ruby Red*, did really well in Australia. Around that time, we were touring the States, and Joan met Jeff Buckley, who she dated, and we became friends with him, and we toured Australia, opening for him, which was amazing.

You know, when Jeff was alive, he wasn't that famous but was somebody that everybody spoke about as like, "This guy's going to be huge." I got to know him, and while touring Australia, just watching him play live was insane. It couldn't have been a more perfect situation for us. Our songs got played on national radio, and we played to some really big crowds, and it kind of rejuvenated our faith in the band.

Joan Wasser: We did some shows opening for Jeff Buckley, who was my boyfriend for the last three years of his life. The Dambuilders and The Grifters were on a headlining tour together for, like, six weeks or something, in the U.S., and right in the middle there was this show in Iowa

The Dambuilders on the southeastern shore of Oahu, 1993.
Courtesy of Mike Miller/EastWest Records

City that we did with Jeff Buckley, and it was the only show we did with anyone else. So we met that night and we really hit it off. It was a mutually exciting time for us. There were a lot of pay phone calls. Wow. We both racked up a lot of charges on hotel phones and pay phones.

Dave Derby: We started working on our last record, *Against the Stars*, which is actually my favorite record of all. We worked really hard on it, and a song for that record, "Burn This Bridge" was poised to hit, but the label didn't pay for a video, and because we didn't have a video timed with the release of the record, a lot of the stations that were going to add it didn't add it. We thought it was probably going to be our last record, and it was really frustrating.

I remember I had this conversation with Joan, which was like, "Why are you just a violin player? I think you need to sing more, and you need to play other instruments other than violin." And it's funny because she got really pissed off when I said this, but I was just trying to push her towards being the frontperson because she is and was a total rock star and a really iconic presence; beautiful and super talented.

At first, I think she wasn't sure about it but then totally embraced it. I love that about the record. In terms of the singing, there's the Joan part of the record and there's the me part of the record, and it was a really great, positive, collaborative experience.

Joan Wasser: You know, we made that record and then Jeff died, and I just sort of died inside. I was in so much pain, and I had nowhere to put it, and it was not getting fulfilled by playing violin. It was then that I was actually trying to write songs, started playing guitar, started playing keys, started trying to sing. It was an incredibly difficult time for me. The pain was too much. We were engaged to be married.

Dave Derby: Jeff died, which really fucked us up, and it was super hard for Joan, obviously, who just tried to kind of white-knuckle through it. Then there were some interpersonal, weird dynamics in the band that got kind of poisonous. We broke up in the middle of the tour. I think we were in Minneapolis, actually, and just decided, "All right, that's it," and had our last show in Chicago. In a way, that's kind of the shame of the record. I think it's really good and we just didn't get to promote it.

18

PRESS FORWARD

In September 1988, an earnest but somewhat slapdash underground newspaper appeared on the scene. *Scrawling Wall*, cobbled together in the offices above Jelly's on Pi'ikoi Street, was established by Norm Winter as a public outlet for creative expression. Subsidized by his Jelly's shop, it covered everything you might find on the Jelly's sales floor: comics, books, and music, along with important, thought-provoking topics and reader submissions thrown in for good measure. Although it lasted only a year, it yielded a template for free-thinking, would-be publishers on Oahu.

Local indies *Metropolis* and *Kaos* followed soon after in 1989 and 1990, respectively. Both focused heavily on music, but *Kaos* was the more contentious of the two, making matters of controversy—abortion, geothermal energy, U.S. intervention in Central America, etc.—its primary focus. By comparison, *Metropolis* spent a good amount of column space on hard rock and hair metal before pivoting with the swiftly changing times—and new publishers—to include alt-rock, hip-hop, and rising local musicians in a glossy-cover newsprint magazine format. In time, *Deep* entered the fray with a hectic, computer-generated layout and ample coverage of Oahu's rave and nightclub scenes. Despite the resolve of these autonomous publications, they could seem rather uneven in content as they often relied on unpaid contributors who sometimes possessed more zeal for their subject matter than actual writing ability.

The most accomplished and ambitious of these periodicals was *Honolulu Weekly*, which featured an array of skilled and experienced freelance writers and a circulation upward of 35,000. Founded in the summer of 1991 with the financial backing of a hodgepodge of local investors, the *Weekly* quickly became Hawaii's most influential and widely read independent paper. Like many of America's top alternative newspapers, it took aim at issues and politics in its own backyard and routinely spotlighted topics either missed or ignored by larger media outlets. Throughout its existence, *Honolulu Weekly* maintained a steadfast regard for culture, counterculture, and the arts, and for many years its arts calendar was the go-to source for happenings on Oahu.

In the early 1990s, nightclubs and events dedicated to such growing sounds as industrial, goth, jungle, and techno popped up in areas outside the usual Waikiki haunts to include warehouses, bars, and late-night eateries across Oahu. In response, *Honolulu Weekly* established a nightclub column in the winter of 1994. It was penned by a succession of scenesters before Mark Chittom assumed the post the following summer. Chittom, whose caustic gibes knew no bounds, quickly amassed an avid readership, half of whom either laughed out loud or howled with outrage at his depictions of the local nightlife.

In one particularly pointed piece, Chittom's column compared the island's punk rockers to obsessive Civil War reenactors, the only difference being "Civil War reenactors know the Civil War is over." There was also the time he implored the U.S. military to torment its enemies with the musical renderings of a cover band that had been making the rounds on the local circuit. When Chittom ran into the group's lead singer weeks later, he found himself at the threshold of physical harm. "He really wanted to fight me," remembers Chittom.

Once, after attending a touristy luau with a group of friends, he dashed off another snippy review. Not long after, two drunk workers from the luau company recognized the group imbibing at Magoo's, the popular University-area watering hole, and approached them, demanding to know which of them wrote the article. Without hesitation, Chittom's friends pointed his way. "They could've just said, 'He's not here,'" he gripes. "These guys were gonna fuckin' beat me up right there."

Fortunately, sitting at the group's table was a Norwegian dock worker who had come to Hawaii to blow his lottery winnings. As tensions rose, the beefy Norseman created a barrier between Chittom and his would-be assailants. "If you got a problem with him, you got a problem with me," he told the pair, who quietly backed down. The encounter still titillates Chittom, who recounts the face-off with a degree of glee: "I was like, '*Norwaaaaaaaay!*'"

Those fast, loose times and the tales they spawned, however, would not last forever. As with all good things, the golden age of alt-weeklies and their bodacious content would come to an end. In the new millennium, as the Internet began to reshape the world's consumption of media, and free online news and entertainment sources became much more common, readership and circulation of newspapers, both alternative and traditional, steadily declined. Many of these properties were bought, sold, and resold, and while some have managed to transition to a digital format, nearly all have toiled mightily to stay afloat.

Most have gutted their newsrooms, while others have ceased operations altogether. Locally, the *Honolulu Advertiser* and *Honolulu Star-Bulletin* merged in 2010, weathering cutbacks and layoffs over the years; the independently owned *Hawaii Island Journal*, established in 1992, boasted for a time the widest distribution of any paper on the Big Island of Hawaii. Acquired by *Honolulu Weekly* in 2005, it ceased operations in 2008.

As for the *Weekly* itself, in June of 2013, it printed its last issue. Several online entities have since tried to fill the void left by its closure, though its staunchest supporters would argue none have succeeded in merging advocacy of the underexposed and coverage of the arts with the insight, commitment, or daring of the *Honolulu Weekly* in its day.

Derek Ferrar (writer/editor: *Honolulu Weekly*, *Scrawling Wall*, *Hana Hou!* etc.; DJ at KTUH): I grew up in New York City until I was about fifteen or so and then I got involved in basically an Indian guru cult. My whole family did. And I did that for about ten years. My parents were involved first. You know, it was New York in the '70s, and Eastern spirituality was really big. We'd had a bad car accident, and everyone survived, but it was really scary, and it sort of made my parents reexamine a lot of things. I think they were taking a yoga class, and through their teacher, they heard about this guru and started to go to programs on meditation, things like that. I eventually agreed to go to a program, and the moment I walked in the door, I had sort of an instantaneous conversion experience, which is kind of a common thing.

I'd visited Hawaii several times, actually. I first came in 1979, when the guru, whose name was Muktananda, was on his tour and came here for a couple months. I actually became a traditional Indian monk when I was nineteen, and I was in charge of a little meditation center they had on Makiki Street.

Over the years, it transpired that it was really a cult of personality. It was all about this one person, the guru, who was seen as infallible. But then things came out that conflicted with that, and there were all kinds of scandals, the standard kind of stuff, and there was a big schism.

When that guru died, he was succeeded by two young people who I knew too well, probably. My belief in it was going away, but it's a hard thing to leave when it's your whole world. When I first joined,

I swallowed the whole thing, hook, line, and sinker, and I was a true believer. But over years you become a somewhat more jaded and experienced person who takes the whole thing with a grain of salt but still believes. Then I basically found out that the guru was having sexual practices with very young women, and he was supposed to be a celibate monk as well. He was not practicing what he preached, and that made me feel liberated from the whole thing.

The new gurus basically split up, and it all just kind of blew up, and as part of that, I was made an example of and got defrocked. I could have stayed and eaten humble pie, probably, but I didn't really believe in it anymore and took that as an opportunity to exit. Once I got out, pretty quickly, over a period of just a few months, I realized I didn't believe in the whole thing anymore.

So when I came back to Hawaii in late 1985, it was basically like catching up on my missed adolescence, and the whole experience had left me with a deep distrust of humankind and what we're capable of doing when we become true believers. It made me skeptical of authority. That basically set the stage for getting involved in the alternative scene and alternative press.

When I was twenty-five, I'd already been through this ten-year headfuck with this spiritual group, so when I got out of that, I decided to move to the North Shore with friends. I was really trying to figure out who I was going to be, you know? Reinvent myself, I guess. I wound up going back towards the person I was headed for in my earlier years, I think: the secular, "question authority" type of person I've become.

I eventually wound up at UH and got involved with KTUH, where I was a DJ, beginning in '87. I majored in journalism, and again, I was trying to find my voice. I felt like I had something to say about power and the power structure. I was also on the UH Campus Center Activities Council with Julia Steele. She was in Journalism as well. We promoted shows like Camper Van Beethoven and Jello Biafra, and we worked on several events with Mari Matsuoka.

Julia Steele (writer/editor: *Honolulu Weekly*, *Scrawling Wall*, *Hana Hou!*, etc.; DJ at KTUH): We also brought in a lot of interesting speakers to UH, which I think sort of contributed to the zeitgeist of the university at that time. It felt like such a vibrant institution. We had Jesse Jackson come and speak, we had Carl Sagan come and speak on a beautiful night under the stars at Andrews Amphitheater, and we had Andrew Weil come and speak when he was really looking at the War on Drugs and trying to be a voice for a more expansive view of what drugs are and why people take them as opposed to this Nancy Reagan "Just Say No" or Bill Bennett "lock them up" approach that was very much alive in the country. We had Michael Parenti come; we brought Daniel Ellsberg and Howard Zinn to speak; Galen Rowell, who's quite a famous photographer, came to speak.

These people wanted to come to Hawaii. They were interested in Hawaii, and they were grateful to come to UH. People would show up with really interesting questions and answers. It was a way of looking at this reality of Hawaii that was outside of its place as a military base or tourist destination and as a home to a lot of very creative and thoughtful people with a really fascinating and important history.

Mark Chittom (writer/nightclub columnist: *Honolulu Weekly*): I grew up in the Mississippi Delta in a town called Greenwood, and that's where Robert Johnson is buried. I'd been failing out of college at Mississippi State and had undiagnosed ADD, which back then basically meant that you were just a fuckup, and you didn't care. So I went into the Navy because I thought if I joined the Army, I might end up on some Fort-something in Alabama or Indiana. I'm like, "If I'm gonna join one of the branches of the service, I wanna join one that can take me all over the world and see some places."

I got stationed at the Marine base in Kaneohe as a hospital corpsman, which in everyday terms is a combat medic. Believe it or not, I wanted to be a Navy SEAL. Knowing me, you're like, "How the fuck could you be a SEAL?" except back then I was really into endurance sports. I was a long-distance runner, and I would go out and ride my bike fifty miles. Just aside from being a young guy and having more energy than I knew what to do with, I liked what happened to me when I got into that zone. My mind was different. But then I came to Hawaii and started taking acid, and I stopped doing that. I was like, "This is a much easier way to get there."

SCRAWLING WALL

Deb Aoki (visual artist; cartoonist/writer/reviewer: *Honolulu Weekly*, *Honolulu Advertiser*, *Kaos*, *Scrawling Wall*, etc.): When I came back home after spending some time on the mainland, I realized you can make shit happen in Hawaii. You don't need to treat Hawaii like a waystation, like a layover until you've moved on to something cooler. I appreciated what people like Robert and Arnie from the Dervishes had done years earlier. Like, "Oh yeah, this place is a blank canvas, and you can make anything fun happen because no one else is."

I went back to school at UH, and there was *Ka Leo*, the school newspaper. I said, "Fuck it, I'm gonna draw a comic strip." I got paid maybe five bucks a strip, but it got me recognized, right? Then I got approached to do drawings for *Scrawling Wall*.

Scrawling Wall was a place for people to really express themselves, get published, and share what they were passionate about. This was before anybody had smartphones or even access to the Internet. People wanted to be seen and heard.

Derek Ferrar: *Scrawling Wall* was punk rock in the sense that everything about it was chaos. Norm named Mari Matsuoka the editor-in-chief, initially, and through our association with Mari, Julia and I began writing for *Scrawling Wall*.

Norm Winter: Mari had come into Jelly's saying, "We gotta change the world; we gotta do something about this society." The first thing she came to me about was getting local bands places to play. Then *Scrawling Wall* started up with funding from Jelly's. It cost us about $5,000 a month, something like that. It was to help the kids express themselves, I guess. It was charity. It started with an idea I had, but Mari took the baton and went berserk on it. She really got the word out on the street. Mari became the ringleader of the whole thing.

Scrawling Wall, August 1989.

Deb Aoki: Mari and Norm were the resident adults. They were also the people who made stuff happen. They found the funds, and they had the know-how and the can-do attitude that most of us who were younger couldn't muster. Norm, even to this day, is a bit of a rabble-rouser, and Mari comes from this revolutionary communist mindset. I remember our nickname for Mari was "Commie Mommy."

Derek Ferrar: I think Mari really wanted to politicize the youth, and so she was into youth culture for that reason. I mean, she hung around with skaters; she hung around graffiti artists, punks, and all the young people who felt like they were under people's thumb. She wanted to make them feel empowered and strong. I think that, ultimately, she would hope that young people would rise up and overturn the system.

Julia Steele: I had graduated with a degree in journalism, and Derek and I were coming at it with some training for what we were doing. I wrote my first story on homelessness, and looking at it now with the whole redevelopment of Kaka'ako and the line of how it was going to be housing for the people, and the willingness of a number of those in power in Hawaii to sell out the people—it's heartbreaking. Again, when I came to Hawaii—and it continues to this day—I see it as a place where there's so much injustice.

Raoul Vehill: Crazy George was very involved in *Scrawling Wall* too. He used to stay downstairs in the record department at Jelly's, keeping track of stock and working behind the counter. Crazy George had an encyclopedic knowledge of music, especially all the new anti-music.

Derek Ferrar: There was a bulletin board in front of Jelly's at 404 Pi'ikoi with white cards where anyone could write or draw anything on the cards, and it functioned like a wall for people's graffiti. Then we'd basically take an image of the board for the center spread of *Scrawling Wall*. People started posting some pretty vile and racist things on there, in our opinion, and we did not want to amplify that and we objected. But Norm insisted that we had to give the people a voice, whatever it was. We had a big fight about it, and we said we had to have the right to edit, and he said editing is censorship. We all quit.

Norm Winter: There were things that they didn't agree with. It wasn't racist; it was just dark...it was dark. Kids would scribble and scrawl on our wall and send us stories about a killing spree at McDonald's, necrophilia poetry, weird stuff.

Raoul Vehill: Norm had sent me to rehab, and I straightened out some.

I was building and staining bookshelves for his store, and it kinda turned into me becoming the new editor of *Scrawling Wall.* That's what I mostly did for pocket money. The whole thing lasted until the end of '89, maybe early '90. I figured out around then, I guess, that I needed to not be on Oahu anymore. I needed to move on.

Norm Winter: The biggest thing with Raoul was his stripper girlfriend. Oh my God, he practically died over her. She came to me worried about him because he was getting crazy, doing all these crazy things, and he wasn't sounding or acting normal. He was in a bad state, but I never notice things like that. He was utterly obsessed with that girl.

KAOS

Deb Aoki: There was a graphic design company called InDesign that was owned by Guy Brandwen. It was in a little house across the street from the McCully Zippy's. I was told, "Hey, come over, we can use some help with illustrations and stuff." Guy did logo design and graphic design for different businesses. That was when I first learned how to use desktop publishing tools: Photoshop, Illustrator, PageMaker, whatever.

Guy was fascinating. He was younger than me, barely nineteen or twenty, and he had this successful business. At the time, we were all into 4AD Records and that whole graphic design style, but Guy was also really into Einstürzende Neubauten and Ministry and the loudest, most obnoxious industrial music as well as Japanese noise rock like the Boredoms. He would blast that stuff super loud while we were working.

So out of the InDesign offices came *Kaos,* which sort of picked up where *Scrawling Wall* left off. *Scrawling Wall* was largely underwritten by Jelly's and *Kaos* by InDesign, but I don't know if either paper had real business goals or if they even thought of things like return on investment. They just did it because it was fun and cool.

Compared to other U.S. metro cities, though, we didn't really have a true alternative paper then. There was the *Honolulu Star-Bulletin* and the *Honolulu Advertiser, MidWeek,* and tourism tabloids on one side, and these small, short-lived papers like *Scrawling Wall* and *Kaos* on the other end. But there was nothing like your *East Bay Express* or *Village Voice* or anything like that.

HONOLULU WEEKLY

Laurie Carlson (publisher: *Honolulu Weekly*): It was while doing this master's program on the East Coast that I read the *New York Times* every morning, and I loved having a great newspaper. When I came back to Hawaii, it was very clear to me there was nothing that connected my community, and we kind of needed that to become politically active, to make changes in the community, and to have some political authority and power.

There were these regional newspapers on the East Coast that connected me with people who had business plans, and I got a lot of support from all of these alternative newsweeklies. There was a big one called the *San Francisco Bay Guardian*, and Bruce Brugmann, who ran that, invited me to come and get anything I wanted. There was another fellow up in Seattle who had the *Seattle Weekly* and said, "Come to any meeting, copy anything you want—we'll help you get started." So there was this whole community, not unlike the food cooperative community that I knew and loved, where there were all these independent publications helping each other. That was really sweet.

I remember there was a woman named Mari that Julia worked for at *Scrawling Wall* who said to me, "Julia is the woman you want," and she was absolutely right.

Derek Ferrar: Our role in *Scrawling Wall* had fallen apart, and when Laurie Carlson was going to start *Honolulu Weekly*, she got in touch with Julia, who got in touch with me when she became editor, and I started doing the calendar and became arts editor. That paper was a struggle, financially.

Laurie Carlson: It took a lot of persistence, more than anything, to find the people in town who had money and could afford to lose it and wouldn't bother me, editorially speaking. I certainly couldn't fund it myself, but finally, I found ten or twelve people, and it was a very strange group in a lot of ways. They were all so different from one another. One was an immigrant from China who had a photo shop in Chinatown; there was a missionary descendant; there was a trust fund baby whose grandfather started Bergdorf Goodman; there were some local attorneys who had graduated from Punahou. It was really an amalgamation of these people who were willing to take a chance and put money into this unknown venture. Most of them got their money back, I think, after about five or ten years, when I was able to repay them.

Derek Ferrar: Laurie was kind of a new age entrepreneur, I guess you could say. She was very involved in Kokua Market in the days before there was any Whole Foods in Hawaii and health food itself was an alternative culture. Those were the days of the joint advertising agreement between the *Honolulu Advertiser* and the *Honolulu Star-Bulletin*, where they shared everything but editorial, and they basically had a huge monopoly on print advertising. As someone running a market, I think she felt she didn't have any choice but to work with them back in the day.

Laurie Carlson: I really saw the *Weekly* as very similar to Kokua, which was the model of natural foods, not Safeway. It was the model for alternative journalism, and not the dailies. In fact, when we first started, we had some swag created that said, "If you love the dailies, you'll hate the *Weekly*." And it's kind of true.

Julia Steele: There were two big daily papers then: the *Honolulu Advertiser* and the *Honolulu Star-Bulletin*. This is not to take anything away from them because they had some great reporters and they were important papers, but they were in some ways pretty conservative. They were—what can I say?—they were the American establishment newspapers. And I think in the same way we wanted to bring Daniel Ellsberg and Howard Zinn to speak at UH, *Honolulu Weekly* was also about that youthful idea of "Let's shake it up a little bit" combined with "Wow, look what's going on here, and look at the land and power monopolization, look at the racism and colonialism that's hard-baked into this system and how these things are manifesting into the minutiae of people's daily lives but not really being talked about." It felt like there was a lot that could be said, so why not speak up and see if we can make some good happen?

We had a tiny staff. I mean, on the editorial staff it was just me and Derek. There was an art director and a production person, a couple of people who sold ads, then there was Laurie and that's it. It was a real challenge.

Laurie Carlson: The *Weekly* was never very profitable, and part of that, I think, stems from the fact that Honolulu does not have a lot of independent retailers. It's not like Seattle; it's not like San Francisco. It's a real struggle to have a business here, but we did manage to successfully publish for twenty-three years. It was hand-to-mouth, but we never missed a payroll and somehow we managed.

Ultimately, I really feel that it contributed to an influence on politics in the state that didn't exist before and didn't exist after. When we delivered the paper to Honolulu Hale on Thursdays, people rushed down to get it. They wanted to know if they were in it.

We covered a lot of anti-development kinds of stories, and whenever I'd see a photograph or video of a community meeting, even on the neighbor islands, I'd see they'd have a copy of the *Weekly* with the cover story about that particular issue. Also, because of our coverage of the arts, we were able to work with a variety of arts-related events as sponsors, and it was a great source of satisfaction to shine a light on these interests and events and people that maybe wouldn't get that exposure otherwise.

Mark Chittom: Oh, I read the *Weekly* religiously. I would read it cover to cover. I would even read the articles about things I wasn't particularly interested in because they had such good writers.

Julia Steele: You know, I wanted it to be really good journalism, where people were never quite sure where it was going to be coming from, but it was going to be really good, in-depth writing. So that was the goal.

Laurie had a friend, Bob Green, and Bob was the film reviewer, and I had a friend, Alan Young, and Alan was the restaurant reviewer. The writers were freelancers. Liza Simon wrote some stories for us; there was Curt Sanburn, who became the editor of the *Weekly* for a while; Franco Salmoiraghi, who believed in our mission, would do photography a lot of times for us. Some of these people who were heaven sent would freelance more frequently, so you could call them up and say, "Would you do a story?"

Deb Aoki: *Honolulu Weekly* was like a freelance illustration job for me. Then for a while, I covered the nightclub scene just because I could, you know? At the time, I considered myself to be an oldster. People in the club scene were eighteen to twenty-two or twenty-three, and I didn't want to be the person who stuck around too long in the scene and only celebrated my pals from back in the day and never paid attention to what the kids were doing.

I was having fun, but it wasn't the be-all end-all for me, and I gladly left my space to let someone else do what they wanted with it. Mark Chittom took it next. He was a little more cynical because that's his personality, right? But that's what a good alternative paper does; it lets people write with their own voice.

Mark Chittom: My first assignment for *Honolulu Weekly* was a review of the Dambuilders show at Access in Puck's Alley. That was kind of when I realized that maybe I didn't have the chops for writing because when I sat down to do it, I found that I didn't have anything interesting to say. I was like, "Well, there's no way that they're going to print what I'm about to give them, but at least I'll make the deadline." I was fully prepared for it to be a failure, but then I got a call from a friend who said, "Oh my God, Mark, everybody's talking about your article."

I was like, "Really? Oh shit!"

Shawn "Speedy" Lopes: As a reader, you could never know what to expect from Mark Chittom. His Dambuilders review was about almost everything but their music. He talked about how he punched some guy in the back and ran away and hid, and how he had an instant crush on Joan Wasser when he saw her on stage. It was like he could never write straight; he always had an unusual take on things, which made for great reading. I loved pretty much anything Mark wrote because he was so unconventional. Plus he was entertaining because he either didn't realize or didn't care who he offended.

Mark Chittom: With ADD and ADHD, when you have a mind like that, it's just lots of chaos, which is great for creativity. You have all of these thoughts that really seem to not have anything to do with each other, and you see relationships between things that a lot of people don't see. Over time, you become this naturally out-of-the-box thinker because thinking inside the box doesn't work. It's just not how your mind works. I enjoyed pushing the boundaries at the *Weekly,* even though, really, they never said, "This is too much." The more weird it was, the more they liked it.

Laurie Carlson: It was very clear to me, over time, that I was there to protect the editorial staff, and unless there was something that was factually wrong, there would be no apology for anything. People were invited to write their letters to the editor. If there was a factual mistake, we would print a correction. We did very, very little of that over the twenty-three years I had the paper.

Julia Steele: Now, Laurie had a budget to pay writers ten cents a word. And that was the hardest thing about being the editor of the *Weekly.* I felt like I was between a rock and a hard place because the writers, in my view, were simply not getting paid what they should have been paid to do the quantity and quality of work that I wanted them to do. I mean, I was paid so little to be the editor, but I felt the paper, had its business model been structured differently, would have been better capitalized and people would have been better compensated.

I came to feel like, "How can I, on one hand, say yes, we're running a progressive newspaper, and yet at the same time we're paying people so little it feels like exploitation?" We would try to look at it in a really democratic way, like, "This paper is a success, people are reading it, so how can we be creative here and make it work for everyone?" and I feel like when we would seek to have conversations like that, we were totally shut down. I think everyone who went into the *Weekly* experienced that without fail. It became known by anyone who ever worked there that you were going to run into that brick wall.

Laurie Carlson: I think the one mistake I really made was not trying to find more funding so that Julia could have an assistant, because Julia was the best editor we ever had. If we had done that, I think she would have stayed. That's what she really wanted more than a better wage, and I just didn't feel that the resources were there to do that.

Derek Ferrar: We had differences with Laurie over many things. *Honolulu Weekly* was a good springboard for talent, but it wasn't a living wage, and I think that's what upset us the most. I believe the writers never went up, in the entire history of the *Weekly*, past ten cents a word. We were asking them to go above and beyond for starvation wages, and that was our primary frustration. The good ones would be developing a resume, and some of them got hired by the *Honolulu Advertiser* or other jobs to pay their bills.

Laurie Carlson: I have to say, I feel good that we gave people a leg up in terms of their careers and getting them launched. We've even got legislators who were interns at the *Weekly* who are still serving. But it was very frustrating not to have the money to be able to really pay people what they deserved or give them what they needed.

You know, at one point, towards the end of the *Weekly*, I knew it wasn't doing well, and I tried to get Civil Beat interested in the *Weekly*. And to me, it would have been a brilliant marriage because we had a paper product, they had an online product. We had arts and entertainment and kind of the heart of the community to offer, and if Pierre Omidyar, who started Civil Beat, had been a little bit more humble and a little bit more able to see the brilliance of it, it would have worked so well to have Civil Beat combined with *Honolulu Weekly* to do all the things Civil Beat doesn't do now and to have a paper product that, at least initially, would have promoted the online product. That was a big disappointment to me. I never got past his minions to give him the *Weekly* to have it continue. That was very disappointing. But I do think the *Weekly* made a difference in Honolulu, and it was really important for us to aim to do that. It was a wonderful life's work.

19

THE RADIO REVOLUTION

Several years before Norm Winter transformed Jelly's from a modest book and record shop to Hawaii's premier used-and-new retail chain, he launched an audacious venture that he believed, with some imagination and a little luck, would revolutionize the music industry.

It was in 1979, when the almighty AM band still ruled the airwaves, that Winter, with backing from local retailers, struck a $2,000-a-month deal with KIKI-AM to broadcast the Hawaiian Island Music Report, a weekly countdown of Hawaii's most popular songs as determined by ballots cast at various voting boxes around Oahu.

By agreement, songs from the countdown were integrated into the station's playlist, thereby shifting a good portion of KIKI's programming from a single program director to the public at large. It was a radical move. To further empower the people, Winter also encouraged "song discoveries"—underexposed tracks submitted by listeners—to be voted on live on the air, with winning selections guaranteed airplay the following week.

The countdown, which aired 10 a.m.-2 p.m. Saturdays, was an immediate hit. "Woolworth's would be open after the show, and I'd go down there and it was unbelievable," remembers Winter. "There'd be lines of people waiting to fill out a ballot. We had a lot of ballots from maybe five or six different locations, and I counted them all."

Most of the votes favored soft rock, leftover disco, and contemporary ballads by the likes of Earth, Wind & Fire; Rex Smith; and Melissa Manchester, though under-the-radar tracks by then-rising acts like Triumph and The Police occasionally found their way onto the countdown. Once, upon hearing The Clash's "London's Burning" breach the airwaves, Program Director Austin Valli stormed the control room and snatched the record off the turntable mid-song. Valli was fired shortly thereafter by station management, and the Hawaiian Island Music Report was allowed to continue unimpeded.

In the twentieth week of the show, KIKI learned it had skyrocketed from a 4.4 share to an astonishing 12.1 in the October–November 1979 ratings period, good for second place in the Honolulu market. Sensing a winning formula, the station's owner, Jim Gabbert, asked Winter to sign over the rights to the Hawaiian Island Music Report so that he might take the concept nationwide. When Winter refused, Gabbert changed the name to the Official Hawaii Music Report and carried on without him. "But of course, they didn't count the ballots, and it fell apart," says Winter.

Winter's next foray into radio came in 1985 at KWAI, a hits-oriented AM outlet struggling to keep pace in a market now dominated by FM properties. Though management promised to include the program's ten biggest vote-getters in its weekly rotation, it often balked at playing anything that strayed too far from the mainstream. "I got really excited when they finally agreed to add songs from Depeche Mode and Siouxsie & the Banshees," Winter remembers. "But they got really upset about Metallica's 'Ride the Lightning' and said they couldn't play it because McDonald's didn't like it, which was bullshit."

When Suicidal Tendencies' "Institutionalized" cracked the countdown at No. 20, Program Director Stan Cook could not believe his ears. "That's not a song," he told Winter. "That doesn't go on the radio ever again." Two weeks later, however, voters moved "Institutionalized" up to the No. 8 position, ensuring it steady airplay for the coming week. Cook was hysterical. "That's when, in a rage, he pinned me up against a wall like he was gonna hit me," recalls Winter, who watched Cook's fist fly past his head and straight through the door behind him. "He couldn't get it back out, and he's the only one who could run the sound board, so we had dead air for five to seven minutes while I tried to get it out of there without hurting his hand." Ultimately, KWAI did not survive the year, and Winter's concept once again went dormant.

When he took another shot at radio in 1991, the musical landscape was much different. It was brimming with alternative rock, post-punk, thrash metal, and hardcore rap that had long been brewing beneath the surface. For years, Winter watched as groups like N.W.A., Slayer, Jane's Addiction, and The Cure consistently outsold many of the biggest pop artists at his Jelly's stores. Meanwhile, techno, acid house, industrial, noise rock, Miami bass, and other peripheral sounds helped his music department clear millions of dollars annually with virtually no airplay. "The world had changed so much in those six years, and yet the suppression of music on the radio had just gotten worse and worse," he says.

With Jelly's on firm financial footing and enjoying record profits, Winter obtained the financing to launch a new enterprise. This time, instead of hoping for cooperation by radio executives, he hammered out a deal which gave him total programming control of KDEO, a station that had been simulcasting country music on AM and FM.

He christened this project Radio Free Hawaii and instituted the slogan "The Radio Revolution." With scores of ballot boxes planted across the island and a TV commercial in circulation, an entirely new audience, most of whom were unaware of his stint on KWAI or too young to remember his time at KIKI, eagerly participated in Winter's concept. "It was insanity," he recalls. "By the time we got on air, we had 17,000 different songs voted for. People wanted variety."

Again, Winter gave his audience exactly what they asked for, and it paid dividends. By playing music other stations refused to acknowledge and showcasing vital, upsurging musical acts in concert, Radio Free Hawaii earned itself an allegiant following. Remarkably, KDEO-FM placed among a handful of America's favorite stations in the *Rolling Stone* Readers' Poll every year it was eligible.

Still, funding such an operation without corporate backing was a constant challenge, and in late 1994, the station succumbed to the bottom line, albeit briefly. Against great odds, it returned from the dead six months later, though there were forces Winter could not entirely outmaneuver, and in 1997, it finally folded for good. To its supporters, Radio Free Hawaii became a symbol of the great musical shakeout of the 1990s, and by turning over the airwaves to the people, it delivered a radically diverse and authentic soundtrack to a transformative decade.

THE LIBERATOR

Norm Winter: Nobody understands the power of radio. When people share music through a radio station, wonderful things happen. New, exciting music appears and everything falls into place, just like in the '60s.

All I really wanted to do was stop the record companies' control of what gets played on the radio, and I thought a ballot system was the answer. I wanted to know what the people really wanted to hear without influence from the record labels.

Pete Vidito: Norm was a risk taker. Props to him for having that impulse to circumvent this tendency by the music industry to dictate what people are exposed to. He gave the people what they really wanted and didn't condescend to them. It's like, "You want this? Great. I'm not going to tell you what you like; you tell me what *you* want." He did that with Jelly's; he did that with Radio Free. It was always bottom up. Norm is a populist at heart.

Norm Winter: Actually, it was Pete and his best friend, Tom Williams, who were in the music department at Jelly's. They heard my idea for the station and kind of pushed me to do it. I had so many things going on that it wasn't the number one thing I was thinking of doing.

I eventually talked to Bob Loew at KDEO about getting on the air and he said, "Well, I'm going belly up, so I'm not sure I'll be able to hang on." Then I found a way to get the money to lease the station, but Bob insisted I take over the AM side as well as the FM. He was desperate. He would have never done it under normal conditions.

Jenifer Winter (Radio Free Hawaii promotions director and research coordinator): As you know, Norm is my biological father. I was born in Los Angeles, and my parents had separated and then ultimately divorced, and I would spend my summers with him in Hawaii as a child. We would live at the Y or at some weird boardinghouse or these really creepy places. He'd been living in the brush in Haleiwa at one point, he told me.

One time I remember we didn't have any money, and he told me we would only eat orange things for two weeks, so we literally had this giant bag of carrots and a giant bag of oranges. I mentioned it to him as an adult and he goes, "Oh yeah…that probably wasn't a good idea, right?" But he's a very sweet person, generally. Like an overgrown child in some ways.

Pete Vidito: Norm had long gray hair and wore aloha shirts and a beret, and he always evoked this hippie sensibility, but he was actually more of a Yippie prankster. You know, like a hippie, but a lot more like, "Let's jam the system!"

Norm was always really kind and decent to me, but he could also be kind of erratic. Jelly's and Radio Free were always a bit chaotic. You never really knew who the fuck was in charge, but I kinda liked that anarchism. It seemed non-hierarchical and very democratic.

Jenifer Winter: My dad loves chaos. He grew up kind of an unusual kid, so he's always related to and rooted for the underdog. He really wants people to not be bound by societal conventions and to understand who they are through music and art. He's really a liberator, I think.

Cary Hayashikawa (Radio Free Hawaii station manager): You know, when I first met Norm, I was working at Muntz Stereo, and we had, like, a dozen locations or something. I would take him to the stores with me and bet people that he would know the catalog number of any record or eight-track tape they pulled off the shelf, and everybody would say, "No fucking way," right? So I wound up winning plenty money. That was amazing because he memorized every single number of every album and could order everything by the number. Nobody could stump him. But that's Norm. I know sometimes it doesn't even look like he's paying attention to anybody, like he's ignoring people, but it's because he's so single-minded.

Jenifer Winter: He's not, to my knowledge, autistic, but he kind of presents in that way to some people because he becomes obsessed with certain things. He can be emotionally connected to somebody, but he can also come across as sort of disconnected or having his head in the clouds. He's just a creative, mystical person who has these really grand visions, the radio station being one of them.

Kai Han a.k.a. Jus' Kai (Radio Free Hawaii DJ): I believe Norm's a genius. I don't think I ever heard of quantum mechanics before talking to him, or any of these things he had going on in his head. His mind is up there in the ether. He's rooted to this realm, I believe, but he's also on another level in the way he thinks, and sometimes it's beyond what other people can imagine. He kind of reminds me of Doc in *Back to the*

Future, where he's this creative genius and other people look at him like he's crazy, but his mind is just so far ahead of where everyone else is.

THE FIRST DJS

Norm Winter: As far as hiring DJs, people had told me to listen to Mohammad, and I just heard him for ten minutes. I didn't need to hear any more. I was so excited, you have no idea. He was the first one I went after. The first week he was on, people told me, "Norm, this is incredible." I had listened to Dave O'Day and wanted to have him on too. Then I listened to Franchon and got her to work part time. Tom and Pete were so adamant about being involved, I put 'em on in the afternoon, and they only stayed a few months. Weird. After they made me start the damn station. Unbelievable.

Tim Pagan a.k.a. Dave O'Day (DJ at Radio Free Hawaii, KTUH): I remember getting the call from Norm when I was on the air at KTUH. I think I was doing the midnight-to-three shift. He calls me and says, "Hey, I'm starting a radio station—you wanna work for me?" and I'm all like, "Yeah! Fuck yeah!"

Franchon Luke: I'd see Norm whenever I went to Jelly's, but I never talked to him, so I don't think he knew me or even listened to me before, but Pete and Tom recommended me. It seemed like a big opportunity.

Radio Free Hawaii started with a lot of college DJs from KTUH, and because I was in the KTUH production department, I did train a lot of them on the basics, but they totally took it to the next level. I just adored these kids who were so smart and had an intense love of music: Pete and Tom, Dave O'Day, Shawn Lopes, Cathy Chang, Kimo Nichols. They were some of Radio Free Hawaii's first DJs.

The way Norm explained it when we all got hired was this station would play all genres of music, but he wanted people to vote on it. I was thinking, *How is that even going to work?* because I was used to the way it was at KTUH at the time, where you would have three-hour blocks

Cocteau Twins' Robin Guthrie signs a concert poster during an interview at Radio Free Hawaii. *Courtesy of Shawn Lopes*

of certain types of music like classical, jazz, or rock. KTUH did have freeform programming after midnight where it was okay for the DJ to play anything and everything, but Norm said Radio Free Hawaii was going to do that all day; just mix it up and play every style of music back-to-back. I was thinking, *How are you going to do that?*

Mohammad Rouf: The first meeting I remember very well. There was a small shack on King Street, right across from Zippy's restaurant. I walked in and I saw this guy with a blue beret, and when I heard him talk, I thought, *Wow, this is interesting idea!* People gonna vote for music, people gonna cast ballots, and we gonna tally them on Saturday morning?

The concept was unbelievable. I just thought, *Wow, this guy Norm is genius!* And that's how I learned about Radio Free Hawaii.

Shawn "Speedy" Lopes: By the time the DJs were chosen, the only opening left was the weekend overnight slot, midnight to six, but that was cool with me if I could just get in there. Then something opened up which entailed basically manning the equipment for Mohammad's show on weeknights because I guess he couldn't handle the technical stuff himself. It wasn't that complicated, but it was too much for him to deal with somehow. That job was like putting out fires all night because he could go off on some tangent, start yelling into the mic, and forget all about the music. I'd have to adjust his volume, keep track of the playlist, take calls, make sure the ads got played, and basically keep him focused. That's where the nickname "Speedy" came from: running back and forth in the studio, trying to keep Mohammad's show from devolving into chaos, pretty much.

People would constantly call the station, curious about this weird guy on the air, wondering if he was putting on a fake accent. I was like, "No, seriously, he's for real." Mohammad even looked like he might work in some office cubicle. You know, this slim Bangladeshi dude in a button-down shirt, khakis, loafers, and a middle part in his hair. He was actually a substitute teacher in his spare time, but over the phone he'd tell callers stuff like, "Well, I'm about four hundred pounds, dreadlocks, maggots in my hair. Why? Do you want to meet Mohammad?"

Don "Lips" Fujiyama (Radio Free Hawaii DJ): I heard Mohammad's show and thought he was fucking crazy because it was all ranting, right? I thought he was nuts for a long time. His thing was, "I don't care; I'm just gonna talk, and I'm gonna challenge people!" He would just go off on social and political topics if you let him.

I couldn't even tell who the real Mohammad was because when he would talk to you, he'd talk to you differently than when he was on the radio. In person, he was laid back and talked slowly and seemed almost sorta like drunk. He never drank a drop of liquor, though.

Norm Winter: Lips was one who kept bugging me for a job, and when I was desperate I finally let him in. I always appreciate persistence, and he bugged me for a long time. I didn't want to do it, to tell you the truth, but everybody liked him, and he was so good with our interns. Cary and a couple of DJs like Kathy With a K were really supportive of him.

Before I put her on the air, Kathy was doing sales for us and setting up ballot boxes in stores on the island. She did a very good job of that, by the way. She's still on the radio today.

UNPREDICTABLE RADIO

Jenifer Winter: We had hundreds of ballot boxes around the island that anyone could vote at. They were in stores, restaurants, and bars, and eventually we got them in a few high schools as well.

Early on, someone had created a very well-intentioned but poorly performing program to type in all of the votes and then tabulate them in this little Macintosh computer. It did not work. There was no authority control, so you'd have fifty variants of the same song, and we couldn't merge them. It was a nightmare. That didn't last more than a few weeks before we scrapped it and did everything by hand.

This was happening in the last moments before the Internet, so it's hard for people now to understand that there was an actual physical network of people working behind the scenes. We'd have teams of people driving around the island collecting paper ballots and sorting through them by the thousands. Pat Ohta and I were working together at that point, with Mari Matsuoka as our supervisor.

For a whole week's worth of ballots, it could take a whole day of just sitting somewhere, looking over everything. I would say on average, we went through 3,500 to about 5,000 ballots a week, and I saw all of the ballots every week. Norm typically handled the ballots after double-checking our work, and it took a lot of concentration to literally go ballot by ballot by ballot and then go through them again. I'm sure there are more efficient ways to do it now, but at the time, it worked pretty well, to be honest.

Shawn "Speedy" Lopes: Every once in a while, someone might ask you, "What kind of music do you like?" and what do most people usually say? "Oh, I listen to all kinds of music." If that's true, then you probably listened to Radio Free Hawaii in the '90s. I mean, nothing was off-limits. We played punk, pop, electronic stuff, hip-hop, reggae, ska, you name it. If it got votes, we'd play it. If it got lots of votes, we'd play it more often.

It was probably mind-blowing for people to hear their favorite grind-core or Belgian techno song on the radio for the first time. I'd say pretty quickly we had a lot of diehard fans because we were playing all the stuff other stations refused to play, and the only reason we were playing it is because listeners were telling us with their ballots, "This is what we really want to hear." Plus it made for really unpredictable radio.

Norm wasn't even trying to start a cool or cutting-edge station; he just wanted to give the people what they wanted. In fact, our first T-shirts we handed out at events said "102.7 FM" on the front and "Program Director" in the upper left corner because we were actually programmed by the people, not by some guy taking calls in his office, listening to record labels tell him what songs the station should play each week. We gave away tons of those shirts. You used to see them everywhere back then. Our bumper stickers too.

Franchon Luke: Compared to the '80s, it just seemed like there was way more music in the '90s. There were so many more concerts and new venues to see bands. You'd also see a lot more local bands starting up because there were more opportunities to get out there and play. There were more indie labels getting wider distribution and people putting stuff out on their own. It was a cool thing to watch this expansion of music, and in Hawaii, Radio Free was right there, helping it grow.

Pete Vidito: I really think Nirvana's "Smells Like Teen Spirit" changed the course of music, you know? It blew up mainstream radio in America and set the whole '90s alternative movement in motion. Aesthetically, I'm not, like, the hugest fan of the song, but its role of awakening all these kids en masse…it was kind of like a new punk rock. I think it was a straight-up zeitgeist thing; right time, right place. The mood was just shifting for whatever reason or reasons. Kids, or at least a certain large subset of the youth, didn't want the glossy shit anymore. No more Wilson Phillips or Amy Grant. They were just ready for *realness*. All of a sudden this smelly-looking band appears, and they're devastating and they're singing about all these dark feelings that I feel, and it's making millions of dollars? Sick!

Shawn "Speedy" Lopes: It was a weird setup, though. There were these very seasoned country music DJs down the hall being relegated to AM radio by us. We were just having a blast at the other end of the building, cranking anything and everything from Anthrax to De La Soul to the Pixies, and I'm sure there was some bitterness there because we were just kids with barely any radio experience taking over their FM signal. For a while, we were getting bomb threats on the office phone line from some disgruntled country listener. Maybe it was one of their DJs, I don't know.

To kind of break the tension, Norm, being a big football fan, had this idea of broadcasting this ridiculous football game between the two stations with the winner taking over the loser's signal for twenty-four hours. There were some really kooky rules involved, like playing on an L-shaped field and using props like fishing nets and swim fins. We lost the game and had country music blaring over our station the following day. Can you imagine something like that happening these days with these gigantic media conglomerates and multimillion-dollar radio properties? There's no way. It was so bizarre it made it into the newspaper. We started to get some media attention because we were just so unlike anything out there.

DANCEFLOOR DEMOCRACY

Dave O'Day: There was a BBC TV program in the '90s called *Rough Guide*. It was this British travel show that went around the world to show you what was really bumpin' in different places. I think you could watch it on PBS in the U.S. They came to Hawaii one year, and they were really intrigued by what we were doing on the air because a lot of the artists we played were British. They did a segment on the station and showed the lines outside Pink's Garage for our Dancefloor Democracy event and said, "Look what this radio station's doing!"

Shawn "Speedy" Lopes: Pink's Garage was a nightclub on the backstreets of Kaka'ako that needed a boost in clientele. Some of the Pink Cadillac people had taken over a warehouse space on Waimanu Street, but it was in this industrial area that was too far to walk to from Waikiki or Restaurant Row, so there wasn't a lot of nightlife around there except for a few dive bars. Then someone had the idea to take what we were doing on air and bring that whole ballot system into a nightclub and broadcast the whole thing live. They called it Dancefloor Democracy because most of what was played that night was read off ballots from people in the club.

The first night, a handful of people showed up, not more than thirty. I remember producing ads for it, and it was a really disappointing night because we all had high hopes for it. But we had no idea what was about to come.

Chris Esteron: I was one of the lighting guys at Pink's Garage, and I remember that conversation about how much money was spent and how they had brought in all this extra alcohol. They thought this was gonna be the night that set it all off and it didn't. Everybody was kind of hopeful but not expectant the second week, like, "I'm gonna put on a happy face, but I don't think this is gonna work." And then, oh, it did. The second time, the whole place was packed, like you-couldn't-even-dance packed. I remember cops came at one point because you couldn't even drive your car down the street.

Shawn "Speedy" Lopes: What nobody knew was that a massive amount of people were actually tuned in the first night, and so the following Friday there were over a thousand people trying to get inside, and a huge crowd spilled out onto Waimanu Street. It was really a shocking turnaround from the week before. From there, it just took off. Other clubs suddenly popped up nearby like the Faktory, Zone 24, and Sanctuary.

Cary Hayashikawa: In order to go live from Pink's Garage, we needed a special direct telephone line that ran from the club all the way to our studios in Waipahu. You pay by the mile, so I think the Garage paid $800 a month for that telephone line. It was only used on Fridays, but it was great for the station because we got the money at the door, and it was during a time slot that we couldn't sell anyway because who wants to advertise at that hour of the night? Now that I think about it, we were probably the first station in Hawaii to do this kind of all-night live broadcast from a nightclub.

Don "Lips" Fujiyama: Richard Blade from KROQ in LA came to one of our Dancefloor Democracy events and DJ'd there, and he was so blown away by how many people were outside the club on a Friday night that he went back to KROQ and started throwing live Friday night parties at the Palace in Hollywood, and they got the same kind of result. Huge crowds.

Dave O'Day: Tons of people would show up every Friday, and they would fill out ballots, send 'em up to the DJ booth above the bar in a little basket, and we'd read out their names and play songs they voted for.

Mohammad started out hosting it with Daniel J as DJ. The thing is, Mohammad didn't know to wait for the break to open the mic, and he would talk all over the music. He had no concept of working around the mix, so he lasted two Fridays. Daniel said, "I can't work with him. Keep him off the mic. He can't be on the mic. Just…no." So I stepped in for Mohammad, emceeing, giving T-shirts away, keeping it interactive.

There'd be some deep house, some techno; we'd throw in some Fugazi, Nirvana, or Cypress Hill. Then someone might vote for KMFDM or Poor Righteous Teachers, and people are hearing this insane mix on the radio, like, "Fuck, this party is kickin'!"

Shawn "Speedy" Lopes: Dave O'Day was the perfect host for Dancefloor Democracy because he's like everybody's party bro from Kailua, the class clown, always down for fun. If someone asked you, "Where's the party at?" you'd point to Dave and go, "Stick with that guy!" He worked great with Daniel J.

Norm Winter: Daniel turned out to be a godsend for me. He was the number one DJ in Hawaii and probably one of the top DJs in the country at the time. He DJ'd all over the world, yet he never wanted any money to get involved with the station.

GOLDENVOICE

Cary Hayashikawa: Then Goldenvoice came into the picture. Rick Van Santen was co-president of Goldenvoice, and they were going to come in and work with Matt and Mike Grim to bring in some really good but maybe lesser-known groups from the mainland.

Matt Grim: Gary Tovar ended up getting busted for selling weed, and his underlings, Paul Tollett and Rick Van Santen, wound up owning Goldenvoice. I knew them through Gary Tovar, but when they took it over, they weren't loyal to me and my brother. They were using us for our connections. We got all these people involved and ended up getting screwed out of everything.

Cary Hayashikawa: When I met Rick, I thought, *Wow, this guy's really trying to do something here, and we're the only station playing a lot of that stuff.* So Rick and I made a deal. I said, "I know you gotta bring in groups that might not sell in order to get the bigger ones." So I said, "You pay me advertising money for the groups that you know will sell, and I'll give you free advertising for the groups the record labels make you take."

Shawn "Speedy" Lopes: Seeing Tantra Monsters, Dread Ashanti, Elvis '77, B.Y.K., Spiny Norman, and a bunch of other local bands get voted onto our weekly playlists inspired kids to start making music. It gave bands a way to reach a wider audience, and a lot of them got to open up for major concerts, which was something tangible to shoot for.

Franchon Luke: I remember some of our DJs would help greet visiting bands at the airport with Mari when she was working with Goldenvoice, and I'd also worked for Rico Lago when he was promoting concerts.

I'd do things like pick up Red Hot Chili Peppers and get them checked in to their hotel, then take them to Club Rose and sit at a table in the back as all the strippers came out. I didn't want to touch anything because it was my first time there. Oh, God. Everybody had told them that's where all the beautiful girls were, and of course, they'd come back and say, "I met a girl," and it was like, "Okay, you can go, but don't miss the show!" You'd have to keep an eye on them and keep them out of trouble.

Don "Lips" Fujiyama: Don Ho was performing at the Waikiki Beachcomber, and because I knew Don and everybody at the door, we'd take bands like Lush and Blink 182 to his show when they came to town. They'd take pictures, hang out with Don Ho, have a drink, and *hele on.* Everybody loved him. He was an icon. He was like Elvis, you know? Guys like the Mighty Mighty Bosstones and NOFX loved meeting Don Ho. They got off on it.

Dave O'Day: One time, Ozzy Osbourne called up from his limo while I was on the air. He was in town for a concert and was wondering what our station was all about. He said he never heard anything like it before. He thought it was some kind of pirate radio.

RADIO FREE SYDNEY?

Norm Winter: There was an Australian woman named Belinda Bradford who was our promotions and marketing director. Well, in 1993 she went to Australia to license our concept with 2 Triple M FM. They broke off talks, but they started using the name "Radio Free Sydney" and were planning to use our format. She called Cary when she found out, and they went to a lawyer, and I joined them out there, and we had a court battle. The judge made this station settle for $40,000 and they eventually canned the whole project.

Shawn "Speedy" Lopes: When Norm came back from Australia, he told us airport security had asked him to state his purpose of coming to Australia. So with a big smile, he lifts his index finger into the air and says, "I'm gonna start a revolution!" Wrong choice of words. They detained him for four hours.

A REAL PRESENCE

Chessa Au (Radio Free Hawaii intern): The biggest thing back then was the Big Mele. *Mele*, of course, meaning song or music in Hawaiian. Every year, Goldenvoice and Radio Free would put on this gigantic music festival at Kualoa Ranch that caused major traffic jams in all directions. Oh my god, you're beside a mountain with a beautiful view of the ocean, rocking out with all of your friends to Tool or Fishbone or Social Distortion or Primus. You'd hear about Lollapalooza and other music festivals on the continent, so for us to have our own version, you felt recognized. Like, we have a real scene here. We have a presence.

Franchon Luke: It was totally different from the decade before. I remember interning at KPOI and going to rock concerts at the Blaisdell in the '80s and seeing the typical groupies, and it really depressed me. I'd get to go backstage and it's like, "That's so sad." Even the roadies were gross.

But in the '90s, seeing Bikini Kill and meeting Kim Gordon from Sonic Youth, it's like, "You're so groundbreaking!" All these female-fronted bands were coming to town: Breeders, L7, The Muffs, Belly, Shonen Knife, Veruca Salt. The opportunities for females were suddenly so much better.

Even the opportunities for our interns were better. They started out as fans of the station and became friends with the DJs and came in to help; then they learned to run our equipment and got to go to concerts. Some of them even got on the air as DJs.

Chessa Au: Even as an intern, the people at the station always treated me like a person and not like some kid. One year I was asked to stay at the station and run the soundboard for Norm while everybody else was off at the Big Mele. I didn't have an FCC license or even know what that

The Big Mele music festivals were held beneath the majestic Koʻolau mountain range. *Courtesy of Shawn Lopes*

meant. I was thinking, *How come the owner of the station doesn't know how to operate the equipment? I'm only fifteen!*

Jenifer Winter: I was driving the station van in Kaneohe, and this whole group of skater kids chased it and grabbed onto the rear, and we kind of went cruising. That van would attract all sorts of people. I'd be trying to collect ballots, and people would come up and sometimes you'd even hear a squeal. They didn't care that I wasn't a DJ. They were just excited to see the Radio Free Hawaii van.

Chessa Au: All you had to do was go to a Radio Free Hawaii concert and see how many thousands of people would show up every time. That's how you knew the station was a big deal.

Norm Winter: What people didn't know was I was behind with my payments to Bob Loew. I was paying him $20,000 a month instead of $36,000. At the time, I had to move the Jelly's store on Pi'ikoi Street to a $60,000-a-month place several blocks over on Ke'eaumoku. We were supposed to have other tenants move in to help cover the costs, but they all fell through. Then the comic book and baseball card markets totally collapsed, and we owed our comics distributor $500,000. If I had to do it over again, I would have just closed that store and kept the one out in Aiea.

I ran out of money completely and didn't even have money for Christmas. I had my wife and other family members telling me I ruined their lives. I just couldn't afford the station anymore, and Bob decided to put a classic rock station on our signal. That was in 1994, and we were off the air for six months until Cary found this guy in New York to get us on the air again.

Cary Hayashikawa: One of the labels we helped out was Quality Records, which was owned by this guy named Adam Levy. He also had a rap label on the East Coast. His dad was Morris Levy, who owned Roulette Records, which had a bunch of hits by Tommy James and the Shondells and a lot of famous artists in the '50s and '60s. There was a book that was put out about the big crooks in the music business, and his father was the main guy in it. Adam and his dad didn't get along.

I was looking for a way to start the whole thing up again and I asked Adam if he wanted to own a radio station and he said, "Sure!" Then I went to visit him, and he had this check for over $2,000,000 on his desk and I went, "Whoa, what the hell is that for?" And he explained that it had something to do with a Mariah Carey song he either wrote or had publishing rights to.

Well, when I had started negotiating with Bob Loew to get the station back, Adam flew out to Hawaii to meet me and had me meet him at some strip club in Waikiki, at the back end of the old International Marketplace. So he sits these two girls in my lap and he goes, "Okay, what do we need?"

And I said, "I think we can get it rolling if you can write me a check for twenty-five grand." I went to Bob Loew, threw the check on his desk, and we were ready to start it up again.

THE RATINGS GAME

Don "Lips" Fujiyama: If we wanted to have higher ratings—and I tried to express this to Norm—you really gotta pound the music. You gotta play the hits. Play them every hour because there are certain songs that represent a generation, and you can sing them in your sleep. You have to sell your soul to some extent. Norm wasn't willing to, and as staff, we were fine with that because it really is brainwashing, and I don't think he likes that aspect of radio.

Norm Winter: I did call-out research and each time, we either came in number one or number two, KIKI or us. We were one of the dominant stations, and in the 18-34 group we were definitely number one. Only when we started getting more votes for punk and played more Rancid and Pennywise and all that stuff, we dropped to four. Yet the Arbitron rating service had us way down at eleven, and the big advertisers only buy the top five. Our research said we were a landslide number one with males 18-24. Landslide. That was our hardcore demographic.

I checked the other stations that made the *Rolling Stone* Readers' Poll in our category, and all of them were number one in 18-34. So that's another reason I'm damn sure we were number one in 18-34. We might not have been number one in 12-34 because KIKI ranked higher with listeners under eighteen. That's the way I looked at it. Someone was lying and it wasn't us.

Shawn "Speedy" Lopes: A lot of us had questions about Arbitron's ratings. I mean, we never subscribed to their rating service because according to Norm, it cost tens of thousands of dollars to get the official results. Is that why we never got great ratings? Would they ever give a station who never bought their service good ratings over stations who consistently paid them tens or hundreds of thousands of dollars year after year? What if a successful station just decided to stop buying their results? Would they still get great ratings? And if so, what motivation would that station have to ever pay these huge sums of money to Arbitron again? It made us wonder.

Jenifer Winter: At one point, I took over our in-house call-out research. We had six people that we would hire, and they'd come out to the station at night to use the phones, randomly selecting names from the phone book. We'd ask people—obviously without telling them where we were calling from—the exact same questions that Arbitron asked: "During the past week, what radio stations have you listened to?" and "How many hours did you spend listening?" or "What demographic are you in?" What we found was, particularly with young males, we were dominating the market, and it was probably the most sought-after group because they were active listeners and spent money on stuff, typically. We'd also heard from people who were advertising with us that they knew the station was a really hot thing with their customers, but it was never reflected in the Arbitron ratings.

Cary Hayashikawa: You know that surf shop, Hawaiian Island Creations? They advertised through their ad agency, but they also did their own in-store survey, and we actually came in second to KIKI-FM when Arbitron had us way down the list. So they told their own ad agency they had to advertise with us.

Jenifer Winter: I thought it was suspicious because the things that we were seeing in our research were not what the ratings were saying. We had a lot of evidence that I think was very systematic, and I personally saw firsthand the data collection all the way through, so I'm very confident that what we found was very scientific and trustworthy.

Cary Hayashikawa: I told Adam, "If I don't show up in Arbitron, I'll keep struggling trying to get advertisers."

So he goes, "How much is Arbitron?"

I told him, "Fifty grand."

So he wrote Arbitron a check for fifty grand, and that's the first time we got decent ratings in Arbitron.

Norm Winter: And suddenly we were number one with males 18-24. Suddenly. After being number six for four years.

Cary Hayashikawa: We found out what we needed to find out about Arbitron, so Adam bounced the check. Even if people knew Arbitron was fake, there was nothing we could do about it because that was the only ratings company around. They're the only guys in town. That's how ad agencies buy radio time for their clients, and advertisers went by what Arbitron said. There used to be other rating services, but Arbitron ended up buying them all.

Norm Winter: I had no idea what I was facing, you know that? I just had no idea. At one time, you could only own two stations in a market. When the government passed the Telecommunications Act of 1996, it was supposed to open up competition in radio, but all it did was let the bigger companies swallow up the smaller guys. Bob Loew wound up selling the station soon after. Someone told me it was for $3.5 million, but I have no confirmation. Then we were off the air for good. That was it.

Cary Hayashikawa: Actually, I should have made our staff worry more. Then they would have cared more. It was just, "Oh, we're still gonna get our paycheck," blah, blah. It was such a struggle I just decided, "I don't think I want to do this anymore. I'm going to let it go its way."

To be honest, we actually had enough money on the books to show we were making money. But we weren't collecting the money fast enough to pay our bills, and everybody was taking it for granted. It just wasn't fun anymore.

At the beginning, we were bringing in all these bands to Hawaii with Goldenvoice and doing broadcasts from Pink's Garage, and by the end, even though we had a talented staff, I don't think everyone was using their talents to the fullest. I also saw Goldenvoice getting bigger and bigger, and I thought, *This concert promotion company that helped us kick things off is gonna get too big for us.* I think I ended up being right when you look at Coachella and how huge Goldenvoice got.

LIVES CHANGED

Jenifer Winter: I would hear things like, "Oh, your dad's really stressed about this" or "He's really worried about the station." I have one of Norm's ballots that he wrote one time. It's a very personal message to the universe. People would write heartfelt things on their ballots—it was amazing—about how much Radio Free meant to them, people saying, "My life has been changed by the station; don't ever leave." Those kinds of things made me realize this was a real cultural and social phenomenon that was really important to a lot of people and worth supporting.

Could something like Radio Free exist now? Probably not, for a lot of reasons. I don't know how it could have lived on in today's world without some type of corporate influence, which would have probably corrupted it in some way. So it was beautiful in its brevity, in a sense.

Shawn "Speedy" Lopes: If you were young and living in Hawaii in the '90s and you loved music, there was no better job to have than working at Radio Free Hawaii. None. I mean, we may not have been paid much, but it's still the best job I ever had. When it first went on the air in 1991, people didn't think it would even last six months, but it ended up lasting six years.

Franchon Luke: It was probably the most unique commercial station ever, and it happened at the right time with the right people, right here in Hawaii, and I don't think it could ever happen again. It was one man's crazy dream that became bigger than anyone thought it could ever be. A whole new generation of teens grew into adulthood with it. It really changed lives.

20

DARK CORNERS

With the grand opening of Pink's Garage in the fall of 1990, Honolulu could at last lay claim to a warehouse-style nightclub of its own, similar in spirit to those found in cities like New York, Detroit, Berlin, Manchester, and London. Though just one block south of bustling Kapiolani Boulevard, Pink's Garage sat on a dark, flood-prone tract of storehouses where the only activity after nightfall revolved around a trio of conjoined Korean hostess bars. This was a strip of town unlikely to attract fashionable crowds. Earlier in the year, a man dropped off his female passenger in a parking lot nearby and took a fatal shot to the temple from an unknown gunman. "It was a complete shithole, that whole area," recalls DJ and promoter Matt Grim, who nevertheless saw exciting possibilities with the arrival of Pink's Garage to the neighborhood.

Its ample floor space and relative isolation, blocks away from any residential plots, made Pink's Garage an ideal concert venue and nightclub. It quickly carved itself a niche by booking touring acts either too big for local bars or too raucous for the Waikiki Shell, yet not quite popular enough to fill nearby Blaisdell Arena. Some of its earliest bills included a diverse slate of artists such as Megadeth, Concrete Blonde, Social Distortion, the La's, Nirvana, Pantera, Book of Love, and Public Enemy. Its DJs were given freedom to branch out and explore bold new sounds other nightclubs forbade. This kind of daring and diversity made Pink's Garage the perfect partner for the no-holds-barred Radio Free Hawaii, whose on-site Friday night FM broadcasts and close ties with LA-based concert promoters Goldenvoice exposed new partiers to the club, many of whom swarmed up and down Waimanu Street when the venue was too packed to allow more patrons through its doors.

Never one to let a prime opportunity pass, in April of 1992, Grim opened the Faktory, an all-ages, anything-goes nightspot just a short walk from Pink's Garage. Hastily outfitted with the help of business partner Guy Brandwen in only four days, the Faktory, despite the rough edges and wet paint, was immediately popular with nightlifers. Some patrons, streetwise and punk-hardened, were unbothered by the indoor chain-link fencing and dusty digs; others, open-minded and artsy, came curious. Most of the remaining hordes were too young to get into proper nightclubs, yet quite willing to slum it on the backstreets of Kaka'ako for a taste of the underground nightlife.

By the end of 1993, After Dark, a competing two-story nightspot with twice the square footage of the Garage (by then officially shortened from Pink's Garage), opened for business in a neighboring industrial parcel across from Pier 38 on Nimitz Highway. As Goldenvoice hit its stride in the Islands, it booked more of its Honolulu shows there with brand-name bands that would come to define '90s rock: the Breeders, Rage Against the Machine, Foo Fighters, Sublime, Primus, Tool, White Zombie, Nine Inch Nails, and Helmet among them. In 1995, After Dark switched hands and became the Groove, then Nimitz Hall, and finally World Cafe in 1998. Live shows at the capacious nightspot became less frequent as World Cafe began to function more as a proper mainstream nightclub. Meanwhile, a new site, Pipeline Cafe, looked to lead the way for mid-sized concert venues when it opened in a former warehouse on Pohukaina Street the following year.

All through the '90s, as the more extreme forms of popular music began to gain acceptance worldwide, a number of metal, punk, post-punk, grunge, and industrial bands toured the globe, often stopping in the Islands en route to or from Asia, Australia, and the mainland U.S. Musical acts which would have been big money-losers to fly out to Hawaii just years earlier became some of Honolulu's hottest tickets. As with the hybridization seen with metal and punk in the 1980s, there was growing overlap between the goth, industrial, rock, and electronic music scenes in the 1990s, evidenced by the diverse crowds attending My Life With the Thrill Kill Kult and Nine Inch Nails at After Dark, two nights each of KMFDM and Skinny Puppy at Pink's Garage, and Ministry at Richardson Field.

In addition to this musical crossover, certain subcultures began to intermingle with adjacent scenes. Submission, a fetish boutique on Kapiolani Boulevard, beckoned to a new, provocatively dressed breed of goth who at times flirted with BDSM and other sexual taboos. Body piercing, an activity that once existed only on the extreme fringes of society, grew quickly in the '90s with support from various cultural subgroups. The Dark Side, a Waimanu Street shop that thrived off sales of heavy metal T-shirts, spiked wristbands, and jacket patches in the 1980s, adapted over time to also carry a stylish assortment of body jewelry, funky nail polish, Doc Martens footwear, and goth makeup. Body piercing would eventually become so accepted by the mainstream that in 2000, Britney Spears received her first belly ring while vacationing in Hawaii. Gus Diamond, who had the honor of piercing the pop princess, had established himself throughout the decade as an authority of the practice through his shops: Paragon Piercing, which shared floorspace with Submission; and Provocative Piercing, which he operated alongside Erin Figueroa, known in piercing circles as "The Piercing Elf," widely regarded as the first body piercer to set up shop in the Islands.

Figueroa, a California transplant whose brother Rod "China" Figueroa was a drummer with Los Angeles death rock legends Christian Death, packed her bags for Hawaii in the late '80s in a timely move that narrowly predated an epochal turn of events. The decade ahead would bring about major developments, not just in music but for society at large, as alternative subcultures, incorporated by big business, would leave an improbable but lasting mark on pop culture. "The timing of everything coming together was absolutely perfect," asserts Figueroa. "It all went hand in hand."

THE FAKTORY

Matt Grim: When Pink's Garage opened up, my brother and I started bringing in all kinds of groups there like Run-DMC and The Romantics and Dark Angel. I remember I went to put an ad in either *Scrawling Wall* or *Kaos*, and Guy Brandwen was the computer whiz and ad layout guy. I hit it off with him and started using him for my fliers. There were some PC-type people there that hated me and my brother, but Guy and me got along real well. He wasn't a club guy or anything; he was a dork. But we started hanging out more, and he found out he kinda liked the club life and the girls, 'cause up to then he was a full-on doofus. We started looking for places to start up our own nightclub, and the old Kodak Building was one of 'em. We both put up $1,200 to open the Faktory there and made our money back almost immediately.

Deb Aoki: The Faktory was an abandoned Kodak processing plant. How the hell did they get the landlord to let them use that building? I remember walking into that place and thinking, *Okay, there was actual chemical processing going on in here, and some of this looks scary.*

Matt Grim: It was 3,500 square feet, maybe more, and there was this area connected by a door that no one was renting out, so we just put an art gallery in there because nobody paid attention to it. That gave us another 1,800 or 2,000 square feet. There were also these massive roll-up doors that opened up to a huge space that we'd take over to do raves, and that gave us 8,000 square feet. Volcom even had an event there with huge skate ramps. There were live wires in there I didn't know about, though. One day we were cleaning up, and I accidentally touched a wire to something while I was putting more tape on it, and it sounded like a fuckin' stick of dynamite went off. I can't imagine—I mean, if somebody would've touched that, they would've been fuckin' dead, guaranteed.

Deb Aoki: At the time, one of the other circles I was in was the art scene in Hawaii, which deals with fine art and exhibits and stuff. I called in my connections at different arts organizations and explained the vision for this place: It's going to be like Area, or those world-famous nightclubs where you have these outrageous club kids and art installations where artists can do whatever they want in these spaces and make it a real happening, right? And I remember James Jensen from the Honolulu Academy of Arts and a couple of bigwigs from the arts community came and walked around with us, and they were just like, "Are you serious?" And yet, when it was hoppin', I saw those people there—they were all at the Faktory.

Matt Grim: We somehow got a crazy deal to have our ads played on Radio Free Hawaii, and that really blew us up. And because people heard about us through listening to Radio Free, when they came to the Faktory, they would be okay with dancing to the Bosstones, then "Hip Hop Hooray" by Naughty By Nature, and then some grunge song or any and every kind of music that was popular then. That was a really good time when there was really no musical bigotry, and even mokes would dance to Skankin' Pickle and shit. Like, that's fuckin' cool.

We also made a beer cage so that people could drink and BYOB, and because we kept them separated from the under-twenty-ones, for the most part, we let everybody in and made an outrageous amount of money, I'm not joking. The taxes we paid on it were insane, and that's what made me hate taxes. It was a fuckin' cash cow. After that, I realized, "Holy shit, we're not even serving alcohol!" This was all from collecting money at the door.

Romell Regulacion (Vocalist/multi-instrumentalist: Razed in Black, Lost Souls, Rime, etc.): There were no signs to tell you it was a night-club. You just had to know, or know somebody who knew, and it almost felt illegal, but I think that was the allure of the Faktory and that whole underground club scene at the time. You could go and hang out all night at some old warehouse, even if you were underage. I was one of those kids, and yet now that I'm a dad, it's like, "Oh, that's so wrong!"

Nelson Nakamoto (bassist: Knumbskulls, Days/Weeks/Months): I remember I was fourteen years old, and because my dad would never be home, pretty much I could do whatever I wanted. One night, my cousin picked me up with all of his friends and they took me to the Faktory. Shit, that kinda changed my life, you know? I remember I walked in there, and kids were skateboarding inside. I'm pretty sure it was a B.Y.K. show, but you could go into another section, and they would be playing hip-hop at the same time, stuff like Fu-Schnickens and Cypress Hill.

It amazed me how young everyone was. I used to trip out because some of these guys had spray-painted cars covered in stickers and shit. They would be throwing bottles against the wall in the parking lot or at other people. I was like, "Wow, everybody does whatever they want here." The Faktory made a big impression on me, but right after, it pretty much closed down. It was hard to go back to school after that. I actually didn't go past the ninth grade. I just stopped going to school at that point.

MY FAVORITE EGGPLANT

Matt Grim: Eventually I was served papers and got kicked out, but I got a good lawyer and managed to keep it going for four additional months. It cost a lot of money to fight it, but the Faktory was still making good money. Then Guy left to start up My Favorite Eggplant and some other things.

Deb Aoki: With My Favorite Eggplant, Guy turned another warehouse into a performance art and dance space because he could. He basically took that "If no one else is, I will" vibe to the next level. Then he said, "Next, I'm going to start this thing called Animals Ate Them where I'm going to import weird and obscure music and have my own store-within-a-store at Jelly's" and "If no one else will, I'm also going to start a skateboard and clothing shop called Funk Pistol that's going to be right above Jelly's because I can."

Right next door to Funk Pistol was a bowling shirt company, and he'd go in there and see shirts that people wouldn't pick up or were out of style and ask the guy, "Can you change the name tag on the shirts to 'Fucker' or 'Dumbass' or something?" and they would dutifully embroider it in beautiful script near the pocket on the shirt, and he would sell it at a three or four hundred percent markup. I still am in awe of his spirit of entrepreneurship.

Guy would just try things out and do it until someone said, "No, don't do that anymore." He and Matt Grim knew how to deal with grownups by giving them just enough information to get a yes, but not so much information that they would get a no.

ZONE 24

Matt Grim: So then I moved around the corner to the Sultan Building. It was a jewelry store that was vacant for years before I took it over. The storefront was on Kapiolani Boulevard, across from Blaisdell Arena, but the parking and our main entrance were in the back, across from Pink's Garage over on Waimanu Street. I called it Zone 24, and if you look at my old fliers, the "e" in Zone 24 was shaped like an ecstasy pill, and "x" is the twenty-fourth letter of the alphabet. Ecstasy and techno were what I was into at the time. That was my shit.

The crowds were good periodically, and there were some nights where it was rocking, but it never really kicked off like the Faktory. It was a struggle too, because I partnered with another guy who had no idea about nightclubs, and he turned into a dick. He thought he knew everything, and we started getting ugly crowds and gangster hip-hop shit happening. You'd think people from the Garage would walk across the street to Zone 24, but it never became the rave spot I was hoping for. I think the rent may have been eight or ten grand a month. It was a lot of fucking money. It lasted for at least six months but definitely not more than a year.

Deb Aoki: Let's face it, I mean, there's a troublemaker element in Hawaii. We also have tourists and a ton of military people living in Hawaii who are looking for a good time. Now, I don't want to paint everyone with a broad brush, but a small faction of outsiders treat every town like their personal shore leave where they feel they can make a big mess but don't have to clean it up. It's when the normies start getting wind of the underground that things start going to shit.

Gus Diamond (owner of Paragon Piercing; Provocative Piercing co-owner): There's three main reasons a person moves from the mainland to Hawaii. Reason number one is they're in the military. Reason number two is they're going to school, maybe UH or whatever. And reason number three is they're running from something. If someone told me they moved to Hawaii just because they wanted to, that was a red flag. You should probably keep an eye on that person.

Erin L. Figueroa a.k.a. Elf (owner of the Piercing Elf; Provocative Piercing co-owner): I came to Hawaii because I have family over here, and they rescued me from LA when I was strung out on heroin. I came over here October 22, 1988. I got really immersed with heroin, and things were getting really dangerous. Between '84 and '88 is when people first started getting killed with guns in Hollywood, and drive-by shootings and all that kind of stuff started exploding. It escalated fairly quickly. At that point, I was carrying guns and being involved with the Salvadorans and the Mexicans who were running heroin, and that's only going to end a couple of ways, especially 'cause I was in over my head in dope and owing people and everything else going on. I'm so glad I got plucked out of there when I did.

My backstory from my Hollywood days is pretty darn colorful. Like, I lived with Jane's Addiction, and I was the first bass player in L7. I'd been playing music up and down the West Coast already for a decade before I got here. I got involved with Jane's Addiction in probably '85 or '86, when they were first starting out. The guy I was going out with, Edino, was their first guitar player. He's since died of a heroin overdose. We got in a fight, and he chased me into the band room with a gun, and I moved out of the house. Everything in the song "Jane Says" is 100 percent true. Jane was actually my brother's girlfriend, who lived in the room I lived in after she moved out. My brother China was the drummer for Christian Death. You know, I don't really speak a lot about those times in Hollywood because it verges on the unbelievable.

PIERCING PLACES

Gus Diamond: For me, Hawaii was as far away as I could get from Texas and still be in the United States. It was the Navy that brought me over in '92. I left the punk rock stuff behind me, but I still had that sense of rebellion. It's just that now I had a haircut and a uniform. When I started looking for the underground scene in Hawaii, one of the first places I found was the Dark Side. They started doing piercings at some point. I'd already been doing body piercing for a few years while I was in the Navy because Navy divers got their nipples pierced and they got their penises pierced. It was a secret society-type thing amongst divers.

Anne Love a.k.a. DJ Nocturna (KTUH DJ; podcaster, promoter): The Dark Side was a little store near Jelly's when Jelly's was on Pi'ikoi Street. They sold jewelry, leather gloves, sunglasses, things like that. But I remember they were really big on piercing. I got my piercings there. At one point, I had ten in one ear and another twelve in the other ear.

Erin L. Figueroa: The Dark Side's owner, Hugo Okonogi, had originally hired me to do piercings out of there, but he reneged on me, and I went and did it elsewhere. My boyfriend rode for Devil's Breed, and I was living in a motorcycle shop in Waipahu and started piercing out of there probably in '89 or '90. That's where it all began for me. The Dark Side didn't start piercing until years later.

Gus Diamond: I'd heard of a person out there in Hawaii and one of the body jewelry companies told me they called her the Piercing Elf. I wanted to meet the Piercing Elf.

Erin L. Figueroa: I've been piercing myself since seventh grade. By the time I was fourteen or fifteen years old, I already had a dozen piercings. Then sometime in the early '80s I fell in with the S&M communities in Hollywood and in San Francisco, which were pretty much dominated by gay men back then, but I was a peculiar little person and I was accepted by them. So I learned the art of body piercing from the LA underground and later by Fakir Musafar, who was one of the early authorities on modern body modification. I was going to the Gauntlet, which was the first piercing place in Hollywood, and hanging with the Gauntlet people before bringing that over to Hawaii.

I was going to shows here heavily pierced, and word soon got around, and because I was well-versed in piercing male genitals through my association with the underground gay S&M scene, I was getting all the freaks on the island. Even Yakuza came over from Japan. Boy, oh boy, I had some really hairy situations early on because the people who were being pierced then were really hardcore fetish people.

From there, I bought an old barber's chair and opened up a shop on Waipahu Depot Road next to Banzai Tattoo in 1990 or 1991. I was a functioning drug addict then. Not just functioning, I was constructive. My parents were dope dealers, so I came from that background, and my dad taught me how to be a working member of society while I dealt dope and to always have a business to cover my tracks. I was, off and on, a dope fiend all through my shop in Waipahu and my shop in Waikiki. You know, I just held it together. Very few people knew. I went in and out of being a heroin addict, but I've been clean for years and years and years now. When L7 came to perform in '93, they came over to the shop, and fuck, I scored the whole band dope before they did the show at the Garage.

I hadn't really met Gus yet, but there was this guy coming to shows and throwing his piercing fliers on the ground, and at that point, I was the only piercer here. I'm like, "Who the fuck is this guy?" It was crazy because then Gus and I met when he offered to buy me a drink at Pink's Garage, and from that very minute, we were on the same page; we were like bros. Nobody knew that Gus and I were friends, and people were trying to pit us against each other, and we just weren't having none of that.

Gus Diamond: We became friends and business partners. Provocative Piercing was our shop in Waikiki that we opened in '94, near the Hilton Hawaiian Village resort and the Ilikai Hotel. We had a lot of stars come through over the years: Shaq, Snoop Dogg, Britney Spears. That's where I pierced Britney.

Erin L. Figueroa: Nipples, navels, and tongues paid our bills. Gus and I were making thousands and thousands of dollars. It was crazy how much the business was taking in. Sometimes we'd walk out of there at the end of the day with two or three thousand dollars each.

SANCTUARY

Matt Grim: After Zone 24, I moved across Waimanu Street to a warehouse a door or two from Pink's Garage, and I got that place for 2,000 bucks a month. That became the Sanctuary, which never took off as a techno club like I imagined, but that's where I met Courtney. Courtney was this skinny haole guy—and I actually know his full name, but he's always just gone by Courtney—who tried to present me with a goth night idea, and I was like, "Are you kidding me? It's not the eighties anymore." Like, "Dude, that is yesterday's news. That will never work!" He'd come up to me in the rickety DJ booth on the second floor with meticulous notes about what he wanted to do at my club, and I told him, "You're gonna fuckin' lose your ass, but I'll give you Wednesday night." He wanted to go 50-50 and I said, "You're not gonna make any money, so I don't want fifty percent of nothing."

Nelson Nakamoto: I knew the Sanctuary when it was kind of a gothic/industrial club. At first, they weren't gonna let me in because I was too young, but I was with my friend Michelle, and they knew her. She said, "Oh, you gotta meet this guy Courtney!" He was bartending there at the time, and when I met him I was like, "Why?" I just thought he was a fucking weird-looking guy, you know? He had a dog collar on with really black, pointy, Siouxsie and the Banshees makeup on and this T-shirt of a nun with her tits hanging out.

Gus Diamond: I don't know how this worked out, but I would meet a lot of strippers for some reason, and a couple of them were my first real friends on the island. They worked at the Wild Horse, right there by Axxtion Video on Kapiolani Boulevard. They were the ones who first introduced me to Courtney, who, at the time, was doing his Propaganda nights on Wednesdays, at Matt Grim's nightclub right by the Garage. I remember it was Halloween '93 that he held the first Dungeon there, and that became a regular thing on the scene for years.

Matt Grim: Courtney wanted to do a Halloween night, and I suggested a sexy bondage and fetish-themed party where hot bitches would dress up, and he found some rope bondage and body-piercing people, so I said, "Let's call it the Dungeon, and we can get a bunch of chicks that wanna dress sexy for Halloween to show up." Dude, it went *off the hook*! I said, "We gotta do these every two months!" That started to help build his own nights to where we started making Wednesday money as well. So Courtney is for sure the guy who single-handedly brought goth back to Hawaii and created a scene where there was no scene.

Gus Diamond: With this fetish lifestyle, some of us would play at home with floggers and stuff like that. It was just part of who we were and what we were doing at the time. Now there was a club with a sound system where you could go do this stuff.

Romell Regulacion: I went to places like the Faktory and the Garage, but most of my nightclubbing then would be at Courtney and Matt's goth nights. That was my home away from home. Those were the days

Radio Free Hawaii DJs Pinkie, Franchon, and Caraigh at the Dungeon.
Courtesy of Franchon Luke

when these underground clubs would suddenly pop up out of nowhere, here and there, real short-lived. I never realized it was the same group of guys running most of them. It was a trip too, because the Hawaii goth scene at that time grew to where E! Entertainment even came out and did a TV segment on it. That's how good it was then.

Erin L. Figueroa: The shows that happened at that time were incredible. They were *amazing* shows. All the bands loved coming to Hawaii and playing because our scene was so thriving and heavy over here.

Nelson Nakamoto: I would go to a lot of punk shows and all kinds of concerts. Courtney kind of took to me because I would go to the club afterwards with my friends and talk to him about bands like Pigface and Pailhead. The cover charge was eight to ten bucks, and that's a lot of money to spend to go somewhere when you're fourteen, but he would say, "Hey, do me a favor. I'll let you in for free and I'll give you some money. Just take this stack of fliers and after the next concert, just hand 'em out."

One night, their DJ quit and Courtney showed me how to run the mixer, and he gave me a couple hundred bucks to go buy CDs from Jelly's or wherever, and told me to come back next Friday and play some music. Then he would have me play Saturdays.

I didn't even meet Matt Grim at that point because Matt Grim would always show up late as hell. The club might run from eight 'til maybe two in the morning or some shit, and then from two in the morning until the sun came up was the afterparty. Sometimes I would go to the club on the weekends and not have a ride home, so I would stay for the afterparty, then fall asleep on the couch, and Courtney would wake me up, like, "Hey, we're closing. Don't you have to be at home at some point?" I was like, "Nah, doesn't matter." I guess since I was hanging out all night anyway, they had me bartending, selling beer and cigarettes and Herbal Ecstasy from behind the counter after hours.

Matt Grim: It wasn't long before the HCDA got Sanctuary kicked out, and they even shut down the Garage. That's the Hawaii Community Development Authority. We were dealing with all kinds of shit in Hawaii.

I remember for the longest time we hated Mark Chittom because he'd fuck our shit up with things he would write in *Honolulu Weekly* and get us on the police radar by joking about seeing "drug piles" and saying stuff like, "The palpable atmosphere of ecstasy almost got me high just walking in…" and "There were cuddle puddles everywhere, everybody's eyes rolling back in their heads, bunch of teenagers…" like, what the fuck? This is going to cause trouble for us! And it wasn't just a one-off thing; it was a whole bunch of snarky shit 'cause he was Mr. Smarty Pants. Nobody knows we spent tens of thousands of dollars defending ourselves with lawyers from all this shit and the mayor sending us a letter saying he was gonna shut us down. Remember, this is when the anti-rave propaganda was at its peak: "Oh, kids are dying from this and they're overheating, and ecstasy is killing people!" They literally used his article to try to shut us down. Meanwhile, we'd brought Mark in, gave him a bunch of drinks, and partied with him. He probably had no idea we were in the middle of a major legal fight, but I was like, "Mark Chittom—fuck him!"

Mark Chittom: My standard was, "Am I laughing when I write this?" and if I could humor myself, then that was good enough. But every now and then, people would complain: "Oh, he never really writes about what actually goes on." Usually, these would be the kind of people who would throw a party with maybe some hardcore drum and bass with no melody, where a dozen guys with hoodies would stand around a DJ booth looking like they weren't having any fun.

Matt Grim: Years later, we ended up doing a bunch of blow together, and I said, "Dude, I thought you were the biggest fuckin' dick. What the fuck was up?" and we hashed it out.

But all these things kind of came and went really quickly then. Within a two-year period, I had the Faktory, Zone 24, Sanctuary, and also a new version of the Sub Club. When I started up the Sub Club that second time, it was on Koapaka Street, where the Backdoor used to be.

SUB CLUB 2

Romell Regulacion: The Sub Club was literally a warehouse near the airport, where there were no signs or anything. If you'd never been there before, you would have to just listen for the bass and follow people to this one building with a blue light. Then you'd walk through a fence with black plastic tarp, and there'd be no one to check IDs or anything. As the evening progressed, it would get hot and people would start to strip off their vinyl and leather, alcohol would kick in, and couples might head for the dark corners. They even had whipping stations where a guy would have his pants pulled down with his back end showing, and there'd be girls spanking him with a whip. It was seedy and shocking, but it was so great.

Gus Diamond: Once, we brought in TSD, which stands for Traumatic Stress Discipline. It's a group founded by Allen Falkner, who was my mentor in body piercing. We did hook suspensions and flesh hook pulls where you're putting hooks in two different people who end up pulling on each other. It was a rite of passage-type thing for me, but it was more of a performance art and a show for the people who came out. There was also a kavadi, which is like a cage that goes over you, and you've got these big skewers with objects on the end of them that dig into your skin, and the more you dance around, the more they wiggle and stimulate the piercings.

Erin L. Figueroa: Gus and I were doing crazy stuff back then. We went from piercings to doing suspensions. We did a tug-of-war by putting flesh hooks in us as we were on either side of the stage, and we pulled against each other, and whoever ripped out first lost. Gus was so much bigger than me that my pulling on him barely did anything, so it ripped out of me first. Mind you, I was completely sober and not using, so for me, it was mind over matter, and my threshold for pain, I found out, was high. After the first two to four hooks, you've in a sense left your body, and there's a very big detachment that happens and you're running on endorphins.

Gus Diamond: Everybody wanted to go to these Dungeon events. I just remember showing up late sometimes, and there'd be a super long line to get in. I was like, "This is amazing!" Courtney would go to the military bases and put fliers in everybody's doors, and he would even bring some girls with him to drop off these fliers. One of them was in the Army, so she could get them on base. There were a lot of females who would go to the Dungeon and even work at the Dungeon.

Nelson Nakamoto: I remember going to a Dungeon party and seeing all these fuckin' high school girls walking around with duct tape on their nipples and stockings and panties. It was the craziest shit I ever seen, especially if you're fourteen or fifteen years old yourself, you know? Like, this is fucking insane!

I remember meeting Priya and Kayla, and those two were fuckin' crazy. Priya looked exactly like Bettie Page, and Kayla was, like, this tall Amazon chick, you know? They fucking scared the shit out of me. The first time I met Kayla, she had on a trench coat, a dog collar, and bra and panties. My friend introduced me to her and she's like, "Oh, hi!" and she just gave me a kiss on the lips, and I was like, "Whoa."

Chessa Au: I remember walking from my car to the venue and trying to ignore getting catcalled. I had an outfit from Submission that was sheer. I would never show my ass; I'd always have shorts on, with maybe a sheer bra and jacket, but you might see my nipple piercing. That was me being bold as a teenager.

Gus Diamond: The Dungeon was geared towards people who didn't fit in with mainstream culture. The young people who showed up were very much rebelling, and it was kind of a shocker to see some there because I don't think that could happen nowadays.

DJ Nocturna: I think everybody has a dark side, I do. Some people are just drawn to the look and sound of this lifestyle, and I'm not saying they're outcasts, but they're different, and when you're different, you embrace other people who are just like you. You feel a sense of belonging.

Nelson Nakamoto: People would trip out at school because I always had money from working the bar. I would go home with $300 a night. Being fifteen years old and having $600 cash on you for the week was kinda crazy. I would walk into class with eyebrow piercings, two piercings in my nose, one in my lip, fuckin' eyeliner from the night before, and fishnet pantyhose as a T-shirt under my shirt. What's funny is I was always chubby and kinda fat, but for some reason, this is when a lot of girls went out with me, and I made a lot of friends. They were like, "Man, this guy just does not give a fuck!"

RAZED IN BLACK

Romell Regulacion: I had sent Cleopatra Records a couple of songs on a cassette demo, a photo of my band, and a bio along with a video clip of a performance we did at Sub Club. That's when they called me and said they wanted to sign me. They didn't use those words, though. They just said, "You wanna make a record?"

Nelson Nakamoto: I remember I went to Romell's first show at Sub Club when he was still performing as Lost Souls. When I saw him play,

A '90s lineup of Razed in Black featuring Rommell Regulacion, bottom right. *Courtesy of Romell Regulacion*

I was like, "How is he making this music?" To have all that electronic equipment and to have it all organized to play live, I was kind of blown away. I think a lot of people, even the punk musicians, have a lot of respect for Razed in Black.

Gus Diamond: I really dug Razed in Black. We knew them as a local band, but it was really cool to see somebody from Hawaii make it to that level and have the success they did. Truthfully, they may be the only people I actually know who have done that.

Romell Regulacion: The first tour we did, we toured with Switchblade Symphony and went all over the nation riding their coattails, basically, because they were huge at the time. Wherever we went, the shows became a big goth event in that city, and I remember tripping out because it made me realize that Hawaii's goth scene was actually bigger and much better than a lot of these places around the country.

Every interview I've had as Razed in Black is prefaced with how weird it is to have the kind of music I do coming out of Hawaii, but the fetish shows back home, I felt, were just so much more legit. People really dressed up and took it to another level. We talked about it while we were on the road, just how raunchy it would get back home. So for Courtney and Matt to eventually take this goth/fetish/industrial event to LA, the mecca of entertainment, and have the kind of success they did, that actually says a lot about the scene in Hawaii.

Matt Grim: We did Sub Club for six months to a year before Courtney bought us out. Me and Guy moved away because there was a lot of money to be made in LA at the time, and we were looking at doing bigger clubs and movies. I was meeting all kinds of mega-DJs and hanging out with top promoters in LA, so I sold Courtney the Dungeon name for $3,500 and I bought it back from him in 2000 for ten grand.

When I moved back to LA in 2005, he invited me to his Bondage Ball and it was incredible. It was a mind-blowing, packed event at the Avalon, one of the top venues in LA, and he sold me the Bondage Ball for $10,000. He said, "I just want out of here, and I wanna move to Wisconsin." That was a *great* investment for me.

Erin L. Figueroa: At the time, my mom and dad couldn't understand what I was doing with my life and thought this piercing thing was leading nowhere, but it really gave me a future. The '90s is my most favorite era of my lifetime. We had the best shows. I met the best people, made the best money—it was the best everything. Those were some of the absolute greatest years and times of my life.

Gus Diamond: All the places I went to are gone now, but I am one of the luckiest people in the world because I was in a time and place where I could be me. We made our scene in the middle of the ocean, in the middle of nowhere, and it was a "lightning in a bottle"-type thing. I miss what we had.

21

SKANKIN' IN THE ISLES

When the late summer sun began its ascent over Honolulu on August 20, 1994, not a soul could have foreknown the momentous events soon to unfold. Several thousand spectators, mostly children, had gathered that afternoon for the last of a weeklong string of shows for Circus International at Blaisdell Arena. Behind the scenes, twenty-year-old Dallas Beckwith, a newly hired stable boy, prepared for the grand finale. As the circus' lauded five-elephant act was set to enter the spotlight, there was a commotion backstage as an elephant named Tyke suddenly turned on Beckwith, tossing him through the curtains and onto the arena floor, flipping his helpless body across the stage. Elephant trainer Allen Campbell immediately sprang into action, stepping in front of the massive creature with outstretched arms, barking orders for Tyke to back off. Instead, the three-ton behemoth lowered her head, toppled Campbell, and, behind the weight of her enormous skull, quickly crushed the life from her trainer.

As a confused and panicked crowd scrambled for safety, Tyke bounded off stage, bulldozed through an arena doorframe and onto the streets of Honolulu. She rushed across Kapiolani Boulevard, lost and disoriented, turning down Kamake'e Street and onto Waimanu Street, where she cornered herself into a fenced lot. A publicist for the circus, spotting an opportunity to gain control of the situation, attempted to close the lot gate on Tyke, but she charged through, hurling him into the street on his back where she pummeled him with her trunk. As she hovered threateningly over him, Honolulu police ran toward her, firing their handguns. Though the shots failed to subdue her, they sent Tyke scampering in the opposite direction. She rambled through the Kaka'ako neighborhood for nearly thirty minutes with a growing throng of police and curious spectators on her tail. It was near the corner of Ward Avenue and Ilaniwai Street that Tyke was finally stopped in her tracks, assailed with a barrage of gunfire. With grievous wounds to her nerves and organs, she slowly crumpled to the pavement, no doubt bewildered by her quickly worsening fate. A total of eighty-seven shots had riddled her body and head. Bloodied and drained of her life force, Tyke eventually succumbed to her injuries, her circus headdress still strapped to her face.

The following year, a gravestone quietly appeared at the Valley of the Temples Pet Cemetery in honor of Tyke, though not much is known about how it came to be or the individuals involved. Another memorial to the fallen elephant came in the form of "(Elephant Song) Tyke" by local ska combo Red Session. A lively number that details a version of events, it features a rollicking horn section, circus melodies, and elephant-like trumpeting. It quickly earned spins on Radio Free Hawaii, whose vote-driven format at times afforded homegrown bands access to radio airplay.

From the outset, ska figured prominently on Radio Free Hawaii as ska-punk pioneers Operation Ivy and third-wave ska bands like Skankin' Pickle and Dance Hall Crashers became mainstays on its weekly playlists. The result was near-superstar status in Hawaii for a number of ska acts who began to visit the Islands regularly, including Fishbone, Hepcat, Let's Go Bowling, Mephiskapheles, and others. This predated the American ska explosion by several years and foreshadowed the feeding frenzy of the mid- to late 1990s when, in an attempt to hit on the next big music trend, major record labels gave third-wave ska a considerable corporate push nationally. "Even before the ska thing went mainstream in the nineties, I felt like Hawaii was way ahead of the curve," discloses Skankin' Pickle frontman Mike Park, who first performed in Honolulu in 1992 when members of Hawaiian ska outfit Mr. Simon discovered a Skankin' Pickle hotline in the liner notes of the Pickles' *Skafunkrastapunk* album and rang the band with an invitation to play the fiftieth state. "I found out Hawaii had a huge scene," Park says. "For a little island like Oahu, it was pretty incredible."

Norm Winter: I still have people approaching me on the street, raving about a ska or punk song we played thirty-five years ago. When you have a radio station that actually plays what people want to hear, you're going to break songs long before all the other stations know what's really going on.

Operation Ivy was already established with a certain crowd by the time Radio Free Hawaii got on the air in '91. They were one of the earliest ones to get voted onto the station. Dance Hall Crashers was pretty early too. Later on, bands like Mephiskapheles and Checkered Cabs were huge here as well as the local groups like Red Session and Tantra Monsters.

They got voted onto our playlists pretty regularly. Then after we went off the air, ska got really popular all around the country. But we were always a step ahead.

Karina Denike (vocalist: Dance Hall Crashers, NOFX, etc.): I heard Dance Hall Crashers were going to be going to Hawaii, and having grown up in England, it was my dream to go there. It was like, *Oh my God, we're going to paradise!* On arriving, we had such an amazing response from everybody. We did an interview on the air with Dave O'Day, and we did some in-store signings at record stores with people wanting us to sign their album, the full rock star treatment. We were getting recognized by people on the street, by people going through security and the ticket agent at the airport. It was really shocking and we were really confused and elated because we were not that famous at all anywhere else. We were told we were doing pretty well out there, but when we actually got to Honolulu, it was like, "What is going on? This is really crazy!" We were completely flabbergasted.

Elyse Rogers, Karina Denike, and Mikey Weiss of Dance Hall Crashers at After Dark, 1994. *Courtesy of Ed Holt*

Mike Park (singer/saxophonist/multi-instrumentalist: Skankin' Pickle, Bruce Lee Band, The Chinkees, etc.; co-owner of Dill Records; founder of Asian Man Records): I remember when we first came to Hawaii, there was a place called the Faktory that we played at. We went there a day before our show, and when the DJ put on "Fakin' Jamaican," everyone went crazy. The whole place started skanking, and I was like, "Whooooa!" but that was all because of Radio Free Hawaii. It was such a unique format that allowed independent bands like Skankin' Pickle to get airplay on commercial radio, which was pretty rare. Hawaii had an underground scene that was just poppin'.

TANTRA MONSTERS

Ty Kroll (bassist: Tantra Monsters, Mr. Simon): The thing with Mr. Simon was Bronsy and Russell, who were our singers, started dating at some point, and that kind of went south, and they started being a problem. But what's funny is that the Skankin' Pickle show at the Faktory that we did with Duke of Prunes changed everything. Warren Young was such a great frontman for Duke of Prunes that we started thinking we should get him as our singer, which we somehow did. That's how the Tantra Monsters started. It was basically Mr. Simon minus the singers, with the singer of Duke of Prunes instead. It happened pretty quick.

Ryan Kunimura (trombonist: Tantra Monsters, Go Jimmy Go, Mr. Simon; bassist: M.U.G., Freak Hunt, etc.): With Tantra Monsters, ska was the vehicle that we could all get together on, but I don't think anybody in the band was listening to much ska. Our drummer Jonny was into Epitaph bands like Pennywise and Rancid; me and Caesar Mercado, our other horn player, were into jazz and early soul music like Stax Records. We were super inspired by all the different music we were listening to.

Me and Caesar would watch videos of James Brown and his band, and we learned about how disciplined they were and how James Brown charged them money every time they made a mistake, so we took our live performances seriously too. We had band practice three times a week, and I practiced several hours every day.

Eric White (saxophonist: Go Jimmy Go, The Elevations, etc.): Local bands with horn sections like Tantra Monsters really made me perk up. We'd see them at shows in the early '90s, and we were in awe of them. Back then, the musicianship and showmanship were so high that you couldn't get on stage at the bigger venues without real talent. They really raised the bar.

Ty Kroll: When we would play the Garage, it would be complete madness. We played a show at the Cannon Club on the side of the mountain, next to Diamond Head, just us and a few other local bands, and we charged five bucks and got a thousand people there and made some money. We got to where we could pull 500 to a thousand people to a venue, which we thought was pretty crazy.

Ryan Kunimura: Tantra Monsters got a lot of offers to play, but I was super adamant that we would never perform more than once a month, and I was a total cop about it, like, "We're not gonna be like a restaurant or bar band that plays regularly, no way. We won't play more than once a month, max." Because of that, we would always get a big turnout, and we'd get calls to open all kinds of shows, including any ska band that came to town: Fishbone, Dance Hall Crashers, Skankin' Pickle, Let's Go Bowling, Hepcat.

Karina Denike: From our visits to Hawaii, we got to be very good friends with these really cool Radio Free DJs—hanging out in this great scene, having barbecues, swimming at the beach, and partying. You didn't get that in the Bay Area or anywhere, really. The industry was a bit colder. We became very close with the Tantra Monsters too. I think they played on every bill we played there, at one point.

Ty Kroll: All the bands that came to town and hung out became our really good friends and advocates. Dance Hall Crashers took us on our first little tour of the States with them and a few other bands that they knew. It was like a week or two of shows in LA and Tahoe. We were super green. We didn't even have any merchandise to sell.

Mike Park: It must've been the second time Skankin' Pickle went to Hawaii that we caught Tantra Monsters. When we saw them play, we just knew. I mean, Mr. Simon was cool, but with Tantra Monsters it was like, "Oh, *yeah*." They had such great songs. They were the first band we saw and said, "Man, we should put out their record on our label!" They were just so good.

Ryan Kunimura: We finished recording our album, and Dill Records— Skankin' Pickle's label—put it out. The idea was, "Hey, we'll press this and we'll go on tour together because this is how you sell your record." I feel like the deal Dill Records cut with us was pretty fair. I don't remember the actual numbers, but it wasn't the usual bullshit you get with a major record label.

Mike Park: It's just a profit share and it's still what I do today. So after costs, we just split everything 50-50. It's a good deal, for sure. Nothing like what you'd get with a major label. From there, the next goal was to get their name out and let people see them.

Ryan Kunimura: We went on tour in direct support of Skankin' Pickle across the whole U.S. for two months, which is pretty legit. Skankin' Pickle are road dogs, though. They'd already toured a bunch of times, so they knew what they were doing. The thing is, they were also doing it completely DIY, punk rock style. It was right before the Internet and cell phones and stuff, so there was a lot of legwork involved: networking, calling people on actual pay phones and shit. Running a tour like that is mental, but I fucking loved it.

Mike Park: I know the first shows were pretty big, and they were like, "Wow, this is so great!" thinking every show was gonna be just as big, but it's not like that once you get to these smaller towns.

Ty Kroll: I think the first show we played was a giant ska-punk festival with the Voodoo Glow Skulls in Riverside with 5,000 people or something. When we got there we had a box of Tantra Monsters shirts and a hundred CDs to sell, and they were gone within a minute of the first show. We just weren't prepared.

The Skankin' Pickle guys were like, "You Hawaiians don't know nothin' about touring—you're gonna die out here! Skankin' Pickle is a hardcore touring band!" and we're like, "Oh yeah?" We were gonna show them. We were determined to be as feral as possible, and we were. Our tour rider asked for just one hotel room, $100, and all the beer we could drink at the venue. We each had a per diem of $8 a day or something. We were so broke. They were right that we didn't know that much about touring, but we could definitely hang. We didn't need sleep or anything; we'd just *go*.

Mike Park: The worst part of touring is being away from home and being broke. I remember Tantra having no money and eating beans out of a can because it cost eighty-nine cents to get their stomachs full. They were doing whatever it took to survive.

Ryan Kunimura: By that time, there were already tensions within the band. It was getting to the point where Warren would be driving, and only certain people would ride with him. I was fine with Warren, but other members might've had issues with him or maybe they were just grumpy. You know, you go on tour and it's hard living. That might've moved us in the direction of a breakup because I think we called it quits pretty soon after that, which was kind of a bummer. I don't think we had the maturity to continue and make something better of it, so it's probably better that we moved on when we did.

Ty Kroll: Maybe at the time, we had deluded ideas that we could go further and get bigger, but in hindsight I think we were probably a little bit too odd. If you look at all the other ska bands that made it big in the '90s like Reel Big Fish or Save Ferris, they had a specific sound, and they all sounded the same. We would have had to either move away, which nobody wanted to do, or change our sound, which nobody wanted to do except Warren, whose direction was even less commercial. That wouldn't have made any sense.

Mike Park: There's no reason why Tantra Monsters couldn't have been as big as any of those other ska bands that got signed by majors. It's really just luck of the draw a lot of times.

RED SESSION

Cam Wright (bassist: Go Jimmy Go): The first time I saw Tantra Monsters on stage, they were going full-on apeshit. Seeing a band with horns going bananas like that is probably what first piqued my curiosity in ska. Then I ended up at a house party in Kailua where Red Session was playing and I remember thinking, *What is this?* I was like Steve Martin in *The Jerk* where he starts snapping his fingers, stomping around the room, yelling, "This music speaks to me!"

Ty Kroll: We definitely felt Red Session was our main competition and that we had to be better than them. They were very eclectic like us, but they had a much more consistent sound, and their songs made sense together, whereas we must've seemed like a big mess by comparison.

Jamie Winpenny (guitarist: Red Session): We just had to be at the top of our game because Tantra Monsters were so badass. Everybody loved them, they had such energy in their shows, and they came out with a record before we did.

Shon Gregory (drummer: Red Session, Go Jimmy Go, etc.): Tantra Monsters are my favorite local band that ever lived. They were the guys who played all the major concerts. Meanwhile, we were just taking gigs anywhere and everywhere we could, several times a month, for sure. As our name spread, Goldenvoice took a liking to us, and we started to open for big-time bands too: The Selecter, Voodoo Glow Skulls, Mighty Mighty Bosstones, Reel Big Fish. Once our album came out, Radio Free Hawaii started playing it, and the song about Tyke the elephant was the one that got played the most.

Jamie Winpenny: The guy who was shown on the news trying to hold Tyke behind the fence before getting his ankle broken was a good friend of my dad's, actually. It was so shocking to see that footage on TV. It was just crazy. We were like, "We gotta write a song about this!" Our album ended up selling 10,000 units through our distribution deal and however many units we sold at all of our shows.

Fernando Pacheco (trombonist: Exit 24, Go Jimmy Go, Pimpbot, etc.): I was a music major and in the UH marching band with Chad Tamashiro from Red Session. I went to watch Red Session open up for Homegrown and Hepcat one night, and as soon as I saw Chad on stage, I thought, *Hell yeah, that's what I need to do!* I figured the way to get into a band was to play trombone, even though I played tuba at the time. I borrowed a trombone from my uncle and bought a booklet and a mouthpiece from the music store, and I just started teaching myself trombone. Then I met guys from bands like The Creepers and Happy Campers and we formed Exit 24.

Richard Detty a.k.a. Colonel Reehotch (manager: Red Session, Phenomenauts; vocalist: the Noiz; audio engineer): Red Session's sound was so approachable and danceable that it wasn't hard for them to grow a fanbase. I had a ton of connections that could get them into Anna Bannana's, into places out on the North Shore, and even over to Maui and the Big Island where they could be seen by different audiences. The band played everywhere, trying to make money to fund a move to the mainland

Shon Gregory: The first couple of times Red Session went out to California, we stayed at a warehouse in Oakland. It was just a freak show over there. So much wide-open, hippie, punk rock, anything-goes shit going on with drugs and wild people in the neighborhood. Rancid had their own warehouse down the street too, so it would go berserk with street parties. It was quite a circus. It was deserted and dangerous too, so you wouldn't fuck around with walking the street by yourself. For some of the guys, like our horn players, it flipped them out.

Jamie Winpenny: We got ourselves a house in the Bay Area in November of '97, and we lived together as a band for three years. We figured we'd have a better shot at success if we were touring on the mainland. The house, I named it Strange Manor, and it's still there. It was a seven-bedroom place with a view of the Bay Bridge and the Golden Gate Bridge from our living room. We built a studio downstairs and a loft above the garage. It became kind of a nexus for indie touring bands—largely from the ska scene—without resources. They'd come and stay with us whenever they'd come through, and that favor would be returned whenever we were on the road.

Shon Gregory: We wanted, just like any young band, to establish ourselves on a good record label and not necessarily get rich and famous but make a living off playing music. You could be one of the top bands in your area, but you go to a bigger city and, holy shit, everyone's talented and working just as hard as you. It's not an easy business.

We hooked up with a booking agent who would get us these great gigs in snow towns in Colorado, Montana, places like that. These were club and bar shows at or just outside these ski resorts where they put you up and paid you well. They had a great scene in these places. They were not giant concerts, but they were super fun and they'd make us good money.

Jamie Winpenny: We'd show up with our aloha shirts and our big van that said "Hawaii" on it. We were always something of a spectacle, like space aliens. Vail, Breckenridge, Winter Park, Steamboat Springs, Aspen, Crested Butte—we did all the ski resorts. We did a weekend residency at the Snow King in Jackson Hole, Wyoming, with free rooms, free booze, and, like, 500 bucks a night. For us, it was like, "Yeah! We're making real money now!" We weren't, in retrospect, but it felt like it at the time.

Shon Gregory: In the late '90s, the circuits started to slow down. I loved playing places in the city like Slim's and the Fillmore, but we were playing once a month, twice a month, maybe, and I didn't want to just live there and work. I decided to come home. I was done being on the mainland. Red Session carried on for a few more years without me.

GO JIMMY GO

Eric White: I was at a Hepcat and Buck-O-Nine concert at the Groove, and I saw my old friend Larry Gordon, who also played saxophone when we were both in high school. He was in a suit and everything, and he

Go Jimmy Go. From left to right: Fernando Pacheco, Shon Gregory, Jason "Bison" Friedmann, Ian Ashley, Eric White, and Cam Wright. *Courtesy of Eric White*

goes, "Hey, man, you still got your saxophone? I'm starting up a new band called Go Jimmy Go. We're gonna play ska, but in a more traditional style. You wanna play?"

I was like, "You mean in front of real people?" I had never thought about playing in an actual working band before. My paradigm totally shifted.

Cam Wright: In the mid-'90s, Thursday night was always Ska Night at the Vybe in Puck's Alley. DJ Skarry from Radio Free would be there spinning records, and all the ska kids would go and hang out. That's where you would find Larry Gordon, who was the most ska out of all of us, with that classic rude boy look, dancing with a porkpie hat and suit and tie. He started to put this band together with guys from the local scene. Somebody told me, "Yeah, that guy's starting a band, and I heard you're the bass player." I'd never even met him.

One day, around sunset, I'm driving past Kalani High School and I see Larry sitting at the bus stop with his boots and rude boy outfit on.

I pull off the road real fast and pop out of the car, like, "Hey, you're Larry, right?"

He says, "Yeah."

"Yeah, I'm Cam. I heard I'm in a band with you!"

Eric White: We started to record, and we got some play on Radio Free Hawaii, and from there it was just show after show and all kinds of opportunities: opening up for Goldfinger, playing with Dance Hall Crashers, Hepcat, and Save Ferris. It just opened up my eyes to the bigger picture.

Fernando Pacheco: I thought Go Jimmy Go was cool beyond a level I could conceive. I sent them an email to let them know I was aware that they were recording and that things were slowing down with Exit 24, so if they needed a trombone player, reach out. I was just offering to play on their next album, but I got an email shortly after that saying, "You're in the band now. Here are the rehearsal dates. The next show is at Nick's Fishmarket, so get ready."

Shon Gregory: I was in Anna Bannana's one night, and Cameron said Go Jimmy Go was looking for a new drummer. I'd always had respect for that band, so I said, "Yeah, I'll play but I won't tour." I wasn't leaving Hawaii again. But I didn't realize how much I would connect with their music. Go Jimmy Go had really great songwriters with songs that, to me, went straight to the heart. I just really fell in love with playing for them.

Mike Park: When I visited Hawaii again in the late '90s with the Bruce Lee Band, I met Go Jimmy Go. They were good too. That was a band that just got better and better, and they worked real hard. The problem for Go Jimmy Go was they probably came along a bit too late. When they started, that era of ska was on the way out. If they had started a few years earlier, it could have been a totally different story for them.

Karina Denike: They were doing more classic, old-school ska, which I've always loved. It was probably one of the times Dance Hall Crashers played Honolulu that Tina Lau, a friend of ours who was working in promotions out there, asked me if I could sing on a track for Go Jimmy Go. They had a studio they were recording at somewhere up in the hills, and I laid down vocals there. I grew up on stuff like Toots & the Maytals and early Bob Marley as a kid, so it's kind of in my blood.

Shon Gregory: Our manager at the time, Tina Lau, was involved with people from the Vans Warped Tour. She had the contacts. She asked us, "You guys wanna play the Warped Tour?"

Eric White: We did the whole western leg of the Vans Warped Tour. We flew to the mainland, picked up our tour van in LA, and drove twenty fucking hours to Nampa, Idaho. Right off the airplane. The next day we drove ourselves to Salt Lake City, then on to places you never thought you'd visit, like Iowa and Kansas. We made it to St. Louis, then cut down and played all through Texas, then Arizona. You're with the band twenty-four hours a day, not much money, under really stressful conditions, then keep driving, driving, driving. But we made a ton of fans and a ton of connections, and the tours just got better and better.

Cam Wright: The Warped Tour was a lot to take in all at once. Every day, it's a ten-hour festival. You wake up to an open field, and you see it morph into a sea of bodies, as if it's a time lapse. There was more of a free and fearless vibe then. It's what I imagined the '70s to be when I was in the '90s, and I didn't know I was actually living it in real time.

Fernando Pacheco: As tired and dirty as I felt that summer, watching bands like Flogging Molly and Reel Big Fish every day never got old. It was a crash course in stage presence and live performance. To greet Dickie Barrett from Mighty Mighty Bosstones every morning and talk with guys from these bands I really looked up to and learned from was amazing

Eric White: In 2004, we all quit our jobs to tour full time as an independent band. We started going out to the Midwest and East Coast, playing upstate New York, Milwaukee, Tennessee, just all kinds of places. We even went to Japan. To me, getting to Japan and having an actual record label there for support was awesome. You could finally see the next level. We had released our music there through Ska in the World, a subsidiary of Disk Union, which is a ginormous Japanese record label.

Cam Wright: Japan was a lot to take in. Two weeks. Tokyo, Nagoya, all the way to Fukuoka too. I almost couldn't handle the sensory overload. We were running around playing here and there. The ska fans in Japan are wilder than anywhere else. One guy got naked in front of us at one of the shows.

Fernando Pacheco: This guy was so excited he didn't know what to do with himself, so he just pulled his pants down to his ankles and started screaming. I've never seen anyone get that into it at a show. We saw everything, you know? It's forever left an impression on me.

Eric White: We finally got to tour Europe for the first time in 2007 as the main support for the Toasters. It was the first time Go Jimmy Go ever got around in a tour bus. Seven weeks living out of a suitcase. A lot of bands tour Europe, but we went to places like Croatia, Serbia, Bosnia, and Montenegro. We missed our shows in Macedonia because we got lost in Albania. I had a travel book to help me know where I was and the history of some of these places, but in this book, Albania was completely blacked out. The deeper you get into the Balkans, the more dire and war-ravaged everything looks. Coming from Hawaii, it was like, *Oh, fuck...I just don't wanna die.* These are the kinds of places you could just disappear.

Cam Wright: All I know is I woke up on the tour bus and found out we were lost in the mountains. Imagine being in the upper bunk, riding in a bus, and all you see is a valley right below you. I'm surprised we didn't roll off and die right there. We could hear the tour bus driver screaming beneath us, trying to navigate around a cliff with rocks crumbling off the side of the road.

Eric White: Finally, we make it to the southern border of Bosnia and Herzegovina. It's nighttime and we see what looks like a pizza joint or a bar. Mind you, we're from Hawaii, so we're all mixed with haole, Hawaiian, Asian, *any kine.* The Toasters are too: Black guys, white guys, dreads, whatever. When we walk in the place, it's like a needle scratching across a record. Everybody stops talking and looks at us. They stare at us for a really long time too, so we're feeling uncomfortable. These guys have slicked-back, greasy hair and black leather jackets. It's all dudes, no girls. The bartender comes to take our order, and Bucket from the Toasters somehow communicates with him. The bartender starts laughing out loud, basically saying, "No, it's not a gay bar; we're just all Muslim, and the women stay home while the guys hang out here!" We were all laughing so hard over that. I thought we were gonna have to fight our way out.

Fernando Pacheco: I swear there was some Cher or Cher-adjacent music playing in the background, though, so I was like, "Okay, you do you, bro. So when's that pizza coming out?"

Eric White: In Bosnia, buildings were blown up, burned, bullet holes everywhere. It was crazy. The trombone player for the Toasters, Greg Robinson, was a writer for *Jazz Times*, so he's inquisitive. We were talking about the show there the night before and he says, "I was sitting there looking at everybody, thinking everyone in this room was probably a kid or a teenager during the Bosnian War. I wanted to know more, so I finally built up the courage to introduce myself to one guy and ask him what it was like in those times." The guy told him, "You see that bouncer over there? That bouncer was my best friend growing up as a kid. He ended up being a guard at my concentration camp." Mic drop, right? Heavy, bro.

Fernando Pacheco: Driving through there, it was still 50-50. You'd see one building that was operational, but the next building over was still blacked out and bombed out. Packs of wild dogs were running through the streets. That place hadn't fully recovered by any means, but Bucket said it best when he told us, "Even if they've got just a roof or just a couple of walls, no matter what, we're gonna play for them."

Eric White: In 2007, we went back to tour Japan, flew to Hong Kong, did some gigs there, and even played in mainland China. By 2009, we did our last U.S. tour with the Phenomenauts, and we were done. Something happened between 2005 and 2009, when we stopped touring. Local shows were drying up. They weren't supporting us anymore, and it was becoming more rare to have a really nice, packed event. After 2009, we'd only play two or three times a year and do our best to turn those shows into big parties. Eventually, we decided to call it quits.

PIMPBOT

Fernando Pacheco: There wasn't much songwriting opportunity for me in Go Jimmy Go. I was just filling a slot as a horn player, and that's all they needed from me. So in putting together Pimpbot, I really wanted it to be more of a collaborative ska-punk band like Exit 24 was, but I ended up writing all of the music while the other guys were down to just be along for the ride and to support me and all of my musical decisions.

In the end, I have no regrets. I know that I sacrificed a lot. In the corporate world there are guys my age who are managers and directors, and I realize I'm not at their level because I sacrificed many years being on the road chasing a dream, and I wasn't at home climbing corporate ladders. I'm at peace with that. I don't have to worry about any "what ifs" because I tried everything there is to try. Even if it all ended today, I've got a big smile on my face, and I can thank music for that.

22

FIST CITY

Nestled on the agricultural plains between the Ko'olau and Waianae mountain ranges is Wahiawa, a quirky, somewhat timeworn community in the center of Oahu. It's known as the last town on the road to the North Shore, that world-famous mecca of surfing. Although several modern fast-food outlets now line Wahiawa's entrance on Kamehameha Highway, many of its buildings are leftover relics of a bygone era, some nearly 100 years old.

In ancient times, nearby Kukaniloko was the birthing place of chiefs and chiefesses of the highest rank; a sacred site reserved for royalty, warriors, and priests. These days, warriors of a different sort surround Wahiawa on U.S. military installations such as Wheeler Army Airfield and Schofield Barracks to the south and east, and the U.S. Navy's NCTAMS PAC and Helemano Military Reservation to the north.

Today, Wahiawa is inhabited by kin of the original immigrant laborers of the area's pineapple fields, military personnel from across America and their dependents, as well as local families who came seeking humble habitation at the heart of the island's interior. Naturally, the area's high school, Leilehua, reflects this cultural patchwork. Jeff Chmolack, a 1993 graduate of Leilehua High who grew up in Wahiawa, recalls when members of these factions clashed in a near-riot on the school's campus.

At the time, Chmolack had been delving into the local punk scene and encountered a New Yorker by the name of Dave Telese, who was stationed in Hawaii through the Air Force. Telese—who had introduced a number of scene kids to New York hardcore bands like Agnostic Front and Warzone and the skinhead lifestyle that often accompanied this music—made certain to explain that the original skinheads, who are largely ignored by the media, have historically been anti-racist and admirers of vintage Jamaican and soul music.

Meanwhile, the racist skins who often made headlines with their violent attacks on minorities are the mortal enemy of true skinheads and a scourge to their way of life. "I'm not gonna bullshit you, it was almost overnight from meeting this dude I looked up to that I wanted to be like him," confesses Chmolack. "If he's a skinhead, then I'm gonna be a skinhead."

Chmolack soon adopted the classic skinhead wardrobe—boots, suspenders, and a button-down shirt—and went to school decked out one day when he was accosted by a fellow student he'd not met before.

"What the fuck are you?" he asked Chmolack.

"What do you mean, what am I? I'm a skinhead" was the reply.

"You're not a fuckin' skinhead."

"Excuse me?"

"You're not even white," the student scoffed. "You can't be a skinhead!"

"Well, I'm standing here in front of you," Chmolack retorted.

His challenger laughed in response and promptly walked off, leaving Chmolack fuming. He'd just met another skinhead at school, and to Chmolack's confoundment, it appeared he was of the white supremacist sort that he'd only read about in newspaper articles or heard of through the rumor mill. And here in Hawaii, of all places. "It just stewed in my head that night," remembers Chmolack. "I thought, *I have to defend this. We can't both be here; one of us has to go.* I already knew the next time I saw him, we were gonna fight."

It was the following morning, in fact, as students grabbed a quick breakfast in the school cafeteria before class that a standoff between the two kicked off. They were quickly separated before Chmolack's opponent, who had outfitted himself that day in racist skinhead regalia—red boot laces, red braces, and a Skrewdriver T-shirt—spluttered a threat: "After school, you're fuckin' dead!" Throughout the day, Chmolack received morsels of intel on his antagonist, who was a leader in the school's ROTC program. As his ROTC cohorts had no inkling of his racist beliefs, they were quite willing to back him in a fight. For his part, Chmolack enlisted his skateboarding pals to stand against the xenophobe and his would-be soldiers at the field where the ROTC building stood. "We were outnumbered, and the skateboard kids stood their ground, but most of 'em were basically punching bags," remembers Chmolack. "The thing is, we used to get along with the Samoan kids from Whitmore Village, and one of 'em was a metalhead, and earlier he'd said, 'If it gets out of control, don't worry, we got you guys.' We ended up getting the worst end of it and then the Samoans jumped in and we got the upper hand."

For their trouble, Chmolack says, he and a number of combatants were suspended, while his foe was ultimately expelled from school. It didn't end there, however. That afternoon,

Chmolack and his friends responded to a warning of further violence from his nemesis by tracking him to Schofield Barracks, where he hung out with older Army buddies and reignited their skirmish. "We put a good one on 'em," says Chmolack. "When the MPs came, we gave them our side of the story, and they had no choice but to investigate it. The thing about a racist is they're proud; they're not gonna hide it and they don't deny it. Sure as shit, when they went to some of these guys' rooms in the barracks, they found these swastikas and fuckin' Hitler paraphernalia, the whole nine. So those dudes ended up getting discharged from the Army."

Damon Cabral (vocalist: The Pugilist): There were some white power fuckers, a bunch of GIs and Aryans coming around, and you had to hold it down for the anti-racist skins. We were colorful; you had Hawaiians, locals, Filipinos, haoles, from all sides of the island. So when those outside cats tried to come around and form that Aryan movement, that didn't last too long.

Jeff Chmolack (bassist: The Pugilist): Most people wouldn't know that in the early '90s, there was actually a crew of racist skinheads, and they came through the military. Those military guys recruited some of the outcast punk rock kids who were hanging out in Hawaii at that time and were banished from the scene for whatever different reasons. The next thing you know, they had a crew of ten to twelve white power skinheads running around the island for a little bit.

Chris Esteron: One night there was a Coffeeline show, and there were these jarheads there who I had never seen before: three guys, two girls. One of the girls came walking up to me, like, "Hi, how are you?" You know, small talk: "Yeah, we have a meeting next week, and you seem like somebody who might be interested." I had no idea where she was going with this, but then she handed me a flier, and it was a fucking white power thing. Right at that moment, I looked up and I realized one of them had approached Eric Humphreys from Omnicide, and one of them had approached Jesse Perrin—you know, like, the only five white people in the whole room were the only people who got approached.

I'm not gonna say who did what, but one of those military dudes just got *lit up*. I mean, he was out cold. But what was so funny was Eric and Les Hernandez were drinking Bacardi 151, and one of them poured some on him and lit a fucking match, and the girl was screaming, "Put it out! Put it out!" On cue, everybody dropped their pants and pissed on the guy to put it out.

Jeff Chmolack: We had friends who were in the military too, so they'd tell us things like, "Hey, there's this dude in Kaneohe and he's a racist skinhead."

"Oh, well, let's go find him."

We'd go hunt those guys down and try to keep the island free of that shit. You just can't have that. We'd find them all the time and we'd take 'em. We'd beat 'em and take their stuff. If they were wearing boots, we'd take their boots, we'd take their jackets. We'd take anything that represented our culture.

Damon Cabral: We looked up to the old HARSH crew, basically. Guys like Jesse, Mike Silva, Ray Bala. Jesse was hard and you knew you would have to stand up for the crew when he was around. He would scare the shit out of me. He had that no-mess-no-fuss attitude. Just the way he would handle shit, he was fierce. Mike Silva had sincerity and understanding, you know? He would always say, "You guys are the next generation." He talks like a leader, not really talking down to you, but reaching you at your level, giving you knowledge and advice that was from bruddah to bruddah, you know? I ended up committing my life to the skinhead thing and shaving my head because this is what I wanted to do. It was a way of life.

Jeff Chmolack: Dave Suzuki was welcoming and accepting and just a fucking cool guy, and he really brought me into the skinhead scene. As the older guys are letting me hang out and I'm earning my place, I get this illusion that this is the way it's going to be: "Oh, everybody's so fucking cool," right? Like, "I'm a skinhead now." Nah, nah, nah. Doesn't work that way. There's always going to be the enforcers like Jesse and some of the other guys, and they didn't let just anybody hang out.

Ray Bala: I never really tested anybody. If anybody came into the scene saying, "Oh, I'm a skinhead," I'm like, "All right, cool." But in the back of my mind I'm thinking, *Well, you better not fuck up.*

Jeff Chmolack: At the beginning, I didn't understand, but it wasn't easy to be different back when the older guys were building the Hawaii punk rock scene. They were taking shit and getting beat up by mokes who would walk by a club, go inside and see dudes in a circle pit, and think the object's just to go knock everybody out. Then when you retaliate, they beat the fuck out of you.

Mike Silva: I went to this one show, and I saw this moke guy deck this short Japanese girl because he thought that's how we danced. So I got into it with him because that's fucked up. Obviously, he didn't know how to behave, and he didn't belong there. My whole outlook on the scene just got tainted with all of this negative stuff, and I didn't want to go to those shows anymore because it was depressing.

And then when I went to the Specials show at After Dark, I got into a huge fight with the security. It was the security versus the skinheads, and I got into it because I saw security beating up on people when they shouldn't have. They can say what they want, but their jurisdiction is only the nightclub, not across the street from it. You're not a police force, you're a bouncer. I was trying to leave the place, and I got run down by two security guards in a golf cart, right on the sidewalk, on Nimitz Highway. They pinned me to a truck and stomped on my face a few times.

Jeff Chmolack: We were fighting Goldenvoice security guards, all 300-pound Samoans. That was kind of the night all the older guys were like, "Okay, anybody who had the balls to get involved with that is fucking down with us." They stopped giving us shit 'cause for a while we would come around, and there would be some dudes that would throw shit at you or fucking slap you or whatever. You can't be the whipping boy and let them berate you, but you definitely don't want to pipe up or you're going to get your ass kicked inside and out. You kind of have to stand your ground.

Damon Cabral: It wasn't like a gang where you walk the line, get beat down, and you're in. No, you're proving your shit constantly. You gotta weed out the weak. That's how the family of skins in Hawaii was. When shit goes down, you're gonna look around and see who's there with you. It was one for all and all for one, and I wanted my older brothers to know, man, I ain't going nowhere.

Ryan Kunimura: Sometimes bruddahs would come to the shows and start causing trouble or whatever, and the skins were always the first to stand up to them and fight back. I was like, "I wanna hang out with these guys!"

Ray Bala: We were never a gang, despite what people thought or authorities said. We were just a bunch of fuckin' hooligans who hung out. The only thing that we organized was where to get beer and socialize, basically. But over time, you find out who's down for you and who isn't. It becomes a matter of "Who can I trust?" and "Who can I not trust?" My whole philosophy is, I have friends and I have acquaintances, and they're two distinctly different groups of people. Just because I know somebody doesn't make them my friend. You realize who's the shit talkers and who's the fuckin' doers.

With HARSH, it wasn't entirely a skinhead thing. It was punks and some longhairs too; people who were down for the scene, or people at the time who we thought were down for the scene. After HARSH slowly faded away, FCS started more or less as a way of policing the scene. Like if somebody came in from outside of the scene and started doing stupid shit, we were always the ones to take care of the problem.

FCS, at the time of its inception, stood for Fuckin' Chaos Skins. Then later on, it became Fist City Skins. There were a lot of different acronyms. The Hawaii scene then was all about settling arguments with your fists, basically.

Jeff Chmolack: At some point, guys got together and decided, "Hey, we're going to keep doing our thing, but we can't let these outsiders come around and just fuck everybody up because people are going to be scared to come to these shows." And it got like that for a while. Mokes would frequent certain places, and you'd have to watch your back. So through that, you got the weeding-out process, like, "Hey, I have to be able to trust that if shit goes down, you're not just looking the part, and then when a bunch of guys come to fucking smash us, you run away and now we're outnumbered."

I just refused to go away. If you still don't like me, I get it, it's cool, but I'm gonna keep showing up. I wasn't the best fighter, but I definitely wasn't scared of getting beat up. Through that, I earned my place.

The Fast Zone on Fort Street Mall was kind of our version of the Backdoor, and we knew from what happened at the Backdoor that we needed to protect it. If you go to any punk rock scene, the skinheads are usually going to be the enforcers of the scene, and traditional skinheads are not dicks or trying to be tough guys, beating up everyone who comes to a show. They're just making sure that the people who don't belong there don't come and make trouble. Skinheads get a bad rap for that, especially in Hawaii, but when nobody else steps up, those kinds of dudes will keep coming. That's what happened to the Faktory. It got overtaken by mokes because no one would protect that thing.

Whenever we fought other locals, it's because they were always the aggressors. So we made it a point that regardless of whether it was one on ten, ten on one, ten on ten, it didn't matter. We're not starting anything with anyone, so if anybody starts anything with us, we're just gonna beat 'em so fucking bad that they're not going to want to fuck with us. We just didn't want to have these ongoing wars. If anybody came to square up against us, there's no words anymore. We'd just beat you up, right? We were gonna win. And that builds a reputation. That reputation got out, unbeknownst to us. We didn't know until people started to come around asking for us by name.

Damon Cabral: The Brown Boys, that's what they started calling our crew. Mostly skins and some punks. We got named that from these girls we were partying with who just coined that phrase. It was like, "Oh yeah, let's go hang out with the brown boys." And it just stuck.

Derek "Nos" Okazaki (vocalist: Freak Hunt, Pongoids): I don't care what anyone tells you, this is where their name came from: At the time,

Pongoids were one of several Hawaiian skinhead bands of the 1990s.
Courtesy of Rafael Dongon

the Faktory was the happening, all-ages spot on Kapiolani Boulevard. We noticed this bunch of younger guys who all dressed the same—same flight jacket, jeans, shaved head—coming around, and before we really knew 'em, we used to call 'em the "Brown and Downs" because they were all kind of brown and they were down for anything. They started getting somewhat infamous. People would be like, "Dude, what's up with your 'brown guy' friends? They came to this party and beat everybody up!" We just thought it was funny. Eventually, everybody started calling them the Brown Boys.

Jeff Chmolack: We fuckin' hated it. We couldn't stand the name. We were FCS. But if we got into something, it was a way for the older guys who were still left in Hawaii then to disassociate from us, like, "What? Some skinheads were involved? Oh, you mean the Brown Boys got into a fight, right? That wasn't us." By that time, we ended up making friends with a group of guys who were slightly younger than me, a couple years younger. They would eventually take on the lifestyle, and we had this new crew of maybe eight to ten.

This one time, we got trapped in the After Dark parking lot. We got set up by, I'd say, easily eighteen guys on four or five of us. Like, seven carloads of dudes. They had it fully planned out. They were these Filipino kids from Kalihi who were metalheads, and I think they were a gang, to tell you the truth.

We went to a show at the After Dark, sitting in a parking lot at the end of the road, drinking, and we saw this punk rock kid that we vaguely knew, running down the street for his life, towards the community college. He just blows by us. And three seconds behind, there's ten of these kids chasing him, and they've got sticks, skateboards, whatever. You could tell the dude just got tired. We were watching this whole thing go down and I'm like, "Dude, if this guy turns around and runs at these guys, we have to go help him." It was almost like he heard me, but really, he was winded. He stopped, turned around, and full sprinted, just war cry, bro, like, right back at these dudes. They started to just beat him, and I was like, "Yo, boys…" There were seven of us and him, so they still outnumbered us. We really put it on those guys, but during that fight, one of those dudes hit our buddy Chris Spence in the throat with a skateboard and collapsed his windpipe. He didn't know the extent of his injuries, just that his throat was sore. Luckily, we got him to the hospital, and he went into surgery immediately. The doctor was like, "Dude, you would have died if you went home and went to bed."

Nobody knew who these guys were. We asked around the scene, and nobody knew them, but somebody said they lived in Kalihi, where only a dumb fuck would go searching around, looking to get jumped by the neighborhood. So that's all we knew.

Then one day, maybe two months later, Damon and I went to a skateboard contest at A'ala Park to watch some of our friends skate. It was probably 11:30, noon, we're watching everybody skate, and Damon goes, "Oh, fuck, there's those guys!" They just got off the city bus in front of A'ala Park, and there's four of 'em. Damon says, "There's the fuckin' guy that hit Chris in the throat with the skateboard—we're gettin' these motherfuckers!" We were on the field side of the skate park, watching 'em, and they were on the street side, and one of them caught sight of us. I know he remembered us because of the look on the guy's face when he pointed at us. We were like, "Yup!" and pointed back at him. Damon ran around one side of the park, and I ran around the other, and we just started going at 'em, beat the shit outta these guys, and it was one of the funniest things that I'd seen: Damon did, like, this judo throw, and one of these kids flew out into the street, and the bus almost ran him over, but the reaction of the people on the bus was just the greatest.

By this time, the whole contest had stopped, and all the people were watching us fight. Two of 'em ran into the middle of the park where the skate contest was actually happening, and one of them starts flipping me and Damon off like it was protection or something and we're like, "You know that fence has a gate, and we're walking right through that thing, dude." We walked right into the middle and beat the shit out of the two remaining dudes and we just left. No cops came or anything.

Now, that's two altercations, and these guys are plotting, right? So there was a show, Pongoids with some kind of M.U.G. reunion or something like that, not too far from the After Dark. These guys came, and three of us ended up getting in a fight with three of them. Later, a bunch of us see them at the entrance to the After Dark, where the parking lot was, and they were like, "Fuck you guys, man!" and kept calling after us, then walked into that garage. We walked in after them, and they were like, "Fuck you!" and kept luring us further inside, and once we got to the end where their backs were against the wall and we got close to them, one dude lifted up his hands and all you heard were car doors opening. I turned around and we were instantly outnumbered, trapped in this parking garage. We somehow ended up winning that fight and fucked these dudes up. One of us got a bottle broken over his head, but those dudes got super hurt, to the point where that was finally the end of that.

Like I said, at our best, we were ten, and we weren't always together. Sometimes we got caught off guard. We got caught once at Puck's Alley, and we got smoked within five seconds. We didn't know if these were guys we had beef with, but they saw five of us smoking a joint in the alley. These dudes came up out of nowhere and just put a fucking beating on us. By 1995, I'm sure 50 percent of the scene hated us, hated the sight of us, and fuckin' despised everything about us.

Jesse Perrin: Hawaii was rough around the edges compared to what was going on in the Bay, which was way more sophisticated. But at the same time, there wasn't that same blood-in, blood-out attitude there. Anybody from LA or Hawaii who was staying with me in San Francisco, the Bay Area skins were like, "Jesus, your friends always cause a bunch of shit!" Well, sorry. Meanwhile, all the LA transplants who lived in San Francisco then really got along with all the Hawaii skinheads, like, "Dude, these guys are fucking crazy!"

Damon Cabral: A lot of the old-timers, the old HARSH crew, actually moved away to the mainland. Seattle, the Bay, Florida, New York, places like that.

Jeff Chmolack: The first bunch of us got to the mainland in the mid-'90s. Jesse and them came up here in '96. Me and my wife got here in '98. Ray Bala produced a skinhead magazine out of Hawaii called *A Way of Life*. He did that out of his house, and that thing had worldwide distribution, so through that, we met a lot of skinheads who came through Hawaii. After reading that thing, they would fly out to Hawaii to try and find Ray, meet him, and associate with him. We were getting skinheads from all over the globe coming to Hawaii.

The first time I came up to San Francisco was when I graduated high school in '93, and I met the skinheads over here, and they were full traditional skinheads, man. Right out of 1969, you know? Sta-Prest pants, nice, button-down shirts. It's cold in San Francisco, so they're wearing Crombie jackets with ascots and scarves, like full fuckin' traditional skinheads, man. And here I am with, like, boots and braces and a Dinosaur Jr. T-shirt on. They're like, "Where the fuck are you from, man?" and I'm like, "I'm from Hawaii," and instantly, they vibed, right? They were like, "Oh shit! You're the skinheads they were talking about in the *Skinhead Bible*!" By the time I met 'em, they were called the Bay City Firm. They were thirty deep, maybe eighteen skinhead guys and twelve skinhead girls who looked proper, with skirts and suits. But they vibed with me.

Back then, San Francisco also had a fuckin' crazy white power scene from the late '80s into the early '90s, and this crew had moved from Santa Cruz to San Francisco with the goal of eradicating all the Nazis from the scene. These guys were into brawling and fought all the time; that's how many Nazi skinheads were in the scene. They let me hang out with them, and we got into some shit with some Nazis.

There were other skinhead factions nearby, but they had more of a gang mentality, and they were from Sacramento. That scene in 2001 was huge. Fuckin' Sacramento—I don't mean to be an asshole, but they might as well have been white power because that was their mentality, right? They were all bullies who would recruit picked-on kids and then turn them into fuckin' bullies and give them an outlet, but dress 'em up as skinheads and come to shows and make trouble.

The thing is, the guy who started that crew was friends with the Bay City Firm guys and so were the Hawaii skins. But when we all got here, we decided we weren't going to join anyone's crew because we represented Hawaii. They asked us to join up, but at that point in time, we were all FCS, and we still backed them up big-time anyway. Those guys had been skinheads since 1985, when they were teenagers, and they were as legit as it comes. They could fight and they did. But by 2001, they felt like they weren't enforcing like that anymore, and they didn't really have an issue with us being that, but then shit broke out when those guys from Sacramento started coming out in droves.

It all started with a small fight at a club up here, and it was Jesse Perrin, me, Ray Bala, Dave Suzuki, and Joel Apostol. During that time period, Jesse was into that whole suedehead version of the skinhead. He had this '70s shoulder-length, like, feathered hair, almost like a Farah Fawcett 'do, with these huge fucking sideburns, and he would wear these steel frame aviator glasses and a Levi's jacket with the wool, Sta-Prest pants and Dr. Marten boots. He looked fucking intimidating to me. Jesse's a gnarly guy; he's as tough as they come.

But we're at this show and these Sacramento skins see Jesse up towards the front, and me and Ray are by the bar, and these guys are talking and pointing his way. I was like, "Oh, check it out, Ray. I think these fuckin' kids think that Jesse's like some weirdo." We were laughing and I was like, "They're gonna find out they're gonna fuck with the wrong guy, watch."

Ray Bala: Some fucking fresh cuts from Sacramento thought they were tough, messing with some guy with hair, and found out real fast they fucked up.

Jeff Chmolack: Sure as shit, Jesse's singing along to the band, and these two skinhead kids went towards him and kept bumping into him from behind and got a little more aggressive with it to the point where Jesse took notice of it. He looked at one of 'em and shrugged it off and went back to watching the show until the other one came around and did it again, and the switch flipped. He just motors these two kids, just fucks them up. One dude just beats the shit out of these two guys, and everybody was like, *holy fuck*, right?

So these kids didn't take that well, and when they went back to Sacramento, they told this tall tale about getting jumped by Hawaii skinheads because they couldn't go back and tell their friends that one guy beat up both of 'em to that extent. Anybody at that show will tell you it was complete bullshit.

The next time there's a show, there's a bunch of those guys, including the two that Jesse beat up. They wanted it, so we gave it to 'em. We fucked these dudes up. I'm telling you, man, Jesse's one of the best fighters I've ever seen in my life. He would easily, every fight, take out a couple of guys, so it didn't matter if we were outnumbered.

Ray Bala: It's just his upbringing, I guess. Just like anything else, if you set your mind to something, you're gonna be good at it, and he has rock-solid dedication to the martial arts. I'm just glad he was on our side.

Jeff Chmolack: So we smoke these dudes, and that story grows, right? They go back and say, "We gotta go back because we're getting jumped by these Hawaii skinheads." I don't know what their version of "jumped" is, but I always thought it meant you were outnumbered or in a surprise attack. It isn't confronting three guys when you have seven, and the three guys beat you up. They didn't jump you; they just beat you up and won the fight.

Ray Bala: We met one of the older skins from Sacramento. It just so happens he was the singer for Pressure Point, who I corresponded with previously when I was doing my magazine. He was like, "You're the guy that does *A Way of Life*!" He's all, "Yeah, don't worry about those fuckers, they're stupid."

So it wasn't us versus Sacramento, in general. From what I perceived, these were some fresh cuts who had no affiliation with anybody, and got their asses handed to them too many times that they had to link up with a crew from Sacramento. It was like they needed protection from the bogeyman, which was us, a small handful of Hawaii skins.

Chris Esteron: At the time, the Bay Area had a pretty decent collection of Hawaii expats: Dave Suzuki was there, Mark Peralta from Tweaked was there, Ray Bala, some others. Jesse Perrin moved away just before I got there, but there was a pretty solid group of Hawaii people there. I love Hawaii, but I just wanted to know what it was like to be somewhere else. I ended up staying for six years. There were so many amazing shows happening there, and I just wanted to experience it while I was still young enough to enjoy it all.

Jeff Chmolack: There's an oi band out of New York City called the Templars, one of the best, and they were playing in San Francisco at a club called Bottom of the Hill. There were seven of us there. So Bay City Firm, who were thirty deep, don't want anything to do with any of this, but there's three skinheads who hang out with the Bay City Firm guys that are originally from LA with mutual friends that we took care of while they were in Hawaii who were like, "When shit happens, we got your back."

So we go to this show, and it's sold out. Bottom of the Hill's capacity, I'd say, is 250, and there were at least 300-something skinheads at this show, most from California, some from Nevada or other places. Me and my wife, then-girlfriend, were standing up by the merch table with Chris Esteron, and there were these skinheads nearby, maybe four or five of them, all being super cool, sharing the same enthusiasm for the show with us.

There was this one guy they called Slick Rick, and he was just a fucking troublemaker. He was an instigator who would always get his ass kicked, but it wouldn't deter him from causing trouble. He was always a witness to these fights, and he would always egg people on. Right before the Templars are about to go on, I see the two guys from the original fight. This Rick guy, who was standing next to Ray, threw a beer at one of those kids walking in the door. That kid gets hit by a beer and he looks, and all he sees—because he doesn't know Rick—is Ray. So he and that other dude start bolting for Ray, through the crowd. Esteron's taller than me, so he sees this and he's like, "Oh, dude, there it goes!"

Ray Bala: It was gonna go off regardless that night. When the guy got hit in the head with the beer and it splashed all over him, he turned around, and I think I kind of smirked. I was just leaning against the bar, and I had no idea Rick was gonna throw that shit. They came charging, and it just went off from there.

Jeff Chmolack: They got to Ray, and he started swinging, and I was like, "Oh shit, we gotta go!" As soon as I say that, one of those dudes in front of me that we were talking to all night turns around and fucking grabs me by the collar. I'm starting to see it: He winds up, ready to lay me out, and he swings and I duck, and he knocks out a dude standing behind me watching the Templars coming onto the stage. I can hear the punch just explode onto this dude's face, right? I had brass knuckles in my pocket and end up hitting the guy, and he lets me go when his three friends start jumping me. So now I'm on the ground, on my knees, with three dudes punching down on me, and I'm holding onto the guy that I hit with the brass knuckles, just hitting this dude. I remember getting punched on two sides and on top of my head until I hear a snap and the guy on the left falls down. It was Chris Esteron. I think it might've been the first punch he'd thrown in his adult life, and he knocked this fuckin' guy out. That was just enough to let me get out of the grasp of the other guys, but by the time I turned around there were now four or five guys jumping my buddy Ray. While we were on our way to Ray, I saw the bouncer grab him and throw him out the door, and in the process, he also let four of those guys out. They were gonna kill him.

Ray Bala: From there, it's just a whirlwind. In fact, I don't even know what happened to Rick. I don't know where he went, the fucker. While I was fighting one guy, I got rocked from behind, and luckily, I didn't black out all the way. So I just got up and started hitting anybody around me. At that point, I didn't know who we were fighting.

Jeff Chmolack: There were four dudes kicking Ray on the ground, and we just laid four of those dudes out. The next thing you know, more of those dudes from Sacramento got let out, and now we're stuck in the street, a handful of us, surrounded. This shit got pretty crazy. We ended up fighting, I wanna say, a good twenty-plus guys. From the start of it inside to the end of the fight, which is when the cops showed up, was probably about five minutes. This was a long one, enough for two people to get stabbed, enough for a couple people to lose teeth or be unconscious.

Chris Esteron: The cops were literally grabbing everybody by the shoulders and throwing them on the ground. I didn't want them to throw me, so I just sat down near my boys. A cop looks at me and I'll never forget it—his name tag said "Hernandez"—he says, "What the fuck are you doing, man?" and I didn't know how to respond to him, so I just kinda looked at him. He's like, "Dude, get the fuck outta here; you're white." Here's a brown man with a Black man behind him telling me I can leave this mess because I'm white. I didn't know what to do with that. Then Jeff kind of gave me a way out and told me to go find his girlfriend Nicole. He saved my ass on that one.

Jeff Chmolack: The whole thing ended up putting a giant rift in the San Francisco scene. Anybody who looked like a skinhead from Hawaii didn't get into any shows. We were barred from the San Francisco club scene. A lot of bands had problems booking shows at what used to be a city that was easy to book shows in because of the level of violence that happened at that club, and we took the rap for it. Everybody hated us for it after that, even a good portion of the Bay City Firm. I'm still friends with a better part of 'em, but there was a handful who thought we were the cause of it. We were jumped every single fucking time, so how are we the cause of this? There was an issue of *Maximum Rocknroll* later that year, in 2001, that mentioned the Hawaii skinheads, what happened that night, and how we were the cause of SF's halting of punk rock.

Ray Bala: We got blamed for all kinds of shit. It doesn't matter; it's all talk by a bunch of elitist wannabes. The people who know what really happened know the truth.

Chris Esteron: It's not fair, but it affected my friends more than it did me. I probably wouldn't have been recognized if I went out after that. I would've been just another white boy, whereas they were very recognizable. You know, bald, tattooed brown guys.

Derek "Nos" Okazaki: I was in San Francisco once and I went to a club, and because I had a shaved head and a Hawaii ID, I wasn't allowed in. I was like, "What the fuck?"

They said, "No, we know all about you guys."

I'm like, "I'm on vacation, dude—I don't even live here!"

23

TOO LOUD, TOO MUCH, TOO FAST

The 1990s were a time of growing pains for all manner of alternative music. Once hailed as commercial rock's great foil, alt-rock found itself in the paradoxical position of becoming the new mainstream. Red Hot Chili Peppers' *Blood Sugar Sex Magik* and Pearl Jam's *Ten* were counted among Billboard's top fifteen albums of 1991, while Nirvana's breakthrough masterstroke *Nevermind* cracked the top three the following year, popularizing the grunge subgenre and paving the way for numerous bands from Seattle's ascendant music scene. In subsequent years, albums by Smashing Pumpkins, Stone Temple Pilots, Nine Inch Nails, Green Day, and others went multi-platinum. Major labels, in a race to find the next Nirvana, Pearl Jam, Alice in Chains, or Soundgarden, trotted out an assortment of grunge-lite soundalikes such as Bush, Collective Soul, Candlebox, Creed, and Nickelback. Such endorsements may have cast a wider net with consumers, but it also engendered a growing dissatisfaction among untold music fans who felt the loss of the underground more acutely with each passing year.

Increasingly, music from the more immoderate flanks of rock intersected with the world of commerce. It was not uncommon for alternative rock acts and their songs to be used in ads hawking everything from beer to soft drinks to clothes and cars. Hip-hop, rave culture, skate culture and streetwear were no more impervious to such commercial overtures.

When SoCal-based surfing, skateboarding, and snowboarding apparel company Volcom entered the music industry in 1995 with the creation of the Volcom Entertainment recording label, a number of Hawaii bands eagerly aligned with the blossoming lifestyle brand by offering their recordings for Volcom projects and performing live at various functions.

As overseer of many of the company's events in Hawaii, Volcom regional sales agent Clint Moncata was responsible for some of the most rambunctious soirees across the island chain.

The Volcom House, which housed visiting team riders from around the world and touring bands flown in for Volcom shows, was an infamous party spot that regularly switched addresses up and down Oahu's North Shore, though not often by choice. "We got kicked out of every house, pretty much," says Moncata.

Despite corporate America's widespread investment in counterculture at the time, Moncata maintains that Volcom's engagement with the local underground was not so much business as making genuine connections and having a blast. "It was authentic and real and 'core and rebellious," he insists. "There was no fluff involved, and I was living as hard as everyone else."

With the upsurge in interest in alternative rock came an expanding local underground music scene and the need for additional venues. While a good number of bands were hand-picked by Goldenvoice's Honolulu branch to open for well-known musical acts performing in town, many more startup bands needed places to hone their craft and exhibit their talents. DIY promoters began booking irregular venues such as restaurants, dance clubs, and even Kalaheo High School to showcase Oahu's quickly growing inventory of young, aspirational bands. Of all the new live venues in the mid-'90s, Fast Zone, perhaps more than any other, became a point of convergence for Honolulu's punk scene.

FAST ZONE

Kevin Jones a.k.a. Kevin Catalog (bassist: The Catalogs; vocalist: A Young Poisoner's Handbook): When Fast Zone came along, it became the main place to see local punk shows. There were already a few spots like CD Cafe and the University YWCA where it was easy to book your band and invite your friends' bands to play, but Fast Zone was it for a while.

Dave "Noodle" Heulitt a.k.a. Addison: (vocalist/guitarist: The Sticklers, Temporary Lovers, Das Muchachos, etc.; host of Radio Free Hawaii's *Punkaholic Session*): Fast Zone was a great place in a crappy area. Fort Street Mall at night was not a good place to hang out, and you didn't dare venture too far down Fort Street Mall by yourself. But at the time it really was the mecca of Hawaii punk rock. In fact, The Sticklers formed because our whole goal was to play the Fast Zone. Everybody wanted to play there.

Mike Silva: Unless you were a bum from around the area, you probably wouldn't even know there was a music venue on Fort Street Mall.

Chris Esteron: The importance of the Fast Zone at that point in time cannot be overstated. There were occasional shows at Wo Fat, which was another great venue just a few blocks away, and Formula 660 in Kaka'ako, but Fast Zone became an anchor for the scene and fostered some really great music. It was glorious. All credit to Dave Frye for jumping on that place early.

Dave Frye (vocalist: Generic; promoter): Since I was already putting on my own shows, I got asked by Fast Zone to take care of the Bikini Kill show that was about to happen there, so I put my band and a bunch of others on the bill. On the day of the show, Bikini Kill gets there early, and Kathleen Hanna, the singer, comes up to me, and we greet each other. I welcome her to Hawaii and tell her a lot of people are coming out to see them. The band is like, "Yeah, we're excited too, but we got a problem. There's a band on the bill that we don't want to play." I had a feeling it was going to be us.

We had a song called "Whore," which I wrote when I was fifteen. It was about me getting my heart broken by this girl who cheated on me, and I almost killed myself, actually, by sticking a knife in my chest. Another one was called "March of the Lesbians," which was based on an incident that happened in Waikiki where a gang of butchies on motorcycles in leather jackets were about to kick my ass because they were looking for a bar nearby, and I gave them directions to Hula's. I was a little intimidated, I'm not gonna lie, but we had a conversation, and I let them know I wasn't trying to offend anybody. That's all it was. It was never an anti-lesbian song.

But Kathleen Hanna says, "From what I've heard, Generic is a sexist band, very derogatory towards women." I ask if she knows any of them or knows any of their music, and she says, "No, but this is what I've heard."

I told her, "Well, I hate to tell you this, but they are going to play, and that's my band."

She goes, "What? Oh, ew, you guys are terrible..."

I didn't like the way she demanded that we not play. It felt like someone from the mainland being a rock star, coming to Hawaii, trying to dictate what goes down.

She says, "Well, we're gonna play, but we're gonna play before you."

So because they took our spot, the club wasn't really filled when they played. I mean, there were some riot grrrls there, but by the time we got on, the place was packed. The whole time she's giving me grief: "You know, this is so messed up..." As they got off stage, they tried to unplug our amps, mess with our equipment, and sabotage our set. It made me even madder, and I won't say exactly what I said when I got on stage, but I was pissed and cocky, maybe a little buzzed, and the full local boy comes out, like, "These fuckers come over from the mainland and think they can pick who plays our shows? Fuck you guys and go back to the mainland, you dumb fuckin' haoles!"

Kevin Jones: I mean, there were a lot of young girls there just to see Bikini Kill, so I understand Bikini Kill being protective of their fan base. And then to endure people in the crowd causing trouble or whatever, that's no good for the band either. A lot of the meathead punk rock kids were basically yelling out stupid shit. At least one kid got kicked out. There's still a lot of animosity with some people about that whole episode.

Dave Frye: I was very protective of Hawaii artists, and my whole thing was we're just as good as anyone else, and just because we're not touring doesn't mean you're better than us. We have just as much talent as you guys, so don't come to Hawaii and think you can push us around. In Hawaii, in our culture, we don't care who you think you are. You can be some big shot or whatever, but when you come here, you better be cool.

Cliff Tierra (drummer: Tweaked): Dave was always looking out for different bands, even us. Always energetic, hustling to get shows. He was a super cool dude to me.

Warren Hassett (vocalist: Mistermeaner, Full Send; promoter): If you want to know about Dave Frye, it depends which Dave Frye you're talking about. I have respect for who he's become after everything he's gone through, but we were contentious back in the day. I really liked to party back then too, but I wasn't that kind of partier. So it would depend on which Dave I got. Sober Dave is fuckin' rad; chronic Dave is not.

Dave Frye: The truth is there was a lot of coke, a lot of meth, and some ecstasy in the scene. People would say, "You want drugs? Go ask Dave. He can get it for you." Every member of one of the most popular local groups—except for maybe one—was coming to see me, but they didn't know the others were visiting me too. Even some of the skinheads in the scene would visit me and be like, "Hey, you know you're my bro, but don't tell anybody I came by."

"Gotcha."

Then he'd leave and another one would show up: "Hey, don't let nobody know I was here."

"No worries. Gotcha."

Chris Esteron: You always knew as warm and open as Dave was, he was hiding something. And if you got to know him, you had a pretty good idea of what it was. But he never let it affect his relationship with you as a person. If you were into that other shit, it was just another layer to your relationship. I've met strippers, I've met gangsters, I've met people who never went to shows that knew Dave Frye. And I didn't have to guess how they knew him, but he was every bit as open and cool with them as he was with his friends in the scene. He was a truly lovable guy. Chemicals make weird shit happen, but he never had a bad heart.

GRAPEFRUIT

Justin Mynatt (bassist: Grapefruit): Our band was never involved in some of the stuff that was going on behind the scenes, but that doesn't mean that we weren't aware or concerned about our friends who were. It's not like it was hidden, and we know what was happening at some

Grapefruit at 924 Gilman during an early tour of the West Coast.
Courtesy of Justin Mynatt

of the shows. We weren't naive about it. It bummed us out, though, because we would see promising bands give up because that element took over their lives. Luckily for the three of us, we never got wrapped up in any of that.

Dave "Noodle" Heulitt: Grapefruit were always such good guys. There was no one who played in the '90s that had more energy than Brandon, Justin, and Tom Tom. They were completely different from anything I'd ever heard or seen live. They were frenetic and goofy, going nuts and jumping around, and all three of them were super talented. Grapefruit was a great influence on me as a performer.

Justin Mynatt: We grew up in Kailua, and we started playing music as something to do when there were no waves to surf. We were kind of a fast-paced, energetic band, and people were like, "Wow, okay, Grapefruit's a punk rock band!" But because we don't really use a lot of distortion and we don't have very angry lyrics, we'd laugh, thinking we weren't very punk rock at all. Then we started hearing bands like Operation Ivy and Dead Milkmen and the Minutemen, and that kind of started shaping our sound more.

Chris Esteron: Grapefruit might have thought they didn't fit in because they weren't angry like Pongoids or The Pugilist, but I thought they came at the perfect time. When the surfers and the cute girls and the friendly, normal-type guys started coming to local underground shows in the mid-'90s, you could see how they would be drawn in by bands like Grapefruit, Power Pellets, and The Catalogs.

THE CATALOGS

Cliff Tierra: I remember The Catalogs. I used to dig them because they had that Screeching Weasel-slash-Queers kind of sound, mixed in with the Ramones.

Kevin Jones: There were kids in the '90s who rediscovered the Ramones and all the power pop stuff from the 1970s. That's where The Catalogs were at. That's the sound and attitude we were going for. I'd gotten together with Les Hernandez, who was itching to start a Ramones-style band. At some point, Les and I also decided to promote shows at Fast Zone to fly out-of-state bands to Hawaii. We brought over The Queers and Mr. T Experience, and The Queers liked our song "Another Girl" enough that they recorded it on their *Don't Back Down* record.

Chris Esteron: Les Hernandez could talk to you about history and philosophy and religion, all while cracking dirty jokes and being hysterically irreverent. We need more of that in this world: regular people with a transcendent charisma. That can only come from truly being yourself. Love it or hate it, he was also a pretty high-ranking member of the Church of Satan.

Rolando "Rolo" Dongon: Les was very true to what he believed in. People would see him in dark clothing, wearing a pentagram, and say, "Oh, he's a devil worshiper," but he wasn't dark at all. He's actually a very positive, compassionate, good person. I remember teasing him because his bands always sounded so poppy. I said, "I know why you're playing this music—it's because it gets girls to come to the dark side!" He laughed so hard at that.

Mike Silva: One thing that has to be known is that true Satanists are not devil worshippers. We don't believe in the devil. As members of the Church of Satan, we are atheists. We are our own god. We don't worship any gods or deities; we don't even believe in Satan. Instead, we believe that man created all gods; therefore, they don't really exist; they're made up. What Satan is for us is a symbol of opposition. He is the ultimate rebel. We're staunch individualists.

Les achieved his rank of Reverend because of his work with the Quintessentials, which was his horror-punk band after The Catalogs and Crawling Chaos, which was a band he and I started in between other projects. Just before he passed, he was elevated to the title of Magister. The only ranking above that is High Priest. He lived his life to the fullest all through his fight with cancer, making jokes all the way up to the end.

Chris Esteron: Several years ago, he had a cold that never went away. At first, doctors thought it was allergies, then a sinus infection. I saw him one time and asked if he was all right. He said yeah, but he just couldn't kick whatever it was. Then one day, out of the blue, he made a Facebook post letting everyone know that the cold he couldn't get rid of turned out to be cancer.

One thing to note is that guys like Grapefruit are Christians who are active in their churches, and they came and played Les Hernandez's memorial show. Bro, that's love. That's the realization that within this group of misfits, there's room for all of us. They came, played, and put on a great show as if to say, "Hey, it's really sad why we're here, but let's have some fun."

PUNK'S POPPIER SIDE

Mike Silva: Things really started to change in that era. It was obvious there was a whole new generation of kids who grew up on MTV and listened to Pennywise and The Offspring or even Pegboy. Their music was still fast, but it was a new, more melodic version of punk with actual harmonies. They seemed to be more about having fun with friends than being confrontational and in your face and saying, "Fuck you, society." It was a different attitude.

Richard Detty: Music always evolves, but there was the pop-punk thing that was starting to happen and a lot of it was just crap. So much of it was just bad. So bad, oh my god. There were bands I've seen and worked with that made me think, "I can't believe these kids are popular."

Randy Szucs: To me, that newer punk rock stuff, I hated it. I still don't like it. Punk rock wasn't supposed to be poppy unless you were the Descendants, and there's only one Descendants. I didn't like Green Day or NOFX. They might be great musicians or funny on stage, but I don't go to a concert to laugh at jokes, because in my experience, going to a punk rock show wasn't fucking funny. Where's the *danger*, you know? Fuck.

Cliff Tierra: At first, most of us guys in Tweaked used to like Slayer, Metallica, the old thrash bands, but then we all got influenced by Descendents and All for some reason. Other punk bands too, but we really liked All and Descendents. So all that new pop-punk was cool to us. We liked the melodic stuff too.

Jeff Chmolack: The Pugilist was a fully decked-out skinhead band playing oi music, and oi is catered strictly to skinheads, yet we were playing shows with bands that looked like fucking nerds, but they were cool as shit. We fucking loved it. We went to all the shows, we paid to get in, and we supported all the other bands.

Us younger skinheads felt like we were going to do it our way and just hang out with whoever the fuck we want, and if the older guys accept us, that's cool. If not, that sucks, but it didn't really matter to us. We weren't going to stop hanging out with other people in our age group.

Justin Mynatt: I remember being kind of intimidated by The Pugilist because they were the old-school punk rockers and skinheads with a reputation for being hard guys, and you didn't wanna disappoint them with your music. After a show one night, Mike from The Pugilist rushes straight up to us and slaps Brandon on the chest and goes, "You guys are one of my favorite punk bands now here in Hawaii!" So that was a relief.

BEYOND THE USUAL

Kevin Jones: People will say I'm elitist or whatever, but a lot of us weren't satisfied with the music that was popular or mainstream within the punk scene in the '90s. Things like NOFX and the Offspring and some of the stuff on Lookout Records was not anything we were interested in. A lot of the people I was hanging out with were looking for something else, and we found bands like Antioch Arrow and some of the more artsy hardcore bands that were coming out of the West Coast at the time. We just got bored of the same-old and we were looking for more.

Rafael Dongon (guitarist: Hell Yeah Bowlers, Bangstick, Cooperstown, etc.): Jeff Goo and I were into the new DC and Southern California hardcore. At the time it was a really different sound from what was going on. We were into bands like Downcast and Amenity and all these obscure bands like Struggle and Born Against. It wasn't three-chord punk from 1982 anymore.

Jeff Goo (vocalist: Bangstick, Cooperstown): Progressive hardcore is what it was. I think the direction of music in general then was really interesting. There was an evolution with bands who took music beyond their punk roots.

Nobody talks about that period from 1988 until Nirvana hit it big in '91, but that was the beginning of another generation of underground music when bands like Fugazi and Rollins Band were making music that started to take punk beyond Dead Kennedys and the old hardcore stuff. Then you started to see concerts you thought you would never see come to town.

Rafael Dongon: Goldenvoice started bringing a lot of shows to Hawaii, but some of us were very much anti-Goldenvoice. The way we saw it was they were trying to move in on our scene. We had a DIY ethos, like, do it yourself and fuck corporations, and when Jeff and I were doing bands together, we always said we would never play a Goldenvoice show, ever.

Jeff Goo: This was when you started to see groups like Sonic Youth and Mudhoney come to town, and with Radio Free Hawaii on the air and all this attention on the alternative side of music, you had a whole new wave of kids coming around who had no ties and no roots to the local scene.

Rafael Dongon: I had respect for Radio Free Hawaii, but I still didn't like it. We were already in this thing for four or five years and were looking at all these new kids coming around, thinking, *Are you in this for the long haul or is this just a passing phase for you?* because we were always on the lookout for kids who were gonna be lifers.

FREAK HUNT

Chris Esteron: When I first started going to shows in the late '80s, there was a palpable fear of violence. At my first show ever, I saw guys under a table smoking ice before going on stage, I saw someone pull a knife on somebody at that same show, and I watched someone lose an eye once because he got hit that fucking hard. There was definitely this feeling of chaos among all these people who didn't fit in anywhere else acting wild as fuck, and I accepted that our music couldn't be what it was without that energy.

Fast-forward six years to the Fast Zone, and yeah, it might've been in a little sketchy part of town, but the atmosphere was friendly, there were cute girls in miniskirts hanging out, and it was mostly peaceful. So the night Freak Hunt came out onstage at Fast Zone, I saw all these kids going, "What the fuck...?" There was real fear in their eyes.

Dave Frye: If anyone asked me to name the top five punk rock bands from Hawaii, Freak Hunt would have to be up there. And I don't think they even lasted a whole year. Those guys were nuts.

Freak Hunt at Fast Zone. *Courtesy of Derek Okazaki*

Derek "Nos" Okazaki: It was Ryan Kunimura who said to me, "Man, you know what's missing from shows nowadays? It's all mellow and safe; everybody just runs around in a circle. We need to bring the element of fear back, like when we were kids going to shows and we were terrified of all the gnarly guys from the scene, thinking, *Oh shit, I might get fuckin' worked! Let's just get on stage and assault everybody in the crowd.* It was all the chaos and male nudity that made Freak Hunt even more infamous.

Ryan Kunimura: We just did all kinds of gross shit. I bought a pork tongue from Chinatown and tied it to my face, and Nos stuck a squid to his chest and Saran-Wrapped some kind of snake around him one time.

Derek "Nos" Okazaki: I'd wear a G-string with a baby doll head in the crotch with spikes, and French bread for shoes. Every show, we'd go to Safeway and buy raw meat or seafood to use as stage props just to freak people out. We got banned from every place we played.

Mike Silva: Freak Hunt only lasted a few months because every show that we played would get shut down because of all the damage we did. The infamous show at the Rock Cellar turned into a fiasco.

Chris Esteron: From where I was standing at the Rock Cellar show, I didn't see Ryan undo his overalls, but I noticed at some point he just had a bass guitar covering his crotch. Suddenly, he lifted his bass up and started pissing on stage. All hell broke loose, and I couldn't even tell you what happened next.

Ryan Kunimura: Security started moving towards the stage, a bunch of 'em, and we were like, "Oh shit!" But Randy and the rest of Broken Man kind of surrounded the bouncers and got in the way of them getting to the stage, so we booked it, running through Waikiki with our guitars and shit.

Derek "Nos" Okazaki: This one guy flips over a table and starts kicking shit, yelling, "Riot!" and that's when everybody went nuts. Bouncers were grabbing people, and I just ran out of the club to find my car. Ryan and Mike ran after me and jumped in, and as we tried to find our way out of Waikiki, we drove slowly past the club and saw the cops already had people handcuffed out front.

Kevin Jones: I just remember chairs flying everywhere and people running for safety. That was probably my scariest punk rock moment in Hawaii.

Derek "Nos" Okazaki: We played another show at Euphoria, which was an all-night rave club down the street from where Pink's Garage used to be. That show was oversold by way too much, and as soon as we started playing, somebody threw a five-gallon bucket of salsa they stole from Jack in the Box all over the place. I had these four-foot raw squids on me, and this place just stank so bad because there were too many people in there. I think that was our last show. We were running out of places to play.

Richard Detty: They had a big bag with a whole squid inside with liquid in it, and they threw the bag on the ground where everybody would mosh, and it made the whole floor slippery, and it just stunk to high heaven. The juice went all over my equipment. I had to sit down and wipe it off all my cords. After a couple of shows I said I couldn't do sound for them anymore. It was too much extra work.

Chris Esteron: Mike Silva once said, "The day we make it through a set without getting kicked out is the day we quit."

Mike Silva: Freak Hunt was about putting the "fuck you" back into punk rock. We didn't have a message except that.

PUNK VERSUS THE PARTY SCENE

Dave Frye: There was a major connection to the surf and skate scenes, which brought in way more people to local punk shows. Even though we barely had the Internet back then, word got around pretty quick. You might even hear Generic or Grapefruit on the radio because you could vote for local bands all up and down Radio Free Hawaii's ballots. More and more kids were getting into it because we had a big support system of Radio Free Hawaii, Jelly's, Hungry Ear, and KTUH. Jason Momoa and the crew from *Baywatch Hawaii* were coming to our shows, and people were asking me to sign autographs. I don't think Hawaii will ever have an underground music scene that had that level of support again.

Chris Esteron: I never understood the whole party vibe a lot of guys were on back then. I was never into getting wasted, ramming into a tree, getting into a fight for no good reason, and puking on your girlfriend. I usually had a good time at places like the Cannon Club, but those shows were no longer just about punk rock. There were usually outside elements at those shows mixing with people who weren't accountable for their actions, and that really made things volatile.

Dave Frye: The Cannon Club shows were always huge. One was Unit 101, Tantra Monsters, and us. There must've been over a thousand people at that show. The Cannon Club had these big-ass windows all around, and you could see there was a line of people going down the street. We played first and nobody was really dancing, so I started calling people out, calling them pussies. By the time we got done, people were pumped up, almost in fight mode. I guess some mokes took it the wrong way and just started slamming people. By the time the next group got on, it was nuts. We were outside in this little gazebo watching people getting thrown out the windows. People started running out from the club, and a bunch of cars got their windows smashed. It was even on the news: *Tonight, a riot at the Cannon Club...*

Derek "Nos" Okazaki: There were three groups of people there that night: Waimanalo guys, some west side Waianae guys, and I think some Kalihi guys. More or less gangs of people, huge groups. The reason why we knew where they were from is because they kept chanting stuff like, "'Nalo, 'Nalo!" Total moke invasion. Some guy went through one of the plate glass windows. There was one off-duty cop standing thirty feet away, and he wanted no part of it. He was definitely outnumbered. He just got on his radio and started walking towards the parking lot like, "Yeah, this is way out of control."

Richard Detty: It's that Hawaii machismo, man. You get guys from the west side, other guys from Waimanalo, some from other parts of the island in one place, and they get real territorial. Especially when it's a bunch of young guys in big groups. That's just what happens.

THE VOLCOM FACTOR

Warren Hassett: Volcom was all about the wild, antiestablishment lifestyle: live fast, party hard, chaos, and rock and roll. They were always extremely helpful to the scene. They were super supportive, looking out for us, hooking us up with different things, and helping us get our first record out.

Clint Moncata (Volcom Sales Rep: Hawaii/Tahiti/Guam): When I joined up with Volcom, all they had was a sticker and a poster. Our mantra then was "Youth Against Establishment." Volcom Entertainment started up a few years later, and a record label grew out of that. Pepper was probably the biggest band out of Hawaii that we signed.

Mike Silva: The skateboarders from Volcom built a half pipe in the back-yard of the house I was renting with Randy Szucs from Broken Man and Nos. Most of the time in the mid-'90s, I didn't even go out unless there was something happening at the Fast Zone because everybody would want to come over to our house.

Clint Moncata: The first show I ever did for Volcom was at Pink's Garage. We built a skate ramp in there and had Mr. Simon and Mystery Crash play, and that just kind of set the tone for what was to come. I really wanted to grow the brand and help promote the bands, and if I broke even, I was stoked. We had some pretty wild shows with bands like Generic, Freak Hunt, Ira Hayes, Friend of the Family, Unit 101, and a bunch of others. I was kinda going rogue at the time, building up the company name, but also pulling 700 or 800 people to these events with the Volcom branding behind them.

Dave Frye: Volcom would send us and other bands to the outer islands to play at skate demos. We were doing tours with pro skaters like Bam Margera and Rune Glifberg. We brought the Knumbskulls, Potluck, and some other guys with us to Kauai and Maui, playing these huge shows out there with the team riders. At the same time, we were getting letters from faraway places like France and Switzerland saying things like "We got the Volcom CD, and we love your record!"

Clint Moncata: The Big Island's got a little bit of a scene nowadays that I've been hearing about, and Maui kinda does too, but back then there wasn't much of that going on when you went to the neighbor islands. When we got to Kauai, they'd never seen a mosh pit there before, ever. They didn't even know what it was. When Generic came on and a pit started up, a lot of them didn't know what to do. A couple of kids started fighting, but I made sure the security stopped it, and after a few minutes the crowd finally figured it out.

Warren Hassett: Volcom first flew Mistermeaner to the neighbor islands with a bunch of other bands in '97, and that's about when I started put-ting on my own shows here on Oahu at places like Club Mustang, Ninja

House, 1739, and Club Pauahi. I saw all these young, up-and-coming bands that nobody would take a chance on: National Product, Buckshot Shorty, Exit 24, Lose Money, Potluck, Backwash. I also wanted to give exposure to bands from the outer islands—Last in Line from Kauai, and FFOR and Old Habits Die Hard from the Big Island—trying to get the scene to be statewide.

But I'd say from 1996 to the end of the '90s were a weird few years. There seemed to be a dark cloud over the whole scene itself. Promoters would start to fight over double bookings, and bands were fighting over who played with who and where and what time and "How come we play first?" and all that kind of shit. It got rock star-ish, and it never used to be like that.

There was more competition and a lot of jockeying for attention, if you will. "Why does Mistermeaner get this show?" or "Why does Generic get that show?" and people crying about when they play or who they're playing with. Whatever, brah. I'll play with whoever, whenever, whether it's two people, 2,000 people, or 20,000 people. From two bucks to twenty bucks to 2,000 bucks, it doesn't matter to me, you know what I mean?

Jeff Goo: To be perfectly honest, I left the scene and moved on in '97 because everybody had a fuckin' ego. I'd already seen it among the bands, talking about "Where's my money?" and this and that. What money? This is punk rock. Four bands, three bucks a show? Do the math. Bands were saying they were in it for the kids, but they should've said they were in it for themselves because then I would've had more respect for their honesty. I just wasn't into it anymore.

24

LARGER THAN LIFE

A sampling of Honolulu concerts to kick off 1996 would have seen NOFX and Bikini Kill at the Groove; Bikini Kill jumping onto a local band showcase at Fast Zone the following night; B.Y.K. opening for Primus the next weekend; Jesus Lizard with Mystery Crash just three days later at Wave Waikiki; Porno for Pyros with hometown rockers Spiny Norman at the Groove two days after that; and a triple header the following weekend featuring Green Day at Richardson Field with Reno, Nevada, pop-punk heroes Zoinks! and Grapefruit. Punk and alternative rock, both locally and nationally, looked to be doing swift business.

Fast-forward roughly a year later, and Fast Zone had shut its doors; the Groove, formerly After Dark, switched hands again, and as Nimitz Hall, tried mightily to duplicate the success of its predecessors without the aid of Radio Free Hawaii, which had ceased operations altogether. With fewer trusted community hubs, it seemed the local scene of the late '90s could not sustain the same vigorous pace. "When Radio Free Hawaii went off the air, it just killed the momentum of the Hawaii punk and indie scenes," reasons Grapefruit's Justin Mynatt. "It took even more work to promote shows at the major concert venues, and those bigger concerts started fizzling out." Regarding smaller gigs, he adds, "I think we got kinda comfortable with having shows every single week at places like the Fast Zone, so when they closed down, it was a lot harder for bands to find places to play."

As the Internet quickly grew in scope and influence, the music retail industry also faced an uncertain future. For brick-and-mortar shops, competition from digital downloads, peer-to-peer file sharing services, and competition from online retailers lurked just around the corner. For Norm Winter, ever the staunch believer in traditional, in-person music sales, it was business as usual. Not long after his Jelly's stores were sold off in exchange for debt resolution, Winter pivoted with a new, though much smaller music outlet he called the Radio Free Music Center. Tucked away in a first-floor corner of the Hawaiian Life Building at the intersection of Kapiolani and Pi'ikoi, it was a fraction the size of his Jelly's stores, though it afforded him a shot at rebuilding the music empire he'd forfeited.

Among his ragtag band of shop hands was the surnameless Otto, a mild-mannered individualist who counted roller skating, baking, and punk rock among his favorite diversions. An agreement with Radio Free Hawaii in which his cheesecakes were exchanged for thirty-second ads may have initially helped raise Otto's profile, though it was the sheer delectability of his desserts that truly earned the maverick baker an island-wide reputation over the next several years. In 2001, *Honolulu* magazine declared Otto's creatively flavored cheesecakes the best around, and his award-winning brownies, cookies, pies, and cakes—produced from his home kitchen—were sought after by a number of cafes and eateries across Oahu.

It was not long after the underground celebrity's recruitment into punk combo The Sticklers that Otto began to try his hand at local show promotions both with and independent of bandmate Dave "Noodle" Heulitt. He quickly amassed a small network of bands and venues he hoped would be of aid to all included parties. "He knew all the right people," remembers Heulitt.

Also counted among the more visible promoters of the era was Jason Miller, a shrewd and enterprising Northern California transplant who arrived in Honolulu on a full-ride swimming scholarship to UH in 1992. His first weekend on Oahu, he learned Skankin' Pickle, whose practice space he'd ridden his bike past on many occasions back home, was playing at the Faktory. "It was kind of a nice welcome to Hawaii," Miller notes. As he attended more shows in Honolulu, he would be acquainted with the city's wide-open underground music community. "I soon found out there were so many good bands here in a scene that could go toe-to-toe with a lot of other places," recalls Miller. "I just fell in love with Hawaii."

Taking knowledge gained from his time as promotions director at KTUH, Miller immersed himself in concert promotions, music merchandising, and the creation of the Hawaiian Express recording label, all endeavors that have now spanned more than thirty years. A list of punk rock greats Miller has brought to Hawaii is likely too lengthy to recite, though it includes such luminaries as the Descendents, Misfits, Bouncing Souls, TSOL, Agent Orange, and Dwarves, to name only a few.

As the decade came to a close, independent promoters like Otto and Miller would be entrusted to continue championing up-and-coming bands, secure new venues as old ones fell away, and stave off threats of oversaturation and commercialization in a rapidly changing scene.

OTTO

Scott McDonough a.k.a. Otto (promoter; bassist: The Sticklers, Imminent Riot, 86 List, etc.): I was working at the Radio Free Music Center when The Sticklers came in, and Jackson, their drummer, asked me, "Otto, do you know how to play bass?" and I said. "No."

He goes, "Do you wanna join our band?" and I said, "Sure."

I didn't think they were serious, but we had our first show a week after that.

Dave "Noodle" Heulitt: We brought Otto to practice and just told him, "Okay, put your finger there, now play up and down, then put your finger here and play this four times." The Sticklers were not writing concertos. We were writing three-chord songs we could jump around to. I mean, if you play something fast and loud enough, it just becomes noise anyway.

Noe Bunnell (drummer: Imminent Riot, Sorry, Les Sauvages, Postmodern, etc.): Otto's a very mellow, calm, positive guy, but he can also

Otto, Dave, and Alex of The Sticklers. *Courtesy of Dave Heulitt*

go into some pretty deep depression sometimes. He's had rough times in his life.

Otto was always such a mystery. Like, he would never show us his license, so nobody knew exactly how old he was. I never saw him date anyone, and he never talked about who he liked or who he was interested in, so we were like, "Is he gay or not?" He was fascinating, and nobody could ever peg him.

He was always so open to people and willing to help mentor younger kids in the scene that we would joke about how Otto would get older, but his friends would stay the same age because he'd always have these young friends hanging out with him. He probably felt like he was a similar age mentally. I know he took me to shows and places I would've never been to.

Doug Davidson a.k.a. Doug Upp a.k.a. Tess Tickles (vocalist: Imminent Riot, Patty Judy and the Dirt): I see Otto as sort of an Andy Warhol/Michael Jackson kind of character. He's got this innocence to him and a playful, childlike quality. He's not real book smart, and it took him forever to learn how to read, so he's like this enigma. But he's also super creative.

Noe Bunnell: I remember when he finally got his own bakery on Ualena Street near the airport and he had such a hard time because he couldn't read the lease, you know? We spent a lot of time practicing reading because I was going to school for education, and I was like, "I'm gonna teach you to read!"

Otto: As a kid, I went through special ed at school and met with people who did different types of testing. I was even taken to the hospital, and they did all these tests, and I had to stay there for a week, and they said, "He doesn't have dyslexia." That's all they could come up with.

My mom says, "Yeah, you can read, but you read what you want it to say." So I do get things wrong a lot, but I always figure out a way.

Doug Upp: There was a news story about his bakery closing in 2024, and somebody commented online, "Oh, I walked in there, and he didn't even have a real cash register. How's he going to survive?" Well, he was in business for thirty years! He had a bakery for decades and never needed a computer. Plus he's flown all over the place and toured with all these bands, and people think he can't do things just because he doesn't do it the way they think he should.

Dave "Noodle" Heulitt: Otto's like the Swiss Army knife of human beings. He's so well-rounded and knowledgeable in a million things yet so innocent and almost naive in another million things. He makes the best cheesecake I've ever had in my entire life. The guy was a champion roller skater in his younger days. He's an artist. He can dance and play bass. But he also genuinely cares about people. He taught me a lot about compassion and giving a shit about others. He's just a pure-hearted person who gets shit done.

HAWAIIAN EXPRESS

Jason Miller (promoter; owner of Hawaiian Express Records, 808shows. com): The very first show that I did on my own was in November of '95, and it was Ira Hayes, Tweaked, and Unit 101 because they were three of my favorites at the time. It was at the Campus Center Ballroom at UH. A pit broke out and someone tore down some curtains, so the ballroom people were not happy with me.

Then when I was about to go on tour with Grapefruit, I thought if we were going to spend all this time and energy and money taking their music to the mainland, why not introduce people to all the other bands from Hawaii as well?

I spoke to all the bands I knew that had a demo tape or vinyl record, and for bands that didn't have any recordings, well, what if we printed shirts with their logo as people ordered them? I created this mail order catalog to leave in as many hands as I could along the tour.

Once I get an idea in my head, I start building on it. I started putting out tapes of bands from Hawaii under the Hawaiian Express label and brought a few of those on the road with me. That's kind of how that started. For me, it was just a fun little hobby that I've been paying taxes on since March of '95.

Fernando Pacheco: Jason Miller was *the* local promoter at the time. His shows were a big deal. They were well produced and promoted. Jason put his heart and soul into every event. I think it was the *Honolulu Weekly* that described him as "a punk rock Billy Graham in Vans sneakers."

Kevin Jones: To be honest, during that period, I did not care for Jason Miller at all. He was a total outsider who appeared one day from the mainland, it felt like. He came out of nowhere and decided he was going to be the king of Hawaii punk. He started doing all kinds of promotions in the late '90s. Was it that he felt like he needed to be recognized for doing something important or was he doing it because he genuinely loved the music and the scene? We never really thought of him as part of the scene. He just appeared one day and started booking all these shows.

I mean, I get along with him and I'm friendly with him now, but during the Catalogs period, especially after he started releasing our recordings on his little label, it got kinda hairy between me and him.

Dave "Noodle" Heulitt: Jason Miller helped spread the word on our scene and got a lot of bands to come out to Hawaii, but he and I never saw eye to eye. Essentially, I think there was a difference in opinion on what a band should make versus what a promoter should make. I know when we did our shows, we were not there to make money. We were just gonna play music and divvy up the money to every band.

Jason Miller: There was some division in the scene with a lot of rumors going around that maybe I'm ripping people off or doing something unsavory, and actually, at the Kodak building, there was a meeting that I called one time. I was sick of hearing about all the stuff I was supposedly doing, so I literally said, "At this day, at this time, I'm gonna be there, and anyone who's got a question, comment, or concern, I'll be there to answer them." Probably about a hundred people showed up. I don't think it ever got really ugly, but I showed up with binders of all the accounting, messages of people approving this or that project, and it turned out to be a whole big nothing. I consider myself an open book, and if people have questions, I'm here for it. You may not like the answer, but you'll get an honest answer.

Justin Mynatt: Jason, for us as a band, has put in so much work to help us travel the U.S., put out albums, and get our name out there, even before the Internet could do all of these things. We'd do a show with Jason, then the next week we'd do one with Otto, and there were people who wouldn't go to a show where one or the other was involved. It's unfortunate that there was a split between the two camps at the time. We didn't feel comfortable choosing sides at all.

Clif Chun a.k.a. Clif Knumbskull (guitarist: Knumbskulls, Days/ Weeks/Months): If it wasn't for Otto, we wouldn't have gotten to open for a lot of the big bands that came over since he was working with Goldenvoice. We were the first band on his record label, Ottocake Records. He helped us out so much when we were just getting our legs under us. He was part of our family.

To this day, I still don't know why there was a feud between Otto and Jason, but because we were friends with Otto, we never played a Jason Miller show out of respect to Otto, who had put countless hours into promoting us and putting on shows for us.

One of our favorite bands was Good Riddance, and Jason put us on the bill when they came to play Hawaii. They were on my bucket list as a band to see live, and I would've loved to open for them, but it was just one of those things, you know? Sorry, can't do it.

Jason Miller: If I could emphasize anything, it would be that Otto and I have had a great relationship for a long time now, but there was a brief period of uneasy waters, I think, primarily because enough people wanted to fuel drama. I worked hard to keep that at bay, and it took a little bit of time to dispel the rumors and attempted division.

Fernando Pacheco: I have to say, for Exit 24 to get Jason Miller's attention back then was a big deal for us, like the Temptations trying to get the attention of Berry Gordy. Exit 24 and Go Jimmy Go did a tour date at Johnston Atoll organized by Jason Miller.

Jason Miller: Johnston Atoll is a tiny, remote island claimed by the U.S. military in the middle of nowhere, hundreds of miles from Hawaii. It's about a mile long, just enough to have a runway. They gotta do something to entertain the workers living there, so the military's Morale, Wellness and Recreation department would fly in bands every once in a while, and I managed to get Go Jimmy Go and Exit 24 to come out for a weekend and play there. That led to Go Jimmy Go formally asking me to manage them for a little bit. Those were good times.

I took bands to the outer islands too. In maybe 1999, when Me First and the Gimme Gimmes still had Fat Mike from NOFX and Chris Shiflett from Foo Fighters, they wanted to come to Hawaii and golf on every island, so I had to find them venues on each island. I pulled it off, but the only place on Kauai I could find was a little bar at a heliport that couldn't hold more than eighty people. Somewhere between 400 and 500 people showed up to that show.

JAVA JAVA CAFE

Chris Esteron: If you were a teenager back then, you couldn't get into bars or nightclubs. There was no such thing as social media to tell you what's going on, but if you were lucky, maybe there was an all-ages punk rock show somewhere. So what do you do the rest of the week? You might go to someplace like Java Java, buy a coffee or a smoothie or a bagel, and just hang out.

Clif Knumbskull: Java Java Cafe was on Kapahulu Avenue, a few blocks from Crane Park, where I used to play basketball. I walked in there one day, and Otto was there. My first thought was *Wow, there's a lot of funky-looking people in here.* There were some punk rockers, some pretty-ass white girls with tattoos, you know, you name it. Then I see this guy come up on his motorcycle with some chick, and it was Warren Young from the Tantra Monsters. He looked like a rock star walking through the door.

Upstairs from the cafe was the Lizard Loft, where you could see bands like Elvis '77 and the Bassdads play; all these musicians who were more or less our age. There'd always be a lot of teenagers hanging out there, and they all seemed a little older, more like adults. It was just a really cool, interesting place, you know?

Otto: There was no Starbucks in Hawaii yet, so I would service a lot of different mom-and-pop coffee shops around the island—probably about fifteen of them—with my cheesecakes. Java Java was one of those places. It was a big gathering place for all kinds of people and musicians. I became friends with some of the homeless punk rockers who would hang out at Java Java, and I would help them out by buying them shampoo or shaving supplies and stuff.

KNUMBSKULLS

Clif Knumbskull: After Knumbskulls became a band, that's when we'd get overwhelmed with people hanging out with us. We'd have kids from Kailua and Mililani and other parts of the island dropping by. More and more people started coming around, and next thing you know, Java Java was the hip nighttime spot for all these different types of people: goths, mods, punks, everybody. We had a pretty big fuckin' crew. We'd hang out outside at night, taking up half the block.

Rolando "Rolo" Dongon: Between '98 and 2000, I don't want to say the scene died out, but there was a transition. A lot of musicians realized music wasn't going to be their career and went to school or started exploring backup plans. I even moved to the mainland for a while, and when I came back, oh my gosh, the Knumbskulls were the biggest thing. I never expected that.

Chris Esteron: In '98 and '99, their shows were getting bigger and bigger. It got to the point where they would headline a show at Beach Hall in Puck's Alley and be pretty close to filling the place up the way the Misfits did just a couple years earlier. They were *that* band. It was pretty fucking amazing. They had enough aggro that the hardcore kids loved them, but they tapped into the melodic shit for the other people to catch on to. I've seen AFI live, I've seen Shelter live, I've seen Misfits live, and the Knumbskulls were every bit as good.

Rolando "Rolo" Dongon: I remember being at a Knumbskulls show at Pink Cadillac, and the floor was about to cave in. It was like being on a wooden trampoline, almost. I was like, "Fuck this, I'm not about to fall through the floor!" It felt like an earthquake. The floor was bending and starting to give way. It was scary.

Clif Knumbskull: Pink Cadillac was so packed that night because they oversold our show. They probably broke some fire safety laws, and they still couldn't get everybody in. We're talking probably over 500 people crammed into a small, second-story nightclub in Waikiki, all singing our songs.

Clif Knumbskull on guitar. *Courtesy of Chris Esteron*

After the show, we started counting the money back. Rose, who was the owner at the time, said, "You guys need to come back and do this again—you see all this money? That's big money!" And she gave me a chunk of it too.

It got to the point where people would come up to me randomly and say, "Oh my God, can I get your autograph?" or "You're my girlfriend's favorite Knumbskull—can I take a picture with you?" We were even signing autographs at the end of our sets. That's when certain people started hating us and calling us rock stars or sellouts. But what do we do, tell people, "No, you can't have our autograph"? It felt like this whole thing had grown into something more than just punk rock. We were now idols to these people. It all morphed into something so mainstream that the new generation of kids started to see us as being larger than life.

THE MONSTER OF MALL PUNK

Cliff Tierra: Yeah, things got mainstream after a while. Like, crazy mainstream. Seeing the Misfits' crimson ghost logo popping up all over the place made you think this is all commercialized already. Not the same. Everything used to be underground and do-it-yourself; you used to have to use Kool-Aid to make your hair crazy colors. Then all of a sudden, like, wow, you can just walk into Hot Topic and buy all this stuff. Even the hair dye was all fabricated for you already. That's something you cannot control, yeah?

Dave "Noodle" Heulitt: You start to notice punk rock music and clothing are available in the shopping malls, and they're doing huge festivals that cost so much money to go to, and it all felt so over-commercialized. Bands like Blink-182 and Yellowcard and The Offspring became unbelievably huge and successful, and this monster of mall punk rock was created. Not on purpose, of course; it's just what happens.

Clint Moncata: We had done as much as we could, and there had to be a major shift because it started to feel like that era of punk ran its course already. The big corporate music festivals and the whole scene worldwide just got played out a little bit. I was over it too. It was too much already. It wasn't like it used to be. It wasn't the core underground stuff anymore. After a while, I tried to put on a couple of shows, and I couldn't even pull the people in anymore, you know? It was different. It changed. But it's the same with any brand. You have to reinvent yourself to stay relevant for the next generation.

25

WHO'S OUT THERE?

When Radio Free Hawaii looked to celebrate its female listenership in its first year, it dreamed up the Wild Women's Weekend, a two-day jubilee that essentially banished the men of KDEO-FM from its premises and ceded control of the airwaves to its female contingent. Girls and women were encouraged to listen in and participate in on-air discussions on vital women's topics, local female musicians were brought in as studio guests, and calls for female and female-fronted recording acts jammed the request line. Festivities culminated with a Sunday night concert headlined by Bikini Kill at Pink's Garage. It was the first of three appearances in Honolulu for the insurgent band and the beginning of a slow, progressive tilt toward pluralism and inclusiveness in the local scene.

As frontwoman for local rockers Big Electric Cat, Gail Jeanne says the experience of opening for Bikini Kill that lively weekend in early 1992 was a uniquely enlightening one. "I didn't understand punk rock feminism at the time," she confesses. "But I really learned a lot through the Wild Women's Weekend. It was something a lot of young women probably needed to be exposed to because there were still lots of guys who weren't cool with girls asserting themselves or even being in a band."

Credit goes to Bikini Kill and its devoted network of allied musicians for kick-starting the riot grrrl movement of the 1990s, which advocated self-empowerment for women and girls. Behind this banner, a new generation of young women repurposed punk into a dynamic vehicle for female expression and a platform to speak out against patriarchy, sexism, and violence against women. In defiance of prevailing standards of beauty, some even adopted an unkempt or nerdy appearance, which became visual emblems of a dyed-in-the-wool riot grrrl.

By the mid-'90s, the public had only begun to acquaint itself with the Internet, and fanzines were the primary form of communication and outreach among riot grrrls. Often brimming with impassioned personal essays and calls to action against chauvinism and misogyny, these 'zines also featured poetry, art, and assorted tidbits, including record reviews and advice on sex.

In similar fashion, the queercore movement looked to claim its place in 1990s counterculture. As with women in punk rock, examples of queerness could be found on punk's fringes. Some would even argue that the very term "punk" is a homosexual reference—a slang term for jailhouse submissives. For many, queercore stood as a radical alternative to the gay mainstream, offering a new means of challenging the dominant culture while giving punk rock a much-needed shove and kick back toward its fiercely antiestablishment roots.

There were times, even in the middle of the Pacific, when members of these subcultural groups would collude and form alliances. When Ladyfest, the game-changing women-run arts festival was inaugurated in Olympia, Washington, in 2000, it was intuitively inclusive of the LGBTQ community. Before long, multiple Ladyfests and similar gatherings sprang up worldwide, Hawaii included. In 2003, Girl Fest, a multi-venue gala in much the same vein as Ladyfest, was formed in Honolulu. Ladyfest Hawaii, a local offshoot of the original, was launched a year later. For many, these celebrations were confirmation of the limitless potential of women working together. "Going to Ladyfest in Olympia was mind-blowing and definitely influential to me at that period of my life," affirms drummer Noe Bunnell, whose exposure to the weeklong jamboree with friends sparked an innovative turn among both female and gay punk rockers on Oahu looking to experiment with musicmaking. These young gatecrashers would bring fresh concepts and unprecedented openness to the local scene into the new millennium.

Gail McCracken a.k.a. Gail Jeanne (vocalist: Big Electric Cat): I was very young when the Ramones and Dead Boys were starting out in the '70s. New York was a wild place and pretty scary then. I was going into New York at fifteen or sixteen maybe once a week because the drinking age in New Jersey was eighteen, but in New York they didn't care. All my girlfriends were having sex with either Stiv Bators or one of the Ramones—usually Dee Dee.

I always thought Jayne County was inspirational and a force to be reckoned with. She was a fantastic transgendered singer with unbelievable stage presence, and places like Max's Kansas City and CBGB pretty much welcomed her with open arms.It was such a cool scene

Doug Upp: My dad's Jewish, my mom is Mexican. I'm a queer and I like to cross-dress, but I obsess over things that are against me. Knowing my dad's Jewish, I'm obsessed with Nazism, and because I'm not fully white, I'm obsessed with the Klan and all that hateful stuff only because I want to understand it.

I grew up in the '80s, and I think my damage came from there only being three TV channels, and every Sunday there'd be someone telling me I'm going to hell for being a faggot or not having certain beliefs. I just became fascinated with these things, like why should I hate myself or why do these people hate me? It kind of consumed me.

I wanted to talk about these things, but no one wanted to talk about them, so my way of dealing with all of that was to be in drag and have my hairy belly and legs out in protest and be even more provocative. I wanted to promote conversation in an understanding kind of way, but I don't think people get irony anymore.

Dave "Noodle" Heulitt: Punk rock, to me, was always about bringing in everyone. We are a conglomerate; we are a group. We should share one message, and that message should be positivity towards those on the outside. You are accepted here. At our shows, you'd either accept and respect each other or don't pay the five dollars and get the fuck out.

Doug Upp: People don't always see themselves or their interests reflected in the media, so sometimes they start fanzines. I had certain intentions with my 'zines, but I tried to make it palatable with humor and satire. I wasn't very artful and was probably too overtly sexual, but I guess the punk rock thing to do is be obnoxious and reckless sometimes and regret your execution later.

Otto: My inspiration for doing 'zines was Doug. I would put little advertisements for my cakes in his 'zines. He said some really mean things about everybody in them. Well, maybe not really mean, but funny stuff that could be taken the wrong way.

Doug Upp: I would go to hip-hop shows, drag shows, and punk shows and write about them in my 'zines but make everything very queer. I'd put somebody like Nos on the cover so that all of his friends or anyone who might think it looks interesting would have to read all this gay shit at the same time. I'd write about people like Otto or Nos or anybody who drew attention in the scene. I even wrote a poem about Dave Frye once. I think it said:

> *May I be brave*
> *And say I crave Dave*
> *The man from that Generic band*
> *And you can call me Brandy, honey*
> *Because I wanna go dooooowwwwwn*

I would just objectify boys. I think a lot of people were bothered by it, but not Nos, who was okay with it because he enjoys any kind of attention. I was really obsessed with him.

Lani Teves (vocalist: Sorry, Pomohomo, My Ex Is Dead; guitarist: Frenchie, Postmodern): I don't know how comfortable guys are with talking about their feelings, but girls are celebrated for being able to express themselves honestly, and writing is one way to do that. I think fanzines gave girls a voice that they maybe didn't have in other areas of their life.

Sorry played a variety of shows including a "punk prom"
at the Bunnell residence. *Courtesy of Ipo Bunnell*

Dave "Noodle" Heulitt: When I think about 'zines, I think of people like Noe and Doug. I had one called *Wet Noodle,* and it was a real cut-and-paste hodgepodge, but Noe's was hand-done and you could tell there was real care that went into its creation. There was a purity to her craft and what she was putting out there. *Kytzyl* felt like art to me, in a pamphlet-style paper form.

Noe Bunnell: I was a nerdy kid in high school and liked to write and draw, so *Kytzyl* was an outlet where I didn't have to talk to anybody directly. It was easier to just give them my 'zine and then run away. I was very influenced by *Fuddy Duddy,* which was made by Johnny Jujubee, who did a punk show on KTUH. I idolized him and thought he was so cool and funny. I loved his 'zine and all the music he played on his radio show. I would record his shows and listen to them on my Walkman over and over. He played a lot of pop-punk stuff but also The Misfits and Black Flag, anything punky.

At the time, my best friend Lisa Borsch's older brothers were in Hell Yeah Bowlers, and we were the dorky younger sister and friend who would tag along to shows and stuff. We were not the popular kids at school, but seeing other students from Maryknoll at a Hell Yeah Bowlers show opened up new social pathways because I was scared to talk to people, you know? I just didn't think anyone would like me.

I'd be one of those girls who stood in the back of the room holding boys' hoodies while they went and danced. It was like that a lot at Fast Zone. I'm not saying any of the guys in the bands that played there were misogynistic, but as a whole, they all kinda were. The straight edge hardcore kids were worse, almost. They pretended like they weren't but they kinda were.

Ipo Bunnell (vocalist: Frenchie, Postmodern, Witch Baby, etc.): I was more annoyed going to these shows than anything. It was all dudes. A lot of dummies and kooks and military guys. I was like, "Where are the women?" It just wasn't inclusive.

Lani Teves: Now that I'm older I can see that these were just young guys doing what they do sometimes, but some of them were very cocky, took up a lot of space, and acted like idiots half the time. They might not have meant anything bad, but it just did not feel like there was room for anything different. So we said, "What do we want to do, and how do we go about doing it?"

I went to a Bikini Kill show in '96 at After Dark or whatever it was called then when they opened for NOFX, and I started to gravitate more towards riot grrrl-type stuff and female-fronted bands. I got really into Bikini Kill.

Gail Jeanne: I didn't even know who Bikini Kill were when we opened for them at Pink's Garage in '92. I wasn't sure what they were going to be like either, but Kathleen Hanna was actually really sweet. She gave me her 'zine and a bottle of water, and I got to be friends with her, and we would talk over the phone sometimes or send letters to each other. We kept in touch.

Kevin Jones: I'd say Bikini Kill was foundational for a lot of girls in the '90s, but I don't think it stopped there by any means. Just like me and my friends, they were out to find something that was new and didn't want to get stuck in one place musically. Sleater-Kinney sounds much different than Bikini Kill, who sounds different from Bratmobile, and there was a very diverse soundscape within the riot grrrl scene itself. So I think a lot of the girls who were interested in it then were more adventurous musically than a lot of the dudes who were just listening to the same old stuff. The women definitely brought a new perspective to the punk scene.

Lani Teves: At that point, I think I thought I had nothing to lose, so I just put up a flier at the Radio Free Music Center looking to start a band. I was like, "Who's out there?" I didn't really know what I was doing, but I didn't care. I didn't even know if I would find any girls to make a band with, but I did and we all became friends. We didn't know each other at all.

Ipo Bunnell: I came across that flier and thought, *Fuck yeah, it's time. This needs to happen now. Let's fuck shit up!*

Ipo Bunnell and Lani Teves of Frenchie. *Courtesy of Noe Neumann*

Lani Teves: None of us had much experience playing our instruments. With Frenchie, Noe's sister Ipo was still in high school, and the rest of us were in Leeward Community College, I think. Then Noe decided she was gonna start her own band with girls at UH, and they started Sorry. So now there were two all-girl bands, and I think that, in a way, gave us a feeling of support.

Noe Bunnell: We all took a look at the scene and were like, "No, we don't wanna be this. We're different." And that's the whole thing about punk: It's a reaction to what came before, and you try to break new ground and forge your own path.

Otto: I would put on a show once a year where every band had to have at least one girl in it. The idea was to give the kids something different from what was going on, and this was one way to also give opportunities to females and get more bands to include girls.

Dave "Noodle" Heulitt: Having girl bands playing shows was a huge deal to me. I grew up with a single mom who was a hippie feminist, so my feeling was "Yes, girl power all day long!" I thought all-female or female-fronted bands were cool as shit. That was so punk rock to me. Otto even more so than me. We were like, "Hell yes!"

Noe Bunnell: Sorry was an all-girl group, but we didn't have the same mentality as Frenchie, who took on more of a riot grrrl identity. I remember thinking I didn't really even like girl bands, and that if the boys accepted me, I didn't need to be part of a separate girls' club. But after a while—and I think Lani was a big part of this—I realized there's something to having a special space for girls. Our bands would play together often, and we'd get grouped together all the time.

Doug Upp: What I liked about them was none of them knew how to play. The bass line and the guitar riff and the drums all sounded like they were playing different songs, but they all kind of worked together.

Noe Bunnell: I don't even remember how I got to playing the drums, but I probably thought I didn't have the fine motor skills to play anything else. I tried playing bass and I was terrible. I mean, I wasn't a great drummer either. Every song had the same drumbeat. Our songs had a lot of weird pauses in them, and the drumbeats weren't necessarily punk because it wasn't so much about being loud and fast and jumping around and being crazy like a lot of the boys. We would just practice and play and make fun stuff up. We didn't follow any rules because we didn't know the rules.

Lani Teves: Sometimes we would clear a room. We would even joke, like, "Let's see how many people leave when we get up there," and they would. They would leave. And we were like, "Well, good. We *want* you to leave."

Ipo Bunnell: At first, everybody fucking hated us. Then when people started to come around, it was probably embarrassing for a lot of the macho punk dudes to admit they liked a girl band. Some of them were kind of jerks to us at the beginning. They wouldn't treat us like humans. I'd hear guys talk about women on stage, and they were so fucking sexist. They'd scream at us and yell stupid shit like "Take your shirt off!" Dumb shit like that. Frenchie wasn't the type of band to put on cute outfits and dance around, so if that's what you were looking for, you weren't coming to our shows. We were screaming at everybody about control.

Kevin Jones: Another side of the punk scene is the ethics that comes with it. A lot of my friends were straight edge or vegan; we all read 'zines and were aware of sexism and racism and homelessness, all of that stuff. So for us, it wasn't just about music; it was all of it. I lived with a bunch of those girls at one point. We all shared a house together and were all really close. Ethically, we thought the same way and were of a progressive mindset. My band at the time, A Young Poisoner's Handbook, played almost every show with Sorry.

Ipo Bunnell: The best part was we'd have girls coming to our shows we didn't even know who would tell us how inspired they were and how they could finally come to shows and feel comfortable.

Noe Bunnell: There seemed to be a lot more diversity in terms of the people who started coming to shows. There weren't as many girls or queer kids before or much crossover into other genres of music. Part of that change was Doug. He was involved in everything. I went to my first drag shows with him, and there was a period where bands like The Sticklers and Imminent Riot were playing drag shows because of Doug. We were open to whatever. We'd be like, "Sure, let's go. Sounds like fun!"

Dave "Noodle" Heulitt: The Sticklers got to play alongside Doug in a Miss Understood pageant for drag queens at Fusion Nightclub. I'd never been around anything like that before.

Doug Upp: I performed with The Sticklers for the talent category of the pageant. Other bands started playing there as well, so musicians from the punk scene would hang out at Fusion too. Noe and Lani from Sorry and Frenchie liked it because it was queer, but they were also rockers.

Noe Bunnell: That was about the time period where I was kind of coming out to myself. When I was in high school, I was like, "I don't like girl bands. I don't wanna play music with other girls. I don't wanna do anything with other girls. I only like hanging out with boys," and that was probably because it was so terrifying to be hanging out with girls that maybe I had a crush on or whatever. I mean, I liked boys *and* girls, but it was so scary to like girls because you're not supposed to. So that part of me just got pushed aside. That's just not how I identified at the time. But getting to know Lani and learning about Bikini Kill and the whole riot grrrl movement made it feel a lot more okay, even when I was hanging out with all these punk boys who were constantly making fun of gay people. Actually, I think Lani might've been the first girl I ever kissed. It was at a drunken party and I was like, "Great, got that over with." In retrospect, everybody probably knew before me.

Doug Upp: I had moved away to Hollywood for a few years, and I got into Jackie Beat, Vaginal Davis, and a lot of drag shows and all the high-concept stuff there like Voluptuous Horror of Karen Black and Haunted Garage. I like rock and roll with a lot of costumes and set pieces; big productions that are either real sexy or queer or messy or chaotic. I got into all that gross kind of LA stuff. When I came back to Hawaii, I was LA-damaged, but I also thought I was too cool. Otto, for some reason, asked me to be in Imminent Riot, and immediately I was like, "Oh, cool—I have all these LA bands I can rip off!"

Otto got Imminent Riot to be the first band to play the local band stage at the '99 Warped Tour when it came to Hawaii, and I remember somebody wanted to fight me because I was wearing a bikini and being too gay, probably. My name at that time was Tess Tickles, and it's because I did a drag show at this nightclub in Kaka'ako one night, and I guess my balls were out.

Otto: When you first saw Doug on stage, he would be covered up. Now that I've seen a couple of episodes of *RuPaul's Drag Race* on YouTube, I realize it's called a "reveal." I didn't know there was an actual name for it. He would put on his makeup really ugly too, but on purpose. He wanted to shock you. A guy from one of the other bands on the bill came over to us and said, "I've been on the Warped Tour for a while now, and I've never seen anything like that before!"

Lani Teves: I saw Doug perform and I was like, "Holy shit!" It was inspiring to watch the way he commanded a room and played with the crowd. He just made everybody super uncomfortable.

Otto: This one show, Doug dressed up as a bride—a dead bride—and it was so out of place and over the top because this was at a pool hall. He would show up with these different garments where maybe his balls would be showing but the penis would be hidden. It was so weird.

Noe Bunnell: Imminent Riot was so terrible. I think we maybe only had ten songs, and they'd all be less than a minute long, so our sets would be mostly Doug doing stuff, because otherwise we couldn't fill more than ten minutes.

Otto: Another time—this is gross—we're the first band to play, and Doug is rolling around on the ground. We're all concentrating on our instruments, so we don't see what he's doing down there, but we find out from people afterwards that he had the microphone pushed up against his anus. This is the one microphone for this show, and there were other bands after us. When I asked Doug about it, he just looked at me and said, "Oh yeah, I did that." You just never knew what to expect from him.

A barely-dressed Doug performing with The Sticklers in 1997.
Courtesy of Noe Neumann

Noe Bunnell: There was a lot of overlap in the scene, so even the straight edge kids came out to see Doug, but they were appalled by him at the same time. He loved when they showed up, though, because he loved to antagonize them and make everything weird and confrontational.

Ipo Bunnell: Doug would have his eyebrows shaved off and be taunting someone in the audience, and it would always be the most masculine guy in the crowd. It was so good.

Lani Teves: Then there was the first Ladyfest in Olympia, Washington, which I went to. I think I read about it in *Punk Planet* or *Maximum Rocknroll* or something. I went with Ipo and Noe and some other people. It was the first one ever, before it went worldwide. The idea was to have a women's music festival that encompassed art and other things. They were like, "Now go back to wherever you're from and make a Ladyfest." The idea was not to just travel to go to a Ladyfest but to create a festival and start your own projects where you're at.

Ipo Bunnell: Women controlled everything there, and they laid out all the rules. Everything was run by women. It was the opposite of what was happening at home. There'd be folk stuff, punk stuff, and queercore. All these genres and all female bands. Shows got fucking crazy too, but nobody was a jerk, nobody was an asshole. It all felt really safe. No violence and no aggression.

Noe Bunnell: Olympia was a pretty small place, and it was a very artsy scene with a lot of genre-mixing with electronic music, punk, and queercore. We for sure brought that stuff back with us and applied it to new musical projects like Pomohomo, Postmodern, and Les Sauvages.

Ipo Bunnell: I met a bunch of punk girls who were activists and stuff, and that led me to becoming a social worker. I wanted to do better for the world. My experiences at that time really developed my individuality and my self-esteem. I realized that other people were just like me, trying to figure it all out. It helped me know who I was and who I wanted to be.

Dave "Noodle" Heulitt: Before I got into the scene, I was a quiet haole guy from the Marine Corps. Punk rock made me come out of my shell and made me comfortable in my own skin. It taught me morals and made me more vocal about the things I cared about. The scene defines who I am as a person and what I believe in, and without that I don't know who I'd be, honestly.

Noe Bunnell: I'd say my parents were not particularly happy to find out that I was gay, but in a way, it became kinda cool. It wasn't anything to hide anymore. It was something to celebrate. It's interesting to think about how music and subculture are intertwined with personal identity and how you can figure out who you are through these things. I'd probably be a lot more depressed for a lot more of my life if not for finding my niche of people: all the weirdos in the scene who supported each other, who let each other be themselves and be celebrated for who they are.

AFTERWORD

While this tale concludes sometime around the turn of the millennium, assuredly, the Hawaii punk and indie scenes have not only survived but thrived in the years since. The original concept for *Local Unrest* was to take the story of Hawaiian underground rock from its inception to present day, though with each passing year it became apparent that this was going to be a challenge. After five-plus years assembling this book, another "generation" has already come and gone; many teens and young adults who were introduced to the Honolulu scene when I started this project have, like so many before, gone to shows, started their own bands, dissolved them, and either shipped off to college, moved to the mainland, or simply transitioned to adult life. At the pace I was at, it was clear I'd never catch up.

It seemed appropriate, then, to put a wrap on this book in the early 2000s, just before the advent of social media and the transformative development of the Honolulu arts district. In my mind, the year 2005 always seemed like the dividing line between the B.C. and A.D. of the Honolulu scene when brassy speculators sparked a vital revamp of the troubled, decaying Chinatown neighborhood by introducing a number of dance clubs, art galleries, and hip eateries to the area. On a personal note, it's also the year I left my job as a music and entertainment writer at the *Honolulu Star-Bulletin* to start a University-area record and clothing shop called Stylus Honolulu. It was an endeavor that allowed me to keep close ties to the local scene.

In the decades since, I regularly watched some of my favorite bands like 86 List, Black Square, 13th Legion, Rats, Rotten Blossom, Ragamuffs, and Chryst Moon perform at such Chinatown haunts as Nextdoor, Downbeat Lounge, Ong King Arts Center, and Manifest. From 2015 until the COVID-19 pandemic shut down all live venues in 2020, I produced a local cable TV show, website, and YouTube channel called B-Side HNL, which featured performances by and interviews with Hawaiian underground bands, many of which would have certainly made these pages had I been gifted with more time and space.

I imagine I would have told you all about Dave Frye's imprisonment on federal drug charges in 2016 and his remarkable redemption story; the marriage and subsequent divorce of Radio Free Hawaii intern Chessa Au and Ramones bassist C.J. Ramone; Pimpbot making it to the prestigious South by Southwest festival in 2009 and 2010; and Go Jimmy Go's epic 20th Anniversary farewell concert and documentary in 2016. I would have also explored Gemma Cubero del Barrio's *Ottomaticake*, a film based entirely on Honolulu scenester Otto, which made the rounds on the film festival circuit in 2017; as well as Ragamuffs becoming the latest Hawaii band to be invited to South by Southwest in 2022 on the strength of their impressive Spotify numbers.

Over the years there have been a number of Hawaii-born recording acts like Jack Johnson, Pepper, Chokebore, Kings of Spade, Superfuct, and National Product who saw their stars rise as they became known more widely across the world in the '90s, 2000s, and beyond. One might also include in that group the esteemed alt-rock combo …And You Will Know Us By the Trail of Dead, whose founding core members, Jason Reece and Conrad Keely, first met while attending Kalaheo High School on Oahu's Windward side. Signed to Interscope Records in 2001, the Austin-based outfit released the prog-punk masterpiece *Source Tags & Codes* a year later to great critical acclaim. In an interview for this book, Reece, who details his introduction to Hawaiian punk in Chapter 15, recounted Trail of Dead's meteoric ascent, starting with a fateful invitation to play the All Tomorrow's Parties festival in England in April 2000. "They brought us over, and we met John Peel that same weekend," Reece told me. Peel, the distinguished BBC radio broadcaster whose endorsements of relatively obscure acts has led to great renown for groups such as The Smiths, Sisters of Mercy, and Joy Division, invited Trail of Dead to record a Peel Session in London soon after. "That's when things went bonkers," said Reece, cackling in disbelief at the memory.

Trail of Dead's backstory is fascinating, and perhaps under different circumstances I might have been able to present more of it. I would have also loved to have offered more insight on well-known local institutions like Wave Waikiki, Honolulu Weekly, KTUH, and Radio Free Hawaii, all of which have featured in their own chapters here but whose histories are so wonderfully complex, significant, and absorbing that each would certainly be worthy of full-book treatment. My hope is that there will be books on them someday, though I'd like to savor the completion of this one first before pondering the possibility.

THE CAST

Mark Abramson: guitarist for His Master's Voice, Cosmic Oven

Frank Abreu: guitarist/vocalist for Obscene Routine

Darius Amjadi: DJ at KTUH

John Andreoni: drummer for Sonya & Revoluçion, Fallen Angel, Passion, etc.

Deb Aoki: visual artist; cartoonist/writer/reviewer for *Honolulu Weekly*, *Honolulu Advertiser*, *Kaos*, *Scrawling Wall*, etc.

Dennis Apeles: drummer for Screamin' Jay Hawkins, Bobby & the Rebels, etc.

Chessa Au: intern at Radio Free Hawaii

Ray Bala: drummer for M.U.G., The Pugilist, Pongoids, etc.

Fred Barbaria: KTUH station manager from 1966–1973

Peter Bond: guitarist/vocalist for Hat Makes the Man, Oriental Love Ring, Spiny Norman, etc.

Keiko Bonk: vocalist for His Master's Voice, Cosmic Oven

Ipo Bunnell: vocalist for Frenchie, Postmodern, Witch Baby, etc.

Noe Bunnell: drummer for Imminent Riot, Sorry, Postmodern, etc.

Damon Cabral: vocalist for The Pugilist

Laurie Carlson: publisher of *Honolulu Weekly*

David Carr: drummer for Cringer; vocalist/guitarist for The Vacuum, The Wrong, etc.; Hawaii Punk Museum creator

Jimmy Dee Caterine: guitarist for Sacred Rite, Sabre

Kalea Chapman: guitarist for Poi Dog Pondering, Love Crabs, Food

Mark Chittom: writer/nightlife columnist for *Honolulu Weekly*

Jeff Chmolack: bassist for The Pugilist

Clif Chun a.k.a. Clif Knumbskull: guitarist for Knumbskulls, Days/Weeks/Months

Gary Chun: writer for *Honolulu Star-Bulletin, Novus, Brouhaha;* co-host of KTUH's *Rough Take*

Sean Coffey: drummer for Poi Dog Pondering, Food, Love Crabs, etc.

Michael Corcoran: writer for *Rolling Stone, Creem, Spin, Sunbums, Austin Chronicle, Austin American Statesman,* etc.

Earl Crawford: guitarist/drummer for Luau Guys, Friend of the Family, Ciguatera, Devil Kine Music

Rob Cribley: drummer for Saud, Stage Dive, The Wrong, Hypo-Depression

Jeff Dahl: vocalist/multi-instrumentalist for Jeff Dahl Band, Angry Samoans, Vox Pop, etc.

John Dahlin: vocalist for The Accüsed, ADMS Family, Crib Death, etc.

Doug Davidson a.k.a. Doug Upp a.k.a. Tess Tickles: vocalist for Imminent Riot, Patty Judy and the Dirt

Karina Denike: vocalist for Dance Hall Crashers, NOFX, etc.

Dave Derby: vocalist/bassist for The Dambuilders, The Exactones, Communiqué, etc.

Richard Detty: vocalist for The Noiz; audio engineer; Red Session manager; co-owner of Exclusive Rehearsal Studios

Gus Diamond: owner of Paragon Piercing, co-owner of Provocative Piercing

Patrick Donegan: KTUH Monday Night Live director, Progressive Arts founding member, soundman

Rafael Dongon: guitarist for Hell Yeah Bowlers, Bangstick, Cooperstown, etc.

Rolando "Rolo" Dongon: drummer for Hell Yeah Bowlers, Last Chance; guitarist for Knumbskulls, Generic, etc.

Gerry Ebersbach: bassist for The Squids, Fun and Profit, Pacific Ethno Techno

Kit Ebersbach: pianist/keyboardist/composer for The Squids, The Tourists, Pacific Ethno Techno, Don Tiki

Chris Esteron: vocalist for Devil Kine Music, Days/Weeks/Months

Derek Ferrar: writer/editor for *Honolulu Weekly*, *Scrawling Wall*; DJ at KTUH

Erin L. Figueroa a.k.a. Elf: owner of The Piercing Elf, co-owner of Provocative Piercing

Eric Friedl: vocalist for The Exactones; guitarist/vocalist/multi-instrumentalist for the Oblivians, Dutch Masters, etc.; co-owner/founder of Goner Records

John Friend a.k.a. DJ John John: DJ at Soda Pops, Odyssey, Sub Club, etc.

Willie Fruean: guitarist/vocalist for B.Y.K., North American Bush Band, Rootonics, etc.

Dave Frye: vocalist for Generic, promoter

Don "Lips" Fujiyama: DJ at Radio Free Hawaii

James Ganeko: drummer for Pagan Babies, Cool Runnings, Nuclear Tan, etc.

Daniel Glass: drummer for Royal Crown Revue, Brian Setzer, Mike Ness, etc.

Gerard Gonsalves: drummer for Aaronsrod, Stajefrite

Jeff Goo: vocalist for Bangstick, Cooperstown

Kit Grant: DJ at KTUH

Shon Gregory: drummer for Red Session, Go Jimmy Go, etc.

Lesa Griffith: writer/editor for *Novus*, *Time Out New York*, *Honolulu Weekly*, *Honolulu Advertiser*, *Honolulu Magazine*, etc.

Matthew Grim: promoter/owner/DJ at The Faktory, Zone 24, Sanctuary, Sub Club, etc.

Kai Han: DJ at Radio Free Hawaii

Warren Hassett: vocalist for Mistermeaner, Full Send; promoter

Cary Hayashikawa: general manager at Radio Free Hawaii

Dave "Noodle" Heulitt a.k.a. Addison: vocalist/guitarist for The Sticklers, Temporary Lovers, Das Muchachos, etc.; host of Radio Free Hawaii's *Punkaholic Session*

Jaime Ikeda: guitarist for Saud, Stage Dive, Broken Man, etc.

Angelo Jensen: vocalist for Aaronsrod, bassist for Kaos

Kevin Jones a.k.a. Kevin Catalog: bassist for The Catalogs, vocalist for A Young Poisoner's Handbook

George Kail: owner of 3-D Ballroom, Pink Cadillac, Blue Zebra, etc.

Mark Kaleiwahea: guitarist/vocalist for Sacred Rite, Sabre

Kili Kaohu: drummer for Broken Man

Marti Kerton: vocalist/violinist for Hat Makes the Man, Electric Lunch Band, Henry Kapono, etc.

Jim Kneubuhl: DJ at KTUH; bassist for Mojo Hand, Bobo Handshake, Brainchild, etc.

Robert M. Knight: rock photographer

Johnee Kop: pro skateboarder; drummer for The Sharx, S.R.O., Dana Lynn/Chokebore, etc.

Ty Kroll: bassist for Tantra Monsters, Mr. Simon

Ryan Kunimura: trombonist for Tantra Monsters, Mr. Simon, Go Jimmy Go, etc.; bassist for M.U.G., Freak Hunt, etc.

Byron Lai: guitarist for Hat Makes the Man, New Dreamers/Diamond Hedz, Whitey & the Gooks, etc.

Jon Lange: bassist for The Efekt

Barry Lasit: vocalist/guitarist for Kaos, X-Chaser, Martial Law, Widowmaker, etc.

Jack Law: owner of Wave Waikiki, Hula's Bar & Lei Stand, Malia's Cantina, etc.

Shawn "Speedy" Lopes: DJ at Radio Free Hawaii, KTUH; documentarian; writer/columnist for *Honolulu Star-Bulletin*, *Honolulu Advertiser*, etc.

Anne Love a.k.a. DJ Nocturna: DJ at KTUH, podcaster, promoter

Franchon Luke: DJ at Radio Free Hawaii, KTUH

Burt Lum: founder/publisher of *Novus* and *Brouhaha*, co-host of KTUH's *Rough Take*

Scott Mackenzie: DJ/music director at KTUH

Gail McCracken a.k.a. Gail Jeanne: vocalist for Big Electric Cat

Scott McDonough a.k.a. Otto: promoter; bassist for The Sticklers, Imminent Riot, 86 List, etc.

Sonya Mendez: vocalist/multi-instrumentalist for Sonya & Reveluçion

Jason Miller: promoter; owner of Hawaiian Express Records and 808shows.com

Matthew Miller: bassist for Hat Makes the Man, Poi Dog Pondering

Clint Moncata: Volcom regional sales rep for Hawaii/Tahiti/Guam

Abra Moore: singer/guitarist for Poi Dog Pondering; solo artist

Justin Mynatt: bassist for Grapefruit

Nelson Nakamoto: bassist for Knumbskulls, Days/Weeks/Months

Pat Ohta: promoter, activist, publisher of *Iron Cross*

Derek "Nos" Okazaki: vocalist for Freak Hunt, Pongoids

Craig Okino: bassist/vocalist for Pagan Babies, Cool Runnings

Frank Orrall: drummer/vocalist/multi-instrumentalist for Poi Dog Pondering, Hat Makes the Man, The Squids, Mumbo Jumbo, etc.

Barry Oshiro a.k.a. DJ Barry Freeze: vocalist for The Sharx, Hypo-Depression; DJ at Odyssey, Sub Club

Gary Owens: DJ at 3-D Ballroom

Fernando Pacheco: trombonist for Exit 24, Go Jimmy Go, Pimpbot, etc.

Tim Pagan a.k.a. Dave O'Day: DJ at Radio Free Hawaii, KTUH

Charlie Palumbo: drummer for SRO, Elvis '77, Travel Light, etc.; DJ at KTUH

Mike Park: saxophonist/vocalist for Skankin' Pickle, The Chinkees, Bruce Lee Band; founder of Dill Records, Asian Man Records

Jesse Perrin: co-founder of Hawaii Anti-Racist Skinheads (HARSH)

Chris Planas: guitarist/vocalist for Pagan Babies, Cool Runnings, Nuclear Tan, etc.

Gardner Pope a.k.a. Gardner Maxam: bassist for The Sharx, The Vacuum, J-Church; bassist/vocalist for Cringer;

Ronnie Ravelo: bassist/guitarist for Widow, Collision, Mumbo Jumbo, etc.

Jason Reece: vocalist/multi-instrumentalist for …And You Will Know Us by the Trail of Dead, Ifany, Mukilteo Fairies, etc.

Romell Regulacion: vocalist/multi-instrumentalist for Razed in Black, Lost Souls, Rime, etc.

Dave Rorick a.k.a. Dave Roe: bassist for Al Poe & the Fleas, Whitey & the Gooks; bassist/session player for Johnny Cash, The Pretenders, Dwight Yoakam, Jerry Reed, etc.

Jim Rossi a.k.a. Goopy Rossi: bassist for Mumbo Jumbo, Hat Makes the Man

Mohammad Rouf: DJ at Radio Free Hawaii, KTUH

Arnie Saiki: guitarist for Dervishes, Bad Posture, Castration Anxiety

Victor Sam: nightclub DJ, writer for *Novus*

Robert Scott: vocalist for Mumbo Jumbo, Dervishes, Bad Posture, etc.

Beano Shots: guitarist for The Squids, Hat Makes the Man, Oriental Love Ring, Beano's Black Sheep, etc.

Gabe Silva: guitarist for M.U.G., Pongoids, etc.

Mike Silva: guitarist/bassist/vocalist for M.U.G., The Pugilist, Pongoids, Freak Hunt, etc.

Elwood "Woody" Soueira: bassist for X-Chaser, Optimum Fury, Ciguatera

Brian Spalding: guitarist for Kaos, Aaronsrod

Julia Steele: writer/editor for *Honolulu Weekly*, *Scrawling Wall*, etc.

Randy Szucs: vocalist for Broken Man

Elyce Tajima: keyboardist/vocalist for Pagan Babies

Guy Takaki: bassist for Luau Guys; vocalist for Nocturnal Fear

Ed Tarantino: bassist for Scarred 4 Life, Cringer, Broken Man

Rich Tarantino: guitarist/vocalist for Scarred 4 Life; bassist for Saud, Stage Dive

Lani Teves: guitarist for Frenchie, Postmodern; vocalist for My Ex Is Dead, Sorry, Pomohomo

Cliff Tierra: drummer for Tweaked

David "Rudy" Trubitt: guitarist/vocalist for New Dreamers/Diamond Hedz, The Squids, Fun and Profit; solo artist

Richard Upper: rock photographer

Lloyd Veerman: drummer for The Efekt

Raoul Vehill: vocalist for Devil Dog, Battery Club, The Beasts

Pete Vidito: DJ at Radio Free Hawaii, KTUH; bassist for Tantra Monsters; drummer for Chicken Eats the Worm

Joan Wasser: violinist/vocalist for The Dambuilders; vocalist/multi-instrumentalist for Joan As Police Woman

Eric White: saxophonist for Go Jimmy Go, The Elevations, etc.

Jamie Winpenny: guitarist for Red Session

Jenifer Winter: Radio Free Hawaii research coordinator and promotions director

Norm Winter: founder of Radio Free Hawaii; owner of Jelly's Music and Books

Cam Wright: bassist for Go Jimmy Go

Matt Yoshihara: guitarist for Tarrasque, Travel Light, etc.

www.ingramcontent.com/pod-product-compliance
Lightning Source LLC
Chambersburg PA
CBHW021210130626
46554CB00004B/1159